ON INSIGNIFICANCE

Focusing on the anthropological consequences of the disappearing of materiality and sensory embodiment, *On Insignificance* highlights some of the most perturbing patterns of insignificance that have seeped into our everyday lives. Seeking to explain the semiotic causes of feelings of meaninglessness, Leone posits that caring for the singularities of the world is the most viable way to resist the alienating effects of the digital bureaucratization of meaning. The book will be of interest to scholars of anthropology, cultural studies, semiotics, aesthetics, communication studies, and social theory.

Massimo Leone is Full Professor of Cultural Semiotics at the University of Turin, Italy, and a Visiting Full Professor of Semiotics at Shanghai University, China.

ON INSIGNIFICANCE

The Loss of Meaning
in the Post-Material Age

Massimo Leone

Routledge
Taylor & Francis Group

LONDON AND NEW YORK

First published 2020
by Routledge
4 Park Square, Milton Park, Abingdon, Oxon OX14 4RN
605 Third Avenue, New York, NY 10017

Routledge is an imprint of the Taylor & Francis Group, an Informa business

British Library Cataloguing-in-Publication Data
A catalogue record for this book is available from the British Library

Library of Congress Cataloging-in-Publication Data
A catalog record has been requested for this book

ISBN: 978-1-138-61831-2 (hbk)
ISBN: 978-1-138-61830-5 (pbk)
ISBN: 978-0-429-46127-9 (ebk)

Typeset in Bembo
by codeMantra

To my father, Luigi Raffaele Leone

CONTENTS

List of figures   *ix*
Acknowledgments   *xi*

   Introduction: the significance of insignificance   1

1 Framing insignificance: a semiotic typology
  of meaninglessness   6

2 Trolling insignificance: disrupting the digital
  public discourse   22

3 Contrarian insignificance: wars of position in the
  digital arena   33

4 Picturing insignificance: the utopia of digital perfection   56

5 Shopping insignificance: post–material temples   83

6 Assembling insignificance: post–material crowds   95

7 Eating insignificance: post–material meals   116

8 Recovering significance: the value of singularity   133

9 Negotiating significance: the value of compromise   144

10 Sharing significance: the value of common sense   159

11 Courting significance: the value of interpretation   172

Conclusions: the clash of semiotic civilizations   188

References   *203*
Index   *219*

FIGURES

3.1 A "Je suis taxi legale" poster on the car window of a taxi in
Turin; photo by the author   38

3.2 An image posted anonymously on the web, adapting the
"Je suis Charlie" slogan so as to show support to the terrorists   41

3.3 The semiotic square of ritual opinion formation; scheme
by the author   49

4.1 Alex Tew. As of February 8, 2009. *The Million Dollar
Homepage*. Webpage. 1,000,000 pixels; picture from
www.milliondollarhomepage.com/   58

4.2 Early October 2016. Gravel on the path of Villa Casana,
Novedrate, Italy; picture by the author   62

4.3 Photographs of different kinds of sand: (a) Santorini sand,
(b) Olivine sand, (c) Mars sand, (d) Pink coral sand, and
(e) Pismo beach sand; (pictures from www.geology.com)   65

4.4 Late September 2016. Cobblestones at the Institute of
Philosophy, University of Leuven, Belgium; picture by the author   66

4.5 Different types of asphalt "cracking": (a) fatigue "alligator"
cracking, (b) block cracking, and (c) slippage cracking
(pictures from www.asphaltinstitute.org)   67

4.6 Late September 2016. *Flowerbeds at the Public Library*, Leuven,
Belgium; picture by the author   68

4.7 Ecuadorian carpet from Otovalo market; picture by the author   70

4.8 Mid-September 2016. Ecuadorian Panama-style hat, Quito,
Ecuador; picture by the author   72

4.9 Rings inside a Panama hat; picture by the author   73

4.10 Mid-September 2016. Ecuadorian tapestry, Casa Joaquin
Boutique Hotel, Quito, Ecuador; picture by the author   75
4.11 Fruit salad; picture by the author   76
4.12 Mid-September 2016. Giant screen at Guayaquil Airport,
Guayaquil, Ecuador; picture by the author   77
4.13 LCD screens flickering; picture by the author   79
4.14 Broken flap display at the airport of Belgrade; picture by the author 79
4.15 Arduino split flap display (picture from www.instructables.com)   80
4.16 Late seventeenth-century azulejos: the adoration of the
Eucharist; Lisbon: National Museum of Azulejos; picture
by the author   81
5.1(a–c)   The dome and the main foyer of the Galeries Lafayette,
Paris; pictures by the author   92
6.1 Line of people from Sol to Plaza Mayor, Madrid, in the early
morning of June 4, 2016; picture by the author   96
6.2 Plaza Mayor during a "multitudinous master class of yoga"
on June 4, 2016; picture by the author   102
6.3 Francisco Rizi. 1683. *Auto-da-fé in Plaza Mayor, Madrid*.
Oil on canvas. 277 × 438 cm. Madrid: Museo del Prado   102
6.4 People practicing multitudinous yoga in Plaza Mayor, Madrid,
on June 4, 2016; picture by the author   103
6.5 People practicing multitudinous yoga in Plaza Mayor, Madrid,
on June 4, 2016; picture by the author   105
6.6 Crowd visiting Christo's Floating Piers, Lake of Iseo, Italy, late
June 2016; picture by the author   112
8.1 Rembrandt Harmenszoon van Rijn. 1632. *The Anatomy Lesson
of Dr. Nicolaes Tulp*. 216.5 cm × 169.5 cm (85.2 in × 66.7 in).
Oil on canvas. The Hague: Mauritshuis   137
11.1 The sequence of the vase; photogram from 晩春 [*Banshun*],
Late Spring (1949), by 小津 安二郎, Ozu Yasujirō (1949),
picture from Wikimedia Commons   176

ACKNOWLEDGMENTS

This book conflates questions and answers accumulated over a number of years, often in dialogue with research institutions, colleagues, and friends. I thank the University of Turin, the Department of Philosophy, CIRCE, my research center, and, above all, my fellow semioticians therein. The chapter on "Framing Insignificance" results from a period as visiting professor at the University of Kyoto, Japan. I thank Atsushi Okada for facilitating this experience and for enriching conversation on the cultural semiotics of Japanese ways of life. Chapter 2, "Trolling Insignificance: Disrupting the Digital Public Discourse," stems from a research project on "viral extremism" carried on together with the University of Potsdam, Germany. I thank Eva Kimminich for providing precious feedback on the topic. The third chapter, "Contrarian Insignificance: Wars of Position in the Digital Arena", was first presented as a keynote lecture at the Bologna Congress of the Italian Association of Semiotic Studies, which I thank. The content of Chapter 4 was first delivered as a keynote lecture to the audience of the Technical University of Limassol, Cyprus, in the occasion of an international congress on visual semiotics: I thank Euripides Zantides for providing such an opportunity for exchange. Chapter 5, "Shopping Insignificance: Post-Material Temples," was conceived for a symposium on "contemporary urban sacred space" under the impulse of Mariachiara Giorda, whom I thank. The content of Chapter 4 was first delivered at the Leuven Congress of the European Association for Religious Studies and benefited from feedback from Giusi Viscardi and other colleagues, to whom I am indebted. Chapter 7, "Eating Insignificance: Post-Material Meals," was originally conceived for a publication project on the semiotics of food edited by Simona Stano, whom I thank. The content of Chapter 8, "Recovering Significance: The Value of Singularity," was presented in various versions and in different languages to fellow semioticians around the world, in particular at a semiotic congress organized by Sémir Badir (whom

I am grateful to) and other colleagues at the University of Marrakech, Morocco. It also benefited from feedback offered by participants in a Monash-Turin symposium at the Prato Monash Centre (I thank Richard Mohr for the opportunity). "Negotiating Significance: The Value of Compromise" (Chapter 9) was first published in the *Journal of the American Semiotic Association* under the impulse of Dario Martinelli, whom I thank. The content of Chapters 10 and 11, "Sharing Significance: The Value of Common Sense" and "Courting Significance: The Value of Interpretation," was first delivered to the Chinese Academy of Social Sciences in Shanghai; I thank in particular Zhang Jiang and Zeng Jun for their valuable insights. The final chapter was first conceived for a special issue on Greimas of *Sign Systems Studies*, the semiotic journal of the University of Tartu, which I thank (in particular, Remo Gramigna).

This book has been put together through a period that was professionally blissful but personally tragic. Through composing it, I sought to come to terms also with my intimate experience of insignificance. Throughout this difficult period, I was encouraged in different ways by relatives, friends, and colleagues. It would be impossible to thank them all, but I must mention my mother and brother, my aunt Anna, my colleague Ugo, all my collaborators at CIRCE, my research center, and above all my students, whose enthusiasm and attention gave me strength through hard times.

The first book plan was outlined during a visiting professorship at the Institute of Advanced Study, Durham University. I thank, in particular, Elizabeth Archibald, the principal of the Saint Cuthbert's Society, to which I was honored to be affiliated during my stay. Most of the book was then put together during my visiting fellowship at the IFK Vienna, whose director, Thomas Macho, I thank.

This book is dedicated to my father, who passed away while I was on the verge of completing the book. None of it would exist without the both physical and existential impulse that he gave to my life.

INTRODUCTION

The significance of insignificance

This book describes how insignificance seeps into everyday life. It concentrates on meaningless human behaviors repeatedly performed, although no significance is attached to them. The book expounds on causes, effects, and remedies. It points at how the progressive digitalization of life is turning the relation between subjects and objects, as well as that among individuals, into empty stereotypes; it underlines the causal link between such lack of existential salience and several contemporary "obsessions"; it suggests some strategies to resist the alienating effects of the digital bureaucratization of meaning.

The book engages with some of the most perturbing patterns of insignificance in present-day societies. It focuses, in particular, on the aesthetic sphere and its paradoxical manifestations of meaninglessness. Adopting a view inspired by semiotic anthropology, it reframes the ideologically overloaded concept of alienation in new terms. Unlike the classics of the sociology of reification, it does not tackle the issue of insignificance abstractedly but through the analysis of everyday contexts and activities. The book is expected to cast light on the genesis of insignificance and to indicate a series of lines of diversion from it.

Written avoiding the technical jargon of semiotics, *On Insignificance* is intended for the vast readership of those who feel that their everyday life is increasingly besieged by meaninglessness. The book seeks to explain the semiotic causes of this feeling and propose some antidotes to it.

On Insignificance begins with an introductory chapter entitled "Framing Insignificance: A Semiotic Typology of Meaninglessness". Taking as anecdotic situation of departure a ride on a Japanese bus, the chapter technically explains what "meaningless" means. It pinpoints the linguistic and cultural processes through which human beings pass from total ignorance of meaning to full grasp of it. At the same time, it exposes the modalities through which these patterns are sometimes reversed into their opposite: an inexorable decline into a meaningless existence.

The second chapter, entitled "Trolling Insignificance: Disrupting the Digital Public Discourse", interprets trolling as a violent attempt at reacting against the loss of significance in the digital arena through the disruption of the mechanisms of virtual public conversation. The chapter reads the rampant phenomenon of trolling as a form of nihilism, in which the correspondence between signified thought and signifying word is less important than "the fun" that one proves at witnessing the jamming of social conversation. The chapter singles out and describes the main rhetorical ingredients of trolling through contrasting it with comparable discursive practices: provocation, joke, defensive anonymity, critical public discourse, controversy, and lie. The following elements are found to play a major role in the discursive construction of trolling: topic-insensitive provocation, time-boundless jest, sadistic hierarchy of the sender and the receiver, anonymity of both the troll and her or his audience, choral character of the "actant observer" of trolling, construction of artificial contradictory semantics, disruption of argumentative logics, and irrelevance of the relation between beliefs and expressions. Trolling profoundly disrupts the ethics of human conversation because it severs expression from content, signifier from signified, communication from intention. This digital phenomenon, however, should not be simply stigmatized, but deciphered as a symptom of the existential distortions that the digitalization of social life often entails.

The third chapter, entitled "Contrarian Insignificance: Wars of Position in the Digital Arena", highlights how reactions to the insignificance of the digital conversation do not give rise only to trolling, but also to sterile controversies that unfold syntactically, disregarding the actual subject of contention and creating an empty dialectics among equally narcissistic positions. The traditional social sciences have mostly focused on the formation of social opinions from a semantic point of view: Given a certain semantic field, interviews, statistics, and other analytical instruments are commonly deployed in order to map the distribution of views, their evolution, their conflicts, and their agreements. Socio-semiotics, social semiotics, and the other semiotic branches that bear on social inquiry have contributed to the effort by providing semiotic grids of categorization. These grids too, however, have been mostly related to semantic contents circulating through societies and their cultures. The chapter pursues a different hypothesis. After briefly recalling the events of January 7–9, 2015 in the Parisian area (the terror attacks against Charlie Hebdo), it seeks to survey and map the syntax of progressive differentiation of opinions circulating in the social networks about such events. Some patterns are identified and semiotically described: (1) cleavage, (2) comparative relativizing, (3) blurring sarcasm, (4) anonymity, (5) unfocused responsibility, and (6) conspiracy thought. A new semiotic square is created to visually display these patterns, their positions, their relations, and their evolution. The bitter conclusion that the chapter reaches is that most opinions in the present-day digital conversation are created and defended by contrarians, who seek to escape existential insignificance not as much through expressing a personal and empathic voice as through robotically contrasting the voice of others, whatever its content might be.

The fourth chapter, entitled "Picturing Insignificance: The Utopia of Digital Perfection", deals with another utopia of the present-day digital world: that of regaining significance through the fullness of technical achievement. That is particularly evident in the sphere of digital imagery. The chapter consists in a semiotic critique of the constitutive element of digital life, "the pixel". By contrasting its technical features with those of the constituents of material life (e.g., the knots in a carpet), the chapter points out how, through the alluring image of a smoothly orderable world, digital marketing is stripping everyday life of the surprise of imperfection. In the pre-digital world, art consisted in the asymptotic effort to master a recalcitrant matter; in the digital era, instead, reality is presented as something that, as the philosopher Lévinas would have said, is endowed with a cold façade but lacks any proper visage. The insignificance that digital bureaucracy injects in everyday life, the chapter concludes, consists in surrounding people with an artificial environment, whose aesthetics is strikingly at odds with that involved in the perception of nature.

The following three chapters expound on some new sociocultural obsessions triggered by digital insignificance: People strive to recover the meaningfulness of the material world, yet such longing is hijacked and monetized by the marketing of the digital era and its production of empty simulacra.

Thus, the fifth chapter, entitled "Consuming Insignificance: Post-Material Temples", connects a philosophical reflection on the devaluation of the signifier in culture—and specifically in religion—with the emergence of post-secular temples, which retrieve some elements of the premodern spatial symbology of the sacred in order to host individual liturgies of consumption and meaning-making.

The sixth chapter, entitled "Assembling Insignificance: Post-Material Crowds", concentrates on three examples taken from everyday aesthetics: a multitudinous master class of yoga attracts thousands of young women in Madrid's Plaza Mayor, a crowd applauds at the funeral of a famous university professor, and visitors line up for hours to walk on Christo's installation *The Floating Piers*. If analyzed through semiotics, all these apparently different events reveal a common thread: The demise of embodied rituals has left digital societies with an inextinguishable thirst for communitarian transcendence. The post-religious ways of achieving transcendence, though, taking shape in the empty frameworks of past religious "semiospheres", are constantly in danger of being hijacked by the marketing discourse of post-capitalism, which transforms them into as many occasions for surreptitious spiritual alienation.

The seventh chapter, "Eating Insignificance: Post-Material Meals", interprets and criticizes the present-day economically developed societies' unprecedented attention to food. The culinary discourse, in all its facets, gains increasing centrality in contemporary cultures. Institutions, media, and common people are obsessed with what they eat. Gastronomy turns into the main concern, into the most debated and cared of system of norms. Social phenomena like Slow Food and Zero Kilometer conquer the world, claiming that improving the quality of food is the way for a better planet. But what is the deep cultural meaning of this massive trend? What lies behind the "culinary reason"? Aesthetic neutralization of socioeconomic conflicts, chauvinistic marketing of stereotypes, and anti-intellectual subversion of sensorial hierarchies, the chapter contends, claiming that the sacralization of food is a further marketing trap into which the digital society, bereft of material meaningfulness, shows tendency to fall.

The book intends to denounce the dynamics of insignificance in the post-material world as well as the digital obsessions to which they lead. This *pars destruens* is, however, meant to be conducive to a *pars construens*. The book aims at pointing at some directions along which significance might be recovered. Thus, the eighth chapter, entitled "Recovering Significance: The Value of Singularity", suggests to revalue the singularity of cognitions, emotions, and actions, contrasting the generalizing tendencies of digital bureaucracy and taking as a source of inspiration the singularizing gaze of painting in its dialectics with the generalizing gaze of anatomy and the other technics of taxonomic knowledge.

Another direction for the reactivation of semiosis in the post-material world is indicated by the ninth chapter, which bears the title "Negotiating Significance: The Value of Compromise". Against the sophisticated algorithms of global digital bureaucracy, which constrain the complexity of social life into a series of calculable options, semiotics must suggest that language is always potential exploration of a gray zone among polarities, in which new forms of compromise and co-existence among differences can be found. From this perspective, the approach of humanities must not consist in mimicking the digital arrogance of a technological ordering of the world, but in creating a space of negotiation beyond the constraints of technology. "Please, we urgently need a semiotician!" is certainly not the most common request heard in a situation of emergency, yet a time may come when we realize that there are cases that a physician (or another scientist) cannot effectively deal with. Two passengers fight over the same space on a plane, to the point that the pilot is obliged to land and have the two contenders get off at the closest airport. Each of the humanities has a specific way to frame and seek to find a less disrupting solution to the problem. The chapter argues that the specific contribution semiotics can and must give to present-day societies is that of providing discursive evidence that problems that fall in the domain of language cannot be solved by technology, no matter how smart it might be, but rather can be solved only via communication as such: talking, compromising, and finding agreements.

The tenth chapter, entitled "Sharing Significance: The Value of Common Sense", recommends that significance must be recovered not individually, as the digital marketing of post-material narcissism encourages consumers to do, but rather collectively, through the creation of a new community of interpreters. That which is usually called "common sense" is nothing but the complex deposit of implicit cognitive, emotional, and pragmatic rules through which the members of a society interact with each other and, simultaneously, affirm their belonging to the group. This sense is called "common" both because it is current—meaning that it permeates the daily life of the group in all its manifestations—and because it is shared: It is something that belongs to the community as a whole and something through which, at the same time, the members of the community can belong. What is the relation between "sense" and "common sense"? This question is extremely relevant to semiotics, hermeneutics, and the other disciplines and philosophies of interpretation. Against the mechanical fragmentation of perspectives favored by the dematerialization of public discourse, semiotics must propitiate the elaboration of a new digital philology, meant at recreating a common sense in the virtual arena.

To this regard, the eleventh chapter, entitled "Courting Significance: The Value of Interpretation", questions the role of different hermeneutic stances in coping with the apparent insignificance of everyday life. What is the difference between interpreting a literary text during a university lecture and interpreting reality outside of the academe? And what is the difference between interpreting in natural sciences and interpreting in the humanities? Despite evident and known divergences, humanities too can rank their interpretations and aspire to guide the interpretations of society. Three alternative methods can be used so as to test interpretive hypotheses, depending on whether the author's, the reader's, or the text's meaningful intentionality is primarily investigated. The chapter argues that the third method is superior to the first two, for it leads to the creation of a common meta-discursive space for intersubjective exchange about meaning. Although adopting an appropriate methodology is essential in textual analysis, that which is even more important is supporting the creation of a community of interpreters that, sharing the same method, engage in the constructive comparison and ranking of interpretive moves.

The conclusive chapter of the book, entitled "The Clash of Semiotic Civilizations", adopts a strong view about the need for a politics of significance. The chapter claims that the strength, as well as the weakness, of structural semiotics consists in positing a rational way to determine the range of meanings of a text. Hermeneutic methods that are more aware of the diachronic dimension, such as Eco's interpretive semiotics or Lotman's semiotics of culture, inflect this view by anchoring the rationality of interpretation to the reasonableness of a community of interpreters that is, by definition, changing over time. The chapter claims that, on the one hand, the structuralist theoretical stance is in line with the predominant "culture of meaning" distilled by the Western civilization from the Greeks until the Enlightenment, stressing the value of truth as correspondence between textual evidence and its hermeneutics; on the other hand, the chapter also suggests that Eco's and Lotman's insistence on the dynamic character of hermeneutic communities entails a politics of meaning meant to preserve the core of the Western "semiotic civilization" against threats that aim at deeply subverting it from both the inside and the outside of the semiosphere.

1

FRAMING INSIGNIFICANCE

A semiotic typology of meaninglessness

Le vrai paradoxe est là: à l'échelle cosmique
notre durée de vie est insignifiante, et
pourtant ce bref laps de temps où nous
paraissons sur la scène du monde est le lieu
d'où procède toute question de signifiance.[1]
(Paul Ricoeur, 1984. "Le temps raconté",
Revue de métaphysique et de morale, 4: 440)

Introduction

Riding on a bus abroad can be an instructive semiotic experience. To foreigners with no knowledge of Japanese, buses in Kyoto exude mysterious prospects of significance, each of them a decoding challenge. To Western travelers,
messages in English will appeal first, like life vests in a shipwreck. Characters
in *rōmaji*, as the Japanese call the Latin script, will also pop out here and there,
albeit unfamiliarly interspaced and surrounded by a myriad of unknown signs.
A sign is, indeed, a promise of signification. Most tourists on their way to one
of the Kyoto temples have no knowledge of *hiragana*, *katakana*, or *kanji*—the
three systems of writing that Japanese constantly intermingles—yet they trust
that those "bizarre" arrangements of dots and lines are no simple decoration.
Several contextual elements (the place and structure of their appearing; some
previous, although merely evocative, familiarity with the Japanese script; and,
above all, confidence that the inside of buses is arranged across cultures in a
similar way, offering passengers orderly clues about their functioning) urge
them to look at those marks, believe them to be signs, and even pathetically
try to decode them. Such is human beings' desperate relation with language:
Although there are no chances that they will understand, they cannot help

seeking to understand, assuming that deciphering language will provide better control over the environment.

That is the case with buses. Tourists tend to avoid them, riding on subways as soon as they can, for the latter usually obey more globalized, standard rules, while the former follow local schemes whose decoding is an essential precondition. Where and when should I buy a ticket? How much does it cost and for what category of fare? What should I do with it? How could I realize when my stop is near, and what should I do to signal the driver that I wish to get off? In Kyoto buses, messages in unknown scripts beckon the foreigner by their bright color, perspicuous font, and noticeable size. They all seem to imply: "I am important; read me; understand me; follow my instruction". Yet, to the ignorant foreigner's frustration, they remain like mysterious warnings from a remote, incomprehensible deity.

Learning a new language is, indeed, frustrating, especially when it involves decoding a new system of writing. To most Western visitors, the use of *kanji* logograms in Japanese is a major source of despondence. Yet, for the same reason, learning a new language is exhilarating. Riding on the same bus day after day, and studying the language meanwhile, one experiences over and over again the miraculous moment in which the sign keeps its promise and delivers its content. In the case of Japanese, the syllabic scripts of *hiragana* and *katakana* first reveal their message of sound and, therefore, communication. Eventually *kanji* logograms too, however, cease to appear as jumbled collections of dots and lines and, even before releasing their precise semantic treasure, start looking as patterned configurations underpinned by logic. One does not know what such logic precisely is but is confident that there is one and it can be learned.

Psychoanalysis might suggest that the bittersweet feeling of learning a new language is attractive, for it brings one back to a sort of second childhood, in which language is increasingly absorbed as a means to gain control over the environment and, above all, in the relation to one's parents. After all, learning a new language might mean wanting to talk to one's parents again. Voluntarily putting oneself in a situation of linguistic ignorance might just be the necessary pain that one has to endure in order to subsequently taste—through hard study, of course—the sweet flavor of becoming, again, a linguistic self, embraced by a community of speakers. As polyglots know well, learning languages can be addictive, and the addiction might be related to this unconscious desire of both identity and acceptance.

But it can also be argued, out of the psychoanalytical framework, that the pleasure of learning a new language is intimately related to the instinct of preserving one's life. Surrounded by unknown cultures, human beings keep trusting that what they experience all around is not mere noise but signs, whose deciphering will turn them from potential promises of meaning into actual messages. Learning how to read them will provide a firmer grasp over the environment and, as a consequence, prospects of longer and better survival. *Just as each living being in the natural universe strives to preserve its material existence, so too each semiotic being in the cultural semiosphere strives to preserve its symbolical existence,* seeking to attach meaningfulness to the myriads of unknown signs—yet, still signs—that seem to pop out in the environment at all time. We do not understand anything, yet we believe that we might understand. We shall die, yet we want to survive.

There is a reverse to this parallel. Just as the instinct of survival prevents human beings to fully come to terms with their mortality, so too the semiotic instinct impedes them to entirely becoming aware of that which is, nevertheless, an absolutely central element of both individual and collective life: *insignificance*. The most disturbing aspect of this blindness is that it has affected not only laymen but also those who are supposed to be specialists in the field, that is, semioticians. *It is as if doctors had studied, trained, taught, and worked for millennia in the illusion that the human body is immortal.* Focusing on the sign as the natural object of their inquiry, semioticians have, since the very early prehistory of the discipline, cultivated a bias for the dawn of signification, a taste for the inaugural moment in which reality shows itself as sign, promises to deliver a content, and finally releases it when the appropriate code is established. The entire semiotics of Umberto Eco can be read as an ode to this Sherlock Holmes's anthropology in which living consists in triumphing over the apparent meaninglessness of the environment through shrewd abductions, in mastering the signifying codes of society in order to correctly read and write messages (Eco and Sebeok 1983).

Focusing on the elating moment in which meaninglessness becomes meaningfulness, the potential promise of the sign turns into an actual delivery of content, and cooperation between texts and their ideal readers—perfectly integrated in their communities of interpreters—a hermeneutic, standard semiotics has, however, guiltily overlooked something whose existential proportions are, nevertheless, monstrous. It has cultivated the illusion that meaningfulness is the rule of social life and insignificance its marginal exception. But is it thus? And can semiotics really answer the most urgent human questions about meaning, signification, and communication by adopting such a triumphant attitude? Can a doctor be of any use when believing that death is actually an exception in human life and not the rule? Is not such an overconfident attitude toward insignificance, meaninglessness, misunderstanding, and noise a macroscopic impediment to genuine, empathic, and ultimately useful understanding of society just as it would be for a physician belittling the role of disease, infirmity, and pain in human life?

Unfortunately, authors who knew very well how to communicate have written most semiotic theories, as though physicians with no personal acquaintance with pain, malady, or death had been the protagonists in the history of medicine. Yet, the beginnings of the discipline were infelicitous: on the one hand, a genial American philosopher, who died impoverished and forsaken (Charles S. Peirce), and on the other hand, an equally genial Swiss linguist, with few disciples and a quixotic passion for anagrams (Ferdinand de Saussure). Perhaps, *it is time to take insignificance seriously.*

Undecipherable, incomprehensible, uncanny

First, insignificance and meaninglessness are not the same, although these words, as the corresponding adjectives—"insignificant" and "meaningless"—can sometimes be interchangeably used. Meaningless is that which has no meaning. It can be said of something whose meaning one fails to grasp and understand, or it can be predicated of something whose meaning one is not in agreement with. *In the first case, something in the environment appears as a sign, yet it refuses to deliver its promise of signification. Kanji* instructions on Japanese buses are meaningless to most foreign tourists. Although contextual circumstances contribute to identify them as signs by both locals and visitors, the latter are unable to go beyond their potentially signifying expression and access the actual content that such expression stands for. Therefore, *kanji* instructions are subjectively meaningless and are not objectively so. That is why, while being meaningless to some receivers, they do not cease for that matter to be signs. Should foreigners study hard enough, their perception of meaninglessness would turn into one of meaningfulness, giving rise to the experience of semiotic awareness evoked earlier. In this first acceptance, "meaningless" is a synonym of "indecipherable".

According to a second acceptance, "meaningless" can be said of a sign whose content one understands but fails to connect to a more encompassing logic. Another aspect of Japanese buses that often puzzles foreigners is the behavior of drivers. Every time a new driver enters the bus, he or she (but mostly he) takes off his or her hat and bows in front of passengers. Most foreigners are perfectly able to relate this gestural expression with a semantic content of deference. From this point of view, the gesture is not undecipherable to them. Its code resembles that of many analogous gestural codes one comes across around the globe, where the lowering of some parts of the body is used as a postural or gestural expressive device to mean subjection. Foreign visitors to Japan, however, are likely to find this gesture *incomprehensible*, which is the second facet of meaninglessness. In this case, tourists do not ignore *what* the sign stands for but *whom* the sign stands to. Drivers enter and bow, and nobody bows back (except some awkward foreign tourists); nobody among the locals even pays attention when drivers bow, yet Japanese drivers perform this gesture over and over again with no remissness. Why do they do it, foreigners wonder? That is meaningless!

Of course, that too is meaningless subjectively, not objectively. The fact itself that the gesture is recognized as such, that is, as a sign, indicates that what makes it appear meaningless is not an intrinsic quality but an external factor, namely, the tourist's lack of cultural knowledge. In the first example, *kanji* instructions were meaningless to foreigners qua undecipherable, for they ignored the linguistic code relating those patterns of dots and lines with a precise semantic content. Studying the Japanese language, as pointed out earlier, would turn meaninglessness into its contrary. In the second example, bowing gestures are meaningless to foreigners not qua undecipherable but qua incomprehensible. Foreigners do not ignore the cultural code relating those gestural patterns with a precise semantic content (which is obvious: deference) but the code relating it with a precise *pragmatic* content. Increased familiarity with the Japanese culture will lead tourists to turn this meaninglessness too into its opposite. They will understand, to start with, that entering an enclosed space in the Japanese culture entails a different range of semantic connotations and, as a consequence, pragmatic requirements than in most Western cultures. Spatial thresholds work differently in Japan, and both verbal and gestural formulae must adapt to this different sense of separation.

Peirce's legendary definition of the sign implicitly supports both ways of construing the meaning of meaninglessness seen thus far. If the sign is "something that stands for something, to someone in some capacity", a receiver can fail to associate the "something" of the sign with the "something else" it stands for (meaninglessness as indecipherability); or he or she can fail to understand whom the something of the sign stands for (meaninglessness as incomprehensibility).

This differentiation allows one to better specify the "contextual circumstances" thanks to which a sign is recognized and received as such, although it does not yet fully deliver its promise of content. In the first example, foreign tourists ignore that which *kanji* instructions stand for, but they trust that they stand to someone, that is, local passengers. That is why they still consider them as signs, although *kanji* instructions are meaningless (undecipherable) to them. In the second example, foreign tourists do not know whom salutation ceremonies stand to, but they are confident that they stand for something. They are meaningless (incomprehensible) to them but do not cease for that matter to appear as signs.

What happens, however, when both what a sign stands for and whom it stands to are ignored? A third example, always about Japanese buses, might help elucidate this third, even more complicated circumstance. Can a sign be recognized as such, that is, as a promise of meaning, although one ignores both the semantic and pragmatic codes of its functioning as a sign? Riding on Japanese buses at night, one sees often bits of hemp string knotted to the railings. To most, if not all, foreigners, such bits look meaningless both in the sense of "undecipherable" (it is not clear what the strings stand for) and in that of "incomprehensible" (it is not clear whom the strings stand to). But something in such bits of hemp string will still qualify and present them as signs, that is, as promise of signification. A recurrent bus passenger, indeed, will soon realize that (1) only bits of hemp string appear, not of other materials; (2) they are always knotted around the same railings; and (3) they are always knotted in the same way. Thus, although foreign passengers do not know either what these bits of hemp string stand for or whom they stand to, they will start realizing that their appearance in the world is *patterned*. Bits of hemp string on Japanese buses are meaningless not because they are undecipherable, and not because they are incomprehensible, but because they are both.

That is the third definition of "meaninglessness": something whose both semantic and pragmatic functioning is ignored is meaningless in the sense of "uncanny". This acceptance too is inherently contained in Peirce's definition of the sign. A sign is not only something that stands for something else and not only something that stands to someone but also something that stands "in some capacity". When foreign passengers repeatedly come across bits of hemp string knotted to the railings of Japanese buses, these bits look to them not only meaningless qua undecipherable and not only meaningless qua incomprehensible but also meaningless qua uncanny because of their both indecipherability and incomprehensibility. Yet they still look like signs. They still prompt a subtle, mysterious, even disquieting promise of signification, which results exactly from their patterned nature: Bits of hemp string do not appear in whatever material, shape, or position; ergo, they must signify something. In other words, the fact that only some aspects of their material existence are recurrently selected, while some other aspects are discarded, suggests that such selection is likely to act as the perceptible expression of the capacity wherein a sign stands for something to someone. Passengers ignore the "something" as they ignore the "someone", yet they surmise that those bits of hemp string result from a promise of signification, a promise so feeble, in this case, that only its abstract capacity is beheld. Yet that is sufficient for the sign's foreshadow to appear. Assiduous frequentation of Japanese buses will allow the puzzled passenger to realize that those bits of hemp strings are actually "relics" of the leaflets that are tied to the bus's railings for distribution early in the morning and are mostly all gone at nighttime, taken away by other passengers. The bits of hemp strings are, therefore, indexical relics of this practice of leafleting, customary in Japanese public transport.

If in the first example meaninglessness was turned into its opposite through familiarization with the linguistic code behind the sign and if in the second example that happened through acquaintance with the cultural code behind the sign, in this third example, empirical observation allows the passenger to associate a potential signifying capacity with an actual meaning. Only repeatedly taking the same bus at different times will turn the uncanny into the familiar or even into the banal.

Types of meaninglessness and types of signs

To sum up, *a sign can be meaningless because its semantic content is ignored but not its pragmatic functioning (meaninglessness as indecipherability); it can be meaningless because, vice versa, its pragmatic functioning is ignored but not its semantic content (meaninglessness as incomprehensibility: the colloquial expression "it makes no sense" also captures this version of meaninglessness); or it can be meaningless because both its semantic content and its pragmatic functioning are ignored but not its capacity to act as a sign (meaninglessness as uncanniness).*

This tripartition does not overlap with Peirce's equally tripartite semiotic typology but combines with it in interesting ways. Arguably, a specific sphere of meaninglessness predominates in each typology of sign. Symbols can be meaningless qua undecipherable, but they can hardly be thus qua incomprehensible or uncanny. Recognizing a sign as a symbol, indeed, is tantamount to implying that it must stand to someone, although that which it stands for is ignored (that is the case of *kanji* instructions on Japanese buses). Similarly, recognizing a sign as an icon is equivalent to implying that it must stand for something, although whom it stands to is ignored (that is the case of bowing ceremonies on Japanese buses). Finally, recognizing a sign as an index amounts to implying that it must stand for something to someone in some capacity, although both the "something" it stands for and the "someone" it stands to are ignored (that is the case of bits of hemp strings on Japanese buses).

Meaninglessness *versus* insignificance

Indecipherability, incomprehensibility, and uncanniness, however, are not insignificance. Insignificance is something else. A sign can be meaningless because one fails to access its semantic content, pragmatic functioning, or both. But a sign cannot be insignificant. That would be a contradiction in terms. In order for a sign to be insignificant, it should deny itself, that is, it should deny its own nature of sign. It should appear as something about which one does not only ignore what it stands for, or whom it stands to, but also the capacity in which it stands. An insignificant sign is a sign that stands for nothing, to nobody, in no respect or capacity. It is a non-sign. It is a thing.

The history of modern semiotics, especially from the 1960s on, has constantly overlooked the possibility of such a non-sign, of such a thing. Eminent semioticians have emphatically hammered into the vulgate of the discipline that everything can be studied as a sign (Eco 1976). It does not matter, indeed, that a sign stands to no interpreter as long as it can stand to an *interpretant*, that is, as long as it harbors potentiality for interpretation. Nothing in the entire universe is irremediably insignificant (Goethe), since everything can, given the right circumstances, become part of the joyous chain of unlimited semiosis, of the multifarious snake that enfolds the whole universe and bestows upon it the sparkle of intelligibility. From this point of view, "insignificant" is nothing but the synonym of "meaningless": It is just a matter of time, dedication, and scrutiny, and each object in the world will be awakened from its apparent insignificance and given a place in the splendorous realm of human signification.

But is this really the way in which human beings experience meaning in their valley of tears? Are they really surrounded by a universe of potentially titillating stimuli, each a key to a new adventure of knowledge and interpretation? It is difficult not to suspect that behind such iridescent conception of how signification works lies the bias of scholars who looked at the matter from a particularly privileged point of view, from the perspective granted by an exceptionally gifted, exceptionally curious, and exceptionally inquisitive mind. Semiotics has long extolled the fictional character of Sherlock Holmes as the champion of the discipline, as the herald of abduction, and as the epitome of the tremendous perspicacity of the human mind in the whirlwind of semiosis. *It is perhaps time to suggest that most human beings are not Sherlock Holmes. They are Dr. Watson.* The world to them is a platitude. They themselves are a platitude to the world. Most of what happens in their life is not simply meaningless, in the sense that it is waiting for a stroke of Holmesian genius to be turned into a source of meaningful insights. Most of what happens in their life is beyond meaninglessness. It is irredeemably insignificant. It is not just waiting for the right interpretant to associate it with a semantic content and a pragmatic value, with a linguistic code or a cultural semiosphere. It is just a thing. It is a thing that stands for nothing, a thing that stands to no one, in no respect or capacity. It is a black hole in the supposed entelechy of the universe, a blind corner, a mute sound, a transparency that nobody looks through, a letter that nobody will ever read not only because it is written in a language spoken by none and not only because it is enclosed in a bottle that will never be opened but also, and above all, because nobody ever will recognize it as a letter. It is insignificance. It is that which not even the cleverest semiotician can talk about. It is that which the exuberant liveliness of gaudy scholars instinctively suppresses, covering it with fantasies of encyclopedic gushing. If life is semiosis and semiosis is life, as equally happy-go-lucky bio-semioticians repeat like a mantra, then insignificance is death—death human beings live by.

Insignificance matters

Two questions: If insignificance does not signify, how is it possible to recognize it? And why should we care?

Awakening into significance

Insignificance can be recognized through contrast with significance. The contrast can be perceived both ways. On the one hand, there is the passage from insignificance to significance. Let's go back on a Japanese bus. Most foreign visitors to Japan will be struck by how often locals fall asleep in public transport—buses, metro, and trains, no matter the mode: The foreigner will be often surrounded by Japanese people who drowse, doze, nap, sink in their seats, lean, slant, slope, and then miraculously awake at their stop. Initially, most tourists laugh at that, as when human beings are confronted with that which they do not understand and that, nevertheless, concerns them. Less superficial beholders will hypothesize that Japanese people work too hard, get up too early, or spend too much time in public transport. In some cases, however, this bizarre experience will give rise to a passage from insignificance to significance, one that it would have been impossible without the anthropological experience of traveling into another culture. The passage does not consist simply in interpretation of the Japanese habit of sleeping in public transport. That would be on a par with transition from meaninglessness (in the sense of incomprehensibility) to meaningfulness, through relation of such habit with a certain aspect of the Japanese semiosphere.

On the contrary, in this case, passage from insignificance to significance entails a much more startling revelation about what public space in one's non-Japanese culture is. Seeing how easily and how commonly Japanese people fall asleep in public transport, indeed, will lead some foreigners to think, "I would never feel comfortable doing that in the metro of Paris, or on a bus in Rome, or on Madrid's suburban trains". Japanese people fall asleep in public transport not only because they must, as naïve interpretations suggest (they work too hard, etc.) but also because they can. *They can for they trust their public space.* They trust their society. They trust their fellow Japanese. They trust them to the point that falling asleep in public, at the mercy of other gazes and intentions, does not worry them. That is the passage from insignificance to significance that such anthropological observation leads to. Upon traveling on a bus in Japan, the wake that characterizes riding on public transport in other countries will cease to be insignificant; the alertness by which exhausted passengers struggle to keep vigilant will stop appearing like a natural behavior and look for what it is: a significant choice; the result of a whole social system; and the quotidian, banal, and, for that reason, even more pernicious outcome of a long and complex history of violence and injustice, and of centuries of hunger, poverty, exploitation, and crime, all weighing on the shoulders of each passenger of the metro of Paris, Rome, London, and Madrid, and all whispering to their ears, "Don't fall asleep, it's dangerous".

That is the passage from insignificance to significance. It is the moment in which the color of the air starts to show itself. It is the instant in which voices theretofore unheard begin to whisper their message of truth. It is the institution of a new code, one that breaks the muteness of second nature and reveals it as the burden of history. Traveling frequently entails the adventure of turning meaninglessness into meaningfulness through familiarization with an unknown cultural code; but a rarer and more enlightening outcome of the anthropological experience of traveling is not that of learning or discovering such outward code but that of instituting a new inward code, able to bestow new intelligibility not upon the culture of the other but upon one's own culture. From that moment on, being awake in public transport will not seem so natural anymore; its opposite will not appear as so laughable either. It is like being in a classroom where a noisy overhead projector is switched on: You do not realize how noisy it was until it is switched off, and the quality of silence in the room becomes a significant matter again.

Nevertheless, revelatory passages from insignificance to significance are rare. They arise in circumstances of travel or anthropological exploration, which are activities precluded to most. To most human beings, the violence of public space, as well as hunger, poverty, dirtiness, oppression, and so on, is not simply meaningless. That would be already something. It would mean that, given the appropriate conditions, a search could be launched in order to find the cause of the curse and eradicate it. The problem is that to most human beings, pain, hunger, poverty, dirtiness, oppression, and violence are insignificant. And they are insignificant not as much for their beholders as for those who suffer from them. They hurt but naturally thus; they hurt like cold. For a child who has starved all his or her life, or a woman who has been beaten since she was a teenager, or a worker oppressed and exploited since she or he was an infant, pain is not a semiotic habit. *It is an insignificant, mute condition of existence with no alternative horizon.* That is one of the most serious moral mistakes of modern semiotics: thinking that semiotic habits are innocent per se qua outcome of the unceasingly semiotic labor of a community of interpreters. Not only semiotic habits are not necessarily innocent, but they are also mostly blind, meaning that when they establish themselves, they offer no access to the liberating activity of semiotic interpretation. Only comfortable scholars could have thought that unlimited semiosis is destined to crystallize in the most suitable, most rational, and most equitable habits a community is capable of.

Linguistic anthropology has long established the fruitful distinction between -etic and -emic perspectives (Pike 1967). Bizarrely, semiotics mostly ignores it. To most semioticians, semiotic habits are the close toward which the rationality of the functioning of the sign naturally leads unlimited semiosis. When semioticians analyze a semiotic habit, they see it as the best response a community of interpreters was able to give to the puzzle of signification. Such perspective, oblivious to the anthropological distinction between -emic and -etic, fails to realize that semiotic habits are actually semiotic only from an external point of view. It is from the external point of view of the analyst, indeed, that they can be seen as alive, as cultural constructs that emerge from the tentative configuration of a code, from its progressive establishment and solidification into a stable sign, resisting the fibrillations of history as long as an ideal community of interpreters agrees on its reasonableness. From an internal point of view, instead, semiotic habits are not semiotic anymore. They are insignificant. They are not too different from religious beliefs, or routines, or any other example of human predicament or conduct in which cultural choice is absorbed as second nature, as an unquestionable standard. That is why it would be too generous to say that our semiotic habits are meaningless, in the sense that we do not know what they stand for (they are undecipherable), whom they stand to (they are incomprehensible), or in what capacity they stand (they are uncanny). More disquietingly, our semiotic habits are insignificant because they are the bio-cultural mechanism through which social choices transmogrify into natural selves. Thinking that such transmogrification is always the best possible way or thinking that a stroke of genius could shake it anytime from its semiotic torpor into the revived fizziness of unlimited semiosis is, frankly, an expression of moral naiveté.

The space of public transport in most European cities is unsafe. One could not sleep in it. One can sleep in one's car, or at home, or in one's office in certain cases, and even in such places diminished alertness would sometimes entail danger. Yet Europeans do not miss sleeping in public. They do not know it. They do not think about it. The relation between sleep and public space is insignificant to them, at least as long as their socio-semiotic habits are not revealed as such through encounter with a different civilization, in which the same relation is shown, on the opposite, as significant. Then one realizes not only that a different form of public space is possible but also that this alternative form is preferable.

One becomes aware of the insignificant violence she or he has been subjected to. This is how semiotic habits work: not as refined encyclopedic sedimentations that communities distill through history by means of placid academic dialogue and that individuals absorb upon probing reality through alternative interpretants. Semiotic habits are like little pebbles in one's shoes: It is only on getting rid of them that one realizes how better walking is without them and how better it might have been even before. They are like a pain so engrained in one's body that one forgets about it while still excruciatingly suffering from it. They are a chronic disease one gets accustomed to.

Affirming that semiotic habits tend to become insignificant from an internal perspective is not tantamount to advocating the utopia of life in accordance with unbridled unlimited semiosis. Such an option is precluded to most human beings and viable only to some privileged individuals (e.g., true artists). On the contrary, reflecting on the insignificance of semiotic habits is meant to subvert the idea of their intrinsic reasonableness. It is not true that a community of interpreters always selects the best interpretants as the pragmatic close to the chain of unlimited semiosis, as it is not true that such a close is always temporary, open to reactivation at any moment, should the community believe that alternative interpretants offer a better solution to the riddle of shared meaning. Conversely, *one could redefine violence as the persistence, in a community of interpreters, of semiotic habits that, while invisible for most members of the community, inflict suffering on some of them to the advantage of others.* Slavery too was a semiotic habit. It too was selected as the best suitable representation of humankind from a chain of alternatives in which it crystallized as the close and final interpretant. It gave rise to mentalities, behaviors, trade, and jurisdiction. It inflicted unspeakable pain. Yet it was insignificant to most. It was not meaningless. It was not undecipherable. It was neither incomprehensible nor uncanny. It was part of (second) nature. Yet it was monstrous, and when some courageous minds were able to point at it, and fought against it, and finally outlawed it, then humanity realized how intolerable it had been to turn such a choice into a habit. Perhaps, one day people will realize with the same dismay how blind it was to have people die while attempting to cross national frontiers, or how intolerably invisible a semiotic habit it was to slaughter other animals to feed human beings, and so on and so forth.

Semioticians are not primarily called to fight violence and injustice in the world; yet they are not called either to turn into the detached bards of the reasonableness of semiosis, developing sophisticated theories to justify the status quo. Only from a privileged position in history, society, and life, one can advocate for it. As soon as one steps out from this coddled vantage point, one realizes that human beings often turn violent interpretations into semiotic habits, share them as communities of interpreters, turn them into moral rules and legal norms, inflict pain through them, sponsor intellectuals who depict these semiotic habits as the reasonable outcome of human interpretive rationality, and ultimately create a realm in which violence, injustice, and suffering perpetuate themselves as second nature: unquestioned, mute, and insignificant. Semioticians should show that not all that is significant is right and that not all that is right is significant. They should reveal the insignificant pain of humanity.

Sinking into insignificance

Insignificance, however, can be revealed not only through the passage from insignificant to significant, as in realizing the violence of European public space while riding on a Japanese bus, but also in the symmetric passage from significance to insignificance.

Finding new meaning is always somehow thrilling. It is thrilling when the undecipherable is decoded through intuiting what a sign stands for. It is thrilling when the incomprehensible is understood through grasping whom a sign stands to. It is thrilling when the uncanny is recognized as the capacity in which a sign stands. Yet the most thrilling semiotic experience of all is when a new sign is born, a new sign that one would ignore that it would stand for something else, to someone, and in some capacity. It is the awakening of the world as language. It is the turning of a thing into a being. It is the realization that nature has yet another false bottom, a secret chest in which culture is hidden. The euphoria of the discovery is unrelated to the actual semantic content or pragmatic value of the sign. On the one hand, one can painfully discover the insignificance of violence as a matrix of signs theretofore invisible, such as the nervousness of the body in public space. On the other hand, one can exultantly uncover the joyful significance, for instance, of realizing the value of silence or of having one's body surrounded by natural sounds. In both cases, an innate instinct bestows upon human beings a positive chemistry when they are able to turn yet another mute corner of the world into language, no matter what it says. One could argue, as a counterargument, that obnubilation too is a pleasure—sinking into indistinctiveness, becoming a machine, perceiving the world as a thing and not as language, living an existence with no alternatives, and embracing necessity. Yet that is a dangerous trend. It is a perilous addiction whose moral entailments stand out when one analyzes insignificance not as the point of departure of moral awakening (the realization that a better world is possible) but as the point of arrival of moral sleepiness (the internalization of the idea that one lives in the only possible world). Furthermore, if one develops a taste for sinking into insignificance, it means that he or she is already unable to perceive its thresholds. When human beings start enjoying acting like robots, they do not act like robots anymore; they *are* robots.

Indeed, as long as one keeps faith to one's humanity, that is, to one's biocognitive endowment, one cannot be content with becoming a machine. Every time we realize that what we do or say stands for nothing, to nobody, and in no capacity, we should feel a sharp pain. We should feel an unstoppable longing for escape. We should change. That is not only a moral but also a bio-cognitive imperative. If we accept to live surrounded not by language and meaning but by mere things, then we are abdicating our role in the evolution. We are regressing through the history of the species. Turning the environment into significance is that which grants human beings a better control over it. One might choose to relinquish this capacity for the sake of the utopia of a mystical reunion with nature. In most cases, however, when human beings are pushed to sink into insignificance, to do and say things they do not know what they stand for, to whom, and in what capacity, they are transformed into things not out of their own utopian initiative but so that other human beings might use them as "human tools". Deep down, when some human beings plunge into insignificance, some other human beings profit from it.

What lesson can be drawn from riding on a Japanese bus about the relation between significance and insignificance? This time, it must be a personal lesson. The reason for which the present chapter adopts Japanese buses as a source of semiotic examples is that its author worked as a visiting professor at the University of Kyoto for one sabbatical semester (riding on many Japanese buses back and forth from home to office as a consequence).

A sabbatical can be an enchanted period for an academic. Suddenly, he or she is granted the possibility of spending long hours in libraries, archives, and laboratories; meeting new colleagues; having long, philosophical discussions with them over exotic meals; imparting new knowledge to attentive students; secluding oneself in a little study, unencumbered by too many personal items, in order to read, write, and, above all, think …. But wait a minute: Is not that exactly that which a university professor should be paid for doing all the time, during his or her entire career? Are these not exactly the normal occupations of a scholar?

Those, indeed, are the activities that should make the life of a scholar significant, meaning that he or she exists in the firm conviction that what he or she does stands for something relevant, to someone who cares about it, and in a capacity that is the best one given the personal vocation, training, and skills of the scholar. During a successful sabbatical, a university professor revels in significance. He or she cultivates the trust that his or her efforts are not vain, that they contribute to a better humanity.

But such feeling of significance is in sharp contrast with the predicament most university professors go through at home, working in their own institutions. Of course, some universities are better than others, and some give researchers more freedom than others, more opportunities for scholarly encounter and socialization, a wider and quieter office space, and so on. Nevertheless, that is not the point. A sabbatical is normally destined to be a scholar's better experience, no matter from which institution he or she comes from and no matter in which institution he or she lands. That is the case because, to a scholar, a sabbatical period normally means extracting himself or herself from most of that part of university life that is insignificant.

During the last financial and economic crisis, Italian universities have introduced a complex digital system of evaluation and self-evaluation on multiple levels as a means to progressively rationalize and eliminate unproductive practices and behaviors. Evaluation and self-evaluation are certainly useful in every field of human activity. As it is frequently the case in Italy or in countries with a similar cultural attitude, however, this originally Nordic framework of self-scrutiny has been imported only in its form and not in its substance. As the director of a master's program, the author of the present book must collect every year a long series of statistic data, compile them into a digital preformatted report, assess the situation of the program, and formulate promises for its improvement. All that looks great in appearance. In reality, statistic data are often fake or at least collected in such a poor way that they are totally unrepresentative of the actual state of the program; focusing exclusively on numbers, the report fails to capture that which really matters, that is, the quality of teaching and research in the program; there are no resources to effectively carry on that which is promised in the report; and, worst of all, nobody really reads these reports, except those bureaucrats who content themselves with controlling their formal impeccability. As a consequence, this activity of digital evaluation and self-evaluation (1) stands for nothing, since it does not really represent the status of the program; (2) stands to nobody, since nobody, neither the student nor the professor nor the institution leader, will take it seriously; and (3) stands in no capacity, since it fails to select significant aspects of the object it is meant to signify. Yet collating these reports is compulsory and takes an awful amount of time, a precious time that could be spent doing more significant things, like reading a book or talking to a student.

If life is semiosis and if significance is the destiny of the species, then digital academic bureaucracy is frustrating. Compiling insignificant reports is depressing; it turns one into a robot, into a machine, into a thing. It is tantamount to abdicating that which scholars treasure the most, an amorous relation to language, in order to become the automata of an insignificant way of life. Moreover, as suggested earlier, this transition from significance into insignificance is not innocent. Every time human cognitive energy is diverted from a significant relation to the environment into an insignificant one, someone or somewhat is using that energy as a tool, as a device of stupidity. In the case of digital academic bureaucracy, hypotheses on where such exploitation might lie abound. Who is benefiting from the fact that time of significance is subtracted from the life of professors and students in order to satisfy the hungry demands of bureaucracy and its endless production of digital forms?

Conclusions

Reflecting on the semiotics of insignificance is important not only in order to answer the foregoing question but also to realize that academic bureaucracy is just the tip of the iceberg of digital alienation. That which makes most present-day university professors so acutely nervous—in a way that seems incomprehensible, laughable, or even contemptible from an external point of view—is that most of them can still realize the difference between significance and insignificance. There are, of course, suicidal scholars who embrace digital bureaucracy and even shovel it into their colleagues' free time, but fortunately they are still an exception and probably have long ceased being scholars or were never good at it. Most university professors, on the contrary, are still aware of how luminous their life becomes when they can study a topic in depth before discussing it with their students, when they can read a new book, and when they can take the time to craft a sentence in an article which will survive them. And they can also feel the violence of being obliged to perform insignificant digital tasks. Feeling the nervousness of the passage from significance to insignificance is healthy, as it is healthy of any human being who realizes that things are not as they should be and that they could be better. Protest, migration, and philosophy, they all in different ways point to the same blessed inability to grow accustomed to pain, suffering, injustice, and exploitation.

For most human beings, however, this instinct of semiotic survival has long gone. They have been battered into insignificant forms of digital life, whose insignificance they cannot even realize any longer to the benefit of more significant lives. In the 1960s, utopians dreamed of a world in which there would be no work without creativity and no creativity without work. In the present-day conditions, however, asking for every human being to be given the chance of leading a creative life is probably not only fanciful but also sinful. It is somehow shadowing the awareness that most human lives today are not only uncreative but also insignificant. They consist in a quotidian burning out of time and energy in accomplishing digital activities about which one completely ignores what they stand for, whom they stand to, and in what capacity.

Semiotics must denounce the insignificance of human life and also stigmatize with equal vehemence all its placebos. People are starving for significance: They long for it in the microscopic thrills of egotistic satisfaction that they receive from instants of exposure in digital social networks; they yearn for it when they sink into the irrationality of "strong thoughts", embracing fundamentalism, superstition, and obscurantism; they strive for it through falling for the lure of consumption; they hanker after that golden existential moment in which they will finally believe that their effort means something, means something to someone, and means something to someone in some capacity. Semiotics cannot and must not teach the meaning of life; but it can and it must warn about the death of meaning.

There is a close relation between the rampant upsurge of bureaucracy in most human activities and the increasing digitalization of social life. Many human communities are yielding to the utopia that existential significance can be gained through ordering reality by means of digital calculus, by framing it into a grid of quantifiable parameters. Whereas numbers are an exceptional symbolical device for aptly interacting with the environment, the utopia of turning the whole social reality into the arena of a gigantic digital algorithm is doomed to turn into a dystopia. Significance, indeed, is not a property that stems from the automatic treatment of semiotic habits but, on the contrary, from the creative reactivation of semiosis. In the academic field, for instance, it is not by turning students' attitudes into statistical data that will improve academic life. Statistics are useful, but personally talking to students face-to-face is definitely more important. In general, the reactivation of significance in a world increasingly dominated by digital arrangements demands a courageous return to materiality, in different forms: meeting someone face-to-face instead of sending her or him a digital message, admiring a landscape instead of taking a digital picture of it, writing by hand, painting without the use of a digital device, and admiring the singularities of reality before attempting to categorize them into digital clusters. That is not meant to discard the benefits of digitalization, which are huge, but to balance the new automatic algorithms of social life with material serendipity. Unfortunately, though, such plea for a return to materiality sounds already nostalgic or is appropriated and sold by hipster digital marketing and its pseudomaterial simulacra. Escaping the insignificance of digital bureaucracy will require to fully come to terms not only with the limits of the utopia of total calculus but also with the new violent reactions and sterile obsessions to which such utopia, when perceived as dystopia, gives rise.

The next chapter, thus, devoted to "the art of trolling", focuses on a particularly disquieting social phenomenon, the emergence and proliferation of trolls in present-day digital conversation, and interprets it semiotically, in relation to the topic of insignificance. Trolls violently react to the impossibility of gaining a satisfactory individual and social identity in the new social and semiotic arena of the digital world. Such violence, however, is not physical but virtual: It disrupts the framework of reasonable conversation in order to loudly protest against the lack of significance in everyday digital existence. As a consequence, it should not be simply condemned, despite its being often despicable in mainstream moral terms, but read as an irrational reaction to the void of significance created by the digitalization of social relations in the present-day world.

Note

1 "The true paradox is there: on a cosmic scale, our life span is insignificant, yet this short stretch of time in which we appear on the scene of the world is the place whence any issue of significance proceeds" (transl. by Massimo Leone).

2

TROLLING INSIGNIFICANCE

Disrupting the digital public discourse

Et tamen quis disceptandi finis erit et loquendi
modus, si respondendum esse respondentibus
semper existimemus?[1]
(Augustine of Hippo, *De civitate dei*, II, 1)

Introduction

The relatively new phenomenon of trolling has been often studied from the point
of view of its reception, that is, from the perspective of its victims or "Internet witnesses".[2] A typical semiotic move consists in reversing the direction of analysis so as
to wonder about the fabrication of trolling, that is, the discursive elements and the
contextual conditions that are necessary in order for trolling to take place and be
socially recognized as such. The history of rhetoric, a discipline that can be considered as the ancestor of semiotics, as well as the history of philosophy, especially with
authors like Schopenhauer, have brought about a series of works whose main label
might be "the art of…", works that were intended, indeed, to transmit practical and,
above all, stylistic knowledge about such and such domain of communicative practice, escaping the more cogent instructions of codified grammars. To the series, the
current cultural semiotics might add a further work, entitled "The Art of Trolling".
What are, therefore, the main tenets of this art? A practical way to expose them is to
compare and contrast trolling with similar discursive genres and practices.

Trolling *versus* provocation

An important ingredient in the morphogenesis of trolling is its responsive
character. Trolls are usually never initiators of a new semantic trend of communication. Conversely, they normally respond, parasitically, to a fragment of

discourse that has been created by someone else, someone who is considered as holding no trolling attitude and who can, therefore, be designated as victim of this discursive practice. Trolls do not initiate discourse but respond to it for the simple reason that they do not care about any particular semantic focus. They are not interested in what they write about; they are interested in the cognitive, emotional, and pragmatic reactions that they can obtain from an interlocutor or from a group of interlocutors when these are solicited to participate in a trolled conversation.

That, the fact that trolls are not actually concerned with that about which they communicate, is certainly an unpleasant aspect of their style of communication but is not an exclusive one. From this point of view, indeed, trolling is nothing but the latest manifestation of an older discursive genre: provocation. Every time that we communicatively provoke someone, we are not interested as much in what we provoke about, as in the reactions to provocation. As the Latin etymology of this word suggests, provocation is a communicative action whose purpose is to elicit a voice, meaning an emotional more than a cognitive or pragmatic voice. Provocation, indeed, does not intend to obtain extra knowledge or extra action from an interlocutor but, rather, extra emotion; that is, it is meant to raise the emotional tone by which the interlocutor engages in conversation. It usually aims at increasing the negative emotional tone of an interlocutor's answer, in terms of indignation, anger, or utter rage.

As experts of rhetoric know, however, provocation can be a useful pragmatic device and even produce positive effects in the communicative exchange. When I provoke my partner about an issue, for instance, it is not because I want to see her or him angry but because I esteem that his or her emotional engagement in regard to a certain topic is not sufficient. As it is known, emotions are not entirely separated from cognitions in conversation. A moderate emotional activation, for instance, can lead the communicative exchange to conclusions that would have not been attained, were the participants engaging in it in a purely robotic way. As it is also known, however, excess of emotions in conversation can lead to its paralysis, meaning that the need to express one's altered states of mind takes over the need to express one's ideas. Provocation too, then, is the object of an art; provoking someone can enhance the communicative game; beyond a certain extent, though, provocation can be disruptive. Trolling is *provocation that is indifferent to its conversational topic* and that aims at paroxysmal emotional reactions. The pleasure of moderate provocation consists in seeing that the shape of conversation has been changed, and sometimes even improved, by intentional increase of its emotional tone. The pleasure of trolling, instead, consists in realizing that *the emotional tone of conversation becomes the main focus of conversation itself.*

That is one of the first ingredients of the art of trolling: When trolling someone, I should not care about what I say but about potential emotional responses to what I say, no matter what. In simpler terms, the first communicative goal of a troll is to be able to push the interlocutor's most sensitive buttons. "Pushing someone's buttons" is an appropriate locution here. That which is at stake, indeed, is not to elicit some emotional but nevertheless controlled reactions, in which a cognitive frame of argumentation filters the irrational response. That which is at stake, instead, is to trigger relatively unmediated emotional responses, in which the negative passions of the interlocutor simply explode without regard any longer for the cognitive and rational framework of argumentation. *The ultimate goal of a troll is to be insulted by its victim.*

Trolling *versus* joke

As we have seen, trolling is not simply provoking, but it is not simply joking either. Jest, humor, and other declinations of irony play a fundamental role in human communication (Leone 2015b). Paramount persuasive effects can be obtained through humorously poking fun at an interlocutor. That is, moreover, a pleasurable activity per se. Teasing someone, and realizing that this someone feels teased and responds to it, is the source of an autonomous aesthetic pleasure, which ultimately relates to a desire of control. Whereas the pleasure of persuasion consists in realizing that we can control otherness through changing someone else's mind, the pleasure of irony consists in realizing that otherness can be controlled also through changing someone else's heart, for instance, by producing that mild and usually innocuous irritation that teasing among friends is about. In ironic conversation, I can pretend, in jest, that I maintain opinions that I actually do not seriously hold, since if that were the case, they would probably be unacceptable for my interlocutor. One of the useful communicative purposes of joking is, therefore, that of testing the limits of the conversational relation in which joking takes place. Through saying things that are unacceptable to my interlocutor and, at the same time, through signaling, by means of special conversational markers such as the tone of the voice, the facial expression, gestures, and so on, that I do not actually believe in what I say, and that I'm saying it in jest, I can study the cognitive and, above all, the emotional reactions of my interlocutor outside of the framework of a "serious" communicative exchange, as though jest was a gymnasium in which two contenders train and gauge their strength without actually engaging in violent fight with an unknown rival. The intrinsic aesthetic pleasure of teasing, indeed, consists not only in realizing that I can control the emotions of my interlocutor but also in making sure that communication, as long as teasing is respectful of its limits, will never change into verbal or, worse, physical violence.

Trolling shares some communicative ingredients of verbal jest. In trolling too, one does not believe in what one says or, rather, writes. But whereas the successful ironic conversation requires that both the sender and the receiver realize that the former does not believe in what he or she says to the latter, successful trolling implies that only the sender and his or her community of trolls realize that there is no belief attached to what is being said, whilst the receiver firmly believes in such relation between internal belief and external expression. *Trolling, then, is joke whose communicative nature of joke is never revealed to its addressee,* for the fundamental purpose of trolling is not to make fun *at* someone, but to make fun *of* someone.

In other words, the victim of trolling is debased to an inferior level of the pragmatics of conversation, in which he or she does not participate any longer to the testing of the limits of the communicative scene but turns into the sacrificial victim of a spectacle. In a joke, both the conversation partners come out of jest knowing more about each other and their personalities; in trolling, the sender enjoys precisely the fact that the receiver does not understand and is actually trapped into an "infinite jest" whose nature of jest he or she ignores. Whereas in teasing sender and receiver mutually experiment the power of being able to control the emotions of the other, in trolling this mutuality is disrupted, and the victim turns into a mere puppet into the hands of his or her trolls. As a consequence, trolling does not aim at testing the boundaries of a relation but rather at confirming the sender's narcissistic illusion of omnipotence, as well as the bonds that tie him or her to a community of trolls.

The fact that trolling is both provocation that is oblivious to its topic and jest that is opaque to its receiver entails two important further pragmatic ingredients of this communicative practice: anonymity and choral nature.

Trolling *versus* defensive anonymity

As regards anonymity, trolling would be impossible if its victim knew his or her troll perfectly well. Elaborate jokes are viable among friends, and yet they must, at a certain stage, end up with revelation of what they are, that is, jokes. The longer the joke, the higher the risk that testing the limits of an amiable relation will, in the end, jeopardize the relation itself. Long and complicated jokes are possible, as a consequence, only among good friends and not at all among strangers. The reason is simple: An exceeding amount of communicative energy and action will be needed, after poking fun at a stranger for a long time, in order to "close" the jest and return to the a non-ironic communicative framework. *Trolling, instead, knows no end.* Its aesthetic pleasure exactly derives from the fact that in no moment its victim realizes or expresses a realization that the conversational exchange in which he or she is immersed is actually a joke, a verbal game from which one can exit at any moment.

From this point of view, as we shall see even better later when dealing with the choral dimension of trolling, this practice is a sadistic one, meaning that it produces aesthetic pleasure by debasing the counterpart of conversation to the level of emotional puppet; it is, however, a sadistic practice in which no safe word is given to the victim so as to end the game. The victim, instead, must ignore the ironic frame in which he or she is made fun of and, as a consequence, must not be able to determine that the conversional counterpart is joking. In elaborate jokes among friends, sooner or later the moment of disclosure always arrives. Even before its arrival, however, the victim of the joke cannot completely believe that his or her friend is acting and speaking in a way that is in such a contrast with the customary one. To give an example: In the French comedy *Le Prénom* (Alexandre de La Patellière and Matthieu Delaporte 2012; in English: *What's in a*

Name?), Vincent, a real estate agent, jokingly reveals to two of his closest friends, Claude and Pierre, that he, Vincent, is going to name his first son "Adolph". The friends are shocked at the revelation, and yet they cannot completely believe that what they are hearing is true. When the joke is protracted for too long, then, catastrophic consequences are triggered in the relation among the three men and in those around them, exactly because the conversational face that the main character has displayed to his friends is not compatible at all with the story of their mutual acquaintance. A joke that jeopardizes a relation, either because it overly challenges its boundaries or because it is protracted for an exceeding amount of time, is a bad joke. Its conversational and social result is disruptive. On the contrary, *trolling in which the victim does not realize that he or she is being trolled is a perfect one*, since it can continue endlessly, at mounting levels of emotional tension, each being the source of the troll's equally increasing pleasure. For a troll, there is nothing better that witnessing how a perfect stranger, embodied by his or her social network avatar, enrages more and more over what is being said, falling into a spiral of increasingly violent arguments and, eventually, insults or even threats.

The question remains to determine whether increased possibilities of anonymity have begotten trolling, or whether trolling has begotten increased need for anonymity. As it was pointed out earlier, trolling requires a higher degree of anonymity than a usual ironic conversation would. The discursive modality of trolling, however, is not only the cause but also the effect of enhanced anonymity in digital communication and social networks. Such anonymity must not necessarily been actively sought for. There is, indeed, a more diffused and perhaps even more pernicious form of anonymity, which simply stems from the fact that, in the digital semiosphere, interacting with a huge amount of complete strangers is more and more frequent, when it is not the rule. In digital communication and especially in social networks, people feel invisible and anonymous not only because they act under disguise but also because they feel part of a multitude in which their individual responsibility of speakers disappears. They are irresponsible in the sense that they do not have to respond anymore to anyone for what they write and say. From this point of view, digital communicative arenas have often brought about the same terrifying ethical effect that spatial distance usually implies: Human beings tend not to care about other human beings that they perceive as spatially and, therefore, emotionally far from them; moreover, they also tend to develop sadistic or even violent attitudes when this distance is perceived as asymmetric. Looking at other human beings from the top of a skyscraper or on the monitor of a military drone, one feels no particular negative empathy at the thought of annihilating them, as though they were small noxious insects.

In many circumstances, digital communication and social networks have resulted in the introduction of such unethical consequences of spatial distance in conversational environments in which, on the contrary, all gives participants the impression that they are closely connected, all familiar to each other, and all sharing the same proximity. The combination of ethical distance and virtual closeness is explosive: In these conditions, many human beings develop sadistically violent attitudes toward their digital conversation partners. Trolling is the epitome of it: I talk to you and engage in conversation with you, yet what I have in mind is not to exchange ideas, emotions, and plans of actions with you, but to rejoice at my capacity for pushing your buttons and provoking your rage, ad libitum.

Anonymity is necessary in repressive societies; it allows members of persecuted minorities to express their thoughts and seek to overthrow the regime by acquiring increasing consensus and power. *In non-repressive societies, however, anonymity is not needed in order to shelter oppressed voices but in order to oppress unsheltered voices.* It is not a rhetorical instrument in the hands of the victims of power but rather a rhetorical instrument in their torturers' hands. It is like the hood on the head of the executioner. *Trolling is, in a way, a verbal pillory*, because what it aims at is not to elicit such and such piece of information from a tormented body/soul but to give pleasure through the spectacle of its useless pain.

Trolling *versus* public discourse

That is the reason for which the choral dimension of trolling should not be overlooked. Like torture, trolling is never only a matter between a torturer and a tortured one. In the terms of Greimasian semiotics, one could say that both torture and trolling always imply an actant observer, that is, an instance that beholds the sadistic game and draws pleasure from it. To a certain extent, that is true of a joke as well: Saying something in jest to a friend requires not only a sender of the humorous message and a receiver of it but also a third actant, whose role is to witness the joke and somehow also sanction its discursive appropriateness. That does not mean that a conversation actor must physically observe the scene of irony. In most cases, indeed, the one who jokes will simultaneously be the joke's witness, somehow rejoicing in anticipation at the effect of surprise and hilarity, as well as relief, that the closure of the joke will result in. Similarly, the scene of trolling also implies some observers, who nevertheless share, in most cases, the anonymity of the troll: The troll does not perform in front of him-or herself or in front of a group of friends; he or she, instead, performs for an audience that, being potentially infinite, and potentially coinciding with all those that can come across the troll's words in the web, ipso facto becomes an anonymous public, to which, again, no specific responsibility is attached. Trolling, thus, entails an anonymous torturer's endless and fruitless provocation for the sake of an anonymous audience, a digital crowd that somehow resembles those that, in the past, would elatedly attend the spectacle of public executions.

Trolling *versus* controversy

Through comparison and contrast with similar discursive practices, some of the main semiotic ingredients of trolling have been singled out: topic-insensitive provocation, time-boundless jest, sadistic hierarchy of the sender and the receiver, anonymity of both the troll and his or her audience, choral character of the "actant observer" of trolling, and so on. Although all these pragmatic features are closely linked with a sociocultural context (acting as both their cause and their effect) and although they result in semantic effects, they are not, nevertheless, semantic per se. A separate analysis, therefore, must be developed as regards the semantics of trolling, that is, the specific fields of meaning that trolling usually bears on. Suggesting that trolling is insensitive to topic, indeed, does not mean that this discursive practice can unfold in relation to whatever semantic area. In order for trolling to take place, the field of meaning at the center of digital conversation must be a contentious one.

The level of contentiousness of areas of meaning in the semiosphere ultimately depends on the specific structure of the semiosphere itself (Leone 2016e). No topic is intrinsically immune to contention and no topic is inherently a contentious one. Abstractly put, in order for trolling to happen, it is sufficient that the semantic area that trolling is about be susceptible to give rise to an axiology and, therefore, to a polarization. As soon as a topic whatsoever entails a potentiality for contrasting opinions, that topic becomes a possible semantic area for the activity of trolling. Comparison and contrast, however, are in order here too. Trolling is not simply controversy, as it is not simply provocation or jest. In Greimasian terms, given a certain field of meaning, trolling parasitically constructs its position, so that it results not only contrary but also mirror-like contradictory to the opinion that is voiced by the interlocutor.

One of the socially disquieting aspects of trolling, indeed, is that the troll does not have a mind, but builds it in relation to that of the counterpart and victim of trolling; the troll, moreover, does not pursue the objective of expressing a radically different mind, and convincing the interlocutor and/or the audience of it, but rather seeks to provoke, through a specific choice of arguments, the mounting rage of the conversation partner, for the delight of the sadistic audience of trolling. The troll would like to be utterly outrageous, and often he or she is; in order to be effective, however, the discourse of trolling must also abide by a specific aspectuality.[3] The "art of trolling", indeed, also implies that its perpetrator does not reveal its nature at the onset, through using some initial outrageous arguments or lines. Trolling in which the victim immediately realizes that he or she is being trolled is not a good one, for it does not give rise to that protracted conversation sadism that is at the core of the aesthetics of this digital phenomenon. The aspectuality of this discursive practice, therefore, consists in measuring out the outrageousness of arguments, so that initial contradictory semantic positions do not immediately disclose the real nature of the game but entrap the conversation partner in an emotional spiral, in which progressively more and more intolerable arguments will be used without giving out, for that reason, the fictitiousness of their pragmatics.

Trolling *versus* lying

Trolling is not characterized only by a specific pragmatics and by a particular semantics; its syntactic logic too contributes to the overall semiotic effect of this discursive genre. So as to enrage the counterpart of a conversation, in fact, choosing and endorsing opposite arguments is necessary but not sufficient. A close analysis of trolling, indeed, shows that, often, its victims are increasingly outraged not only because of the arguments that the troll uses but also because of the syntax of the argumentation. In order to achieve its sadistic goal, trolling must be full of non sequitur, repetitions, petitions of principle, arguments *ad personam*, and so on, skillfully displaying an array of logical fallacies that constitute a sort of counter-manual of rhetoric. The pragmatics, the semantics, and the syntax of trolling pinpoint the main features of this phenomenon as discursive practice and text-producing communication. Such internal characterization, nevertheless, is not exhaustive per se but must lead to a better understanding of the sociocultural context of trolling, in terms of both its effects and its causes.

Pain

As regards the former, which are probably easier to observe and analyze, discrepant opinions have been held about the social consequences of trolling. On the one hand, one might think that, by outrageously testing the limits of conversational tolerance, trolling is actually beneficial, since it exposes the paradoxes, the taboos, and the hypocrisies of the present-day digital conversation. From this point of view, trolling might be regarded as a new instance in the series of highly unconventional voices that, from Socrates's gadfly ethics until modern clown aesthetics, have contributed to shake society from its entrenched certainties, favoring, thus, the healthy renewal of its moral energy. A community that is able to react against trolling, indeed, becomes a stronger community, and one with an accrued capability for discriminating among tolerable and intolerable stances. Just to give an example: It is quite common, in trolling, to defile the memory of violently deceased young people, so as to cause extra pain among the relatives of the victim; that is clearly a sadistic behavior, and a morally unacceptable one in all societies; in all cultures, indeed, showing respect, or at least not showing disrespect, for the death of young and innocent people and the grief of their families is a pillar of shared empathy. By ignoring and tramping this taboo, trolls unintentionally point at the crisis of traditional patterns of empathy in the digital arena, as well as at the hypocrisy of global grief; at the same time, through deprecating trolling and reinstating this taboo, societies renew and reinforce their moral boundaries, thus redefining and reinvigorating the distinction between that which is morally permissible and that which is not.

Meta-pain

The most disruptive effect of trolling, however, does not consist in the pain that it causes in such evident cases of conversational sadism: Only a troll would send pictures of the mutilated corpse of the victim of an accident to his or her family. Albeit tragically heinous, such acts, indeed, are not as disruptive as the meta-pain that trolling brings about when its nature of trolling is not as clearly discernible. In more general words, the worst social consequence of trolling is that of making it increasingly hard to single out trolling itself. The possibility of labeling a fragment of discourse as "trolling", indeed, cannot simply depend on the pragmatic, semantic, and syntactic features described above. These are all necessary to define trolling, and trolling systematically features them. Trolling, however, can be fully defined only in terms of intentionality. In other words, only can be defined as "trolling" that provocative, disruptive, and outrageous textual occurrence whose content does not correspond to any of the troll's actual beliefs. That does not mean that trolling is a lie, that is, that its expression is contrary or contradictory in relation to that which the troll actually believes. *That which ultimately defines trolling, indeed, is the unimportance of the relation between that which the troll says in a conversation and that which he or she believes.*

Trolling profoundly disrupts the conversational ethics of the human civilization because it severs expression from content, signifier from signified, communication from intention. That which matters are not the invisible thoughts or emotions that communication signifies but the visible outrage that it prompts. In metaphoric terms, trolling is socially dangerous not because it poisons the water of communication but because it makes it very hard, and increasingly so, to distinguish between drinkable water and undrinkable one, between criticism of mainstream trends and trolling of them. As in the case of conspiracy theories, in that of trolling too, the worst consequence of this sadistic practice of discourse is that of discrediting non-trolling social criticism, which, exactly because of the proliferation of trolling, ends up being difficult to distinguish from it and, therefore, discarded as mere instance of it. As it was pointed out earlier, irony has always been a powerful rhetorical device for the dismantlement of the moral status quo, yet the proliferation of anonymous trolling defuses this device and makes it unavailable in digital arenas, giving rise to the famous law of Nathan Poe: In a world of trolls, satire becomes impossible, because it can always be mistaken, and often is, for a nonsatirical statement, advocating precisely that which it would intend to ironize about.

Imagine a world in which, whenever someone says something that we do not like, we cannot actually determine whether he or she is serious or not. In such world, whose realization might not be thus unrealistic and far in the future, conversation would cease to be a discursive framework for the creation of a community of interpreters and, therefore, the peaceful resolution of conflicts. That is the reason for which, although it is hard to label such typically digital phenomenon as trolling with categories, such as "right-wing" or "Fascist", which belong to a different historical epoch, it is undeniable that, by systematically encouraging sadistic rejoicing at other people's distress, creation and ridiculing of outsiders, and, above all, a disruption of that conversational arena which would precisely grant participants a nonviolent frame for the resolution of conflict, trolling intrinsically is a fascist behavior, in the sense that it thrives on the institution and maintenance of a community whose internal cohesion and aesthetics depends on the painful subjugation of a victim.

Conclusions

The work of the semiotician should be distinguished from that of the sociologist. The former might help the latter by offering an articulate description of the discursive phenomenon of trolling, but then extra-textual information will be required, to the latter, in order to fully understand the effects and, especially, the causes of such disruptive and violent practice. In the present context, only some hypotheses can be ventured, which all stem from the consideration that the pragmatic, semantic, and syntactic features of trolling might actually be a response to a distressful social and existential condition that they seek to compensate for. What pushes a troll to act as such? First of all, trolling might be a particularly spectacular symptom of a more general attitude, which is that which sociologists have already singled out and labeled as the "no syndrome". Today, communities are hard to shape around positive values and projects of sharing and construction; communities more easily take shape around negative projects of opposition to that which is considered "the mainstream" or "the establishment". From this point of view, the appeal of trolling might be seen in its capacity for offering a sense of community, belonging, and entitlement to those who sadistically engage in dismantling the "moral mainstream". Given the fact that this "moral mainstream" becomes more and more narrow in postmodern societies, trolls must resort to increasingly outrageous behaviors in order to define their opposition, to the point that the only way, for them, to generate an existential stance and a community consensus is to openly endorse cruelty. As populism is the revolt of the social outcast against that which he or she deems as the abuse of the system of political representation, so trolling is the revolt of the moral outcast against the community of mainstream morality, which the troll feels and rejoices in feeling morally superior or, simply, indifferent to.

Why should someone, and presumably a young person, experience aesthetic pleasure in triggering the outrage of an interlocutor through adopting preposterous and yet obnoxious stances? The ultimate answer might sound like follows: Trolls feel so utterly impotent in the traditional conversational arena, unable to convince anyone of anything and, worse, unable to be convinced by anyone about anything, that the only source of empowerment they can rely on is that of breaking the machine of conversation itself, exactly like a player who overthrows the chessboard because he or she is unable to escape checkmate or, with an even more appropriate metaphor, like the child who, not being able to understand how a toy works, breaks it into pieces. Unfortunately, the toy that an increasingly number of trolls is disquietingly seeking to destroy is not a minor one: It is public discourse.

The first chapter of the book, on "Framing Insignificance", has proposed a categorization of meaninglessness based on Charles S. Peirce's semiotics. It has also suggested that insignificance is more than meaninglessness, since it coincides with the human withdrawal from language into a domain of mute things. The second chapter, on trolling, has analyzed a current populist reaction against digital insignificance; many (especially young) people nowadays find it very hard to create a significant personal identity in the increasingly digital semiosphere; therefore, they sometimes react violently to their distress, not only through withdrawing from digital conversation but through actually disrupting its discursive mechanisms. If I cannot be significant in the web, I shall turn the web into an insignificant place: That is the troll's pernicious philosophy.

Trolling, however, is just the tip of the iceberg. Internet reactions to the threats of insignificance and loss of identity in digital conversation constantly pollute the construction of public discourse and, through it, that of the public opinion. Since the narcissistic strive for preserving the significance of one's digital self is so desperate, the exchange of ideas, emotions, and plans of action on the Internet often becomes a grotesque pantomime, in which the interplay of violently dialectic oppositions is more important than the actual topic of conversation. That is what the following chapter on "Contrarian Insignificance" seeks to point out through an in-depth study of what happens in the web when opinions start to emerge and be exchanged about controversial topics: Distinguishing oneself as a significant voice, often through violent or even trolling stances, predominates over voicing a significant opinion.

Notes

1 "And yet to what end shall we ever bring our discussions, or what bounds can be set to our discourse, if we proceed on the principle that we must always reply to those who reply to us?" (Engl. trans. Marcus Dodds, 1871).
2 An early study of the legal implications of trolling is (Bond 1999); Revillard (2000) offers a study from the perspective of the sociology of interaction; Hardaker (2010) refers to "impoliteness studies" but seeks to propose an alternative definition of trolling; on the relation between trolling and violence, see Shachaf and Noriko (2010); Walter, Hourizi, Moncur, and Pitsillides (2011) analyses the morbid relation between death and trolling; Herring, Job-Sluder, Scheckler, and Barab (2002) investigates the relation between trolling and female subjects; Krappitz (2012) is a dissertation about the culture of trolling; from a psychological perspective, see Buckels, Trapnell, and Paulhus (2014); the recent practice of trolling in cyberwarfare is the object of Spruds et al. (2016); there is plenty of "gray literature," both in Internet and in traditional media, about trolls, but still not enough scholarly contributions. The most comprehensive (and provocative) study on trolling to date is Phillips (2015). On the visual semiotics of trolling, see Turton-Turner (2013). A semiotic analysis of the relation between trolling and conspiracy theories is in Thibault (2016); a paper on "The Role of Trolling in Shaping Cultural Discourse and Identity: A Case Study of an Anonymous Internet Message Board" was delivered by Mark Lehman at the 18th Annual Michicagoan Graduate Student Conference in Linguistic Anthropology (May 6–7, 2016).
3 In linguistics and semiotics, aspectuality is the way in which discourse reproduces the quality of time, not simply describing *when* things happen in time, but *how* they do so. See Leone (2017).

3

CONTRARIAN INSIGNIFICANCE

Wars of position in the digital arena

Καὶ ἡμῖν δὴ οὖν ἀγῶνα προκεῖσθαι πάντων
ἀγώνων μέγιστον νομίζειν χρεών, ὑπὲρ οὗ
πάντα ποιητέον ἡμῖν καὶ πονητέον εἰς δύναμιν
ἐπὶ τὴν τούτου παρασκευήν, καὶ ποιηταῖς καὶ
λογοποιοῖς καὶ ῥήτορσι καὶ πᾶσιν ἀνθρώποις
ὁμιλητέον ὅθεν ἂν μέλλῃ πρὸς τὴν τῆς ψυχῆς
ἐπιμέλειαν ὠφέλειά τις ἔσεσθαι.[1]
Basil of Caesarea, *Oratio ad adolescentes* [Πρὸς τοὺς νέους,
ὅπως ἂν ἐξ ἑλληνικῶν ὠφελοῖντο λόγων], II, 8

Introduction

Social sciences have mostly focused on the formation of social opinions from
a semantic point of view: Given a certain semantic field, interviews, statistics,
and other analytical instruments are deployed in order to map the distribution
of views, their evolution, their conflicts, and their agreements. Socio-semiotics,
social semiotics, and the other semiotic branches that bear on social inquiry have
contributed to the effort by providing semiotic grids of categorization. These
grids too, however, have been mostly related to semantic contents circulating
through societies and their cultures.

Conversely, the present chapter pursues a different hypothesis: The formation
of opinions in current societies, especially in those that have massively embraced
social networks as a predominant form of personal manifestation, cannot be
studied any more from a semantic point of view only. Individual voices, indeed,
as well as groups and communities of belief, are increasingly turned into the
knots of a gigantic bundle, in which positions take shape more according to a
syntactic logic than according to a semantic one. That is not to say that people do

not believe what they say or do not care about it; they certainly do. Nevertheless, their individual position in the bundle, and as a consequence their range of opinions, stem more from an unquenchable thirst for differentiation than from actual contact with social matters. That partially explains the often extremely conflictive character of the present-day social formation of opinions: Radical negation of previous positions is a more effective path of differentiation than adherence to a mainstream trend. Are the current technology and modality of communication turning most social actors into blind contrarians? That is the main question around which the present chapter revolves, adopting as a case study one of the most controversial and yet central issues of contemporary societies: the terrorist[2] attacks perpetrated by violent jihadist fundamentalists against those who, in their view, dared to satirize Islam.

After briefly recalling the events of January 7–9, 2015 in the Parisian area, the chapter seeks to survey and map the syntax of progressive differentiation of opinions circulating in social networks about such events. Some patterns are identified and semiotically described: (1) cleavage, (2) comparative relativizing, (3) blurring sarcasm, (4) anonymity, (5) unfocused responsibility, and (6) conspiracy thought. A new semiotic square is created to visually display these patterns, their positions, their relations, and their evolution.

The tragedy and the ritual

Like most European citizens, I followed the tragic events of January 7, 2015 with anguish. Being in Lyon as a visiting professor made the news about terrorist attacks in Paris sound even closer and, to a certain extent, surreal. I know Paris very well. I have jogged endless times through the streets where the killings took place. It was unbelievable. Yet, as reports and commentaries proliferated (I was monitoring the media in several languages), I sought to preserve a dimension of detachment. I tried to keep a part of myself calm enough to analyze not the events, which still appear overwhelming to me, but the discourse on the events. While the terrorists were still besieged by the French police special forces, I could not help asking myself, "How long will it take before the usual patterns that structure the reception of news in the present world reproduce themselves? How many days after the events will the usual, recurring voices surface and propose an interpretive grid for what has happened?"

The answer was, "immediately, or almost immediately". Just hours after the shocking news, stereotypical patterns of interpretations were arising, to the extent that I started wondering, as I will be wondering in this chapter, whether the point was not the content of these receptions but their inner structure.[3] The content, indeed, might appear as novel, as the situation to which it reacted seemed to be without precedent. The form of this reception, however, was, in a certain way, ritual.[4] I refer not to the sophisticated comments that started to flourish in the press, with interventions by professionals ranging from military experts to metaphysical philosophers. I am referring, instead, to comments, and comments on comments, in the anonymous, scattered press of our epoch, social networks.[5] I will now try to schematize some of these interpretive trends and formulate hypotheses about why and to what purpose they repetitively exemplify the response to tragic events like the Paris terrorist attacks of January 2015.

Cleavage

The first trend this chapter will point out is progressive differentiation, which in the French press often goes under the somewhat derogatory name of "*clivage*" ["cleavage"]. The emotional response to the extermination of Charlie Hebdo's cartoonists was rapid and, in a way, commensurate with the symbolical kernel of the tragedy.[6] The victims were mostly famous satirical cartoonists; jihadist terrorists murdered them because, to the former's minds, the latter had repetitively dared to represent the Islamic prophet Mohammad, often with heavily sarcastic tones.[7] Messages of emotional proximity to the victims, therefore, took the expressive form that was under attack; cartoons started circulating throughout the web, mostly in social networks. The viral power of responses increased as a result of people initially reacting not verbally but visually. Not everyone can draw, and as a consequence, people mostly spread images that professional cartoonists had made, posting them in their social networks. The visual discourse that initially reacted to the killings concentrated in a few images, widely circulating through the web. They could be analyzed one by one, so as to show their precise perspective on the events, but most tended to coalesce around the same message, which can be verbally summarized as follows: "Cartoons are stronger than weapons; they will eventually triumph". There were other semantic lines, for instance that of cartoons showing the victims in ironic after-life situations, but they were less predominant.

A second, as well as widespread and immediate, reaction was also visual, although including both verbal and graphic elements. People started posting a specific visual rendering of the sentence, "Je suis Charlie" ["I am Charlie"], adopting the traditional lettering of the magazine, usually in black and white, and in various languages.[8] This very simple sentence was rhetorically strong because it was based on empty deictic positions (Benveniste 1966, 1971; Ono 2007; Manetti 2008): an "I" identifying with Charlie, a time coinciding with the enunciation of the sentence itself, and no indication of space. As a consequence, everyone in the world could appropriate this "I", inhabit the time of its enunciation, and transport its content to whatever latitude. What did "Je suis Charlie" mean? In the beginning, a quite unarticulated expression of human proximity and of empathy toward those who had been brutally killed for having visually expressed their ideas of sarcastic contempt toward what they considered Islamic obscurantism. In other words, the many instances of "Je suis Charlie" that proliferated throughout the web would not explicitly mean, "I agree with the ideas of the killed cartoonists" but rather, "I am you since you were killed because what you thought", or even more generally, "I am you because you were brutally killed while doing your work".[9]

These first two orders of reaction, which we might call viral visual response and first-person identification, showed some spontaneity perhaps because they intervened in the first instants after the tragedy, when facts were still evolving.[10] By contrast, in the succeeding phase, when the social reaction to the tragedy turned from an emotional, visual, and intimate monologue to a rational, verbal, and collective dialogue or polyphony, stereotypical patterns started to shape the public discourse. In other words, while the first, emotional reactions were fresh and surprising, what came after was, to a larger extent, perfectly predictable. It was mechanical, and as such it was also often, and sometimes intolerably, inhuman. The cold predictability of social discourse was borne out by the ease with which a moderately expert analyst could foresee, sometimes in detail, what the next move would be. The first of these moves was the simplest move by which human beings usually produce value and, therefore, identity: negation.[11] While millions of people were reproducing the same Titanic cartoons in social networks, as well as adopting the same slogan, soon other people felt compelled to stand out, to display their individuality, and to manifest their being members of a minority.

Arguably, this strategy of opposition and individualization is relatively independent from its actual content and reproduces itself in the semiosphere, especially in social networks, every time that a collective response takes place. In other words, when social networks produce a viral interpretation "A", it is only a matter of seconds before some individuals in the same social networks start to proclaim "non-A". The point, however, is that the latter are not really interested in "A"; they are mostly interested in "non-", that is, they are irresistibly excited by the possibility of empowering, through negation, their own identity. While millions of people take existential comfort in merging their emotional individuality in a collective reaction, some other people feel almost threatened by it (Canetti 1960). They feel the urge to stand out from the crowd no matter what it takes.

Being a contrarian, negating that which everybody is repeating, is the first degree of individualization in digital social networks because it inevitably leads to the necessity of nuances. Indeed, while the slogan "Je suis Charlie" can be embraced without justification (its justification is in its circulation itself, in the almost evolutionary identity of its emotional efficacy), the contrarian must, conversely, justify the reasons for which "Je ne suis pas Charlie" ["I am not Charlie"] is uttered. Disparate arguments were given to justify this first degree of cleavage. The most common of them all was the idea that, while feeling empathy for the tragic destiny of the cartoonists and the other victims, a statement of identification with the satirical magazine was not in order, for people proclaiming "Je ne suis pas Charlie" strongly disapproved of its contents and tone. It was not fair, these voices affirmed, to denigrate religion in the way the magazine did. Therefore, total endorsement of it through a personal statement of identification was impossible. The disquieting aspect of such first-degree cleavage was its coldness: How was it possible, while the corpses of eleven people were still warm, brutally massacred in the name of ideology, concentrating not on the unspeakable violence of murder but on the editorial line of the magazine? That was possible because, in a way, it was not about the magazine. It voiced, on the contrary, a "human, too human" instinct of differentiation. One feels empathy, but nevertheless wants to stand out; one doesn't want to merge with the "Je suis Charlie" crowd. One shouts out, in contrast, the "Je ne suis pas Charlie" slogan. What matters is not the tenability of such a stance but its individuality, the capacity to project an exclusive profile around one's opinion and persona.

But were not these two proclamations, the positive and the negative one, on the same level? Why should the former be considered as an emotional, instinctive, and collective reaction to the tragedy and the latter as a cold, meditated, and individualistic counterreaction to it? There are several reasons for this distinction, but one of them is fundamental. Those who chose "Je ne suis pas Charlie" were not reacting to reality. They were reacting to a discourse on reality. Their relation with the killings was second-degree and, therefore, from a certain point of view, devoid of human empathy. But was not the "Je suis Charlie" partially also reacting to a representation of reality provided by the media? Most of the members of this collectivity, indeed, had not witnessed the tragedy directly but through the nerve-racking storytelling of French and international media. Nevertheless, those displaying unconditioned empathy toward the victims situated their reaction on a hierarchical level that was different from the one hosting the "Je ne suis pas Charlie" statements. As it shall be seen, one of the main discursive complicacies affecting communication in digital social networks nowadays is exactly the widespread incapacity to distinguish between levels of discourse: between a message that bears on the reality of death and a message that bears on a message that bears, in turn, on the reality of death, and so on.

Comparative relativizing

Such incapacity is even more striking in the second form of rhetorical differentiation, which stemmed not simply from cleavage (you say "yes"; therefore, I say "no") but from another stereotypical dynamic of the present-day social discourse. It could be called "comparative relativizing". The structure of this argumentative pattern is extremely common in social networks and can be summarized as follows: Every time that a collective subject expresses empathy or simply proximity to a cause "X", an individual subject will construct its identity by relativizing such proximity through comparison. In the case of the "Je suis Charlie" movement, in a matter of hours after its manifestation on the web, "Je ne suis par Charlie" are proliferating not only through criticism of the magazine's contents (cleavage) but also through relativizing comparison: What about the journalist "Y" persecuted and killed in such and such country? What about the victim "Z" of such and such terror? Why don't people say "Je suis Y" or "Je suis Z" for them? This process of differentiation is, in a way, even more pernicious than the first one, for it projects an ideological grid on empathy. Following this argument, there is always one victim, one massacre, one genocide, and so on that is worthier of consideration than the present one. "Are my victims worse than yours? Then stop complaining", the comparative relativizing argument says. The viral consequence of this rhetorical pattern on the web is a multiplication of instances of empathic redress: In the cacophonic conversation that, minute after minute, expands on social networks, each participant comes up with a cause, a source of injustice, a wound that lies somewhere and sometime else in space and history, and whose message to the current situation is, "Consider me, not Charlie Hebdo; I am as worthy or even worthier of attention".

To give an idea of the surrealist paroxysm to which this argumentative pattern can lead, consider the following example. At the time of the killings, in the city of Turin, Uber, the web-based private transportation network, was becoming increasingly popular, especially with students and young people. Taxi drivers were angry, complaining about losing customers and having their license decrease in value. Thus, they kept protesting, sometimes quite aggressively. During one of these waves of protest, they started pasting on the windows of their taxis a sticker. It was identical to a "Je suis Charlie" sticker, with the same design, colors, and lettering, but "Charlie" had been replaced by "taxi legale" ["legal taxi"] (Figure 3.1). A slogan that had been created to show collective empathy toward the victims of a terrorist attack was therefore used to attract empathy toward taxi drivers endangered by Uber. That is the moral oddity to which the process of comparative relativizing can lead: Myriads of more or less serious grievances are pushed to compete for media attention through the meme of "Je suis Charlie". The problem is that, from a discursive point of view, none of them wins.

FIGURE 3.1 A "Je suis taxi legale" poster on the car window of a taxi in Turin; photo by the author

At a first glance, it might seem that this argumentative structure is additive. "Let's not say only 'je suis Charlie'; let's say also 'je suis Y' or 'je suis Z'". In reality, though, this argumentative pattern is subtractive. It parasitizes the emotional charge that a collectivity is sharing around a certain issue in order to channel away some of that charge elsewhere. The minimal formula of this subtraction is a simple word: "but". It is a word that has equivalents in practically all languages and that logically and above all semantically introduces a negative differentiation.[12] "Je suis Charlie but ...", The semantic configuration that this word prompts is the same that emerges from one of the most paradoxically racist sentences of the contemporary social discourse: "I'm not racist, but..." This "but" actually nullifies any antiracist self-definition, as well as it disintegrates any empathy behind the "Je suis Charlie" identification. Pragmatically, such "but" invites the crowd to snap out from its emotional trance and to cognitively redirect its empathic attention elsewhere.

Is this comparative relativizing justified by the multiplicity of ideological agendas that, as it is natural, circulate through the digital social networks? Attentive observation of this complex discursive arena seems to legitimize the suspicion that such second-degree differentiation too stems more from a formal pattern than from sensibility to a particular content. In other words, what matters seems to be not the urgency to bring to the fore such and such grievance but to somehow downplay the one that is under the spotlight, to break the spell of an enchanted collectivity and to reintroduce a motive for its re-fragmentation. It is as though an ancestral fear of the crowd manifested itself every time that an emotional collectivity forms in the web. An instinctive reflex of individuation leads many to stand out, to speak out their stance of contrarians, and to gain a few seconds of public attention as a result.

There is always a modicum of profiteering behind any differentiation. The simplest form of it is attention: Those who create value through the emergence of difference receive attention. In some cases, value is created not through negative differentiation but through positive creativity. After the terrorist attacks against Charlie Hebdo, a drawing attributed to Banksy (but actually drawn by Lucille Clerc on January 7, 2015) started to spread throughout the global web, in which a "today" and a "tomorrow" were visually compared. "Today" was the image of a broken pencil. "Tomorrow", the picture of the two fragments, turned into two sharpened pencils. The drawing was clever because its message was direct, powerful, and unequivocal: Today, cartoonists are killed; tomorrow, they'll multiply. Freedom and creativity overcome obscurantism and repression. The drawing was immensely successful also because its form embodied its message: (pseudo-) Banksy's creativity was extolling the resilience of creativity. As a result, the image became immensely popular and was widely shared on the Internet (Figure 3.3).

Besides the positive differentiation of creativity, however, whose potential of individuation is huge, there subsist myriads of microscopic instances, which do not create difference through creativity but through negation. Cleavage and comparative relativizing are two examples of it: When "Je ne suis Charlie" is posted on Facebook, or when a "Je suis taxi" sticker is displayed, some of the force of the collective empathy is parasitized in order to gain a moment of attention, be it even an outraged, annoyed attention. But does that entail that the collectivity has a copyright on its slogans and that no minority, alternative stance is possible? Such a claim would be tantamount to advocating a dictatorship of the collectivity. At the same time, a logical difference obtains between those agnostics who simply do not partake in the collective empathy, for instance by not displaying any "Je suis Charlie" sticker, and those who, on the contrary, willingly produce negative deviation from the collective block.

A contemporary scholar's duty is to reflect not only on what happens to a society when it expels any instance of negation, as in the case of dictatorships, but also on what happens to a community when collective empathy is constantly frustrated by operations of cleavage and relativizing. Is this individualism of contrarian reactions conducive to a sort of moral paralysis, in which the continuous juxtaposition of competitive claims disrupts any attempt of moral project? In other words, what happens to a society when it is no longer able to hold a minute of silence for its victims of terror without individual voices to break the void? The narcissism that pervades digital social media is a mighty force, which sometimes works to the detriment of social cohesion.

As pointed out earlier, there is nothing easier than gaining attention through negation. When the crowd says, "Je suis Charlie", I differentiate myself through cleavage or comparative relativizing; I therefore win the attention of a small group of followers, who maybe think what I think but most probably are also eager to differentiate themselves through the paradoxical formation of a minority. In order to integrate a minority I must share the opinions of others (individual minorities are as difficult to conceive as individual languages are). The kind of homologation that the individual suffers in a minority, however, is different from that which the majority or the mainstream impose. It is a homologation that, nevertheless, keeps the value of "differentiation through negation" attached to it.

Blurring sarcasm

A third degree of differentiation exasperates the semantic and pragmatic effects of cleavage and comparative relativizing: In the semiosphere, messages start to proliferate that do not only seek to negate the emotional cohesion of the crowd or to displace its focus toward other domains but also clearly constitute an anti-statement. That is the case of the French satirical comedian and anti-Semitic activist Dieudonné M'bala M'bala.[13] On January 11, 2015, in order to show solidarity to the victims of the terrorist attacks, a giant crowd marched through the boulevards of Paris; the French comedian, a notorious contrarian, conversely tweeted, "*Sachez que ce soir, en ce qui me concerne, Je me sens Charlie Coulibaly*" ["Please notice that tonight, as far as I am concerned, I feel like Charlie Coulibaly"], mixing the name of the satirical magazine with that of one of the terrorists, Amedy Coulibaly.[14] He was therefore prosecuted and condemned by the French authorities for being an apologist of terrorism.

FIGURE 3.2 An image posted anonymously on the web, adapting the "Je suis Charlie" slogan so as to show support to the terrorists

Dieudonné's statement, however, was not isolated. Soon after, other versions of the same slogan started to spread through social networks, sometimes adopting the graphic shape of the "Je suis Charlie" sign. These versions, however, would also replace, like Dieudonné's, the name of the magazine with the name of the terrorists, that is, again Coulibaly or the infamous Kouachi brothers, perpetrators of the Charlie Hebdo massacre[15] (Figure 3.2).

These counter-slogans would also frequently openly endorse violent Jihadism or anti-Semitism. It is quite evident that the degree of differentiation that these slogans sought to bring about was situated on a different level of antagonism. They did not limit themselves to deny the identification of the crowd with the victims, nor did they simply replace the victims with other supposed victims, but they proposed a disquieting identification with the terrorists. As it is evident in the case of Dieudonné, this third degree of differentiation produces scandal, and as a result attention and audience, as well as imitators and supporters. Since the present chapter is about abstract patterns of semantic differentiation in the semiosphere more than about their actual content, what is at stake here is not so much the absurdity of proposing to the media, and especially to social networks, an identification with the assassins, but these statements' capacity for virally spreading throughout the semiosphere. Proposals of this kind, indeed, are certainly worrying because of their semantics of violence, but they are worrying even more because of their pragmatic efficacy: Many people on the Internet were eager to receive and relay them, thus contributing to their diffusion. How can one explain that? Whereas differentiations of the first two sorts (cleavage and negation) defy the crowd through moderate counternarratives, followers of Dieudonné or supporters of the Kouachi brothers endorse a dramatically antisocial view, according to which the crowd that manifests against terrorism and is in solidarity with its victims is not only wrong (we should not be "Charlie", we should be someone else) but turns, de facto, into an enemy. Shouting "Je suis Coulibaly" means designating the whole pro-Charlie crowd as the next potential victim.

To this regard, a further distinction should be made. On the one hand, opinion leaders like Dieudonné openly utter these statements. They are well aware of the legal consequences that they will have to face as a result. Indeed, for as punitive as these consequences might be, they inevitably turn into the most effective megaphone that these opinion leaders might have. That is one of the dilemmas with which Western societies must deal in the present time: on the one side, limiting the diffusion of hate speech and, on the other side, facing the risk that any limitation becomes involuntary propaganda (Bleich 2011; Leone 2011). That is exactly what happened after Dieudonné was prosecuted for his seemingly pro-Coulibaly statement: Thousands of anonymous voices on the Internet started to depict him as a martyr of freedom and as a victim of censorship and repression, even to the point of comparing him with Charlie Hebdo. The evident difference between the cartoonists, who had been brutally killed for what they had drawn, and Dieudonné, who was being prosecuted according to the French law, was totally ignored. Dieudonné, as well as other contrarian and provoking opinion leaders like him, knows well how to use public outrage as a lever to gain popularity and, as a result, political and financial benefits. Hence, it is not difficult to explain the rationale behind these rhetorical patterns of provocation. Unfortunately, the more morally outrageous they sound, the more they attract media attention; therefore, they acquire social status in specific niches. What is more difficult to explain is why these niches proliferate in the present-day political panorama. Why should someone endorse a statement that openly justifies or even glorifies brutal terrorism, if no apparent benefits derive from such endorsement?

Anonymity

The increased anonymity of digital communication introduces paradoxical effects into the semiosphere (Roesler 2007; Stryker 2012; Poletti and Rak 2014). Anonymity is not a modern invention. Anonymous letters, pasquinades, and graffiti with no manifest author have a long tradition, often playing a central role in society (Griffin 2003; Mullan 2007; Pabst 2011): Given the unbalance of power and the social hierarchy in a community, the only way for unrepresented and repressed voices to circulate is to be communicated without apparent attachment to a persona. Anonymity defends the dissident or the minority from the violence of power. What happens, though, when anonymity becomes not the exception but the rule of sociopolitical communication? Internet journals and magazines are full of comments and opinions that react to each other in an infinite chain, and yet few of them are attached to what, in the pre-Internet era, would be called "an author". Fictitious avatars with fantastic names constitute today the bulk of communication on the Internet. Lengthy and complicated investigation is required, even for police forces or secret services, in order to reattach these avatars to the persona of a citizen. In some cases, such reattachment is utterly impossible. The traces that link a body and its Internet voices fade away in the continuously moving ocean of the web.

Proliferation of anonymity in the public arena is not without consequences. As underlined earlier, secrecy allowed dissidents of the past to voice messages that would have been otherwise brutally repressed. In the present time, however, it is not only fear of repression that prompts authors to conceal themselves behind avatars but a new version of the aesthetic thrill that Canetti has recognized in the formation of crowds. On the one hand, there is anonymity in every crowd, at least to a certain extent. Those who marched through the boulevards of Paris shouting, "Je suis Charlie" were also enjoying the aesthetic pleasure of merging into an overwhelming collectivity. On the other hand, fusion in a real crowd is never complete: No matter how much supporters of a political cause or a soccer team stick together, they remain individual bodies, sentient beings, occupying a specific portion of time and space. They might shout outrageous slogans, but they will never be able to totally shed responsibility for that shouting. They might ecstatically lose themselves in the multitude, sometimes with tragic, violent consequences, but they will still exist in it as singularities, and as such they will be faced by police forces, videoed by secret services, and arrested if necessary.

Crowds on the Internet are more powerful. Avatars join causes, express solidarity, manifest concern, incite to hate, side with the victims or with their assassins, call for empathy and action, attract to or distract from such and such goal, practically without boundaries. A brutal message written in a web forum and the actual persona of his or her author, living in a space and time, are so distant that only exceptional circumstances recreate a binding connection between them. At the same time, though, the essentially virtual character of the contemporary Internet crowd also generates some disquieting consequences. What kind of opinion is, indeed, one that is radically disconnected from its body? Threads of comments that develop at the bottom of whatever news in the websites of journals, especially in relation to controversial topics, often feature a particular semantic characteristic: They are syntactically related in the thread, formally connecting to each other through appropriate anaphoric references, but they nevertheless seem to avoid fully engaging with the semantic field opened by others. Solipsism is the meaning effect that emerges from such an arrangement. Is this a consequence of anonymity? It partially is. Avatars do not converse like human beings, not only because—despite the development of more and more sophisticated emoticons—verbal exchange is constantly detached from other systems of signs and languages (facial expressions, intonations, etc.) but also because voices detached from bodies tend to drift in the semiosphere without any hindrance or obstacle to divert their trajectory.

On the one hand, any avatar on the Internet easily finds a constituency: No matter how outrageous a proposal might be, it will sooner or later garner, if not support, at least other avatars' willingness to find differentiation and value in the virtual semiosphere through adhering to that proposal. Avatars and people behind them are starving for value and sometimes find it in the most morally unacceptable stances. On the other hand, given the conformity of the virtual semiosphere, even the most controversial stance will not come across any resistance but develop a sort of a niche in the unlimited semiotic space of the web. Terrorist jihadist web forums justifying the stoning of adulterous women inject into the Western semiosphere criminal ideas, yet they mostly remain unchallenged, inhabited and visited only by those who have already shaped their avatar identity by playing the obscurantist game of the forum.

That should not suggest that no connection exists between the way in which ideas are exchanged on the Internet and the way in which they circulate outside of the web. Controversial leaders like Dieudonné, for instance, gain political and financial status exactly because they are skillfully able to inhabit the ridge between virtual and non-virtual, YouTube and theaters. However, what fuels their political and economic power, that is, their supporters, rarely stand out from the anonymous crowd, manifesting themselves only through vague avatars. The double standard that characterizes the expression of opinions in the Western semiosphere as regards the relation between the square and the web-square accentuates this phenomenon: Since real personae must face censorship and sometimes legal consequences, while avatars mostly develop their personal moral world undisturbed, the former increasingly disappear behind the latter, shaping a social arena in which semantic content is created and communicated without responsibility.

The semiotic analysis of patterns of opinion formation in the virtual semiosphere should not turn, however, into a plea for censorship (Leone 2016f *Censura*). On the contrary, democratic observers cannot but rejoice themselves at the new spaces of expression of ideas that the Internet has offered to human beings. These spaces are absolutely fundamental, especially in those societies in which speaking in person, and not only through an avatar, might be a cause for persecution and even death. At the same time, semiotic analysts must open their eyes, and the eyes of others, vis-à-vis the possible consequences, for a community, of a social conversation and a formation of public opinion that mostly develop virtually, without or with transient connection to a physical and administrative persona. The keyword here is responsibility.

Responsibility

Responsibility is certainly not a syntactic characteristic of communication, although it affects its syntax. The same goes for the semantic level. Responsibility is, however, not simply a moral concept but also a semiotic, and specifically pragmatic, one. Etymologically, it designates the circle of individuals or institutions to which a subject ideally responds, to which a subject is accountable. Who will ideally answer the conversation that I start on the web, and what do I owe to this conversation partner(s)? What are the rules that I have to abide by in order for my statement to receive an appropriate answer? Understanding what responsible communication is can be easier if its negative counterpart is analyzed first, that is, irresponsible communication.

Let us go back to Dieudonné's contrarian statement "Je suis Charlie Coulibaly". In defending himself against the accusation of "apology of terrorism" leveled at him by the French State, Dieudonné declared that his intention was rather that of "avoir voulu dépasser la logique 'des gentils et des méchants'" ["going beyond the logic of 'the kind ones and the evil ones'"]. The degree of responsibility of this statement, and of the statement it seeks to justify, can be measured in relation to the audience to which Dieudonné potentially responds. Such an audience is not simply composed by the comedian's relatives and friends but consists in the vast arena of people who, through theater shows and especially through social networks, are reached every day by Dieudonné's words and performances. Dieudonné's Facebook page is presently followed by more than 1,300,000 supporters; Twitter, 129,000; "Quenel+", Dieudonné's YouTube channel, almost 100,000. At the same time, Dieudonné is not an elected official; he is a private citizen, with the same right of expression as other French citizens. The point here, though, is not legal but pragmatic: What is the force of Dieudonné's voice, his capacity to create contents that, once injected into the semiosphere, circulate through it and even reach its kernel? What is the probability that Dieudonné's anti-Semitic ideas, for instance, "infect" the nucleus of the French society?

Given the position that the comedian holds in the French and Francophone semiosphere, his ironic insights on the Republican March of January 11, 2015— posted on Twitter and other social networks—and especially the infamous sentence of his, "Please notice that tonight, as far as I am concerned, I feel like Charlie Coulibaly". are pragmatically irresponsible. To this regard, the most revealing segment of the sentence is not the repulsive juxtaposition of the name of the victims with that of the assassin, but the incidental clause "as far as I am concerned" ["en ce qui me concerne"]. A public opinion leader with such a grasp over a large part of the French audience cannot qualify his statements with "as far as I am concerned", since it is clear that whatever he publicly does or says will affect hundreds of thousands of people. In order to better gauge the measure of this irresponsibility, three elements must be analyzed: (1) the pattern of opinion formation that this sentence exploits, (2) its "trajectory" in the semiosphere, and (3) the actual semantic content that it circulates in the contemporary French arena.

As regards the first element, it is clear that Dieudonné builds the value of his message and identity not only through simple cleavage ("I am not Charlie Hebdo") or relativizing comparison ("We should not be Charlie Hebdo, we should be Y or Z") but by an ambiguous combination of both, which is essentially sarcastic. Given the tragic situation that Dieudonné's statement comments upon, his sarcasm is desecrating. It precisely consists in blurring the distinction between the innocent and the murderer. It calls its audience for an ambiguous, oxymoronic, and de facto impossible identification, which embraces in the same empathy the victims of terror and its perpetrators. Since this identification is hardly conceivable, especially in the aftermath of the tragic events, the sarcastic character of the message prompting it stands out: Dieudonné's statement does not actually advocate consideration, on the same level, the death of *Charlie Hebdo*'s cartoonists and that of Coulibaly; it is mocking those who express spontaneous identification with the murdered. Therefore, the pattern of opinion formation that this sentence exploits cannot be considered as purely syntactic, as a way to forge, albeit for a minute, the frisson of a contrarian's identity; it is, conversely, a calculated moral chimera, offered to Dieudonné's web audience in order to strengthen the comedian's position as a maverick in the French semiosphere and as an opinion leader who is able to go beyond the mainstream thought imposed by information lobbies.

As regards the second element (the "trajectory" of Dieudonné's sentence in the semiosphere), it developed along three different lines. Along the first one, the sentence immediately generated repulsion and, consequently, a legal action against the comedian, accused and then condemned for apology of terrorism. Along the second line, though, the more the sentence was quoted, and condemned by the political, media, and intellectual establishment, the more copycat versions of it started to circulate in the web, frequently topped by versions that, abandoning the veil of sarcasm contained in the original sentence, would bluntly endorse an identification with Coulibaly, the murderer. There were, it is true, web followers of Dieudonné who expressed concern about the comedian's new provocation (third line), but they were a minority. Overall, he managed to reinforce his image as a contrarian and a victim, persecuted by a repressive establishment.

As regards the third element, that is, the actual content that Dieudonné's statement circulated in the French and Francophone semiosphere, it deploys itself on different levels. First, it seeks and probably succeeds in using irony, or rather sarcasm, in order to break the spell of a nation that unites, in an almost religious moment, to commemorate the victims of brutal murder. Second, it insinuates that such an outpouring of indignation is misplaced, since it should be considered how the perpetrators are themselves victims when considered from a more "enlightened" perspective. Third, it shows a model of desecration, offered to all those that, for such and such reason, might side with the terrorists: muddying the water of moral judgment by blurring the distinction between the murderers and the murdered. Fourth, it pursues a strategy of victimization by provocation, by forcing the French authorities to prosecute the comedian for his statements; the strategy is particularly pernicious since it explicitly proposes a (pseudo)parallel between Dieudonné and Charlie Hebdo, which would equally undergo obscurantism and repression.

Given this analysis, the pragmatic irresponsibility of the comedian also situates itself on several levels. First, as suggested before, Dieudonné is not a common citizen but an opinion leader, albeit a "comic" one, who economically and also politically profits from the growth of his popularity, which in turn is directly proportional to his ability for provocation and for denying the established consensus. But is not provoking laughter the first duty of a comedian, no matter what the situation is? Is not shedding irony and even sarcasm on all sorts of reality the core business of a humorist? It probably is. The questions then are, "Who was supposed to laugh at Dieudonné's 'joke', and who actually did?" "Could relatives and friends of the victims laugh at this 'joke', feeling relieved by it?"

"Could the millions of French mourners rejoice at the humor, thankful for the way it lifted their spirits?" It is difficult not to be firmly convinced that the only audience that could reasonably laugh or smile or feel euphoria at Dieudonné's sarcastic sentence was composed by those somehow siding with the murderers. Dieudonné's "joke" was therefore titillating terrorism sympathizers. That is the first reason of his pragmatic irresponsibility: A comedian should be able to propose the best interpretation of the extent to which a certain pragmatic context is open to laughter or not. Cracking a joke at a funeral can provide relief even for mourners, but if the joke implicitly debases the dead one, then it is not a joke anymore but simply an expression of bad taste.[16] When bad taste is shared with hundreds of thousands of people, then it turns into a bad opinion and sometimes even into a bad plan of action.

On a different level, Dieudonné's statement is irresponsible not only toward the pragmatics of the context but also toward the genre itself to which it purports to refer. As the history of philosophy and semiotics shows, laughter is a serious matter.[17] The one who is able to make people laugh is able to give those people a rare aesthetic and almost physical pleasure, whose rules of creation escape any standardized production. There are, of course, techniques to provoke laughter, but people still rightly consider great comedians as people of talent or even genius, since they can touch other people in a powerful yet mysterious way. From this point of view, humor is a gift, and as such should be cultivated. When a successful humorist transposes this gift from the arena of entertainment to the political one, abusing laughter as an alibi to convey the most controversial stances, then that comedian is implicitly betraying the pact of genre that links the artist and the spectator, the jokes of the former and the laughter of the latter. It is one thing when a comedian, performing in his or her theater, uses humor, irony, sarcasm, and laughter to wittily unveil the unbalances of human life, but it is another when a comedian, having gained through his or her ability the consensus of millions, abuses humor, irony, sarcasm, and laughter to rage on victims of power. That is the ultimate irresponsibility of Dieudonné: By inciting his fellow citizens to joke about Charlie Hebdo's tragedy and to side with its perpetrators, he encouraged them to laugh at the unarmed victims, not at their armed killers.

Conspiracy

Thus far, three patterns of opinion formation in the semiosphere have been analyzed: differentiation through negation, differentiation through relativizing comparison, and opinion leading through sarcasm. The last and fourth pattern that this chapter will analyze is that of conspiracy theories. The first pattern says, "I am not Charlie Hebdo"; the second, "I am not Charlie Hebdo, I am Y"; and the third, "I am Charlie Hebdo's assassin". The fourth pattern explicitly states, "Charlie Hebdo does not exist". Mere hours after the brutal attacks in Paris, statements of this kind started to proliferate in social networks. They often took an elaborate, professional or semi-professional form, aiming at "debunking" the hoax "Charlie Hebdo". Through pointing at details in the dynamic of the events, and especially through (pseudo) analysis of the many pictures and videos representing them and circulating in the media, these theories gained differentiation and, therefore, value by insinuating that there were no terrorist attacks and that, instead, the killings had been staged by some secret and often undefined agencies.[18]

At least in the beginning, several of the circulating conspiracy theories did not propose an identity for these alternative agencies but limited themselves to denying the mainstream hypothesis about who the perpetrators were. Later on, the same conspiracy theorists tried to designate the real instigators of the killings, often indicating the "usual suspects" (Israel, etc.). For instance, only a few hours after the attacks, Mr. Carlo Sibilia[19]—a member of the Italian Parliament elected in the "Five Stars Movement", a political party that sometimes espouses what mainstream commentators define as "conspiracy theories"—declared that it was "Incredibile che a #CharlieHebdo sia rimasto ucciso l'economista Maris che denunciava irregolarità su emissione moneta" ["it is incredible that the economist Maris, who denounced the irregularities in the emission of currency, was killed at Charlie Hebdo"], referring to the tragic death of French economist Bernard Maris[20] during the terrorist attack against Charlie Hebdo. The ambiguous sentence was insinuating ("it is incredible") that the attacks had not been perpetrated by jihadist terrorists but rather orchestrated by obscure agencies whose only aim was to silence a hostile economist. The absurdity of the theory was evident to the point that Sibilia's blog was soon full of sarcastic comments about how, on the contrary, all the other victims of Charlie Hebdo had been "credibly" killed. It is, however, important to underline that the epistemic soundness of conspiracy theories is not the only issue at stake here. The episode, indeed, reveals that there is an audience for these kinds of surreal interpretations and that opinion leaders can differentiate and acquire value by explicitly or implicitly endorsing them.

The range of rhetorical means that conspiracy theories deploy often includes images. Rosario Marcianò, one of the most active supporters of "chemtrail conspiracy theories" in Italy, also close to Beppe Grillo's[21] M5S movement, soon after the killings started "analyzing" pictures and videos of the events; he reached the conclusion that it was all staged and that the video of the brutal murder of peace guardian Ahmed Merabet during the attacks was actually a hoax with an actor. This conspiracy theory and its visual analyses are clearly a fake debunking; not only do they point at absurd "signs" in images and videos, but, above all, they fail to propose a coherent reconstruction of reality: If Ahmed Merabet did not die, who are the relatives crying at his funeral? Are they all actors? But again, the epistemic soundness and rhetorical sophistication of these conspiracy theories is not the main point. What is alarmingly more important is that there is a consistent minority that is ready to endorse and spread these interpretations in the labyrinth of social networks. In other words, for many present-day individuals, desire for a stronger identity, to be created through endorsement of non-mainstream representations of reality, is more compelling than human empathy. While Ahmed Merabet's relatives are still crying around his coffin, anonymous commentators experience the existential thrill of denying the truthfulness of his death. That is why opinion leaders who circulate these kinds of conspiracy theories in order to secure followers and status are as irresponsible as those who side, like Dieudonné, with the murderers. Whereas the former laughs at the victims and promotes emotional proximity with the assassins, the latter divests the victims of their role, turning them into the extras of a bad spy movie.

The semiotic square of ritual opinion formation

The four patterns of opinion formation identified and analyzed thus far can be visually inter-defined through a simple diagram, the "semiotic square" of Greimasian semiotics. First devised by Greek philosophers, the semiotic square was adapted by Greimas and his school in order to articulate and explore the semantic categories of a text (Figure 3.3).[22] From a technical point of view, applying this instrument of micro-textual analysis to the macro-level of opinion social formation is not without risks and methodological uncertainties (Leone 2012a). It is, however, an operation that has been already carried on several times by socio-semiotics, ethno-semiotics, and so on. A difference in the present application, though, must be pointed out. The semiotic square will be used here syntactically more than semantically. In other words, it will show how the social discourse creates value, without attaching a particular importance to the content of that value. In Hjelmslev's terms (1943), the diagram will model the form of opinion patterns, not their substance. Behind this unconventional methodological choice (the semiotic square is usually employed to articulate sememes, that is, semantic patterns and trajectories in a text), there lies a provocative hypothesis: Talk in contemporary society is more ritual than communication; it aims at creating, destroying, reinforcing, or weakening positions of value as empty places,

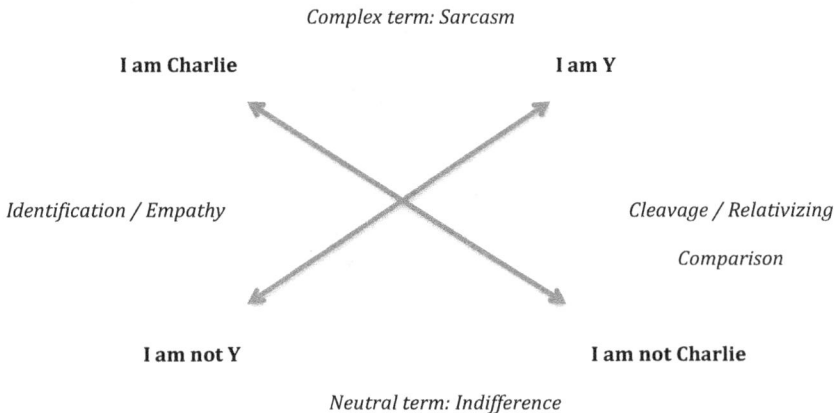

Complex term: Sarcasm

I am Charlie   **I am Y**

Identification / Empathy   *Cleavage / Relativizing*

Comparison

I am not Y   **I am not Charlie**

Neutral term: Indifference

FIGURE 3.3 The semiotic square of ritual opinion formation; scheme by the author

independently from the actual content they hold. But it is exactly this ritual dimension of social discourse that opinion leaders in the new media and especially in the digital social networks can easily manipulate and turn to their favor.

Mixing Lotman's idea of the semiosphere and Greimas's conception of semantic differentiation, the semiosphere can be imagined as composed and recomposed by texts that move along all the trajectories of the semiotic square in order to gain centrality and, therefore, semiotic status and power. That implies the ability to model and remodel all the signs, texts, and fragments of discourse that circulate in the semiosphere. In simpler words, all positions of value seek to become a primary pattern that models other contents according to a predetermined axiology. The expansion of a syntactic position of value therefore coincides with the diffusion of an ideology.

As Greimasian semioticians know, a relation of contradiction underlies the first and simplest movement of differentiation in the semiotic square: A is denied into non-A. This relation of contradiction corresponds to the pattern of opinion formation identified above as "cleavage". I differentiate myself from you by simply denying your content. You say "I am Charlie Hebdo", I say "I am not Charlie Hebdo". The second movement in the semiotic square does not manifest a relation of contradiction but one of contrariety. In such case, I differentiate myself from my interlocutor not simply by denying its position but through qualifying mine as an alternative one. I do not simply acquire a ritual position of value by saying "I am not Charlie Hebdo" but by saying "I am not Charlie Hebdo, I am Y". This movement is certainly more semantically relevant than the first one, since it proposes to "hook" a position of value to an alternative content in the semiosphere. Nevertheless, it retains its predominantly syntactic nature, for it mainly acquires meaning and status through relativizing comparison: What matters in the statement that defines my position is not that I declare my identity with Y but that I define it as contrary to the mainstream identification with Charlie Hebdo. The third trajectory that characteristically brings about and visualizes value in the semiotic square stems from contradiction in order to affirm contrariety: "I am not Charlie Hebdo; therefore, I am Y". The ideological nature of this implication is evident: Although there is no need to deny one's identity with Charlie Hebdo in order to "be" Y, the statement implies that whoever "is" Charlie Hebdo cannot "be" at the same time Y and should therefore cease "being" Charlie Hebdo in order to "be" Y. Again, it is reasonable to hypothesize that what matters in this diversion toward an alternative object of identification and empathy is diversion itself rather than the object.

What about the position of value and the consequent pattern of opinion formation created by statements like the one uttered by Dieudonné? How should they be represented in the semiotic square? Dieudonné's sentence "I am Charlie Coulibaly" does not simply deny identification with the victims, nor does it merely propose different victims to identify with but undermine the idea itself of identification. The value of this ritual position is constructed neither through contradiction ("I am not Charlie") nor through contrariety ("I am not Charlie, I am Y") but through blurring and even suspending the semiotic square itself.

From this point of view, Dieudonné's statement adopts a meta-point of view on the semiotic square of empathy toward the victims and endorses a position in which empathy itself is placed in a network of alternative syntactic positions. Among them, Dieudonné's statement clearly adopts that of "complexity", that is, the position of value manifested in a discourse whose content is "A and B": "I am Charlie, but I am also Charlie's murderers". The adoption of this syntactic position on a meta-level disrupts the semantic category of empathy and turns it into a different genre: sarcasm (Haiman 1998; Rockwell 2006). The statement can be read as a bitter-ironic comment belittling the value of the positions and patterns of opinion formation seen above. It is as though Dieudonné and his followers were saying, "the problem is not to choose the victims to empathize with; the problem, instead, is the status itself of the victim".

The semiotic square includes also a fourth position, which is the one that manifests itself in text and discursive formations in which it is not the complexity of values that is affirmed (A and B) but their neutrality (non-A and non-B). In relation to the case of Charlie Hebdo, this syntactic position too is a meta-one; unlike Dieudonné's stance, though, it is essentially empty. It advocates not the blurring of the distinction between Charlie Hebdo and the murderers (A and B) but indifference. That is the position of those who sleepily receive the news about Charlie Hebdo, listen to the commentaries, and talk to people about the events but are fundamentally impermeable to their tragedy. They feel empathy neither toward the victims nor toward the murderers; they do not deny such empathy either, and neither do they propose an alternative object of compassion. They just live and continue to live their routine existence, anesthetized by indifference or trauma.

The most interesting aspect of the semiotic square is not its capacity for statically visualizing relations of values but its ability to visually render their dynamics, thus turning into a field of tensions. It is, indeed, fundamental to underline that these patterns of opinion formation are not crystallized into an immobile semiosphere but constantly fluctuate under the pressure of corresponding rhetorical strategies. A successful rhetoric of identification, for instance, will convince more and more members of a society that they have to declare their solidarity with the victims without exceptions; conversely, proliferation of cleavages and relativizing comparisons will deflect signs and texts from identification toward non-identification or toward alternative identification. Finally, the two meta-rhetoric patterns of sarcasm (complexity of values) and indifference (neutrality of them) will encourage the semiosphere to actually expel the position itself of empathy and identification.

Conclusions

Semioticians can themselves be indifferent, coldly observing these fluctuations of patterns as if they were the stars of a distant galaxy. Two considerations, however, should at least ripple the surface of this imperturbability. The first might sound moralistic if it is not articulated in a formally acceptable way. Any preference attributed to the positions described above, indeed, is tantamount to advocating an axiology in the semiosphere and therefore embracing an ideology. From the impassible perspective of the scholar, there is no formal reason for which empathizing with the victims of terror should be a more praiseworthy ideology than sponsoring alternative patterns of opinion formation. That is a moral problem, not a strictly semiotic one. Nevertheless, as suggested above, semiotics cannot ignore that a specific responsibility, not only in moral terms but also, above all, in pragmatic terms, is attached to opinions and interpretations that fluctuate in the semiosphere. Semiotics must not endorse such and such opinion but must definitely highlight the asymmetries of the semiosphere, which translate into imbalances in the pragmatic force of stances and statements. As pointed out in relation to the Dieudonné affair, statements hold different pragmatic responsibility in relation to the vantage point from which they are circulated in the semiosphere. Different discursive genres require corresponding care in the manipulation of rhetoric and in the consequence formation of opinion. We do not demand the same interpretive carefulness from the judge and from the sport commentator, as we do not demand the same interpretive carefulness from the bar sport commentator and from the famous sport anchorman. The semiosphere models meaning asymmetrically, and pragmatic responsibility is, in semiotic terms, awareness of one's position in the semiosphere and consequent care in crafting or re-crafting meaning.

The second consideration deploys itself on a meta-level and might seem more abstract. It is actually more disquieting. Semiospheres can be differentiated not only in relation to the axiologies that they allow to predominate through the position held by primary modeling signs, texts, and discursive formations but also in relation to the distinction between syntactic and semantic ideology. As pointed out from the beginning of this chapter, there is something uncannily automatic in the way in which patterns of opinions take shape in the contemporary semiosphere, especially in social networks. The semiotic observer has the impression that relations of contradiction, contrariety, complexity, and neutrality are deployed with no real semantic engagement but in a sort of ritual, where what is at stake, for instance, is not denying identification with Charlie Hebdo, proposing an alternative identification with Y, sarcastically placing Charlie Hebdo and its killers on the same moral level, or manifesting indifference; what matters, on the contrary, is precisely these syntactic moves: contradiction, contrariety, complexity, and neutrality. In other words, what matters to the members of the virtual semiosphere is narcissistically creating a position through these moves, not the specific semantic contents that these moves circulate. The predominance of this syntactic, empty skeleton of patterns of differentiation over the actual semantic contents that they structure bestows a certain cold, inhuman rituality to the formation of public opinion. Opinion leaders act as the skillful priests of this syntactic game, pulling its strings with no real interest in the semantic core.[23]

Is that simply the content of a subjective impression due to an axiological bias? In other words, it might be that attributing a narcissistic etiology to different opinions is merely the outcome of the ideological presuppositions of an observer inclined to embrace the cause of "Western consensus" and oblivious of the alternative voices that, in the world, criticize such mainstream political line, as well as, in the most extreme cases, the "fiction" of democracy itself, and its Arabophobic/Islamophobic nature in the French context. Arguably, though, there are at least three objective elements that can be referred to so as to demonstrate that such accusations of narcissism do not simply result from the ideological biases of the semiotic analyst but actually intrinsically characterize many current patterns of opinion formation in social networks: (1) most of these patterns do not give rise to any attempt at influencing the formation of opinion outside of the digital social networks; those who unconditionally adhered to the "Je suis Charlie" slogan filled the streets of Paris; their objectors, on the contrary, remained a scattered virtual community with no visible off-line manifestation or political project (unless terrorism is considered a political project; see point 3 for that); (2) social networks agents that objected to the "Je suis Charlie" consensus recurrently reappeared, previously and subsequently, in order to manifest the same objections over and over again concerning the most disparate issues; in other terms, there is objective evidence so as to demonstrate that their posts or comments are not specifically critical but generically critical; they are not against the "Je suis Charlie" movement in particular but against whatever is mainstream; that is why they qualify as syntactic, nonspecific, and even ritual patterns of opinion; (3) one could claim that terrorism itself is a way to express one's opinion and that support for terrorist acts is a viable position in a democracy or at least in the global conversation; nevertheless, this argument would be paradoxical not only because it would implicitly deny the democratic framework but also because it would intrinsically annihilate the semiotic framework; equating terrorism and communication, indeed, implicitly endorses a non-semiotic point of view on humanity (from the Peircean perspective, one could claim that terrorist acts are more dyadic than triadic, since they seek to change the world without resort to language; that is, I do not persuade you not to blaspheme my God; I kill you).

Again, semioticians might observe with a cold analytical look this hypertrophy of the level of syntactic ideology to the detriment of the semantic one. At the same time, they should not overlook the risks that this hypertrophy entails. Living, thinking, and producing meaning in a semiosphere where syntactic ideology prevails means existing in a universe where pragmatic responsibility is not an issue anymore, for every opinion is actually not a semantic, twenty-first-century opinion anymore, attached to a body, to a community, to a genre, to a grid, and to a style of interpretation but a syntactic position in a game, where ideas oppose each other in various ways but seem to have lost their earnestness. The proliferation of syntactic ideology and its increasing centrality in the contemporary digital semiosphere may be dangerously conducive to a sort of trolling society, in which what matters is not to define or redefine social relations through exchange of meaning but the simple frisson that sparkles from inconsequential difference, from the creation of—and the permanence in—an echo-chamber. Unveiling the inhuman consequences of such a trolling society is one of the urgent tasks of present-day semiotics and its quest for significance.

Notes

1 "We must need believe that the greatest of all battles lies before us, in preparation for which we must do and suffer all things to gain power. Consequently we must be conversant with poets, with historians, with orators, indeed with all men who may further our soul's salvation" (Engl. trans. Frederick Morgan Padelford. 1902. *Address to Young Men on the Right Use of Greek Literature*).

2 Although the definition of "terrorism" and "terrorist" is highly problematic, it will not be discussed here. For a detailed examination of the semantics of these two terms, see Leone (2014c: 810).

3 The semiotic analysis of public opinion is still a relatively underdeveloped field, especially as regards social networks. See Ehrat (2010) for a semiotic study of the representation of "scandalous" events in the media; see also Gaines (2010). On the one hand, such field is close to the research area on "framing"; for a partially semiotic approach, see Botan and Soto (1998), Zhou and Moy (2006), and Boomgaarden and de Vreese (2007). Research on formation of public opinion regarding terrorism attacks has blossomed after 9/11. See Greenberg (2002); some recent contributions are Gerhards (2011), Frindte and Haussecker (2010), and Archetti (2013). From the theoretical point of view, on the other hand, the topic of the semiotic analysis of opinion formation intersects the area of the semiotics of "lifestyles", "forms of life", and "modes of existence" (see Fontanille 2006; Zilberberg 2011); the French semiotic journal *Nouveaux Actes Sémiotiques* contains several articles devoted to such topic; see, for instance, Landowski (2012). On the formation of interpretive frames in the social networks, see Liu (2007) and in the same journal issue, Lange (2007); see also Adami and Kress (2010).

4 The application of ritual studies to the analysis of contemporary communication is not new, at least since the Manchester school; see, for instance, Handelman (1977) and Liebes and Curran (1998); on "framing" in ritual studies, see Handelman (2006).

5 The formation of opinion in social networks is a matter of increasingly intense research especially in the domain now known as "social informatics"; see Javarone and Galam (2015); a recent survey on n-ethnographic (n-ethnography being the ethnography of the Internet) approaches for the study of social networks is Hine (2015); on trolling as a modality of opinion formation in social networks, see the thought-provoking Phillips (2015) (as well as the previous chapter in the present book); on the spreading of unfounded news through social networks, Aron (2014); on the sociodynamics and psychodynamics of identity in social networks, there exists an abundant and growing literature; recent useful contributions include Balick (2014) and Barbieri (2014); for a survey, see Power and Kirwan (2014).

6 On the conceptualization of terrorism in Western media, see Schwarz-Friesel and Kromminga (2014).

7 Bibliography on the cartoon affair is quite extensive. For a survey, see Klausen (2009); Grenda, Beneke, and Nash (2014); Sniderman, Petersen, Slothuus, and Stubager (2014); on the Danish context, see Sinram (2015); on the German context, see Ata (2011); for a comparative study, see Avon (2010); see also Contemori and Pettinari 1993; Hart and Hassencahl (2002), Giarelli and Tulman (2003), and El Refaie (2009).

8 French graphic designer Joachim Roncin created the slogan and its visual gestalt in the immediate aftermath of the attacks. Roncin chose the typographic style of his own magazine, *Stylist*, for pronoun and verb ("Je suis" ["I am"]) and the typographic style of *Charlie Hebdo* for "Charlie". The slogan spread first on Twitter, then virally everywhere on the web.

9 On the semiotics of empathy, see Koch (1989); on narrative empathy, see Keen (2006) and Boler (1997).

10 For a socio-semiotic analysis of such collective emotional responses, see Landowski (2004).

11 Literature on negation is extensive. For a semiotic perspective, see Centre de recherche sémiologique (1991), Nöth (1994), and Ibo (2012); issue 114 of the *Nouveaux Actes Sé-miotiques* (2011) is also entirely devoted to negation (accessible at http://epublications. unilim.fr/revues/as/2730; last accessed January 17, 2018); see Donà (2004); an early study of the social psychology of negation is Wason (1962); for a general survey, Yang (2005).

12 On "but" as one of the main operators of differentiation, see Greimas (1976).

13 Fontenay-aux-Roses, Hauts-de-Seine, France, February 11, 1966.

14 Juvisy-sur-Orge, Île-de-France, France, February 27, 1982 – Paris, January 9, 2015.

15 Chérif and Saïd Kouachi, born in Paris, November 29, 1982 and September 7, 1980; both died in Dammartin-en-Goële, France, January 9, 2015.

16 For a more detailed analysis of the role of humor, irony, and sarcasm in the present-day sociopolitical panorama, see Leone (2014c). See also Leone (2002, 2015b).

17 Literature on the topic is extensive. An obvious reference is Eco (1985).

18 The bibliography on conspiracy theories is huge; for a survey, see Leone (2016g); for a semiotic perspective, see Leone (2015a).

19 Avellino, febbraio 7, 1986.

20 Toulouse, France, September 23, 1946 – Paris, January 7, 2015.

21 Genoa, July 21, 1948.

22 For an introduction, see Hébert (2006).

23 It should be underlined, nevertheless, that the typology of patterns presented in the present chapter maps the formation of opinions in digital social networks, mainly in response to highly dramatic events. Other patterns (luckily) keep subsisting both on-line and off-line. But as the formation of opinions in social networks more and more becomes *the* formation of opinions in the contemporary world, and as the agenda setting of such formation is increasingly shaped around dramatic events—in certain cases even receiving political legitimation—such model might become central and effective in mapping most short circuits and paradoxes in the present-day creation of the political semiosphere.

4

PICTURING INSIGNIFICANCE

The utopia of digital perfection

So ist der geometrische Punkt in unserer
Vorstellung die höchste und höchst einzelne
Verbindung von Schweigen und Sprechen.
(Wassily Kandinsky (1926)
Punkt und Linie zu Fläche, 17[1])

Introduction

We are surrounded by pixels. And we surround them. As soon as we wake up, we check e-mails, websites, and social networks on our mobiles; we interact with the LCD displays of appliances in our kitchen, bathroom, and car; the screen of our computer "talks" to us through patterns of pixels; when traveling, giant panels in airports and train stations communicate to us the times of arrivals and departures pixel by pixel. Pixels are also the main components of digital craft, for instance in animation movies, or even become the constituents of the so-called "digital art".

Yet, despite their multifarious "accomplishments", pixels remain "hidden" to us, squeezed into the framework of a screen in increasingly high numbers, subserviently absorbed by the configurations of form, color, and brightness in which they inexorably disappear, compressed together by constantly improving technology so that their individual identity literally melts in the beautiful images that they compose.

The present chapter is an attempt at indicating some lines for the possible development of a "semiotics of the pixel". It is a highly speculative enquiry, for it must start with a foundational skeptical question: Are pixels semiotic objects at all? Do they signify autonomously from the image they give shape to? And if that is not the case, if they appear to be simple and inert constituents of digital configurations, what is their status then? According to Umberto Eco's witty definition, everything that can be used to lie can become an object for semiotic enquiry (1976: 18); but can pixels actually "lie"? Or are they bound to produce light and color according to a cold mathematical rule, with no possibility for the randomness of intentional communication? (Mitchell 2005: 87–92).

Reflection on the "semiotics of pixels" here will unfold in between two opposite perspectives, apparently distant and unrelated as regards their historical genesis and theoretical preoccupations. On the one hand, the enquiry will be inspired by one of the most famous classics of modern art theory, Wassily Kandinsky's *Punkt und Linie zu Fläche: Beitrag zur Analyse der malerischen Elemente* (1926). In particular, the chapter tackles the question whether pixels might be considered like points and whether pixels in digital art might assume the same aesthetic value as points in Kandinsky's "metaphysics of graphics".

On the other hand, the chapter reflects on pixels from the somehow alternative framework provided by the so-called "parametricism", that is, the trend of aesthetical reflection that has developed from the adoption of parameters in digital art and especially in digital architecture (Poole and Shvartzberg 2015). The two perspectives are, in a sense, diametrically opposite to each other, given that the former advocates a centrifugal aesthetic view on the pixel—turning it into the origin of a possible "visual expansion" toward a horizon of autonomous signification—whereas the latter tends to turn the pixel into a pure numeric expression, whose semantic potential is completely predetermined by a series of set parameters.

Meditation on points and pixels (or on pixels as possible points of digital visual signification) will be carried on through an unconventional procedure, mainly by reflecting on a series of "visual provocations" that compare pixels with similar aesthetic elements. At the same time, some ground questions will constantly accompany the enquiry; in a nutshell, they are the following:

1. What is the difference between a pixel and a point?
2. Are there pixels in nature and in fine arts?
3. Is digital singularity possible?
4. Is a semiotics of the pixel a viable project?

Money, mirror, temple

A good, provocative point of departure for rethinking the present-day aesthetics of the pixel is *The Million Dollar Homepage*, by Alex Tew (Figure 4.1).

The story of this bizarre web page is known to all digital art aficionados: Indebted British student Alex Tew had the genial idea to create a 1,000 × 1,000 pixel empty web page and to sell the pixels on the Internet in blocks within a limited range of time at the price of 1 $ per pixel; pixels could then be used by purchasers as they pleased. The operation was an incredible, viral success: All pixels were sold within few months, the last block being so coveted that an action

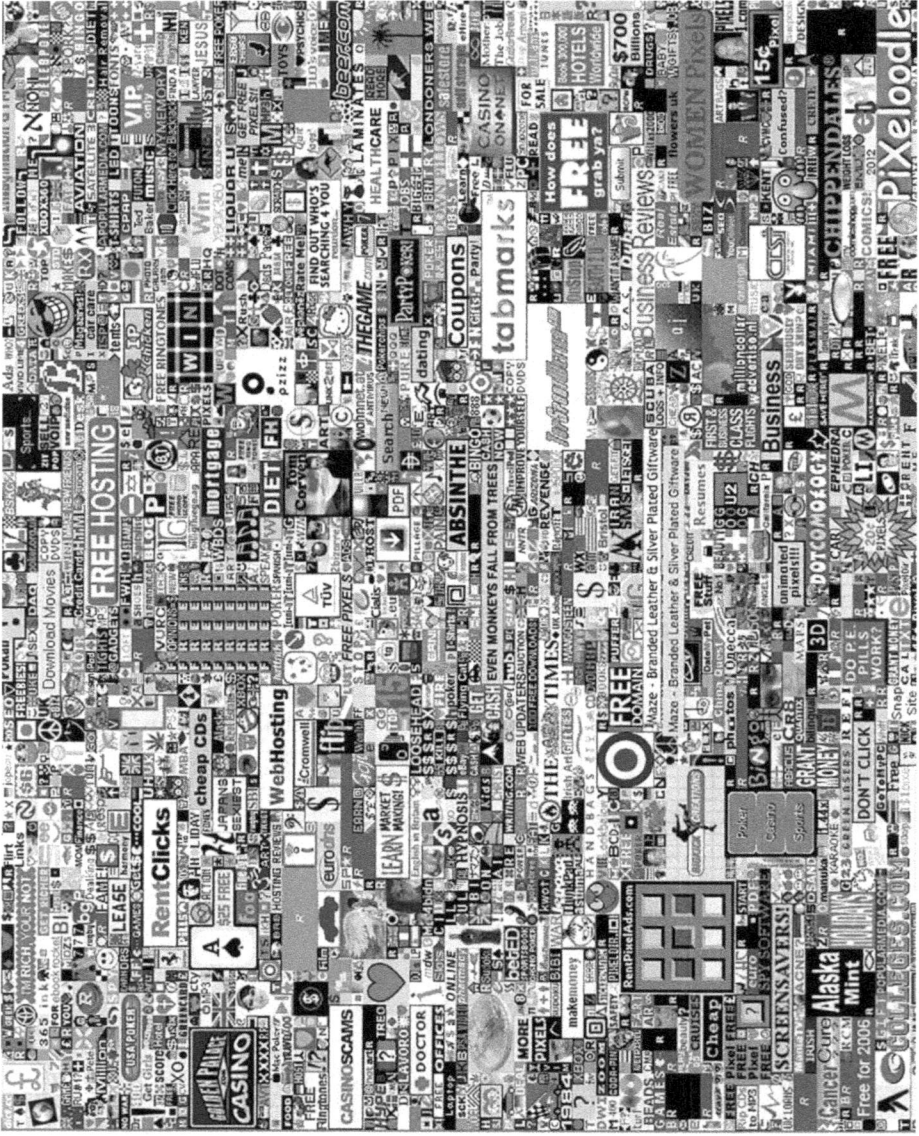

FIGURE 4.1 Alex Tew. As of February 8, 2009. *The Million Dollar Homepage.* Webpage. 1,000,000 pixels; picture from www.milliondollarhomepage.com/

on eBay was organized. Alex Tew suddenly became a wealthy young man, for his funny idea was actually revealing, through provocation, an essential characteristic of the current digitalization of most present-day visual culture. The rhetorical principles underpinning *The Million Dollar Homepage* can be summarized as follows:

1. Pixels are offered in a limited amount;
2. Pixels are offered in a limited time;
3. There is no limit to the quota of pixels that one can buy within the web page;
4. There is no limit to what pixels may express;
5. There are no contextual constraints to what pixels may express;
6. There is competition for visibility (the bigger, the better);
7. Competition requires the finite nature of pixels.

The paradoxical nature of this remunerative provocation stems from the fact that pixels are, per se, infinitely producible: There is no limit to the amount of pixels that can be generated on the Internet, meaning that there is no limit to the amount of different web pages that can be created, each one with a slightly different configuration of pixels. At the same time, the imposition of both a quantitative and a temporal framework triggers competition and, therefore, attributes social and economic value to something that is, at least in principle, valueless (Matrix 2006). But is that not the same dynamics through which most capitalistic discourse works? The imposition, through an appropriate rhetoric, of a meta-frame inducing the idea of a limit of both resources and time ("the special offer") fuels competition and stimulates the demand. René Girard's theory of mimetic desire explains well what happens in these cases: The more the pixels are desired, the more they become desirable (1977). There is no particular reason for which those pixels, and not others, should be sold, desired, and bought; yet the successful "frame of valorization" created by Alex Tew turns the insignificant into the significant, the valueless into the valuable, the banal into the exceptional.

The experiment, however, reveals the social aesthetics of pixels also from another point of view: Purchasers pay not only for the possession of a certain quantity of digital figurative space but also for the possibility of using it in order to signify what they please. That is an essential characteristic of pixels, which to a certain extent makes them comparable with money: Pixels are a protean matter, usable in order to give shape to whatever configuration of form, light, and color. First of all, buyers can express what they wish. To this regard, *The Million Dollar Homepage* unveils one of the most fundamental allures of the aesthetic economy of pixels: Their value characteristically stems from the almost magical ability to grant their possessors the opportunity to "express themselves", to use a certain amount and configuration of pixels as a matrix for voicing one's insatiable narcissism. From this point of view, pixels in Alex Tew's provocation do not work only like money but also like a mirror, in which pixel purchasers indelibly imprint their visual identity.

Second, this manifestation of visual identity is not limited by any contextual constraints: Not only may buyers signify what they want, but they may also do so without any regard for the context; the purchase of a certain number of pixels subtracts buyers to the obligation of "digital sociality". As a consequence, the principle of "the bigger and brighter, the better" affirms itself: The vaster the part of the page that digital egos occupy, the more they will be seen; competition for visibility, then, creates value and eventually even gives rise, at the end of the experiment, to an auction (the ultimate capitalistic mechanism for linking value and money).

At the same time, the frame invented by Alex Tew prodigiously turns the infinite nature of pixels into a finite one. Purchasers pay an extremely high price for something that a) actually exists in almost infinite quantities, like space or time, and b) actually does not exist if not through the display technology of the purchasers' own screens. Whereas *The Million Dollar Homepage* produces value exactly by artificially limiting in spatial and temporal terms the offer of available pixels, the web page achieves its result by selling the idea that pixels will somehow be forced to signify their purchased content without limit of time and on every screen displaying *The Million Dollar Homepage*. This website therefore shows not only that pixels can be as fluid as money and as enticing as a mirror but also promises that they can acquire the seductiveness of a temple, which often also selects a random portion of time and space (the perimeter of the *sancta sanctorum*, the etymology of contemplation) in order to turn emptiness into sacredness. The first man who drew the perimeter of a temple was a genius; the one who proposed an alternative perimeter was a failure or had to fight very hard to impose the alternative. Similarly, as the history of the Internet proves, Alex Tew's experiment could work only once.

Elements and agency

It is worth, at this point, to recall the etymology of the word "pixel"; first appeared in a published document in 1965, it is a contraction of "picture element", literally meaning the element of a picture. A similar concept was expressed in German by the word *Bildpunkt* [literally meaning "image point"], which appeared in early patents related to the development of television technology, such as Paul Nipkow's in 1888. To be precise, though, a picture element and a "picture point" are not exact equivalents (Paul 2016). Whereas the *Bildpunkt* can remind one of the points metaphysically dealt with by Kandinsky in his abovementioned treatise, a pixel is, by definition, an element of something else; precisely, it is the element of a picture.

But what is an element in art? Can an artwork be seen as composed by such things as "elements"? And is the point an element of art? Is the point an element of nature? And what is the difference between points in nature and the pre-digital culture on the one hand and, on the other hand, pixels in the digital culture? "Element" is a common word in several meta-languages, although usually associated with some sort of mechanical functioning; "element" makes one think of the components of a mechanism or of a chemical compound. Metaphorically, its semantics can also be extended to cover the functioning of parts of non-mechanical wholes, yet this extension is a priori limited in scope. Rarely will the word "element", for instance, be used with reference to a limb of the human body, or to the subsection of a novel, or, indeed, to the forms that compose a figurative artwork. What is the semantic rationale behind this difference? It probably consists in the fact that when something is called "an element", this denomination implicitly affirms a diminution of its agency; an element of something is not something that expresses an autonomous intentionality and a self-centered agency but something that is subservient to the agency of a greater whole. That is the reason for which conceiving an artwork as composed of "elements" or, vice versa, thinking that points, lines, surfaces, and colors are the "elements" of an artwork, induces one to think that a static relation holds between the whole of the work of art and the parts that the (analytical) eye somehow singles out in it.

Nevertheless, this use of the word and its semantic implications as regards the functioning of an artwork would be somehow misleading, suggesting, in fact, that such functioning ultimately is non-semiotic. On the contrary, claiming or reclaiming the semiotic functioning of the relation between the parts and the whole of an artwork means underlining that whereas points, lines, and surfaces, together with colors and the general topological structure of the image, are contributing to the overall aesthetic significance of the whole, they are not entirely subsumed by it and in it. They can continue to express an autonomous range of signification, which is nothing but the result of their capacity to exert an individual agency toward the eye of the spectator while somehow contributing this same individual agency to the coalescence of agencies that determines the final gestalt of the artwork. That is a first important difference between a point and a pixel; in Kandinsky's meditation on the visual language of Western art, the point is never simply an element, but a monad that exerts both an individual and a collective visual agency, together with the other points, lines, and surfaces that appear in the graphic or pictorial work.

It is undeniable that the point is a component of visual and sometimes also non-visual artworks, yet most of Kandinsky's reflection about it precisely consists in underlining its autonomous and irreducible agency. That also explains the difficulty of defining the range of this agency and, with it, the topology of the point, which can be expressed only in terms of a tension between the dimension of the point and that of the surface, as Kandinsky correctly suggested. The pixel, on the contrary, is never a point but a square, or a rectangle in the case of some LCD curb screens; it differs from the point precisely because of this consubstantial morphology, which entails a whole series of aesthetic consequences. Differences between a point and a pixel are so sharp that they can be arranged in a scheme of structural oppositions. First, whereas in an artwork (even in a pointillist painting), each point is intrinsically different from the others, in a digital picture each pixel must be characterized by exactly the same potential, although this potential is subsequently actualized according to different parameters of color and brightness (Graw and Lajer-Burcharth 2016). Second, whereas the characteristic circularity of the point makes it an essentially centrifugal eidetic component—expanding its visual agency in the surrounding iconic context—the pixel is characterized by a tetragonal structure, whose shape and technological functioning exactly aims at the opposite effect of turning the pixel into a centripetal visual element, unable to expand its visual agency onto adjacent pixels. In a point, color and brightness emerge and seek to irradiate the external visual space; in a pixel, on the contrary, color and brightness are trapped within its squared perimeter, in which they must be activated or deactivated in total subservience to the program. A pixel that does not obey the overall program of the picture is not an element anymore but a malfunctioning pixel (Spieler und Scheuermann 2012).

Vibrating patterns, I: gravel

It is instructive, at this point, to ponder similarities and differences between the functioning of the point in art and the functioning of similar morphological elements in nature.

Figure 4.2 reproduces a photograph of gravel on the path of Villa Casana in Novedrate, a university town in the proximity of Como; it was taken with the digital camera of a mobile phone in early October 2016. A conglomerate of objects

FIGURE 4.2 Early October 2016. Gravel on the path of Villa Casana, Novedrate, Italy; picture by the author

that we would normally look at with indifference, engrossed in our daily routines, acquires a new aesthetic value once it is framed by the "magical" rectangle of a picture and surrounded by a context that attracts the attention of the viewer toward its details. Gravel, then, ceases to be the inert material that we tread on our way to office and becomes a surface endowed with a dignity, a beautiful tapestry composed of little multiform and multicolor stones, all arranged next to each other according to a mysterious yet perceptible order. So as to complete the marvel of the observer, then, tufts of grass of different kinds—shining with several hues of bright green among the gray, white, and reddish little stones—emerge courageously from the gravel, adding a touch of organic asymmetry to its visual configuration.

The aesthetic pleasantness of this visual gestalt, however, does not derive only from the superimposition of a frame; a holistic aesthetic principle seems to be at work herein: The juxtaposition of similar units creates more than their mere sum; a "pleasant" aesthetic effect emerges from the juxtaposition. At a closer look, indeed, we perceive not only the little pebbles with their distinctive variety but also the whole that emerges from their complex arrangement; the interesting aspect of this aesthetic effect is that the two levels of perception and aesthetic agency interact and blur but, at the particular distance singled out by the photograph, never merge into each other: The observer can appreciate the individual qualities of the pebbles at the same time as this perception is somehow energized by the swarming gestalt of the gravel.

What is the origin of this aesthetic pleasure? Why should a visual configuration of this kind induce optical and aesthetic delight? Is that entirely subjective, or there is something objective in the pleasant tingling of the multitude? The key to understand the source of this optical pleasure seems to lie in the tension between similarity and difference, universality and singularity. It is also a matter of scale: As distance from the observer increases, heterogeneity yields to homogeneity. Should we look at the same gravel from a distance of one hundred meters, the perceptibility of its internal eidetic and chromatic difference would be dramatically blurred, the swarming effect of its texture dwindle until, in the end, only a grayish uniform surface would be perceived.

Symmetrically, looking closer and closer at the same configuration, smaller and smaller portions of it would be included in the view, until the visual focus would concentrate solely on a single pebble, or on a portion of it, and, therefore, be confined to the uniformity of one colored surface without morphological variations (these would reappear, of course, if an optical instrument enhancing the human sight, like a microscope, was adopted). Uniformity, homogeneity, and indistinctiveness are the perceptual result of both a too distant and a too close gaze; in the middle between these two opposite but actually adjacent polarities lies the tension between a focus on similarity and a focus on difference, each harbinger of a peculiar aesthetic pleasure. The "holistic aesthetic pleasure" disappears when tension between similarity and difference is no longer perceptible. When it is, however, it is conducive to an oscillation between two cognitive as well as emotional conditions.

On the one hand, a close look entails an adaptive pleasure of aesthetic discovery: Singularity "hides" within universality; approaching the swarming gestalt of the gravel allows the observer to "find out" what its visual components are; the individuality of pebbles is "discovered" and almost "rescued" in their multitude. Why should this pleasure be adaptive? It is not difficult to hypothesize that our ancestors might have benefited from an aesthetic condition giving them cognitive pleasure every time that they could "look closer and better", in order to distinguish the traces of a predator in the sand, for instance, or the eyes of an enemy in a bush. The semiotic energy of the secret operates in this visual dynamics, wherein the particular, the individual, and the singular are as though "hidden" in the general, in the collective, and in the plural: Looking closer allows one to uncover a level of reality that is not immediately manifested.

On the other hand, a distant look loses this sense of individuality and progressively attributes more visual weight to the whole; the vibrating energy that it receives from its parts starts to dwindle and a feeling of compactness emerges; whereas a closer look to multitudes bestows upon the observer the sentiment of an aesthetic discovery, a more distant look entails a pleasure of totality, the bliss of a gaze that, suddenly, seems to encompass more of the reality and understands it better as a consequence. The pleasure of distinctiveness versus the pleasure of indistinctiveness: These two polarities imply diverging cognitive and aesthetic allurements but could not be appreciated as such without their mutual tension, that between the uniqueness of the object and its serial multiplicity.

Vibrating patterns, II: sand

In no other object is this tension as spectacularly visible as in sand. Dunes appear as uniform in color and internal morphology from distance, but the vibration of the multitude of grains that compose them emerges as soon as one's gaze approaches the object, a vibration that, then, diffracts into the surprising individuality of the grains of sand themselves as one looks even closer. Figure 4.3 reproduces photographs of grains of sands from different areas of the world; one of them is actually a specimen of sand from another planet (I'll let the reader the pleasure to find out which one).

Their chromatic difference is immediately evident. At a closer look, however, also their eidetic particularity becomes manifest. The grains in each picture appear as different from those in the adjacent photographs; moreover, even within each of the photographs, at an even closer look, individuality manifests itself as irreducible difference of shape, color, position, and, as a consequence, texture. A closer look redeems the individual dignity of every single grain of sand. Grains do not cease to be part of a larger, vibrant whole but acquire an almost personal beauty, as if they were each created by a dedicated agency.

A phenomenological look at the gestalt of sand makes one appreciate the emotional effects of closeness and distance: As one's gaze gets closer and closer to sand, for instance, particularity emerges in the form of irreducible singularity: each grain of sand is different; as one's gaze recedes, a different aesthetic pleasure, accompanied by a different emotion, becomes predominant: The world turns more easily intelligible; the dune becomes predominant in perception.

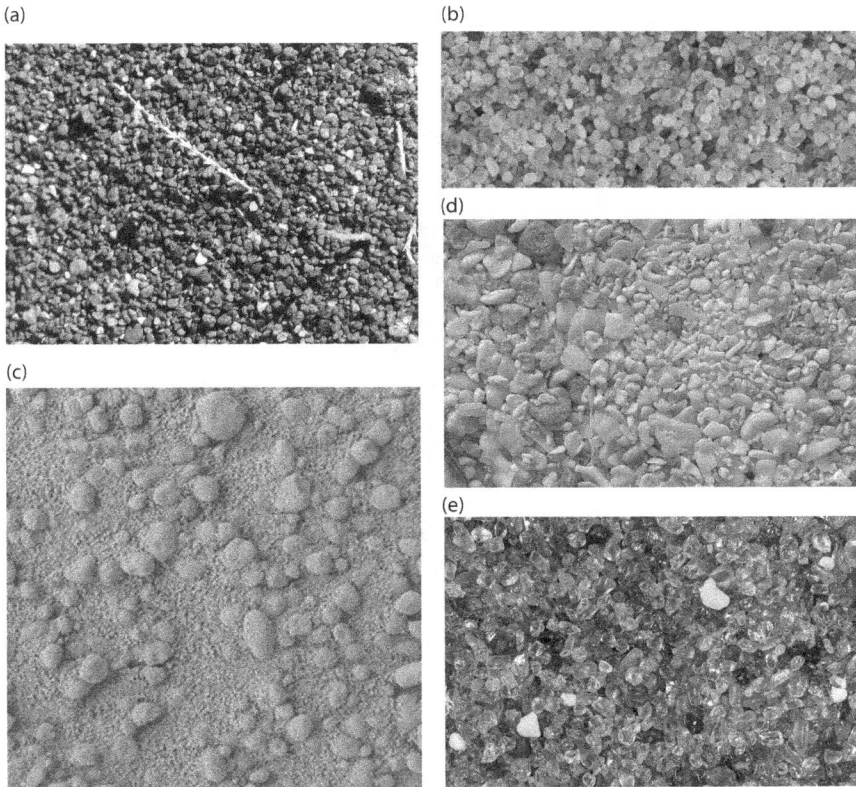

FIGURE 4.3 Photographs of different kinds of sand: (a) Santorini sand, (b) Olivine sand, (c) Mars sand, (d) Pink coral sand, and (e) Pismo beach sand; (pictures from www.geology.com)

Vibrating patterns, III: cobblestones and asphalt

The dialectic tension between the singular and the plural as well as the aesthetic pleasure that it brings about manifest themselves not only in the observation of natural holistic configurations but also in that of human-made visual patterns. Figure 4.4, for instance, reproduces the photograph of a cobblestoned path in the Institute of Philosophy at the University of Leuven, Belgium.

The material texture of the pavement is in part justified by functional purposes: for instance, increasing friction and traction in case of rain; but this material texture entails some aesthetic effects too: Cobblestones are perceived as more "pleasant" than asphalt. On the one hand, such aesthetic connotation is due to historical tradition and social conditions of perception: Cobblestones are an architectural element that immediately sends the viewer back toward the past, when asphalt had not been invented yet or was not systematically used. As a consequence, cobblestones are now included in the common architectural alphabet of cities that want to rediscover their past, or rather reinvent it, and offer it to the aesthetic consumption of

FIGURE 4.4 Late September 2016. Cobblestones at the Institute of Philosophy, University of Leuven, Belgium; picture by the author

tourists and students. On the other hand, though, the pleasantness of cobblestones also derives from the intrinsic perceptual tension implied by their gestalt. That is not as extreme as in the case of gravel or sand, but it is all the more pleasurable as a consequence of that: At a certain distance, cobblestones appear all as very similar and orderly arranged in regular rows; this perception, however, never eliminates the underpinning aesthetic vibration, which is precisely due to small differences among cobblestones and slight imperfection in their alignment (Uffelen 2009). The tension between the orderliness of the square, the homogeneity of the little forms, and their systematic layout on the one hand and, on the other hand, the persistence of subtle "deformities", as well as minute varieties in color and topological disposition, turn this cobblestoned pavement into something that, to a certain extent, *is alive*, meaning that it presents perception with an internal visual tingling that is somehow akin to the movement of organic matter. To the gaze, this cobblestoned road surface swarms as though it was covered with big squared insects.

Other materials do not visually behave in the same way, mainly because of the different texture that characterizes them, a texture which, in turn, is a consequence of their physical structure. In this case too, sociocultural connotations handed down through the history of the material interact with its intrinsic perceptual affordance. Were the road in the Institute of Philosophy of Leuven covered with asphalt, for instance, the enchanting melancholy that cobblestones signify and suggest to the observer would be replaced by an *imaginaire* of parked cars and futuristic efficiency.

Each material, though, has its poetry and conceals in itself the organic aesthetics stemming from the dialectics between uniformity and deformity. It is just a matter of scale and right distance. It is sufficient to observe asphalt from closer, and with an affectionate eye, and this apparently cold material too reveals in itself a beautifully disorderly world. Asphalt engineering looks at cracks in asphalt pavements as if they were mere problems due to wrong fabrication or laying, yet the typology of asphalt "problems" reveals, to the eye of the attentive observer, a multitude of beautiful visual patterns, each traversed by a vibrant dialectics between the uniformity of the material and the chaotic tensions that explode through it (Field and Golubitsky 1992). Figure 4.5 contains images of several types of "asphalt pavement distress"; this technical term itself is interesting, as though asphalt too was able to "suffer" and be "in distress" like living beings are; the denomination of some forms of "asphalt distress", like "fatigue 'alligator' cracking", then, implicitly hints at the fact that this inert material can, under certain conditions of transformation and at the right distance of observation, take on the gestalt of an organic texture, like animal skin.

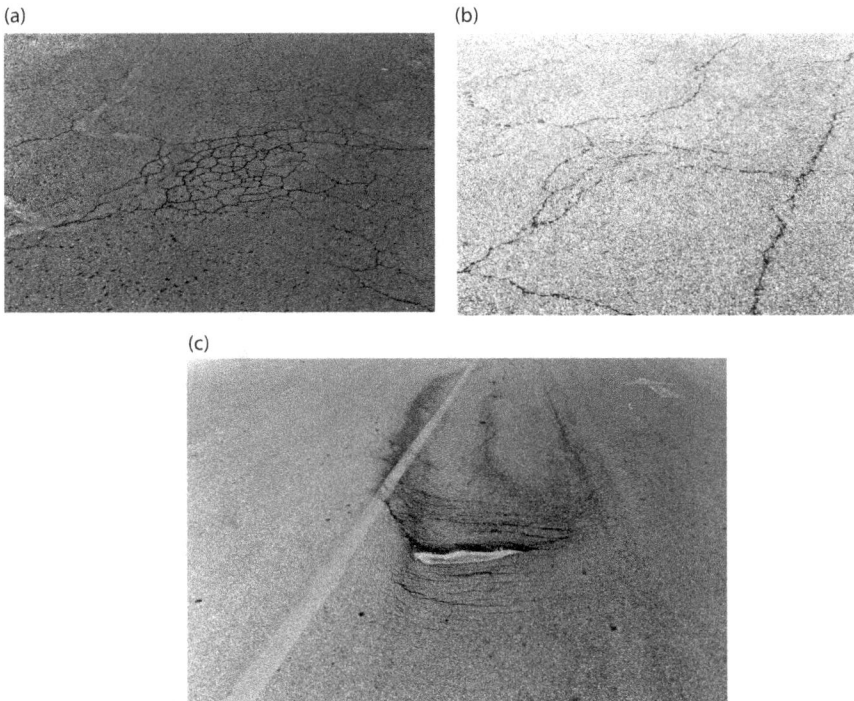

(a)   (b)

(c)

FIGURE 4.5 Different types of asphalt "cracking": (a) fatigue "alligator" cracking, (b) block cracking, and (c) slippage cracking (pictures from www. asphaltinstitute.org)

Aren't all these kinds of cracking "beautiful"? Don't they look, when the frame of a picture surrounds them, isolates them, and invites the viewer to observe them from the "right distance", like the visual configurations that contemporary artists so painstakingly seek to produce in their artworks? Couldn't they be the result of Alberto Burri's imagination? In each of these images, the dialectics between the reassuring uniformity of the material and the insurgence of asphalt grains reemerges, turning the material "elements" of asphalt into as many sources of individual agencies, or at least into as many sources of agency that coalesce into independent subgroups. The fascinating aspect of this "rebellion of the material"—as one could call it with an anthropomorphism—is that a micro-order seems to take shape within the disrupting disorder of the cracking. The cracking introduces deformity in uniformity, yet this deformity too seems to be underpinned by a more complex formula.

Vibrating patterns, IV: a flowerbed

But what is the formula behind the holistic aesthetic effect that emerges from a picture like the one reproduced by Figure 4.6?

FIGURE 4.6 Late September 2016. *Flowerbeds at the Public Library*, Leuven, Belgium; picture by the author

The "holistic" aesthetic effect described above can be observed not only in the inorganic, mineral world (be it "natural" or human-made) but also in the organic, vegetable world. Increase in morphological variety changes the characteristics of this effect; accrued presence of life often implies a more internally various gestalt; that entails extreme difficulty of representing the tension between homogeneity and heterogeneity; hundreds of species gather together in a single flowerbed; that reveals the inadequacy of botanical knowledge and representation. Botany can identify the plants and flowers of the flowerbed as tokens of botanical types, as members of a species, but it does not take into account the singularity of each flower and of each plant. This flowerbed exerts an almost hypnotic optical power exactly because its overall gestalt emerges from the juxtaposition of a very high number of singularities.

As suggested earlier, there is a relation between life and increase in the morphological complexity of a multitude. If life quintessentially coincides with movement, this flowerbed differs from a cobblestoned pavement precisely because its internal visual structure is constantly vibrating under the effect of a myriad of motilities. As a consequence, a Botticelli or another extremely skillful artist would be required in order to render the beauty, but also the morphological intricacy, of hundreds of species competing or cooperating for life not only as species but also as individual members of them. The more one moves forward through natural evolution, the more one comes across species endowed with the ability to accomplish elaborate movements with increasingly higher degrees of freedom and complexity. Were a horse pasturing on this flowerbed, for instance, the very wide range of movements that the animal could easily perform would farther complicate the visual intricacy of the scene. A Michelangelo would be needed to render this holistic visual dynamics in a single static pictorial image.

One might hypothesize that the tension between homogeneity and heterogeneity that, at the right distance, a landscape of dunes or even an asphalted road manifest to the gaze, is in proportional relation with the degree of freedom of movement and, therefore, change that the elements of these visual gestalts can enjoy. As geology suggests, minerals change through time too, yet the speed of this change is mostly invisible to human perception (except in spectacular phenomena like earthquakes or volcanic eruptions); the interplay between sand and wind makes the former much more subject to movement and change than a rock or a cobblestoned pavement might be (indeed, cobblestones and other pavement materials have been invented or adopted exactly in order to limit this mutability and its uncontrollable and undesirable effects: It is easier to travel on cobblestones than on sand). The complexity of this interplay of agency results in visual effects at the macro-level of the gestalt of dunes, which do not appear as immobile blocks of sand grains but as movable, almost living beings. A flowerbed, or even more a flowerbed over which bees noisily hover, is a place in which this interaction of agencies and the aesthetic effect resulting from it become exponentially more complicated. Our gaze is pleased by a flowerbed because it intrinsically is a spectacle of freedom, in which myriads of competing agencies nevertheless find a way to harmoniously occupy the same time and space (Tao 2008). Incidentally, that explains the difficulty of depicting a battle scene. The great pictorial representations of battlegrounds in art history all look like flowerbeds exactly for their static character—as well as their intrinsic aesthetic aim—does not allow the painter to sincerely express the chaos of a battle; the depiction of a battle is always somehow harmonious, as though enemy agencies did, nevertheless, agree in assuming their postures, forms, and colors in order to fit within the frame of the painting.

Vibrating patterns, V: textiles

The pleasant aesthetic effect of the interaction between idiosyncratic agencies and their holistic harmony results from handmade visual configurations too. The cobblestoned pavement was an example of it, although in that case the aesthetic effect was certainly less predominant than the practical purpose. In any case, the aesthetics of a cobblestoned pavement is generally unintentional or follows the aesthetic inertia of architectural fashion. There are, on the contrary, human artifacts that explicitly seek to exploit the dialectics between singularity and universality for aesthetic purposes. Many forms of weaving craft, for instance, consist in the juxtaposition of knots or other weaving units that, although composing a regular pattern and sometimes even a complex figuration (e.g., like in tapestry), maintain nevertheless their subtle individuality and, therefore, contribute to the unpredictable vibration of the whole. Take, as an example, the Ecuadorian alpaca carpet from Otavalo market whose photograph is reproduced in Figure 4.7.

FIGURE 4.7 Ecuadorian carpet from Otavalo market; picture by the author

To a closer look, each of the knots that compose this carpet is different from the others. Without this singularity, the texture of the rug, but also its tactile affordance, would be completely different. Within a certain range of observation distance, the carpet looks as it does exactly because it constantly proposes the interaction between two phenomenological levels: On the one hand, the vibration of a multitude of individual knots, each slightly different from the others in terms of color, topological position, as well as internal morphology and, on the other hand, the emergence of an harmonious but vibrating gestalt from the juxtaposition of these singularities; the individual agency of the knots is not completely eliminated (the fibers that compose the knots twist and turn each with a peculiar bend in space and time), yet it is somehow curbed within the overall gestalt of the rug. This subtle dialectics affects not only the visual configuration of the carpet but also its tactile affordance. Stepping barefoot on such carpet feels like it does because the knots in it have an internal structure and, to a certain extent, a freedom of movement that molecules of marble in a pavement do not have. The material tactility of a carpet is also an expression of the degree of freedom of its internal morphology.

Ghiordes (symmetrical) and *senneh* (asymmetrical) knots; *jufti* (over four warp threads) and Tibetan knots: There is not only a large variety of knots but also an individuality of them, for they are made by hand; as a result, the aesthetics of handmade rugs is different from that of machine-made rugs. The variety of the internal morphology of a rug is increased by the possibility to choose among different kinds of types of knots, exactly like the internal visual variety of a flowerbed depends on the possibility to choose among different species of plants and flowers; a handmade rug somehow imitates a flowerbed also because its internal morphology vibrates as a consequence of the fact that no knot is exactly like the others, in the same way as each rose shows micro-morphological peculiarities while belonging to the same species as all other roses (Bahamón and Pérez 2008). The hand of the rug-maker strives for perfection, yet its intentionality translates into movements that are never completely standardized. Fatigue, state of mind, and conditions of work change throughout the hours, the days, the months, and the years, thus introducing slight perturbations in the movement of the hand that knots a rug. The unpredictability of the human hand's agency somehow transfers into that of the knots of a rug, exactly like a mysterious variation is constantly introduced into the morphology of rocks, animals, and human beings. "Creating" a handmade rug is different from "fabricating" one by machine because the former operation reminds one of the unpredictable creativities of nature, whereas the latter seems awkward in its dealing with the tension between perfect universality and idiosyncratic singularities.

The comparison between the gestalt of a machine-made rug and that of a hand-knotted one reveals the paradoxical dialectics between perfection, imperfection, authenticity, and aesthetic quality: An authentically handmade rug is knotted so as to minimize imperfections; yet imperfections persist and constitute the uniqueness of the rug, as well as its value and mark of authenticity;

machine-rugs are less expensive because they are too perfect. Fake imperfections intentionally introduced in rugs by human rug-makers tend to be stereotypical, but anyway more creative than intentional machine-produced imperfections. The mastery of rug-making, which is based on the mastery over knots, consists in the ability of arranging the potential motility of warp threads into regular patterns; this reduction of complexity is never exhaustive, and that is exactly what makes the difference with a machine-made rug. In a handmade rug, the regularity of knots constraints their material singularities, yet these singularities, and the agency that they evoke, never cease to vibrate under the surface of the visual pattern, as if they were tiny servants constantly on the verge of bursting into a rebellion. In general, the tension between struggle to perfectly subdue the idiosyncrasy of matter and the constant possibility of an emergence of imperfection seems to generate an aesthetic pleasure that is akin to that enjoyed by the beholder of a dune, of a flowerbed, or of a cobblestoned pavement but enhances even more the dialectics between individual agencies and overarching gestalt.

Figure 4.8 reproduces the photograph of a Panama from Ecuador. At this stage of the chapter, it is quite easy to observe that, in this hat too, when it is looked at from an appropriate distance range, a dialectics between singularity and universality, heterogeneity and homogeneity emerges. *Mutatis mutandis*, a Panama hat aesthetically works like a rug: In a limited amount of space, determined by

FIGURE 4.8 Mid-September 2016. Ecuadorian Panama-style hat, Quito, Ecuador; picture by the author

the framework of the hat's shape, single compositional units must be juxtaposed and woven together so as to fill and at the same time create the form. In this case too, the manual work of the hatter strives to reduce the idiosyncrasy of the straw fibers, to subdue them into a regular order; yet each fiber "behaves" both morphologically and chromatically in a peculiar way, yielding to the general scheme followed and enforced by the hatter yet constantly menacing to subvert it. As a consequence, the threat of small imperfections makes an authentic panama hat vibrate with the dialectics between the plan of human creativity and the resistance of matter. Differently from a Persian rug, though, this plan does not involve bidimensional figuration but three-dimensional shape. Straw fibers must give rise to the shape of the hat.

Hats and screens

So as to gradually return to a "semiotics of the pixel", it might be interesting to wonder what the difference is between buying a new digital screen and buying a new Panama hat. First of all, how does one assess the quality of a Panama hat?

On the one hand, the quality of a Panama hat depends on some objective, countable features, such as the number of rings inside the hat or the number of straw fibers per inch. Figure 4.9 reproduces two photographs of these countable signs of the quality of a Panama hat. They are functional qualities too: A tightly

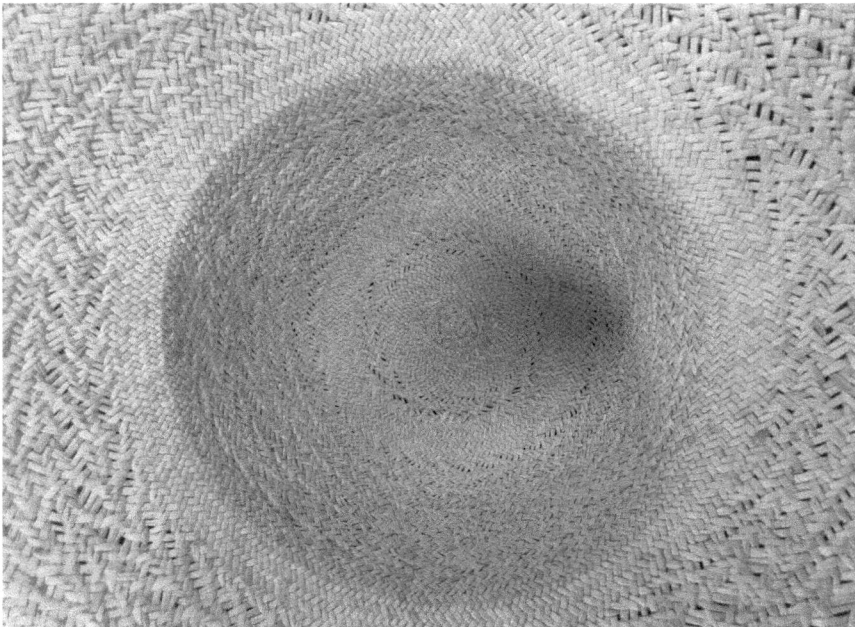

FIGURE 4.9 Rings inside a Panama hat; picture by the author

woven Panama hat will be more resistant, resilient, and, in general, capable of maintaining its shape against the hostile agency of external forces (rain, wind, someone sitting on the hat, etc.).

On the other hand, though, the quality of a Panama hat also depends on some inter-subjective, uncountable features: the shape of weaving, for instance; or the color of straw. Panama hat connoisseurs usually prefer straw weaving with impeccable regularity (at least at the right distance of observation), in contrast with irregularly woven textures.

In this case, however, the criterion at the center of the evaluation is not objective, meaning that there is no quantitative, countable way to determine which straw arrangement is better, which one is worse. Stereotypical aesthetic evaluations in this domain take shape as a consequence of the complex and mostly implicit negotiation within a community of interpreters, a community guided by a group of experts. As a result of these negotiations, Panama hats with regular arrangements of straw fibers become part of the canon, and are sold at higher prices, whereas Panama hats with irregular fiber arrangements are less favorably judged and less expensive. A simple question to ask in order to distinguish between countable and uncountable criteria of aesthetic evaluation, between objective and inter-subjective standards is, "Will it change in time and space?" As regards the number of straw fibers woven in a Panama hat, the answer is negative: One day we might value a loosely woven Panama hat more than a tightly woven one, yet the former will always have more fibers than the latter in the same amount of space; in this domain, its superiority will always be measurable. In the second case, instead, the answer is positive: One day, the community of interpreters that evaluate the quality of Panama hats might change in such a way that hats with irregularly arranged straw fibers might look more "authentic" than hats with regular fibers (e.g., as a consequence of the massive diffusion of splendidly woven machine-made hats). That is even more evident as regards color: There is no objective reason for which straw fibers with a certain hue of color should be valued more than the others.

Whereas the first criterion is quantitative, the second is qualitative. It does not bear on a perception that can translate the qualities of a phenomenon into quantifiable measures and, ultimately, comparable numbers. It bears on an aesthetic appreciation that, again, is able to receive aesthetic pleasure from the dialectics between uniformity and deformity, between the smooth surface of a Panama hat and the subtle imperfections that make its texture vibrate at both sight and touch. A Panama hat is a result of creation as much as a rug is. They both "imitate" the complex way in which natural agencies and, ultimately, life give rise to a sand dune or to a flowerbed. They reproduce, in their internal morphology, the struggle between idiosyncratic mutation and collective order that seems to characterize the patterns of evolution (Romero and Machado 2008).

Deconstructive pleasures

Figure 4.10 reproduces the photograph of a tapestry currently hanging in a boutique hotel of Quito, Ecuador. From a semiotic point of view, a tapestry is a carpet in which the plastic level is "forced" to express a figurative level. The plastic level of a tapestry, however, never completely disappears but contributes to the aesthetic effect of the figurative level. In a tapestry, a constant plastic vibration underlies images. The quality of this "vibration", though, changes depending on how the tapestry is woven. The way in which the single knots are knotted, and give rise to the overall figure, influences its perception by the beholder. The same principle is observable, with different modalities, in everyday decorative arrangements, such as the one of the fruit salad of Figure 4.11.

There are no compelling functional reasons for which fruits should be cut and presented in this way (except, perhaps, making it easy to pick them up with a fork or spoon). The aesthetic quality of such arrangement derives, again, from the pleasure that human beings feel in deconstructing the figurative level of reality into combinable ingredients, such as the colorful geometric shapes of this fruit salad. Like in a rug, or in a tapestry, or in a Panama hat, the idea that tiny units might coalesce into an overall effect of shape and sometimes even figure is, for

FIGURE 4.10 Mid-September 2016. Ecuadorian tapestry, Casa Joaquin Boutique Hotel, Quito, Ecuador; picture by the author

FIGURE 4.11 Fruit salad; picture by the author

some reason, enthralling. In a fruit salad, human beings play with the dynamics of order and disorder, homogeneity and heterogeneity, deconstruction and reconstruction that underpin the natural world and its perception.

The aesthetics of pixels

Is the same dialectics clearly visible in LCD screens too? Is the quality of such objects gauged in the same way as that of Panama hats is, by conflating countable and uncountable criteria of evaluation? Does a digital screen decompose and recompose an image of reality in the same way as a rug or a mosaic do it? And, last but not least, is a screen too the visual framework of a creative production of icons, reminiscent of the way in which nature itself manifests its visual morphology in minerals, plants, and animals?

Figure 4.12 reproduces the photograph of a giant screen displaying arrival times at the airport of Guayaquil, Ecuador. Similar screens have been installed in almost every airport or train station around the globalized and cosmopolitan world. Is the aesthetic functioning of this LCD screen somehow comparable to that of the natural patterns or the visual artifacts that have been mentioned so far? When comparing several digital LCD screens among them, the only thing that really matters is a countable criterion, that is, the number of pixels that

FIGURE 4.12 Mid-September 2016. Giant screen at Guayaquil Airport, Guayaquil, Ecuador; picture by the author

are squeezed within the framework of the display. Indeed, there cannot be an alternative criterion, for pixels actually *are* elements, as the etymology of their name suggests. They completely abdicate any autonomous aesthetic agency in order to become totally subservient to the project of the overall picture. They are not round—a feature that Kandinsky would deem essential in the visual metaphysical force of the point—but squared or, at the most, quadrangular, like in the most recent curb LCD screens. Most importantly, they do not express any singularity, not only for their shape is always exactly the same but also because their value of brightness and hue can be determined by a numeric value, with no margin for idiosyncrasy. A pixel that does not abide by the mathematical rules of the figurative project which it is an element of, is a malfunctioning pixel.

Pixels, therefore, do not aesthetically function like grains of sands, or cobblestones, for their individuality is thwarted at the moment itself of their fabrication. They also starkly differ from the knots of a rug or the tiles of a mosaic, not only because of their lack of "deformity" and, therefore, singularity, but also and above all because the enunciation of a pixel must coincide with the disappearing of it. In a carpet, the dexterous hand of the rug-maker has juxtaposed very tiny knots, so that they might almost melt into elaborate figurative patterns; yet the individuality and singularity of knots, as it was underlined earlier, persists, and contributes to the aesthetic effect that this chapter has singled out and described both in nature and culture.

On the contrary, the possibility of a digital art of the screen is somehow limited by the way in which its constituents, the pixels, are hidden from sight and reduced to total obedience, for such is the quantitative promise of the market to LCD purchasers (Castelli, Festspiele, and Martin-Gropius-Bau 2007). The rhetoric of pixels does not reveal their semiotic nature but their robotic perfection, their cold splendor, as Lévinas would have said. Whereas paintings, tapestries, rugs, and even Panama hats retain something of the liveliness of the face, with its dazzling vibration of imperfections, the LCD screen is a façade, a surface that, like a mirror, subtracts itself to any semiotic functioning in order to yield to the reassuring regularity of a mathematical ratio. An image displayed by an LCD screen appears as perfect to the gaze, even more perfect that its content does to sight in real life; yet this content is somehow deprived of life, since it is stripped of that dialectics between the regular and the eccentric that underpins most beholding of a visual multitude in both nature and culture. That does not mean that LCD screens are intrinsically unable to reveal such dialectics. To this regard, a semiotics of flickering is in order. Lagom LCD monitor test pages so define this instance of technological idiosyncrasy:

> In a pixel on an LCD monitor, the amount of light that is transmitted from the backlight depends on the voltage applied to the pixel. For the amount of light, it doesn't matter whether that voltage is negative or positive. However, applying the same voltage for a long period would damage the pixel. For example, electricity decomposes water into oxygen and hydrogen gas. A comparable similar effect could happen inside the liquid crystals that are in the pixels. In order to prevent damage, LCD displays quickly alternate the voltage between positive and negative for each pixel, which is called 'polarity inversion'. Ideally, the rapid polarity inversion wouldn't be noticeable because every pixel has the same brightness whether a positive or a negative voltage is applied. However, in practice, there is a small difference, which means that every pixel flickers at about 30 hertz.
>
> *(Available at www.lagom.nl/lcd-test/inversion.php)*

It is extraordinary how the flickering of light bulbs or, more recently, of LCD screens stereotypically intervenes in the climactic moments of horror movies. Flickering, indeed, signals the arrival of the uncanny, the monstrous, and the horrific through the idiosyncratic malfunctioning of that which, by definition, should be as reliable as a machine. Flickering, therefore, signifies the manifestation of a mysterious, often malign agency in a mechanism that should not have one. All of a sudden, the pixels of an LCD screen cease to be picture elements—subservient to the cold perfection of the image to which they are supposed to give shape through renouncing any individuality—and turn into quixotic mavericks, possessed by a dangerous force.

The flickering of LCD screens (Figure 4.13) is the digital equivalent of the malfunctioning of flap displays, less and less in use around the world and almost

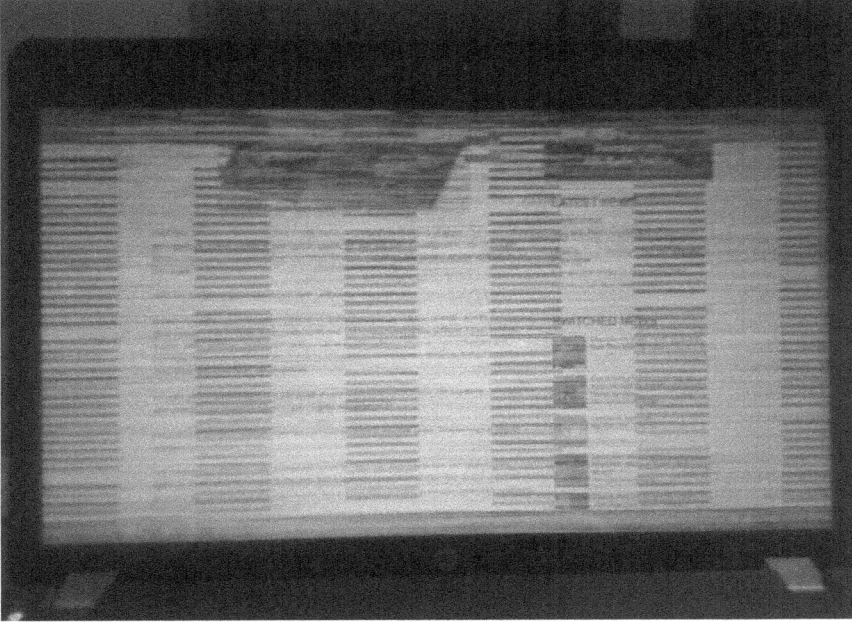

FIGURE 4.13   LCD screens flickering; picture by the author

FIGURE 4.14   Broken flap display at the airport of Belgrade; picture by the author

entirely replaced by digital screens. The latter, however, would entail a strong narrative dimension—a sort of suspense—and deploy an aesthetics of imper-fection that was heavily dependent on the essentially mechanical nature of the display (Hagener and Hediger 2015) (in Figure 4.14, a split flap display in the arrival area of the airport of Belgrade, Serbia, with "Dadaist" malfunctioning).

FIGURE 4.15 Arduino split flap display (picture from www.instructables.com)

The fact that the era of a possible "poetics of the mechanical error" is somehow lost forever is emphasized by vintage, hipster, and nostalgic efforts of recuperation, such as the split flap display reconstituted through Arduino materials and visible in Figure 4.15. The description of the project is extremely telling of its nostalgic connotations:

> With three-letter abbreviations like BRB, LOL, OMG and SMH commonplace in today's smartphone and online conversations, the Maker decided to bring text and animation back to its mechanical roots with his own split flap display. As you can see in the video below, an arcade button under each frame enables him to cycle through all 26 letters to spell out his thoughts in acronym form, while a fourth frame reveals an animation of the very first cat video (by Eadweard Muybridge).
>
> *(Available at https://blog.arduino.cc/2016/07/15/ omg-this-diy-split-flap-display-is-awesome/)*

Conclusions

Are there any chances to turn LCD screens and, more generally, visual digital technology into a matrix for aesthetic effects at least reminiscent of those induced by more traditional "raster surfaces", such as rugs or mosaics? Although the pixels of LCD screens can potentially malfunction and misfire, like in flickering, such possibility is so deeply embedded in sophisticated technology that it can rarely give rise to unpredictable aesthetic effects. A very interesting term in digital screen technology is "demosaicing" (also "de-mosaicing", "demosaicking", or "debayering"), an operation that, through appropriate algorithms, reconstructs a full-color image from the incomplete color sample outputs of an image sensor overlaid with a color filter array (CFA). Demosaising is the ontological and aesthetic opposite of the mosaic: Whereas in a Byzantine mosaic, the tiles contribute to the splendor of the image but at the same time do not entirely melt into it—their irreducible singularity farther enhancing the golden vibration of the whole—in a demosaised digital image, the multitudinous matrix of the screen is concealed behind a numeric, impenetrable smoothness.

Figure 4.16 reproduces the photograph of a splendid *Adoration of the Eucharist* composed of Portuguese *azulejos* (National Museum of Azulejos, Lisbon). In this and similar images, the tiled fragmentation of the picture is not an obstacle to its visual composition, but underlays it without ever completely disappearing, so conferring to it a sort of geometric subtext, a connotation of order and regularity (Marks 2010). The gaze enjoys recomposing the image from the single tiles, yet

FIGURE 4.16 Late seventeenth-century azulejos: the adoration of the Eucharist; Lisbon: National Museum of Azulejos; picture by the author

the singularity of the tiles does not vanish in this visual exercise of reconstitution of the image, since they continue to geometrically vibrate under the figurative surface of the representation. This effect, which turns the composition of azulejos into an effort of creativity non-dissimilar from that which nature deploys in a flowerbed, is completely absent in a correctly functioning LCD screen.

We are more and more surrounded by pixels. Yet the only possibility for this digital environment to resemble a human fabric of singularities and order, regularities and imperfection, would be delving into the deep technology of the current displaying matrixes so as to introduce therein a dynamic of pixilation. In filmmaking, pixilation is a technique, dating from the beginnings of cinema, in which live actors are posed frame by frame and photographed to create stop-motion animation. The word derives from an archaic British word meaning "possession by spirits" (pixies) (then used to describe the animation process since the early 1950s).

Animating a digital image means turning the subservient logics of the pixels into the semiotics of the pixies, that is, of elements that cease to be such for, possessed by mysterious forces, reclaim the freedom of the singular into the collective project of the digital image, into the subservience of its eternal transmission and marketing allure. Pixies, not pixels, are the equivalent of the unpredictable agencies that move creativity in nature and that the human species has sought for millennia to reproduce in the paradoxical weaving of its visual artifacts. Forgetting about the beauty of a constantly reemerging imperfection leads to a domain of the cold displaying surface, to the imposition of a framework that is destined to remain inexorably empty.

The first chapter of the book categorized meaninglessness and insignificance, arguing that, in present-day societies, the latter increasingly results from the alienating frameworks imposed by digital bureaucracy in more and more domains of existence. The second and the third chapter (respectively, on "trolling" and "contrarian insignificance") interpreted current forms of virtual violence as reactions to the impossibility of fully belonging to the digital arena. The fourth chapter, focusing on pixels as the most constitutive elements of the visual digital world, has pointed out the origins of alienation in the post-material era: Whereas in pre-digital visual artifacts, beholders experience a soothing and even enlivening echo of the natural world, in digital environments, the dialectics between the randomness of natural motion and the calculus of cultural forms is impoverished to the detriment of the former so as to extol the latter. The quantitative perfection of displays turns the vision too into the domain of inhumanity, where no creativity is possible and any serendipity is eliminated at the onset through the cold programming of the machine. The following chapters will dwell on present-day desperate attempts at recovering the aesthetics of the pre-digital world and its material mysteries, attempts that give rise to as many post-material obsessions and their marketing exploitation.

Note

1 "We look upon the geometric point as the ultimate and most singular union of silence and speech" (Engl. trans. Howard Dearstyne and Hilla Rebay).

5

SHOPPING INSIGNIFICANCE

Post-material temples

> [...] these errand-boys and furtive and fugitive
> girls who, ignoring their doom, look in at shop
> windows? But I am aware of our ephemeral
> passage.
> Virginia Woolf, *The Waves* (1931)

Introduction

The present chapter connects a philosophical reflection on the devaluation of the material signifier in culture—and specifically in religion—with the emergence of post-secular temples, which retrieve some elements of the premodern spatial symbology of the sacred in order to host individual liturgies of consumption and meaning-making.

Semioticians often think in terms of oppositions.[1] They question beauty through ugliness, good through evil, and word through silence. Various concepts are opposed to that of spirituality, but one of them stands out because of its heuristic potential: materiality.[2] It designates, among other things, everything that is tangible, offers itself to the senses, and can be an object of perception and manipulation. In the last quarter of the twentieth century, the label "materialism" has also stigmatized the unbridled passion for the acquisition of tangibility: the possession of goods, consumerism, and the unconstrained valorization of the sensual appetites to the detriment of that which is ethereal, intangible, and impalpable.[3] "Materialism", then, in a higher philosophical register, has been referred to an epistemological framework deemed as excessive qua able to seize the nature of things and phenomena uniquely in their brutal, mechanical aspect.[4] Religion too has been among the victims of such materialism, often in its "pop" versions, which would belittle spirituality through equaling it to an outcome of such and such down-to-earth dynamic. Many will perhaps remember the etiology—fortunately today outmoded and also a little risible—by which socio-biology would seek to explain the religious impulse.[5] Anti-spiritual materialism, however, has given rise to reactions too, for instance to the call for rediscovering interiority, the secret of intimacy, and a religious self free from any external determination.[6] In its protean genius, yet, the market insinuated itself in this trend too, transforming it into a paradox: The escape from materialism toward *new age* has led to a large-scale production of *spiritual gadgets*.[7]

In the first decade of the new millennium, however, neither consumerist and ideological materialism nor new age spiritualism dominates the current cultural trends, but a diffused tendency of taste that might be defined "anti-materiality".[8] Such is, perhaps, the term of comparison and contrast that better defines contemporary spirituality. What does "anti-materiality" mean? In order to answer this question, two approaches will be followed: the first rather historical and sociological, and the second, semiotic.

The digitalization of signifiers

From the historical and sociological point of view, inclination toward anti-materiality is double bound with the development of new technologies of communication, which simultaneously cause it and result from it, in a self-feeding circuit. On the one hand, the long period of globalization has encouraged the search and the development of increasingly sophisticated forms of dematerialization of the signifier.[9] The desire—often underpinned by ambitions of commercial or military conquest—for annihilating spatial and temporal distances, for making the world smaller until it becomes manipulable, constituted the context for the exponential evolution of a more and more efficient *ideology of the signal*: That which counts in a letter is neither paper nor ink that traces characters on it but the content of such characters, which must be extracted from its material expression, translated into numbers, transformed into signal, and, therefore, transmitted. During the last quarter of the twentieth century, the binary drive—which tends to conceive and transform every phenomenon of meaning into a series of zeros and ones, of switching on and switching off, of presence and absence—has become so predominant as to influence even the epistemology of humanities: The mind too, it was hypothesized, is nothing but a computer, and the body its operational machinery.[10] As the hypotheses of sociobiological materialism, so also those of the ideology of the signal have been superseded by subtler thoughts. What persisted of this binary anxiety is an emphasis on dematerialization, a eulogy of anti-materiality. With increasing technological acceleration, more and more extensive areas of the human action have been freed from the yoke of materiality so as to be diluted into the digital ocean of telecommunication. Behind this technological twisting, though, an anthropological turn was maturing, which semiotic was able to seize at least since Baudrillard (1981).

In the 1960s, talking to someone on the phone was certainly not like talking to him or her face-to-face. That which the interlocutor would hear was not the body of the other, but a reverberation of such body produced through a system of correspondences. The voice of a body could be recognized for that of the phone would echo it. This correspondence, nevertheless, was not arithmetical but geometrical. It was a correspondence of sizes, not of numbers. In semiotic terms, the analogical telephone would still function like an imprint. It was, from a certain point of view, nothing but the electrical version of a drum: By hitting harder, by yelling into the handset, the interlocutor would receive a wave of that force, an echo of the body that had produced it. In the technical terms of semiotics, the sign communicating the voice was an index, that is, a communicative artifact wherein the signifier and the signified, the sign and its object were related through a tie of physical contiguity and causality. There is smoke; therefore, there must be fire, for the latter produces the former and the former emanates from the latter.

From digital phones, instead, one receives no indexes any longer but symbols, that is, sound impulses that faithfully correspond to the source that generated them—even more faithfully than in analogical communication—yet this faithfulness is not dictated anymore by causal necessity but by the arbitrariness of translation, of a mathematical code that turns the body into numbers and numbers into a body without no proportion or correspondence except those of pure artificiality and simulation. Hence, the progressive digitalization of the signifier turned it into a simulacrum, which does not represent its object as a geometrical projection but as arithmetic reinvention.[11]

The symbolic essence of communication, wherein the relation between signifiers and signified is not the outcome of a cause but of a law,[12] has subsequently more and more cannibalized not only the production of indexical signs but also that of iconic signs, in which the relation between signifiers and signified is normally due to resemblance. Analogical images have progressively disappeared from Western cultures, inexorably replaced by images that numerically reconstruct the appearances of reality. The advantages of such numeric colonization of the signifier have been evident, exactly in the terms of that "signal ideology" inaugurated by binary engineering: If a present-day researcher can consult on his or her screen the digital image of a manuscript far both in time and in space, such possibility is due to this revolution.[13]

Digital religions

As any deep revolution in the domain of production and reception of meaning, this too will probably have an impact on the religious sphere, a decisive influence that, at the moment, can only be surmised. As the genesis of monotheism would have been unthinkable without the invention of writing, and as the birth of Protestantism would have been impossible without the development of mobile type printing, so the progressive digitalization of the signifier will lead to new religious lifestyles, perhaps even to new religions (Campbell 2012). That is not the case because religions are a byproduct of communicative technology; it would be an oversimplifying hypothesis. Rather, both religions and communication technologies translate the slow and inexorable evolution of the way in which the human species relates to the world and to itself through its characteristic interface, that is, language (Leone 2013d). It is difficult to establish where this evolution will lead, and whether long-term regularities and trends can be detected in it, especially for the human cultural memory is still poor and badly organized. One can attempt, though, at singling out some tendencies. An effective strategy for doing it is, paradoxically, that of grasping the symptoms of cultural countertrends.

It has been already underlined that the progressive digitalization of signifiers, caused by an increasingly domineering "signal ideology"—a product, in its turn, of a more general tendency, resulting in the globalization of the late twentieth century, in the progressive annihilation of spatial distances among individuals and groups—has led to a gradual but inexorable devaluation of materiality in many domains of human existence. Such phenomenon is macroscopic as regards the technologies of information transmission. Not only the human voice is, nowadays, a digital simulacrum, but phone handsets also themselves eliminate any analogical driver, including keys, so as to translate them into numeric representation. One of the reasons for the success of brands like Apple has consisted in embracing with no hesitation and in smartly promoting a boundless search for de-materialized meaning, in which technology has no indexical relation any longer with the necessity of its usage but becomes sheer design, outcome of arbitrary imagination. Not only communication devices, though, but also all the traditional supports of culture have been digitalized. The paper book becomes more and more a relic, especially in the domain of sciences, and so does vinyl as regards sound reproduction, not to speak of cinematographic images, which are increasingly after a perfect simulative reconstruction of digital bodies.

Such devaluation of materiality and the simultaneous proclamation of the protean power of numbers have indirectly affected also other spheres of existence. A diffused advertising discourse, not unrelated with this logic, let many, and especially the younger generations, believe that one could, and actually should, live a "lighter" life, in the pursuit of miniaturization and, therefore, transportability. Not only books and records should vanish in the few cubic centimeters of a little box, but also travel, friendship, and even love should get rid of superfluous materiality (Van der Ploeg and Pridmore 2016). In other terms, the ideology of signal and the consequent dematerialization of signifiers have brought about an increasing digitalization of relations, the clearest example of which is constituted by social networks. Not only should I not have my friends hear the voice of my body, but its digital translation too is, nowadays, outdated. Friendship itself, indeed, has become electrical signal, simulative tie among avatars in which a correspondence whatsoever with any "material" reality is less and less at stake (Meise 2015). Living without a body, living without a space, living as a numerical flux that constantly flows around the world, surfacing here or there with the visage of an icon, a sound, or a friend: that is the utopia of our times, a utopia that is not entirely devoid of a certain mystical élan, of a sort of numerical *cupio dissolvi*.

As it was pointed out before, it is especially by contrast with minority and marginal countertrends that this background macro-tendency stands out. In the musical domain as in the cinematographic one, the unbridled and subcultural quest for the analogical (Leone 2014b) and the hipster collecting of vintage equipment (Greif 2012) does nothing but underlining the opposite, prevailing inclination for a devaluation of matter to the benefit of a numerical spirit, translatable at will in such and such artifact. The balance of power between macro-tendency and subcultural countertrends is, then, overtly unmasked by the present-day existence of a growing market for the simulation of materiality: digital covers that simulate the imperfections of the paper ones with extraordinary adroitness; CDs that imitate the sound of vinyl records; digital images that stage a perfect imperfection so as to satisfy the niche taste for the material, or better, for the matter-like (Johnston 2015). Numbers triumph over matter through simulating their disappearing to the benefit of an artificially reconstructed materiality, exactly like the artificial mistakes introduced on purpose in the machine-made carpets whose aesthetics was the object of the previous chapter.

It is superfluous to underline that the ideology of the signal and the progressive dematerialization of existence are not innocent. Precise socioeconomic strategies have pushed and are still pushing whole generations to embrace the idea of a sort of Matrix, of a digital mold that can translate either in the entertainment of a movie downloaded from a pirate website or in political representativeness, constructed by clicking on an icon. The loss of aura prophesized by Walter Benjamin as being a result of the introduction of the technical reproducibility of culture (1936) has given rise to a sort of numeric aura: One neither desires the uniqueness of a painting nor suffers the lack of it; one revels in the precision by which Leonardo's *Last Supper* relives in a digital projection.[14] The ultimate horizon of this drive for digitalization is in the imaginary of science fiction (the specter of Matrix is now faraway, turned into current reality). Transforming individual conscience into reproducible, transportable, and, therefore, marketable number: that is the ultimate narrative core of movies such as *Her*[15] or *Transcendence*,[16] or of series like *Black Mirror*.[17]

A history of convergence

That which has just been impressionistically discerned through a historical and sociological approach to the evolution of the ideologies of meaning can be described also in the formal metalanguage of semiotics. The "transversal gaze" of this discipline can not only conceive the history of religions as evolution of the attempts at representing transcendence but also proposing a comparison between the above described ideology of signal—which produces the current numeric frenzy—and the death of ritual. What is it that these two processes share, and where do they lead in their shared devaluation of materiality?

Every great communicative revolution in the history of humanity has coincided with an exponential increase of convergence. With the invention of writing, kinds of oral discourse theretofore separated, as well as distinct fragments of the same kind of discourse, were given the opportunity and were therefore encouraged to conflate in a single medium (Goody 1986). A great part of the Socratic philosophy as reported by Plato reflects on the cultural consequences of such convergence. The storage of contents through a new sign technology enabled communities to centralize their handling and control, for such contents were subtracted from individual consciences and deposited in an externalized memory, the access to which was regulated not only through a technique—writing—but also through a policy: Not all would master writing, and opening and closing the doors of this technology of communication would be tantamount to regulating the circulation of power. That does not mean that the dichotomy "oral cultures/cultures of writing" must correspond to the opposition between democratic and dictatorial societies, quite the opposite! Only writing allowed the accounting of opinions and, eventually, both the free interplay of political forces and their administrative and juridical control. What matters here is something else: With the birth of writing, memory was no longer a personal matter, but socially handled sharing, for instance through the invention and maintenance of knowledge in libraries.

Ritual existed well before writing, yet it was only with writing that the tale that establishes rituality could crystallize into a text that was not simply shared but also controllable by a community: It was up to the "priests" of every religion, indeed, to preside over the passage of the sacred writing from generation to generation and, above all, to hand down and cultivate the techniques that are required to "extract" religious meaning from writing. Hence, with the invention of writing, religions could become a sophisticated tool for controlling the access to the tale of transcendence throughout space and time.

The invention of mobile type printing did not entail a qualitative leap in relation to that of writing but a quantitative one, with important cultural consequences. An even greater amount of contents could converge into the same support, and be preserved as a huge quantity of data. Academic education as it has developed since early Renaissance on would have been unthinkable without the possibility of storing and minutely distributing knowledge. The power of defense and interpretation held by sacerdotal casts, though, could only weaken as a result: Large-scale printing handed out the Scriptures to myriads of faithful, and with this technical possibility a new semiotic ideology simultaneously arose, that which unties the signifier from the signified. Whereas earlier transposing the word of transcendence into a different language from that of Revelation would have been an unthinkable absurdity, now it started to be accepted as normality. Man could translate Revelation, which could subsequently circulate in the world independently from its linguistic origin. That was not the miraculous overcoming of Babel accomplished in the Pentecostal myth: There, the source of the divine message would remain linguistically unique, and it was only through a paradoxical miracle that it was subsequently understood by all, each in their own language. As in the Eucharist, so also in the Pentecost, Christianity has reconciled tradition and universalism through dogmatic paradox. With the invention of printing, however, it was transcendence itself that started to be polyglot. Or, better, it started not to matter any longer whether transcendence would speak an idiom instead of another, in Aramaic rather than in German.

It is only our total immersion in the cultural semiosphere produced by movable type printing that does not allow us to presently realize the vertiginous leap of this passage: from a religious ideology in which meaning should incarnate into a precise tongue—that of a certain historically, geographically, and, above all, ethnically determined community—to a religious ideology in which the letter does not count any longer, and vanishes in an extolling of the spirit that accepts the confusion of Babel as intrinsic not only to humanity but also to divinity.

In this domain too, tendencies often become more visible if one attentively studies countertrends; in religions that globalize meaning through a devaluation of the signifier, it is the marginal forms of "popular religion" that seek to instill new life into the religious discourse, to remotivate it in the sense of diminishing its arbitrariness, for instance through "magical" conceptions of the sacred word. The accusation of primitiveness leveled, especially from the Renaissance on, at these practices is nothing but a frontier traced to defend the boundaries of modernity: It is modern all that which does not fetishize the signifier, which accepts as "natural" that the meaning of divine revelation can express itself not only in whatever language but also to whatever interlocutor (Keane 2007). The figure of the prophet, of the human intermediary of transcendence, to whom religious traditions for this reason often attribute semi-divine connotations, disappears or is diluted into multiplicity: Everyone becomes the prophet of a personal revelation, shared with small groups or even in the minuscule space of one's spiritual intimacy. The Scriptures become portable and so does the ritual that presides over their reading. From a certain point of view, iconoclasm itself is a consequence of this devaluation of the signifier, since in Protestant modernity it does not present itself as the Jewish attempt at marking, through the Law, the empty perimeter of transcendence, of that emptiness that establishes the fullness of communitarian ritual. In the modern iconoclasm of Protestantism, instead, icons are devaluated for they establish the signifier according to the rule of resemblance, through subjecting it to a criterion that is not that of the free agreement among immanent wills (Leone 2016d). Images cannot represent transcendence because any representation of it must be irrelevant, the valueless signifier of an unfathomable signified. There is, therefore, something mystical in the protean semiotic ideology that has stemmed from modernity, but there is also a certain inclination to that which could be defined "semiotic perfectionism": Since nothing is worthy of saying god, then nothing can say it, or else everything can do it, for what matters is preserving, against any attachment to such and such signifier, the sheer idea of transcendence (Leone and Parmentier 2014). Passing through Calvin and culminating in Kant, such attitude has led to a dismantlement of religious language as it had been shaped within human communities in the previous centuries.

Communities without distinction

Kant's religion completes the process of universalization of religious meaning started with Christianity and prolonged in its Protestant version: Through constituting the utopia of a universal community, it *de facto* dissolves the idea itself of community (Leone 2012c). Philosophers of the modern idea of religion such Esposito swear that a community without immunity is possible, and that the axiology between good and evil, as well as that between justice and injustice, can be measured exactly along the watershed separating exclusive from inclusive communities (Esposito 1988). But can a community without immunity, and a transcendence that transcends even the differences among humans, really exist? This dream translates that of a language that abdicates its function of creator of differences in order to solely act as generator of commonalities (Bhatti and Kimmich 2015). But language genetically is not only communion but, on the contrary, both communion and differentiation. It is instrument of sharing as well as frontier, shibboleth. Therefore, the myth of a universal divinity, which speaks to the heart of each without passing through divisive writing, simultaneously gives rise to a desire for differentiation, exclusion, and primacy. From a certain point of view, the anthropology of anti–Semitism, rooted in Christianity, is based on that: the refusal of a form of religious life that shatters, by its own presence, the myth of an universal god, a god that speaks to all in spirit, that reveals itself in all languages, in all spaces, and in all times; Judaism as the living evidence that the sacred is not only communion but also exclusion (Sacks 2003).

The semiotic ideology that materializes in the technology of printing frees the access to religious meaning from any intermediation but removes from the modern anthropology of community a fundamental element, that of distinction. The content of revelation should travel ethereal from language to language and disclose itself with no hindrance to the conscience of each, yet something in this universal communication of the sacred is amiss. An aspect of human anthropology, not a legacy of previous steps in cultural evolution, but a perennial need, leaves unsatisfied those who receive such disembodied word, indifferent to its signifier. Indeed, only the extraordinary success of the semiotic ideology of modernity could make acceptable, or even pleonastic, the idea, in itself absurd, that content is indifferent to its expression (Keane 1997). Upon thorough reflection, the very idea of a separation of these two planes, which is the fundament of the whole methodological project of semiotics itself, is an absurdity if it is observed from the point of view of premodern religions and civilizations. How could divine Revelation live again in a language that is not its? In a language that it has not chosen and that it has not shaped since the mists of time?

That is the reason for which, in the very long period, devaluating the language of transcendence, that is, the material necessities of ritual and its exclusive character, has led to a devaluation of transcendence itself. The steps of this process are easy to define: First, it is excluded that the deity speaks a language that is not its'; afterward, it is accepted that the deity speaks in the language of each of its believers; eventually, the conclusion is reached that each is the language of the deity, and that the deity, deep down, is nothing but a reflex of the individual conscience, a transcendent dream by which the ancients would coat the immanence of human interiority. Whereas Augustine had sought to preserve a difficult equilibrium between exaltation of interiority as source of true divinity and necessity of semiotic sharing through communitarian ritual (Cary 2008), the Protestant, Kantian, and even more the postmodern inheritors of the bishop of Hippo have shattered such equilibrium.

The current stage of such process consists in the passage from God to self. If modernity would present human beings with a disembodied transcendence, without rituals, postmodernity is experienced as ritual without transcendence, as frantic desire for recuperating the non-arbitrariness and the exclusivity of religious language in private temples, in sacred idiolects, and in semiotic configurations in which the self celebrates itself exactly as deity, with its own language, following its own liturgical calendar. The only community that resists in this reaggregation of the sacred around the self is fashion. Fashion is the liturgy of postmodernity. The present chapter will therefore conclude with a sketch of analysis of a sacred space in the *saeculum* (worldliness) of postmodernity.

Conclusions

In 1894, Théophile Bader[18] and Alphonse Kahn, two cousins from a Jewish family of Alsace, inaugurated a clothes shop at the corner of rue La Fayette and rue de la Chaussée-d'Antin, in Paris. The commercial endeavor met such a great success that the two cousins purchased, in the following years, the whole block, turning it into one of the biggest shopping malls in the world. Between 1907 and 1912, then, some spectacular initiatives of architectural requalification transformed the huge store into the present-day building of *Les Galeries Lafayette* in boulevard Haussmann (Figure 5.1(a–c)).

The topology of the dome and the morphology of the interior decorations surround customers with an atmosphere that is comparable with that of a temple. That is not fortuitous but a planned effect of meaning. Théophile Bader, about whom it is know that he was a practicing member of the Alsatian Jewish community and that he would regularly attend the synagogue, explicitly requested Georges Chedanne, the architect entrusted with the project, that a golden light, coming from the dome, would flood the great hall, with its staircase of honor, and make the merchandise sparkle. The shape and the materials of the dome, as well as those of the walls of the central body of the building below were, therefore, selected on purpose so as to give rise to this particular phenomenology of light, which reminds one of that of a revelation: a luminous energy bursts from above in the enclosed space of the shopping mall in order to enlighten and simultaneously transfigure the merchandise into solid light, golden sparkle, and shining.

FIGURE 5.1(a–c)   The dome and the main foyer of the Galeries Lafayette, Paris; pictures by the author

It is worthy noticing that the architect of this *art nouveau* dome—composed of ten wedges of painted stain-glass windows caged by a metallic trestle richly decorated with flowery motives—had won the *Prix de Rome* [Price of Rome] in 1887, and as a consequence has sojourned in the eternal city at length, studying the architecture of the Pantheon. The drawings of the majestic Roman building's interiors executed by Chedanne during his stay in the eternal city are, indeed, still a reference for historians of architecture. The dome of the Galeries Lafayette borrows from the Pantheon the topological and chromatic configuration of light shed as golden and fine dust on the internal emptiness of the building, transfiguring it in an almost mystical way.[19] But it draws also from some other stylistic solutions of sacred architecture. Because of a disagreement between Théophile Bader, the owner of the Galeries Lafayette, and the architect Chedanne, the execution of the dome was entrusted, from 1912 on, to his assistant Ferdinand Chanut, who modified the structure of the dome through explicitly drawing inspiration from that of byzantine architecture.

A light that, coming from above, floods and transfigures the merchandise; the reference to the Roman Pantheon; the intention of situating, on top of the biggest commercial building of Paris, a stained glass dome of Byzantine shape, wherein the gold of mosaics is transferred to the flowery balustrades designed by Louis Majorelle, thus grafting the optics of the theater on that of the temple (the *Opéra* theater is behind the corner) and replacing both the altar and the stage with the spectacle of purchase and consumption[20]: Such transfer of plastic configurations from the architecture and fine arts of the premodern sacred space of praying to those of the modern and postmodern profane space of buying can and must awake the interest of the student of sacred spaces,[21] especially if they are analyzed within the key environment of modern civilizations, that is, the city. In 2009,[22] the Galeries Lafayette Haussmann attracted 25 million visitors and customers, 100,000 per day. Obviously, only few of them have had the explicit feeling of accessing, through entering the central building of the Galeries, a sacred space. Yet it is indubitable that the complex architectural machine set up by Théophile Bader and his architects submerges the visitor in a spatial, chromatic, material, and luminous atmosphere that reminds the visitor of that of a temple, wherein a golden light transubstantiates the merchandise from mere object into the furnishing of an individual rite, into the relic of the mute pilgrimage through which, purchase after purchase, men and women without community nor transcendence can stage, through the liturgy of fashion, the celebration of their solipsistic cults.

Notes

1 That is the case especially as regards structural semiotics; for an introduction to this approach to meaning, see Greimas (1966, 1970, 1983).
2 Materiality is currently a buzzword in the humanities as well as in religious studies; see, for instance, the book series "Routledge Research in Religion, Media, and Culture" as well as the journal "Material Religion: The Journal of Objects, Art and Belief," published by Taylor & Francis; among the most recent contributions in the field, Pongratz-Leisten and Sonik (2015). Materiality has always been among the concerns of semiotics; see, for instance, Floch (1984); more recently, and in a rather Peircean paradigm, see Keane (2003).
3 For a recent rearticulation of such dialectics, see Esposito (2014).
4 For a recent survey, see Comte-Sponville (2015).
5 For instance, Dawkins (2008).
6 For a very recent inquiry and historical reconstruction, see Campion (2016).
7 But on the religious roots of merchandizing itself, see Valeri (2010).
8 For an extensive treatment of this concept, see Leone (2014a).
9 For a historical and sociological account of this phenomenon, see Graham and Dutton (2014).
10 See, for instance, Johnson-Laird (1988).
11 On post-digital aesthetics, see Berry and Dieter (2015).
12 According to the US semiotician and philosopher Charles S.S. Peirce's famous tripartite categorization of signs (Peirce 1982–2000).
13 For a survey of the philosophy of "emerging media", see Floyd and Katz (2016).
14 See Greenaway (2008) and Werner (2010).

15 Spike Jonze (2013).
16 Wally Pfister (2014).
17 Charlier Brooker for Endemol, from 2011 on. See in particular the sixth episode of the fourth series, "Black Museum", directed by Colm McCarthy.
18 Dambach-la-Ville, Alsace, April 24, 1864–Paris, March 16, 1942; on Bader, see Stehlé (1982).
19 For an introduction to the history of the religious connotations of gold, see Spineto (2014).
20 See Böhme (2012).
21 For an example of such interdisciplinary approach, see Giorda and Hejazi (2013).
22 Last publicly available statistics at the moment of writing the present chapter.

6

ASSEMBLING INSIGNIFICANCE

Post-material crowds

τίσιν οὖν τὰ πολυτελέστερα, ἂν αἱρῶνται
πάντες τὰ εὐτελέστερα
(Clement of Alexandria, *Paedagogus*
[Παιδαγωγός, "The Instructor"], II, 13, 268)

Introduction

It is 8:30 AM in Madrid, on a splendid late spring Saturday, still quite early for a city that wakes up much later on weekends. I walk from the neighborhood of La Latina toward the Biblioteca Nacional, eager to spend a few hours in that gorgeous library. In one of the streets that wind down between Plaza Mayor and Sol, I come across a long line of people. They are mostly women, of all ages but predominantly young. They all wear colorful comfortable clothes and hold rubber mats. Occasionally, I also see men standing in order, some in silence, some others exchanging a few words with their neighbors. As I follow the line, I realize that it is longer than I first thought: It actually forms soon after the metro station of Sol and stretches along the entire street up to the proximities of Plaza Mayor. I curiously observe it for a few minutes, seeking to understand its finality. It seems quite different from the early morning lines that take shape in front of the yet-to-open doors of offices, medical laboratories, or consulates. I know too well how people stand in line waiting for submitting their visa applications: usually tired, annoyed, holding boring folders of documents in their hands, their faces emotionless with sleep and resignation. On the contrary, this is a fresh, joyous line, emanating confidence and colorful energy. What are all these people doing standing in line so early in the morning between the two most famous squares of Madrid (Figure 6.1)?

FIGURE 6.1 Line of people from Sol to Plaza Mayor, Madrid, in the early morning of June 4, 2016; picture by the author

I politely start chatting with a few of them. A woman tells me that a big yoga event is going to happen in Plaza Mayor. I ask her at what time. "At 11:00 AM, they are going to open the doors", she answers. At 11:00 AM? That means that all these people will stand in line for more than two and a half hours before they can enter the square and join the yoga event. It is not summer yet, but they will soon be standing under the strong sun of Madrid. I ask whether a big yoga guru will lead the event, but I soon realize from the expression of people that my question is irrelevant. No, they answer, they don't know who will guide the yoga session. They tell me that this event happens once every year and that they are eager to participate in it. I discreetly take a couple of pictures and depart.

As I proceed toward the Biblioteca Nacional, I pass in front of several beautiful baroque churches, their doors already open, their pews occupied by a few elderly devotees. It occurs to me that, on this day, the Catholic liturgical calendar celebrates the Feast of the Immaculate Heart of Mary, promoted and instituted by the French seventeenth-century Saint Jean Eudes[1] through his book on *La dévotion au très saint Cœur de la bienheureuse vierge Marie* [The devotion to the very saintly heart of the blessed Virgin Mary] (1648). In that liturgical treatise, the Saint would dwell at length on the synergy between the heart of Jesus and that of Mary. I wonder whether that synergy is somehow transmogrified into that which runs through the long line that I have just come across. I also wonder whether the spiritual concept of the human heart of a young mother beating in synchronicity with that of her divine child might not be too abstract for the present time, replaced by the physical synchronicity of a multitude of women and men moving their limbs according to a spiritual tradition coming from a more distant East, beyond the origins of Christianity. As I ponder this theological thought, I finally reach my destination, climb the marble steps at the entrance of the library, and enter the quiet reading hall on the second floor. Nobody is there, except an elderly woman taking notes from a massive folio volume. I wonder whether I too should better be standing in line at the doors of Plaza Mayor, waiting to stretch my body together with thousands of young and beautiful people.

It is precisely in attempting to make this kind of public phenomena more intelligible that the area of study called "Language and Religion" must extend beyond an exclusively linguistic focus to a more encompassing—but also, inevitably, vaguer—semiotic field. Several aspects of this Madrid event contain elements of verbal language and, thus, concern linguistics. First of all, communication of the event must have taken place primarily—although not exclusively—through verbal language. A quick search in the web reveals that the event was promoted through a professional website, www.freeyoga.es/, and that the website belongs to OYSHO, a Spanish clothing retailer specializing in women's homewear and undergarments. OYSHO is one of the many brands owned by the Spanish corporation Inditex, the biggest fashion group in the world (comprising world-famous brands like Zara, Mango, Zara Home, Massimo Dutti, Bershka, Pull and Bear, Stradivarius, and Uterqüe). On the web page, the event is advertised as "*free masterclass de yoga multitudinaria*" [free master class of multitudinous yoga]. The linguistic analysis of this announcement should not miss the semantic connotations of its precise choice of words. A description like "free master class of mass yoga", for instance, or one like "free master class of collective yoga", would have transmitted different messages. On the one hand, nobody today likes to be considered as part of a "mass". The expression "mass yoga" would, indeed, sound derogatory, like "mass market" and would sound like a second-class, nonexclusive experience. On the other hand, "collective yoga" would remind one of the free activities organized in a occupied building of Berlin or, indeed, in the *Fábrica de Tabacos* in Madrid. "Multitude", instead, is the spiritual keyword of the announcement: It gives people the feeling that they will empower their identity in harmony with thousands of germane yoga practitioners. It sets an astute equilibrium between egocentrism and fusion.[2] Most importantly, it does not contradict the subtle but, nevertheless, central commercial nature of the event: People must forget that they are stretching their limbs encouraged by a global undergarment retailer; but they must simultaneously and surreptitiously have that in mind: While a supreme calm descends upon the enormous crowd—yoga posture after yoga posture—participants must somehow connect the otherworldly flexibility of their limbs with the qualities of OYSHO's underwear.

What does it all have to do with religion? The verbal language of the event's website carefully avoids presenting the "multitude yoga master class" as a religious or even as a blandly spiritual happening. If religion plays a role in the analysis of this text, it is a negative and contrastive one. No reference is made to the East, to India, to secluded ashrams or to the mystical *om*. The website insists, instead, on trivial practicalities and mainly on how to dress properly for the event. The reason for it is clear and even made boldly explicit at the bottom of the web page: Slender, headless models display a series of subdued underwear and sportswear, under the label "*Te sugerimos estos looks básicos de OYSHO para practicar yoga*" [We suggest these basic looks by OYSHO for practicing yoga]. There are no precise indications on either the origin of the brand name or its intended connotation. It is undeniable, however, that "OYSHO" sounds quite similar to Osho,[3] the name of the world-famous guru, mystic, and spiritual leader. From a certain point of view, the joyous, liberating, humorous, non-confessional spirituality that the free yoga master class is supposed to associate with the underwear brand is akin to the astute content that one finds in many of Osho's books.

The connection between "OYSHO" and "Osho" is one that a linguistic study of spiritual and religious phenomena is able to grasp, as it is able to analyze the verbal discourse that surrounds and permeates the event: What people say while waiting in line before the opening of Plaza Mayor is certainly an important part of it. Most people I briefly "interviewed" along the line, for instance, would emphasize the fact that the event would "happen once a year". Such stress on the uniqueness of the event, as well as on its recurrence, immediately configures a sort of liturgical occasion, whose schedule is likely to produce expectation and desire.

This or similar events, however, cannot be fully understood if one neglects the fact that their spiritual aura derives not only and not much from the verbal language that announces, describes, comments on, and permeates the event but also, and above all, from the other systems of signs that accompany the verbal one and that connote the cognitive, pragmatic, and especially the emotional meaning of the multitude yoga session. On the one hand, it is evident that the analysis on nonverbal aspects of this phenomenon cannot equal the level of articulation that the close reading of its verbal discourse can achieve; verbal language remains a "primary modeling system" of most religious or spiritual or quasi-spiritual experiences, as Yuri M. Lotman[4] would put it (1985). On the other hand, reducing the comprehension of a spiritual event to its mere linguistic dimension would be impoverishing, especially in those cases, such as the yoga gathering in Madrid, in which verbal language does not follow a predetermined liturgy and features complex contamination among different genres (the spiritual and the commercial, sport and meditation discourse, etc.).

In keeping with Ferdinand de Saussure's[5] seminal definition of semiology, the semiotics of religion must consider the interaction between verbal language and other expressive devices, as they co-determine the framework of meaning and experience of spiritual phenomena. In an event like the one evoked above, for example, numerous configurations of signs contribute to bring about its array of semantic connotations and emotional flavors. The first element to take into account is the line itself. Staying in line is something that happens on many occasions in people's lives. A semiotics of waiting in line is still to be developed, and should be treated as a particular instance of a more general semiotics of waiting.[6]

In Greimasian terms,[7] waiting constitutes both a pragmatic and a temporal arrangement in the relation between a subject and an object: A subject who waits is already in a significant relation with an object. Waiting, however, results from the fact that the subject does not possess yet the appropriate competence to attain the object, so this is put on hold until the competence is achieved. From the temporal point of view, waiting is, therefore, characterized by durativity, that is, by a regime of temporality whose predominant aspectual characteristic is that of stretching throughout time without being interrupted by [external?] events. The relation between the subject's desire, its distance from the object, and the durative temporality of waiting is what determines its cognitive, pragmatic, and emotional flavor, together with the euphoria/dysphoria of the object itself (Greimas and Fontanille 1991).

On the one hand, a subject can be impatient to stop waiting in order to attain the object, as it happens when lovers wait for a rendezvous with their beloved. On the other hand, a subject might want to prolong waiting, if the subject itself is actually the object of other negative subjects, for instance when people condemned to death wish to increase the temporal gap separating them from their execution. In both cases, though, waiting can be such an excruciating experience in itself as to turn into a secondary object: Lovers can paradoxically decide to leave before meeting their beloved ones because they cannot stand the anxiety of being waiting for them, and—symmetrically—people on the death row might want to accelerate their own execution for the same reason.

But waiting *in line* is not simply waiting. It is waiting *together with* other people. These multiple actors of waiting might feel in competition with each other. That is the case when one is waiting to be attended to by a bank clerk. In such circumstance, those ahead of us are closer to attaining the object, whereas those behind are farther away from the goal. One usually feels offensive hostility toward the former (wishing to be closer to the object than them) and defensive hostility toward the latter (wishing to keep being closer to the object than them). In these conditions, jumping lines is usually experienced as the ultimate injustice, since it unpredictably disrupts the chronological and existential hierarchy of waiting. A waiting line in such competitive settings urgently requires organization and supervision so as not to turn into an occasion of continuous conflict and, potentially, violence.

Nevertheless, there are also occasions in which the actors of waiting do not feel that they wait *against* each other, as when they are in line before an office or a hospital. Sometimes, they might feel, on the contrary, that they are waiting *together*. In Greimasian terms, they pass from being individual waiting actors to merging into a collective waiting "actant" (Greimas 1979). In such cases, although people are still in line and are still organized in a hierarchy of "before" and "after", they also feel that their object can only be attained if all the people in line attain it as a multitude and not as mere individuals. That is the difference between waiting in line before a famous restaurant and waiting in line before a stadium. The first waiting line encourages an individual experience of temporality, durativity, and desire. The second waiting line, instead, promotes a synergic experience of them. Young women waiting for the opening of Plaza Mayor were anxious to secure their spot in the square, but they were also, and essentially, waiting to become part of a multitude. They wanted to get in, but they wanted to get in *together with* a large number of other people.

As marketing strategists know well, since people often wait for that which has value for them, making people wait for something frequently increases the perception of the value of what they are waiting for. No Parisian would take seriously a restaurant, an exhibition, or even a political rally that does not require waiting in line for a long time. In this regard, however, a difference must be observed between individual and collective lines. Artificially creating lines in front of a restaurant can boost its desirability for both those who are in line and those who observe it (although a subtle equilibrium must be preserved between titillating and irritating customers in line); in this case, the waiting line improves the value of the object. In collective lines, on the contrary, waiting in line with other people is instrumental and conducive to the creation itself of the collective actant. Being in line for a long time, people progressively divest themselves of their individual immunity and start adhering to the temporal but also to the libidinal rhythm of their elective community (Esposito 1988). In line, they learn how to become a collective subject, to desire together with other people, at the rhythm of other people.

That is the main reason for which the linguistics of religion must be expanded into a semiotics of religion. Without taking into account the narrative structure of waiting, the pragmatics of a waiting line, and the proxemics of its inter-somaticity,[8] wherein bodies start resonating with other bodies for the simple fact that they share the same socially organized space, one cannot grasp the similarity that links waiting in line for a "multitudinous" masterclass of yoga and waiting in line in order to participate in the liturgy of a religious ritual. Although the OYSHO event was a clearly commercial one, staged by astute marketing strategists, it acquired a spiritual connotation by the way it arranged the spatiotemporality of waiting: What was the reason, indeed, for closing the public square of Plaza Mayor, if not the intent to turn it into the target space of a religious waiting line?

The space of the event is another fundamental element that the semiotic analysis of religious phenomena must take into account. Rituals and, more in general, liturgical configurations essentially contain times and spaces of waiting. Scholarship on the structure of rituals usually concentrates on its rhythmic dimension, yet such rhythm could not take shape without the carefully regulated alternation of action and inaction, dynamism and stasis.[9] In many religious cultures, believers are required to wait in two forms: as they adhere to the syntax of the ritual and, even before that, as they wait for entering into the space and time of ritual itself. The marketing of the waiting line, therefore, exploits a semiotic pattern whose origin is essentially religious: Young Madrid women expectantly await the opening of the Plaza Mayor as their grandmothers would await the opening of the church, or the arrival of the priest, or the moment at which the statue of the saint, during processions, would egress the doors of the temple. From this point of view, the semiotics of the waiting line, its proxemics, its slow kinesics, the micro-interactions that punctuate it, and its narrative significance in the symbolical economy of the event can be understood in depth only in the topological dialectics that the waiting line maintains with the space of the performance, where the competence of time and patience required of the individual subject gives rise to a collective reunion with the object of desire. Since this waiting line is a communitarian and noncompetitive one, the time and space into which it flows is a spatial and synchronic one. Whereas in competitive waiting individuals accede one by one—or at the most in small groups—to the space of performance and fulfillment of their desire (e.g., when customers of a restaurant are progressively seated, leaving all the other customers in line, waiting with increasing hunger and nervous expectation), in communitarian waiting the line allows individuals to turn into a multitude that joyously explodes into the area of performance just as soon as the gates of the temple are open. The closure of the gates and the presence of a bidimensional space behind them bestow upon the waiting line an even more emphatic ritual character. The transformation of the human line into a human area marks the passage from two states of the ritual narrative, as well as between the stage of individual subjects and that of the subjects merged into a collective actant.

As photographs of the event point out, the religious characterization of the square is not contradicted by the essentially commercial nature of the event about to take place in it but comes into effect exactly because of its connotation according to the discourse of advertising (Figure 6.2).

In other words, the symbolical syntax of the happening turns the discourse of advertising into that of ritual: The urban and architectural support of this discourse lends itself to such merging of the capitalistic and the sacred. If Sol is the social center of the city, that in which the famous "Kilometro Zero" is to be found (i.e., the point of Madrid from which all distances from the Spanish capital are measured), Plaza Mayor is certainly the historical center of the city, the arena in which the most notable public events in the modern history of both Madrid and Spain have taken place. In particular, since the Spanish court moved to the city in 1560, Plaza Mayor has been constantly playing the role of public space in which ritual communities come into being. Here, Spaniards have staged public acts, bullfights, and *autos-da-fé* (see Figure 6.3).

Countless executions took place in this *plaza*, each with a precise topology of violence: The scaffold was situated in the *portal de pañeros* if the execution was by club; facing the *Casa de la Panadería*, if it was by hanging; and, ironically, in front

FIGURE 6.2 Plaza Mayor during a "multitudinous master class of yoga" on June 4, 2016; picture by the author

FIGURE 6.3 Francisco Rizi. 1683. *Auto-da-fé in Plaza Mayor, Madrid.* Oil on canvas. 277 × 438 cm. Madrid: Museo del Prado

of the *Casa de la Carnicería* [literally meaning "the butcher's house"], if it was by knife or axe. Over several centuries, Madrid citizens have learned to consider this squared *plaza*, with its geometric architecture, its statues, its plaques, and the complex topology of its openings, as the place where collective ritual agents take shape in order to experience the staged ecstasy of violence and the controlled frenzy of bodily destruction. In other, more explicit words, throughout the history of Madrid, Plaza Mayor has been identified with the arena of the secular sacrifice, which happens outside of the Church and outside of the strictly religious space but bears nonetheless all the symbolical marks of a sacrifice. Whether the source of it was an unlucky bull or an unfortunate human being, blood has been violently shed in this square in order to cement the Spanish collectivity as communitarian agent obedient to the sacred hierarchy of the state and the monarchy.

On June 4, 2016, monochrome burgundy mats carrying the sober, Oriental-like logo of OYSHO replaced the rich tapestries of the Spanish royal family, usually displayed during collective ritual events in the plaza. On such day, no bodies were dismembered or burned or executed in the square, but a multitude of bodies manifested itself in torsions, twists, and controlled grimaces of pain (Figure 6.4).

FIGURE 6.4 People practicing multitudinous yoga in Plaza Mayor, Madrid, on June 4, 2016; picture by the author

No king, moreover, was to preside over the sacrifice, enjoying the ritual subjection of the frantic multitude to the violence staged by the royal apparatus. But weren't these thousands of women in line, and some men among them, "sacrificing" to the commercial pantheon of postmodern, post-capitalistic consumerism, in which buying is no longer a mere act of allegiance to the market and to its persuasive power but disguises itself as act of "liberation", involving not only an individual but an entire community? What, indeed, could push so many people to wake up early in Madrid on a Saturday morning of late spring, if not the expectation of collective deliverance that the discourse of yoga, astutely manipulated and hijacked by the commercial one, promises to grant?

Consequently, the proxemics and the chrono-topology of the two figures of the waiting line and the public square, through the dialectics described above, take on a double, ambiguous nature. The waiting line is reminiscent of the "waiting for" that the rhetoric of marketing and capitalistic consumption adopts as a powerful metaphor of value (i.e., "worth waiting for"). In recent years, the release of each new mobile phone by Apple or, to a lesser extent, Samsung, has been accompanied by a worldwide display of waiting lines, in which potential buyers would compete for the first products on the market and, simultaneously, testify, by the cumulative assertion of their own waiting bodies, the preternatural value of Steve Jobs's artifacts. In the ritual event analyzed above, the post-capitalistic marketing discourse would shrewdly encourage the competitive line to transmogrify into a communitarian one, also through interaction with the symbolic history of the square in which the waiting line would dissolve. In such case, therefore, the waiting line functions as an accumulator of value whose final result, though, is not simply individual attachment to the religious aura of a brand but collective worship of its sublimated, spiritual counterpart. People in Plaza Mayor do not simply want to possess OYSHO underwear and sportswear; they want to belong to the magically synergic world to which the experience staged by OYSHO, like the executions of seventeenth-century Spain, allow them to access.

From this point of view, the experience of the multitudinous yoga event is a transformative one, since it bestows upon individuals—exactly like many religious rituals described and analyzed in the classics of the sociology and the anthropology of religion—the proprioceptive, emotional, and supra-cognitive conviction that these individuals are no longer alone. They wait in line for hours under the sun for that blissful moment in which they feel that the inexorable sensation of existential solitude that curses their digital life, and that empty and elderly churches are no longer able to dispel, vanishes in the simultaneous longing for the collective performance, in the synchronic occupation of the square, and in the fusional exercise of a thousand bodies subtly orchestrated by the priests of the commercial brand (Figure 6.5).

None of these elements, taken alone, could justify the ritual result of the happening: the topology of the square in relation to the line, the sedimentation of symbolic connotations throughout the history of the *plaza*, and the staging of the space of the event through the ambiguous architectural and decorative discourse of post-capitalistic branding. Taken together, however, all these elements constitute

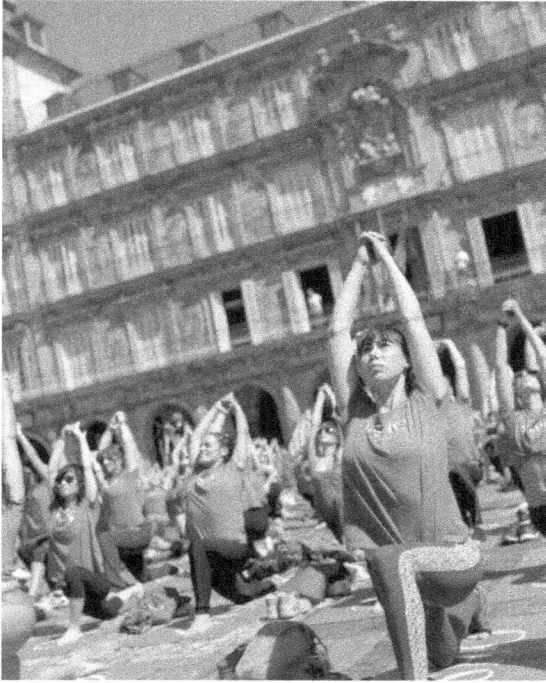

FIGURE 6.5   People practicing multitudinous yoga in Plaza Mayor, Madrid, on June 4, 2016; picture by the author

a semiotic "configuration" that turns a fragment of the space and time of the city into an impromptu religious experience, a "low-intensity ritual" through which attendees feel blandly transformed and bettered through connection with the multitude, its post-secular rituality, and the commercial allegiance that it surreptitiously expresses.

Post-religious burials

A distinguished professor from an Italian university died a few years ago. He was a semiotician. The university organized an honorary burial chamber in the garden of the library of the Faculty of Letters, then situated in a beautiful medieval building. Relatives, disciples, colleagues, and students were all extremely sad and moved. Professor Umberto Eco was there, paying homage to the deceased. A few touching speeches were pronounced by close friends and collaborators, then four colleagues carried the coffin on their shoulders away from the burial chamber. At that precise moment, the large crowd burst into a thunderous applause. At the same moment, however, Umberto Eco yelled at the crowd with his characteristic raucous yet stentorian voice: "One does not applaud at funerals!"

That day, I was devastated by the loss of the dear professor, yet after a few months Umberto Eco's sentence resounded into my mind. Why should one not applaud at funerals? And why have Italians started to systematically applaud at public funerals? Finally, why was Umberto Eco so irritated by such behavior? In traditional, premodern societies, funerals are an intrinsically religious event. Communities spontaneously agree on the fact that the passage from life to death, the commemoration of the deceased, and the process of mourning must be regulated according to a series of codes whose nature is not simply legal or moral but entails a reflection on the afterlife, often on transcendence, or at least on the spiritual dimension of existence.[10] In all the major world religions, funerals, burials, mourning, and the commemoration of the dead are not left to the creativity of individuals and families but are regulated, instead, through a technical apparatus, which is supposed to ritualize every aspect of the painful process. It is only with the so-called "secularization" of societies that the question has arisen of organizing funerals that do not necessarily entail a direct and explicit reference to a religious code. The case of state funerals is, from this point of view, emblematic. What happens when the state wants to publicly and solemnly commemorate the death of a distinguished citizen, without impinging on the principle of the separation between church and state, confession and administration? More generally, how should a funeral be orchestrated, when the deceased had not manifested in life any religious allegiance or had even expressly demanded to be buried with no religious ritual at all? How does a state nonreligious funeral look like?

The question is of extreme relevance since it concerns not only death but also other momentous passages of the human existence in modern and contemporary societies. The embarrassment of having to configure the secular version of a traditional religious ritual manifests itself macroscopically at funerals but also affects other analogous existential thresholds, for instance marriages: How is it possible to attach symbolical solemnity and even magical efficacy to a wedding, when it is stripped of any ritual element referring its validity to a transcendent framework? Will a mayor reading to the bride and groom the section of the constitution that determines their civil rights and duties as a married couple achieve the same symbolical efficacy (for both the newlyweds and their community) as a priest, or a mullah, or a rabbi, reading from sacred texts in which divine words have dictated their view of the metaphysical significance of a loving union? And will the modern architecture of the city hall, with its offices full of obsolete computers and paperwork, host the ceremony in as equally a dignified way as the Romanic chapel in which men and women have been saying "yes" in front of God and his assembly for centuries?

In this circumstance, as in the previous case, a semiotics of religion must work hand in hand with a linguistics of religion. The comparative linguistic analysis of both religious and "secular rituals" is essential in order to develop a contrastive overview of differences and analogies between the two discursive styles. On the one hand, for instance, the formulae that the law prescribes for the accomplishment of the present-day civil marriage in many jurisdictions seem to avoid any reference to the religious sphere, transcendence, and the metaphysical fundament of marriage; on the other hand, though, a subtler stylistic analysis shows that, in many cases, these formulae tend to reproduce the prosody, the rhythm, and the sentential flavor of their religious counterparts. In other words, and more abstractedly, "secularized" ritual formulae keep away from any religious *content* but often even unconsciously resort to quasi-religious sounding *expressions*. That is the case in funerals too: Civil state funerals might exclude explicitly religious utterances from the celebration, yet their tone and general linguistic register are akin to that of religious burials. This observation might perhaps be generalized into a more encompassing hypothesis about the secularization of religious rituals of passage: Although the semantics of their verbal language is systematically purged from any reference to a religious background, the pragmatics of their ritual efficacy still depends on their surreptitious adhesion to religious signification patterns.

The persistence of religious undertexts in secularized rituals, however, cannot be fully grasped from a merely linguistic point of view. The analysis of verbal language is essential in order to determine distances and proximities between strictly religious and post-religious ceremonies; yet, in this case too, it is, above all, the analysis on nonverbal systems of signification that reveals to the fullest extent the ritual anxiety of post-religious, digital societies. The ethnography of present-day rituals such as funerals and weddings is producing an expanding and increasingly sophisticated literature.[11] Thanks to such ethnographic or ethno-methodological accounts, one can distinctively sense the efforts that individuals, groups, and communities make in order to restore the symbolic efficacy of existential rituals while ideologically affirming total severance from past religious frameworks. For instance, how does a post-Christian couple celebrate the birth of a child, if any traditional baptism is to be excluded? More and more, the Christian ritual of baptism is being anticipated and replaced by the "secular" ritual of "baby shower", increasingly diffused in Western societies. Even without indulging in a psychoanalytical analysis that would point out how an explicit reference to purifying water persists in the name itself of this "secular ritual", it is evident that the sociocultural rationale for the genesis and diffusion of baby-showers lies in the necessity to symbolically replacing baptism as a religious ritual that effectively marks the birth of a new individual into the community.

The urgency of a semiotic analysis paralleling the linguistic analysis of religious verbal language is even greater in cases where whole religious rituals have been supposedly deconstructed and reconstructed in an entirely, or rather pseudo-entirely, secular way. I recently attended a post-Catholic wedding (meaning that both the bride and the groom came from Catholic families but professed their agnosticism or atheism) in which the priest had been replaced by a friend, the chapel by the setting of a rural villa, the liturgical formulae by salacious comments on the past of both the groom and bride, and the ceremony eventually ended with all the participants wearing red clown noses. The intention to subvert, deconstruct, and even mock the traditional liturgy of the Catholic wedding was evident. Yet in such cases too, a more in-depth semiotic analysis reveals the nervousness of the subversion. Deconstructive reversal, indeed, presupposes a preceding symbolical status quo, referring to which is essential in order to bring about its parody. Hence, as regards the abovementioned wedding, there was no priest to be seen, yet the priest was still there, precisely through his grotesque counterpart; the solemnity of the wedding had been apparently mocked through the wearing of clown noses, yet it would still linger around the couple as a sort of ghost and as the sad shadow of a lost enchantment. All in the ceremony had been carefully planned to signify disenchantment, yet the ceremonial framework was still there, signaling that enchantment persisted in a negative form, as loss, as caricatural nostalgia.

Such persistence of religious enchantment in the post-religious settings of ritual disenchantment would be difficult to pinpoint without the adoption of a structural methodology of analysis like semiotics. In the clownish wedding, for instance, the linguistic analysis reveals how the tone, the pauses, the overall emotional vibes, and even the syntactic choices of the tongue-in-cheek speech actually betray the nervous persistence of a religious subtext beneath the mockery. The semiotic analysis, however, paralleling the linguistic one, points out that what bestows on the entire setting a religious ceremonial aura—despite its participants' intentions of disenchantment and desecration—precisely is the proxemics of the attendees, with the groom and the bride standing alone in front of the priest-clown and all the other guests orderly sitting behind them. This parody of a Catholic wedding has eliminated the chapel, the priest, the altar, the crucifix, the icons on the walls, and so on but cannot eliminate the proxemics of the Catholic wedding, and that proxemics alone is sufficient to remind one of the material absence, and of the shadowy presence, of all that symbolical apparatus of chapel, priest, altar, etc. It is not so easy to deconstruct and disenchant a religious ritual like a wedding, since its historical and collective imaginary so powerfully refers it to a religious semiosphere that, in order to eliminate that reference, one should eliminate the ritual as well. One can try to get married "secularly" but will end up performing a bricolage with bits and pieces of the traditional religious discourse, with fragments of a past coherence that not only the malign semiotic analyst but also the guests themselves will recognize as religious. To most guests, indeed, the symbolic efficacy of the post-Catholic ritual will look somehow nostalgically pale exactly because it constitutes itself as a vicarious, parasitic counterpart.

The intrinsic dependence of post-religious rituals from the semiotic structure of the symbolical and, above all, the pragmatic efficacy of preexistent, obliterated religious rituals does not exclude that new elements and configurations of signs might emerge in the more or less spontaneous *bricolage* through which individuals and communities seek to redefine, in a secular setting, the rituality of existential watersheds. It is from this perspective that the bizarre behavior of applauding at funerals must be understood. First, it should be underlined that this is not a widespread habit yet but one that has taken roots mostly in Italy. Each society develops peculiar ways of expressing collective feelings, and applauding in Italy enjoys a pragmatic aura that is different from that observable in other societies. Italians show a tendency to applaud plane pilots when they perform a particularly smooth landing in peculiarly difficult weather conditions, for instance. In that case, the applause, which is likely to disconcert non-Italian travelers but usually please non-Italian pilots, is meant to pay tribute to the flying and landing skills of the captain. That, however, is not the only signification of the applause. Besides the primary function of congratulating the pilot, the applause also works as a gestural and sonic code meant to create and manifest a collective feeling of deliverance: "We are alive, and we are alive together; therefore, we clap in glee to signify relief after the stiff moments of landing". During the difficult approach to the airport, everybody is individually anguished, tormented by the idea of the possibility that one's life might so abruptly and tragically end. After landing, these individual anxieties merge into a feeling of collective elation, which must be manifested, hence, not only through individual verbal utterances (congratulating the crew while egressing the plane, for instance) but also through a collective, nonverbal, and rhythmic communication such applauding.

These two elements are also present in the new, and somehow even more disconcerting habit of applauding at funerals. "Who is the primary addressee of this applause?" one might ask. Certainly, people do not applaud death, although death seems to be the real protagonist of the ceremonial event. They applaud, instead, the deceased—especially when the dead one was a somewhat public figure—in order to mark their collective endorsing of a past life. The applause in this case means, "You lived well; hence, we applaud the appropriateness of your past life". In the case of the deceased Italian semiotician, the applause meant, "You were a great professor, and did a lot for your university; therefore, we applaud you". As in the case of plane passengers applauding the smooth landing of their pilots, however, here too clapping serves not only the primary semiotic function of signifying collective approval but also the secondary function of creating, through a simple gestural, rhythmic, and sonic code, a collective agent.[12] The purpose of this creation exceeds that of merely constituting a communitarian subject that positively sanctions the life of a deceased (of a pilot). The collective agent, instead, takes shape at funerals through the applause for the same reason for which it manifests itself in airplanes after a perilous landing: People seek not to be left alone with the thought of death and need to collectively and mutually acknowledge the fact that they persist alive. While they are paying tribute to the dead one, they also unconsciously rejoice at their own survival, in the reciprocal recognition that they keep alive. That is a feeling that only a collective ritual can bestow on individuals. One cannot feel alive alone, especially when experiencing the death of a beloved person. In traditional cultures, rituals of mourning are always collective, since it is only through the interaction of the mourning ones with their social context that the former will be able to be confirmed in the existential conviction that they belong to the living ones and that they can progressively separate themselves from the deceased. Religious rituals of burial play a fundamental role in connecting bereft individuals into a mourning community, often within a framework in which death itself is sublimated into a superior, sometimes transcendent, dimension.

But what happens when, after "secularization" and the parallel fragmentation of societies and communities into digital arenas, religious rituals of burial and mourning are progressively abandoned, and the bereft relatives, friends, and colleagues are left alone, without any ritual guidance, in elaborating the tragic experience of a beloved person's death? How does one mourn, without a ritual and without a community? Mourning by oneself can prove an unbearable experience, and that is exactly why, in secular, post-Catholic societies like the Italian one, a spontaneous symbolical *bricolage* gives rise to new ways of shaping a mourning collectivity in spite of the progressive demise of the traditional apparatus of the religious rituality of death. Hence, when Italians applaud at funerals, they mean not only "we collectively pay homage to an exemplary life" but also "we turn ourselves into a mourning community through the corporeal synchronicity of clapping". But why, then, was Umberto Eco yelling at the clapping crowd?

A subtle thread links the multitudinous experience of the square described earlier with the equally multitudinous manifestation of the applauding crowd at funerals. In both cases, the receding semiotic configuration of the religious ritual leaves behind an empty framework, within which the post-religious bricolage of the community can take place and achieve new modalities of existential rituality. The line of elderly believers expecting the opening of the temple yields to the queue of young yoga aficionados awaiting the disclosing of Plaza Mayor; the orchestrated liturgy of collective mourning leaves room to the spontaneous creation of an applauding community. In both cases, though, the communitarian re-enchantment of the disenchanted post-religious individual is not entirely innocent, meaning that the gap between the digital absentification of the religious ritual and its new presentification in post-religious forms is an empty post-material space that external agencies are always tempted to occupy. In other words, the framework of sacramental power vacated by the traditional religious agencies of a society (e.g., the Catholic Church in Spain) does not disappear with the disappearing of the forces that used to preside over it. The passage from traditional, premodern, religious, and material societies to postmodern, post-religious, "secular", and digital communities leaves behind an empty structure of symbolical hierarchies and patterns of belief, which persist well beyond the demise of traditional religious voices. Post-Catholic communities like Italy, for instance, might reject the dogma of the infallibility of the pope, and might even dismiss the pope himself as a religious institution, yet they unconsciously and surreptitiously continue looking for a pope, although through displaying this search in other domains of life. The eagerness by which Italians fall for the utopia and the enchantment of an infallible political leader, able to effortlessly transport them to a better existential kingdom, for instance, could be hardly explained without reference to the legacy of sacramental hierarchy that the demise of the Catholic way of life has left behind.

Similarly, and more concretely, the expiration of religious assemblies has not simply created a vacuum but an empty symbolical and pragmatic framework of patterns that other agencies can occupy and exploit to achieve efficacy. In the first example, global capitalism, marketing, and consumerism clearly hijacked the semiotic structure of the religious ritual so as to associate the symbolical bricolage of post-religious individuals with a commercial enterprise. In the second case study, the idea itself of spectacle seeps into the post-religious formation of communities. Umberto Eco was objecting the new habit of applauding at funerals because clapping is, by definition, the gestural, rhythmic, and sonic way to positively sanction *a performance*. But death is not a performance. Even when individuals commit suicide, death cannot be possibly seen as their accomplishment but rather as something that they have *passively* suffered. Yet applauding at funerals inevitably creates a semiotic scenario in which the gap between old and new rituals is occupied and somehow exploited by those social agencies that create, present, and, above all, *sell* spectacles to their audiences. By applauding, the mourning crowd somehow denies its own ritually post-religious self-definition by turning a sacramental situation into a simulation. Applauding at funerals somehow strips death, the dead ones, and their bereft relatives of the reality of loss, pain, and mourning, ultimately making it impossible, for the crowd itself, to intimately and collectively realize the existential, ontological abyss that death entails. When a funeral becomes a show, it must perforce turn into an empty one, where the awareness of death and its ritual elaboration yield to an unresolved spectacularization of it.

Post-religious miracles

On June 18, 2016, a new installation by the famous Bulgarian artist Christo opened to the public. It consisted in a temporary floating pier connecting the village of Sulzano, on the Lake of Iseo, Italy, to Monte Isola, on the same lake, and then to a private island in the middle of it, San Paolo. The pier stayed open from June 18 until July 3. It was possible to walk on it both ways at any moment, gratuitously, and with no limits of capacity, treading on the eight-meter wide passage created at the center of the pier (whose total breadth was sixteen meters). The installation was composed of 200,000 high-density parallelepipeds of polyethylene, with a cave section of $50 \times 50 \times 40$ cm, joined together into hundred-meter long floating modules, anchored at hundred meters below the level of the lake through 150 anchors, weighing seven tons each. The total length of the floating pier was 4.5 kilometers, 1.5 on land and three on water. The pier was then closed, dismantled, and recycled on July 3, 2016. Christo, the artist, returning to Italy after a forty years' absence, at the inauguration declared, "I shall make you walk on water; you better come barefoot; it will be a walk during which you'll feel water under your feet".

The irony of an artist whose first name is "Christo" promising his audience that he will make them walk on water is too explicit to deserve detailed semiotic

FIGURE 6.6 Crowd visiting Christo's Floating Piers, Lake of Iseo, Italy, late June 2016; picture by the author

commentary. The incredible crowd that the installation attracted is, on the contrary, more interesting. Literally, tens of thousands of people queued for hours so as to be able to stroll on the placid waters of the lake of Iseo (Figure 6.6).

The brilliance of this aesthetic experiment cannot be the only reason for its enormous success. The fact that so many thousands of people undertook a long journey and stayed in line even longer so as to be admitted to the temporary installation deserves a more encompassing interpretation. In a post-religious society, people are starving for miracles. They are not longing necessarily for religious miracles, like the prodigious healings that one reads about in the Gospels, although those also play an important role in present-day societies, mostly among believers. Even people who claim their total extraneousness to religious belief in the so-called secular societies, however, are increasingly longing for aesthetic miracles, for being immersed in experiential and sensorial conditions that somehow snatch them from their usual semiotic habits and surround them with the sublime. When Christo invites thousands of barefoot citizens to walk on the surface of the Lake of Iseo, what he is granting them is not so much the experience of a religious miracle (that evidently is not one and is not presented as one, given the cold technical explanations that accompany the installation and the tongue-in-cheek way in which its creator alludes to the miraculous anecdote of Jesus's walking on water). Rather, Christo is somehow inserting himself in the empty framework left by the demise of traditional religious rituals in the secular society in order to turn the unbelievable narrative of Jesus's miraculous walking on waters into the subtext for the experience of a post-Christian, secular sublime. Those who flocked to the lake during the few days in which the installation stayed open were encouraged by the impermanence itself of the pier to do whatever they could not to miss the possibility to join a temporary, post-religious community in the collective experience of the sublime.

In this case too, a sophisticated market (but still a market) percolates into the empty gap of the passage from belief in the religious miracle to experience of the artistic sublime. Lonely Planet, as the website of the installation made sure to underline, had listed Christo's *Floating Piers* among the "ten top sights to visit in 2016". The trivial marketing of "top ten lists" mingles with the aesthetic ambitions of the artist so as to introduce the consumerist logic of mass tourism into the empty space of rituality described above. Tourists, the new pilgrims, poured into the cities around the lake, staying in local hotels, eating at local restaurants, accessing the installation gratuitously, exactly as the young women of Madrid were given for free the opportunity to join a multitudinous master class of yoga.

But do these events, these installations, and these applauses really come for free? Don't they come at the expense of a genuine formation of social bonds, replaced by temporary communities whose longing for significance and its collective perception is constantly hijacked by forms of capitalistic exploitation? Is a community possible outside of the religious sphere of ritual but also and simultaneously outside of the marketing placebos that promise to heal its loss in contemporary digital societies?

Conclusions

The present chapter has both a methodological and a thematic concern. First, it points out that, for as much sophisticated the linguistic analysis of a religious phenomenon can be, it can hardly be dissociated from a parallel semiotic scrutiny. In many religious cultures and events, verbal language plays the fundamental role of the "primary modeling system" of the spiritual and religious experience. Yet the isolated study of exclusively verbal structures would somehow miss the resonance between these patterns of signification and their specific nonverbal contexts. Pragmatics has developed extremely sophisticated tools and techniques so as to subtly dissect the contextual features of religious discourse, yet such features most commonly include elements that cannot be fully accounted for without reference to the semiological framework as devised by Saussure, Peirce, Lotman, Eco, and other founding fathers of the discipline. Verbal patterns of signification, for instance, are prominent in the three case studies analyzed above, in the way in which a multitudinous yoga master class is announced, in the way in which a burial is ritually performed, and in the way in which an installation is presented to its audience. Religious or spiritual undertones can be singled out through the linguistic analysis of these verbal texts. Yet, exactly because verbal language is the primary modeling system of most semiospheres, it is also the first one to be purged of any religious content or affectation when a culture undergoes a process of "secularization". Eliminating any religious reference from the legal constitution of a society, for instance, is a relatively easy task. What is more complicated, instead, is monitoring the presence of religious contents within signification patterns that are not as controllable as verbal language.[13] In other words, relics of past states of the same semiosphere often persist and linger incarnated in nonverbal structures of signification, which, nevertheless, constitute the context of verbal discourse and contribute to modify its meaning. The verbal language of a session of yoga might be stripped of any reference to spirituality and religion, yet the topology in which it takes place will continue to bear pre-secularization undertones. Similarly, a burial might well be conducted in a programmatically non-confessional manner, yet the attendees' urge to join in the gestural community of applause betrays a liturgical nostalgia. Finally, an artist's installation speech might well mock the religious undertext of his name and artwork, yet people visiting the installation will long for the experience of the collective sublime in a way that reminds one of the ecstatic rituals of demised religious collectivities.

This first methodological concern is intertwined with the second, thematic issue of the chapter. Incrementing the analytical power of the linguistics of verbal religious language through the adoption of the methodological framework of a semiotics of religious verbal *and* nonverbal languages allows the cultural analyst to realize that a peculiar dynamic takes place in the progressive secularization of a society. On the one hand, its primary modeling systems, verbal language being the foremost of them, are systematically aligned with the symbolical needs of a predominantly non-confessional and plural collectivity; on the other hand, though, the religious past of the secularized society persists in the symbolical and especially in the pragmatic efficacy of secondary modeling systems, such as space (the line, the square), gestures (the applause), and movement (the kinetics of Christo's art installation). It is precisely in this gap between intentional secularization of primary modeling systems and unintentional persistence of the religious or spiritual connotation of secondary modeling systems that external agencies can insert themselves in order to surreptitiously exploit the empty and mostly invisible sacramental framework that past religious states of the semiosphere have left behind in their secular demise, as a sort of invisible shell of communitarian life. Post-material capitalism takes advantage of these symbolical niches in order to bestow a quasi-religious yet inconspicuous force to its marketing strategies: We are sold clothes, yet we believe to join a community of superior wellness; we are sold a show, yet we believe to be overcoming death through the creation of instantaneous social bonds; we are sold a touristy destination, yet we believe to be walking together into the sublime. Semiotics is not necessarily against enchantment. It is against the alienation that inevitably stems from the marketing of enchantment. Only a scrupulous analysis of both verbal and nonverbal signs can uncover the lures of such pseudo re-enchantment in contemporary societies.

Notes

1 Ri, Normandy, Kingdom of France, November 14, 1601–Caen, August 19, 1680.
2 From this point of view, the event represents a marketing exploitation of that social configuration that post-Marxist authors thought to be destined to become the pivot of major social changes in capitalist societies; see Hardt and Negri (2004), which set this trend in political philosophy; see also, along the same line, Virno (2002).
3 Chandra Mohan Jain; Kuchwada Village, Bareli Tehsil, Raisen Dist., Bhopal State, British India (modern-day Madhya Pradesh, India) December 11, 1931–Pune, Maharashtra, India, January 19, 1990.
4 In Russian: Ю́рий Миха́йлович Ло́тман; Petrograd, current Saint Petersburg, February 28, 1922–Tartu, October 28, 1993.
5 Geneva, November 26, 1857–Vufflens-le-Château, Vaud, February 22, 1913.
6 On the anthropology of waiting, see Hage (2009); on the phenomenology of waiting, see Ebbighausen (2010); from a semantic and narrative point of view, see Benz (2013); see also Bompiani (1988) and Cariello (2014).
7 That is, in the terms of the semiotics developed by Franco-Lithuanian semiotician Algirdas J. Greimas (Tula, current Lithuania, March 9, 1917–Paris, February 27, 1992).
8 For a semiotic reading of inter-somaticity, see Landowski (2004).
9 For a semiotic reading of rhythm, see Ceriani (2000).
10 Literature on the anthropology of burials is huge. Classics include Ariès (1974) and (1977), Di Nola (1995a) and (1995b).
11 For an introduction to the concept of "vicarious religion" and a lucid analysis of the show funerals of Marco Simoncelli (Cattolica, Italy, January 20, 1987–Sepang, Malaysia, October 23, 2011), a famous motorcycle rider who tragically died during a motorcycle race in Malaysia, see Berzano (2012).
12 A classic study of the semiotics of the crowd is in Canetti (1960).
13 See Sullivan, Yelle, and Taussig-Rubbo (2011).

7

EATING INSIGNIFICANCE

Post-material meals

αἱ μὲν γὰρ τῶν ποθέντων ἢ βρωθέντων ἡδοναὶ
τὴν ἀνάμνησιν ἀνελεύθερον ἔχουσιν καὶ
ἄλλως ἐξίτηλον, ὥσπερ ὀσμὴν ἕωλον ἢ κνῖσαν
ἐναπολειπομένην [...].[1]
Plutarch, *Moralia*, 686c

Introduction

In 1973 Marco Ferreri's[2] movie *La grande abbuffata*, the four protagonists seclude themselves in a villa and eat themselves to death. Since its first screening at the Cannes Film Festival, the movie was interpreted as ferocious satire of consumerism (Mereghetti 2002: 942; Scandola 2004). Food was a metaphor for the meaningless routines of desire and gratification in late capitalism (Grande 1980; Gantrel 2002; Saponari 2008). But in the first decade of the twentieth century, spasmodic yearning for culinary pleasure has lost its metaphoric patina. It has become the direct embodiment of consumption. Immoderate passion for food is no longer the signifier of late capitalism. It is the signified (Ritzer 2001, 2013).

Even visionary director Marco Ferreri could have hardly foreseen the current cultural panorama in an economically advanced country like Italy: TV and radio channels are replete with programs where skillful chefs or clumsy starlets rattle off recipes (Chaw 2003; Krishnendu 2007; Urroz 2008); reality shows featuring masochistic self-styled cooks in competition and sadistic experts chastising them rank among the most seen broadcasts (Marrone 2013; Moutat 2013); increasingly lavish and preposterous cookbooks invade bookshops (Bower 2004; Ferguson 2012); everybody writes them: not only famous chefs but also actors, football players, and politicians; their sales are, indeed, spectacular; television chefs are venerated more than rock stars; their public appearance requires the deployment of security force; bookshop cafés turn into full restaurants and even sell refined groceries together with—and increasingly instead of—books; a movement called "Slow Food"—which advocates better quality nutrition—conquers first Italy, then the whole world; it turns into a philosophy of life, then into a religion; its founder, Carlo Petrini, is revered as a guru; pope Francis honors him by a personal phone call (Petrini 2003; Wilk 2006; Andrews 2008; Leitch 2009); Slow Food entrepreneur Oscar Farinetti establishes Slow Food grocery stores, called "Eataly", first in Italy, then all over the world; Slow Food opens its own university in Pollenzo, near Turin, attracting food scholars internationally; another trend, "Zero Kilometer"—championing local over global food—inspires a growing number of food producers, grocery stores, and restaurants; serious scholars, including reputed semioticians, write articles, essays, and books on food; scientific journals devote special issues; academic associations organize seminars and congresses; universities devote master programs; the 2015 Milan Universal Exposition chooses as its motto "Feeding the World".

Not only the public space is filled with the scent of food. In private places too, people talk about food; debate about food; describe what they ate, are eating, or will eat; plan to cook food; buy food; and consume food. Purchasing exquisite food; dining at exclusive restaurants; knowing the most elite groceries, the most cliquish street markets, and the most secretive recipes, eating better than other people do is the ultimate status symbol of the twenty-first century. Pictures of magnificent food are among the most common posts in social networks (Mcbride 2010).

This is a global trend in advanced economies. Cookbooks are as massive a success in Italy as in the USA, and in Canada as in Japan. Everywhere, young people of all genders feel morally obliged to retrieve their grandmothers' recipes, recuperate their ancestors' cooking tools from where their feminist mothers had abandoned them, and revel for hours in the preparation of archaic dishes, to be proudly served over the next feast (Holtzman 2006). The present-day obsession with food is particularly spectacular in Italy. A country internationally acclaimed as a source of gastronomic delight, Italy is more and more embracing the cause of spreading good-quality food around the world as a sort of religious mission and as the country's vocation (Kostioukovitch 2009). Preserving premier Italian food from heinous imitations; teaching "barbaric" countries with no food culture how to shop groceries, cook, and eat; waging ferocious battles against abominable fast food coming from abroad; and showing the world that Italy eats better than the rest of the planet, present-day Italy is espousing gastronomic evangelism to the extent that it becomes definitional: If you are Italian, you must eat truly well, and if you don't eat well, you are not a true Italian.

This trend might delight some cultural semioticians, their mouth watering at the fragrance of *tagliatelle* that pervades the Italian and the global semiosphere. Some cultural semioticians might even add to this tendency and draw profit from it, tailoring and selling their expertise to the food industry without asking themselves too many nasty questions (exactly as they did with the fashion industry in the 1980s and the advertising industry in the 1990s). If cultural semioticians aim at being not only gregarious gourmands, and not only nonchalant moneymakers, however, they must ask the simple question that underpins their profession: *What does it mean?* What does it mean when the global semiosphere gets increasingly heated with the frenzy of food? What does it mean when food becomes the main content that is sold and bought in the international cultural market? What does it mean, when Italy jollily accepts the role of "chef of the world", fashioning a great part of its public economy accordingly?

In Marco Ferreri's *La grande abbuffata*, reckless consumption of grotesquely elaborate food was a metaphor for the agony of desire in late capitalism. Today, that preposterous fixation with exquisite food has turned from allegory into reality. After exposing oneself even for a single day to the Italian plethora of signs, discourses, and texts that talk about food, one has the impression that *La grande abbuffata* is now. But what does it mean?

The aesthetic neutralization of social conflict

Jurij M. Lotman's semiotics models cultures as dynamic conglomerates of signs, discourses, and texts called "semiospheres" (1990). The topology of a semiosphere is never stable. External elements constantly press at its frontiers in order to be translated in. At the same time, fragments of signification struggle inside the semiosphere to gain predominance in cultural memory and topological centrality. As new elements are translated into the semiosphere, old ones lose the battle for hegemony. They are marginalized, forgotten, and expelled. Ultimately, the frontier of a semiosphere can be determined only as hypothesis, depending on the point of view the analyst adopts on a culture (Lotman 1985; Leone 2007).

As there is no static semiosphere—safe in the theoretical figment of the analyst—there is no culture without a deontic dimension (Greimas and Courtés 1979, *sub voce* "deontic"). In every semiosphere, a particular category of texts suggests, indicates, or even prescribes what human beings *should* do. Be these texts written or oral or in other forms of expression, they dictate ways for existential improvement. They crystallize dynamic paths of agency within the semiosphere (Leone 2009a). Religious traditions revolve around these texts (Leone 2013a, Part X: "Teleologies of Religious Meaning"). Prompts to change and to gain value in life either as individuals or in collectivity, however, feature as well in philosophical disquisitions, political manifestos, and psychological treatises.

In premodern semiospheres, only philosophy and the arts would dispute religion as the main deontic agency advocating existential change. But philosophers and artists would mostly address the individual, whereas collective teleology was characteristically the core of the religious discourse. With modernity, revolutionary ideologies and psychoanalysis increasingly replaced religion, as well as philosophy and the arts, as the prevailing deontic discourses. In late modernity, however, three main trends supplanted the political and Freudian secularization of the deontic dimension: new age spirituality as bland de-secularization of ethics (Leone 2014d *Spiritualità*), medical science as quantitative standard of individual improvement, and aesthetics as the domain where social value can be gained and lost.

Every deontic discourse entails a foe. In premodern semiospheres, the foe of religion was metaphysical evil. It could be defeated only through collaboration between humans and gods. In modern semiospheres, the villain was not transcendent but immanent: In order to enfranchise themselves, humans should not defeat evil metaphysical agents but other evil human beings. In Marx, the deontic discourse prescribed liberation from an enslaving class and in Freud, from a tyrannizing superego. In late modernity, finally, humans fight neither against bad gods nor against bad humans. They struggle against bad taste (Lipovetsky and Serroy 2013). The present-day frenzy for eschatological food too rests on a deontic text, the "Manifesto for the Defense of- and Right to-Pleasure", that delegates from around the world signed on December 21, 1989 at the Opéra-Comique theater in Paris. It was the symbolical beginning of Slow Food. Here goes the manifesto in its entirety:

> Questo nostro secolo, nato e cresciuto sotto il segno della civiltà industriale, ha prima inventato la macchina e poi ne ha fatto il proprio modello di vita.
>
> La velocità è diventata la nostra catena, tutti siamo in preda allo stesso virus: la vita veloce, che sconvolge le nostre abitudini, ci assale fin nelle nostre case, ci rinchiude a nutrirci nei fast food.
>
> Ma l'uomo sapiens deve recuperare la sua saggezza e liberarsi dalla velocità che può ridurlo a una specie in via d'estinzione.
>
> Perciò, contro la follia universale della "fast life", bisogna scegliere la difesa del tranquillo piacere materiale.
>
> Contro coloro, e sono i più, che confondono l'efficienza con la frenesia, proponiamo il vaccino di un'adeguata porzione di piaceri sensuali assicurati, da praticarsi in lento e prolungato godimento.
>
> Iniziamo proprio a tavola con lo Slow Food, contro l'appiattimento del fast food riscopriamo la ricchezza e gli aromi delle cucine locali.
>
> Se la "fast life" in nome della produttività ha modificato la nostra vita e minaccia l'ambiente e il paesaggio, lo Slow Food è oggi la risposta d'avanguardia.
>
> È qui, nello sviluppo del gusto e non nel suo immiserimento, la vera cultura, di qui può iniziare il progresso, con lo scambio internazionale di storie, conoscenze, progetti. Lo Slow Food assicura un avvenire migliore.
>
> Lo Slow Food è un'idea che ha bisogno di molti sostenitori qualificati, per fare diventare questo moto (lento) un movimento internazionale, di cui la chiocciolina è il simbolo.

> [This century of ours, born and raised in the name of the industrial civilization, first invented the machine, then turned it into its model of life.
>
> Fastness has become our chain, we are all prey to the same virus: fast life, which upsets our habits, assails us even at home, make us eating secluded in fast food restaurants.
>
> But *Homo sapiens* must recuperate their wisdom and free themselves from speed, which can reduce them to an endangered species.

Therefore, against the universal madness of "fast life", one must choose the defense of tranquil material pleasures.

Against those—and they are majority—who mistake efficiency for frenzy, we propose the vaccine of an adequate portion of guaranteed sensual pleasures, to be practiced in slow and prolonged enjoyment.

Let's start at table with Slow Food, against the trivialization of fast food let's rediscover the richness and the aromas of local food.

If "fast life", in the name of productivity, has modified our life and threatens the environment and its landscapes, Slow Food is, today, an avant-garde reply.

True culture is here, in the development of taste and not in its impoverishment; progress can start from here, with the international exchange of stories, knowledge, projects. Slow Food guarantees a better future.

Slow Food is an idea that needs many qualified supporters, in order for this (slow) initiative to become an international movement, whose symbol is the little snail.][3]

Previous deontic semiospheres would have waged their battle against evil food through different texts. They would have identified alternative villains. In the premodern deontic dimension, the religious discourse would have enjoined: "Thou shall not eat from the tree of McDonald's!" Then, exegesis would have clarified that fast food is the terrestrial embodiment of an evil metaphysical force, which feuds with the good divinity over influence on the humankind. Whoever eats from the prohibited tree magnifies the strength of the transcendent foe, while whoever abstains from it adds to the cause of heaven (Röbkes 2013). In the modern, secularized discourse of collective and individual ideology, immanent agencies would have replaced transcendent emissaries. The Freudian mindset would have contended: If you eat fast, you are actually titillating your oral libido. Through a frantic rhythm of ingestion, you seek to compensate your underdeveloped sexuality. You counter the anxiety through which your superego encroaches upon the thought of your ineluctable perishing (Bersani 2006). The Marxian theory would have focused not on psychical but on social structures. Fast Food embodies the exploitation of a socioeconomic class. Abominable food and frenetic consumption are nothing but a travesty. Deprivation of time for physiological needs and infected nourishment are symptoms of a socioeconomic structure where the workforce is fed only for the sake of its reproduction. Marketing is the hegemonic agency that bestows a patina of desirability upon junk food, as Gramscian exegesis would have appended (Albritton 2009).

Albeit very different from each other, these three deontic approaches would share a common quality (Ricoeur 1965). They would all frame food not as evil but as an expression of evil. Moreover, they would all situate the (metaphysical, subconscious, or socioeconomic) wicked agency behind fast food outside the subject's reach. Counterstrategy would have been fashioned accordingly: praying the good divinity for protection against evil food, taming the unconscious through psychoanalytical dialogue, and subverting the socioeconomic structure that impinges on the nutrition of proletarians.

The incipit of Slow Food's manifesto is reminiscent of Marx (most of the delegates would come from leftist experiences): "this century of ours, born and grown in the name of the industrial civilization…". However, no external agency is denounced therein. The industrial civilization does not grow out of thirst for profit but, impersonally, from "this century of ours" (Peace 2006, 2008). The dimming of any specific agency through the evocation of impersonal collectivity continues further: "Fastness has become *our* chain, we are *all* prey to the same virus". In the post-Marxist discourse of Slow Food, what inflicts dementedness to human behaviors is not a wrongful spirit, a repressed libido, or an oppressed social class; it is a metaphoric, generic virus that infects all, no distinctions made. "Fast life […] that assails us even at home": Again, fastness is treated not as a symptom but as autonomous agent that attacks "our" lives independently from whom we are. Fastness itself is the foe of Slow Food's narrative (Osbaldiston 2013). Since there is no external agent behind fast food, betterment of life does not require either the cosmic triumph of the good divinity over the crooked one or deliverance from the tyrannous superego or, God forbid, a revolution that would dethrone the exploitative class. If fast food is the foe, then let's start eating slowly, and everything will be OK.

Since the inception of Slow Food, and more and more with its becoming a global ideology, we have, indeed, sought to eat slow. Not everything, however, is now OK. Why? Did Slow Food overlook an ingredient of the salvific recipe? The date on which Slow Food released its manifesto cannot be left unnoticed: December 21, 1989. The Berlin Wall had started its inexorable fall on November 9. Materially and symbolically marking the end of a terrible seclusion and the epilogue of an era, the Brandenburg Gate was open the day after the manifesto was read at the Parisian *Opéra-Comique*. Is it malicious to discern in the onset of Slow Food the swift reaction of a group of leftist intellectuals to the disruption of an ideological epoch? Answering this question would demand an in-depth study of the manifesto's ideological history and context. But most historians and sociologists have been so busy with subscribing to the Slow Food declaration that little energy has been devoted to its critical assessment. The suspect remains that Slow Food and its manifesto partake of a *Weltanschauung* whose genesis coincided with the downfall of the regimes inspired to Marxism. In the geopolitical circumstances of the late 1980s and early 1990s, any discourse advocating the advancement of the humankind through the radical transformation of socioeconomic structures would sound as inexcusably nostalgic. Leftist ideologues did not abandon the messianic idea of deliverance but turned it into what Marxism would have called a "superstructural" mission: In order to free the world, let's not dismantle the capitalistic engine of fast food; rather, let's slow down food: Aesthetic, sensorial revolution will change humanity for the better (Paxson 2005).

Was that the more or less conscious, disillusioned desertion of a failed ideology? Or was it an attempt at making it survive under aesthetic cover? What is certain is that Slow Food has not changed the humankind. It has certainly contributed to spread awareness about the need of protecting and fostering the production and consumption of healthy and sustainable food. We are aware of the aesthetic relevance of *culatello* as never before. However, aesthetic enhancement has not affected the socioeconomic structure of fast food to the least. For most, *culatello* remains terribly expensive (Simonetti 2010).· A small socioeconomic elite around the world can rejoice about existentially upgrading through the unrushed consumption of refined dishes. But for most people in advanced economies—and increasingly so with the lingering of the economic crisis—fast, cheap, unhealthy, unfair, and unsustainable food is still the answer. Teaching them how good *culatello* is will not suffice, if they do not have money to buy it, and time and space to consume it. Not to speak of the so many that, in the world, starve. For them, the relative speed of food consumption is a secondary problem given that there is hardly any food to be consumed.

Slow Food fans will contend that changing the world was not among its objectives. But again, is it malignant to suspect that aesthetic messianism is actually proving a formidable source of false consciousness (Schneider 2008)? Slow Food grocery stores, *Eataly*, are spread throughout the world like McDonalds, advertise like McDonalds, and hire and employ workers like McDonalds. Are they "using the weapons of the enemy" in order to change the world for the better, as *Eataly* supporters claim (Marrone 2011)? Or, more realistically, are they koshering the socioeconomic unbalances of capitalism through a patina of aesthetic evangelism? Is it being terribly démodé, asking how the delicious, slowly consumed cake will be shared?

The marketing of stereotypes

Cultures devote much energy to define their limits. Lotman's theoretical model, the semiosphere, captures the effort topologically. On the one hand, complex transduction systems determine what signs, discourses, and texts are meaningful in a culture. On the other hand, tensions pervade the semiosphere both internally and at its borders. It is a struggle for identity, authenticity, and belonging (Leone 2012a, 2012b). National cultures are particularly prone to the anxious (re)definition of the authentic, in contrast to the spurious. In the process, shibboleths are constantly created (Leone 2009b). From the semiotic point of view, a shibboleth is a distinctive feature whose perceived presence/absence decides the inclusion/exclusion of a cultural element in/out of a semiosphere. Comparison of a token with a type is the simple semiotic mechanism through which shibboleths work. Does the token match the type? Then it is in. If it does not match, then it is out.

Biases, however, affect the comparison as well as the setting of the type itself. Who decides what is typical in a culture? Who presides over authenticity? Who declares belongingness? Majorities and minorities take ephemeral shape around shibboleths. But semiospheres rarely are democratic. Instead, their topology is irregular, erratic, and even chaotic. Polycentric agencies exert their power so as to influence inclusion and exclusion (Leone 2012c). In nationalisms, political agency and its discourse dictate cultural seams. It is a violent, painful process. It frequently involves not only stigmatization of alien signs but also ostracism of bodies. Those whose meaning is judged as inauthentic are marginalized, cast off. The brutality of it is all the more perplexing, since it has no factual ground. From the semiotic perspective, shibboleths are nothing but habitus. They crystallize discursive lines of acceptance and hostility. That which they decide to exclude, they might as well include, and vice versa. Every community is imaginary. But the rhetoric of authenticity can be so pervasive as to give rise to a second nature. Shibboleths turn from cultural to naturalized thresholds (Leone 2010a). Nevertheless, what rhetoric has done, rhetoric can undo. The most important task of the cultural semiotician is showing how both necessary and illusory every culture is: The semiotician must be a maverick, even a contrarian, and take on the nasty duty of breaking the violent enchantment of culture while certifying the inescapability of language.

In no dimension of existence cultures include and exclude more drastically as in sensorial perception (Stoller 1997). They enjoin individuals to immediately categorize as familiar or alien what they see, hear, smell, touch, and taste (Wise and Velayutham 2009). Cultures exert their secluding agency also in the arena of food. Bio-politically, what is more effective than linking the idea of a community to what is ingested and turned into body? Religion founders sense it immediately: Change the way in which a group of people eat, what they consider as licit or illicit food, and you'll have ipso facto a community (Freidenreich 2011). Dietary rules delineate a religious semiosphere more incisively than verbal commandments. But food turns into shibboleth also when defining "secular" identities: the nation, the region, the city, and the family (Hayes-Conroy and Martin 2010).

Whereas Slow Food has turned the temporality of eating into the criterion of a new community (eat fast, you are out; eat slow, you are in) (Meneley 2004), another major trend of both the Italian and the global culinary semiosphere is focusing on the spatiality of food: Zero Kilometer (*Chilometro Zero*). Slow Food extols the value of slowness over fastness. Zero Kilometer praises proximity over distance. Its environmentalist undertone is evident: If you eat tomatoes that come from your Italian village, instead of those from Morocco, the earth will be spared the pollution caused by useless transportation. But the semiotician's thankless job includes the duty to insinuate that the environmentalist discourse too, for as much unconditionally praiseworthy as it might seem, features multiple ideological nuances. Zero Kilometer dictates to Italian consumers not only that they should prefer local to Moroccan tomatoes but also that they should give up exotic pineapples over familiar apples. Desire to protect the environment from polluting transportation should weigh more than craving for distant pleasures. Zero Kilometer affects grocery shops as well as restaurants. If you eat in a Zero Kilometer *trattoria*, forget about papaya salads: What does not grow in your town's orchard is banned.

Again, faced with this new phenomenon, semioticians should ask their professional question: What does it mean? What does it mean when a community increasingly finds that curiosity for exotic cultures is not worthy of its environmental costs and when proximity is praised over distance, and what is closer to the imaginary center of the community, ideally at "zero kilometers" from it, ipso facto becomes more desirable? The semiotician's malicious suspect is that a marketing of stereotypes underpins the extolment of proximity. It is both political and economic marketing. Zero Kilometer, as well as Slow Food, can be categorized together with the countless trends that flourished around the world at the turn of the millennium, reacting to a supposed globalization of economy, society, and culture. In Lotman's terms, no-global movements consist in the rhetorical attempt at disrupting the idea of a supranational semiosphere. Its frontiers, it is contended, are "unnatural", generated by pernicious agents like the global financial power. In order to counter them, a new discourse should reveal the "naturalness" of smaller, more local semiospheres. Global financial power induces consumers to desire pineapples so that the profit of few is accumulated through exploitation of distant lands and pollution of the environment. Giving up faraway pineapples for closer apples will change the world for the better.

But the deontic message of Zero Kilometer is disputable. Insistence on the environmental noxiousness of overcoming distance is strengthening the cultural habitus of proximity. What is close is good; what is far is bad. Whatever brings distant cultures in closer contact is frowned upon, especially if it entails environment costs. The strenuous battle waged in Italy against the construction of new fast train lines ("No TAV" movement in Piedmont) or new gas pipelines ("No TAP" movement in Apulia) share with Zero Kilometer the idea that sociocultural proximity must be defended over distance and that sustainable virtual connection with remote lands should replace polluting physical binding. But is this replacement of physical through virtual globalism really coming at no cost? And are its benefits as evenly distributed as it is purported?

From the political point of view, Zero Kilometer is dangerously germane to chauvinism; it is its environmentally friendly face. From the economic point of view, its action is not immune from the agency of lobbies. Political populism has hijacked socioeconomic hostility toward the discontents of globalization in Italy as well as in other advanced economies. The demagogic rhetoric of no-global populisms has often resulted in overt xenophobia, with alien food among its targets (Ott 2012). Regional secessionist parties in Italy invented the atavistic primate of local food and recipes while stigmatizing the invasion of food from abroad. Kebab—seen as the gastronomic epitome of the Arab culture—as well as Chinese restaurants turned into enemy number one and two. Top administrators in cosmopolitan Milan promulgated laws against the consumption of kebab in the streets of the metropolis (but were jailed for corruption a few years later); mayors in Tuscany prohibited the display of red lanterns outside the premises of Chinese restaurants; others imposed the presence of local ingredients in restaurants' menus. People have continued consuming tons of kebabs in the streets of Milan, red lanterns made their reappearance soon after they were removed, and Tuscan restaurants kept offering their costumers what their chefs pleased.

But where chauvinism and overt xenophobia failed, the environmental discourse succeeded. Zero Kilometer supporters sincerely care about the environment: That is not the point. The point is that their rhetoric of proximity inevitably leagues with populist localisms. Consumers find it more acceptable to value what is local over what is global and what is closer over what is distant, under the umbrella of an ideology labeled as environmental friendly. They fail to recognize that commerce with distant lands has been for millennia not only one of the greatest sources of profit but also one of the best antidotes to war. Until there is commercial trade between two cultures, there is no war, and vice versa. Certainly, the terms and modalities of trade can be adjusted so as to minimize human exploitation and environment impact. But the idea of a society that consumes only what it produces is not only utopian but dangerous. Echoing the autarchy of twentieth-century regimes, it embodies the dream of a culinary gated community (Modigliani 2007; Leone 2009c). Eating the food of the other, although it might entail some environmental externalities, is a fundamental ritual of peace (Rose 2011).

Zero Kilometer is not economically unbiased either. While grocery stores and restaurants in Italy rhapsodize over the excellence of local food, parallel agencies wage a planetary battle against "the culinary fake" (Stagliano 2006; Doll 2012; Mueller 2012). How do Canadian cheese producers dare call it "Parmesan" and sell it under "Italian-sounding" brands? Only Parmesan cheese produced in Italy should bear this name and be commercialized accordingly. The issue is enticing for semiotics, the discipline that studies everything that can be used to lie (Eco 1976, 1987; Scalabroni 2011). What is "true" Parmesan? What is fake? From the semiotic point of view, no Parmesan is ontologically true (Eco 1987). Rather, complex rhetorics circulate in the global semiosphere so that "communities of belief" take shape apropos the authenticity of food.

Cultural elements deemed to be "unique" and "irreplaceable" often occupy the core of a semiosphere. Much symbolical energy is spent to continuously reproduce this idea of uniqueness. Value indeed stems from it, and the possibility of a hierarchical topology from value. A culture in which nothing is unique, and everything can be reproduced, is without center and therefore without sacredness. The arts play a fundamental role in guaranteeing the uniqueness of value in semiospheres. Artistic signs still substantiate the bulk of a culture's heritage, pace Walter Benjamin's contention on the cultural disease of their technical reproduction in the modern era (1936) and despite the pernicious encroachment of the market on the aesthetic sphere (Berger 1972). The frontiers of a culture's heritage define whom and what is entitled to inhabit the center of a semiosphere. Signs, discourses, and texts that are situated in such center are, by definition, priceless: No effort will be spared to trade their faithful memory to the future.

Yet no cultural heritage, for as much as it is defended, is immune from change and falsification. Everything that is cultural can be falsified; and everything that is falsifiable is culture. *Mona Lisa* irradiates its symbolical aura from the center of the Louvre, which is in the center of Paris, which is in the center of France, which once was in the center of the Western world. But as the geopolitical center of the world moves elsewhere, it is not unthinkable that *Mona Lisa* will one day move as well, not only geographically but also symbolically. Its capacity of defining one of the pillars of French culture, the absorption of Renaissance in Northern Europe, might diminish and perish. The world might one day venerate *Mona Lisa* in Dubai or in Shanghai; or, more realistically, a wall scroll painted by Ma Lin will replace *Mona Lisa* as the global embodiment of artistic sacredness.

Not only external agents erode the central patrimony of a semiosphere. The idea of uniqueness dissolves also internally, through falsification, parody, and trivialization. In premodernity, attempts at falsification would attack the aura of *Mona Lisa*; in the modern era, Duchamp's parody jeopardized the centrality of the painting in the world's cultural heritage; in the postmodern era, neither falsification nor irony is any longer needed to deface Leonardo's portrait. Countless mechanical reproductions undermine its value. *Mona Lisa* is everywhere—on cups, aprons, T-shirts, toilet paper—and therefore is nowhere. It is certainly no longer symbolically in the Louvre, at the center of the European Empire's museum.

Internal strives to corroborate or falsify the heritage of a culture pervade all semiospheres. On the one hand, titanic efforts are made to still-frame as many cultural elements as possible on an immutable Mount Olympus. It is the tendency of nationalistic mindsets, according to which everything, from language to history, from the arts to fashion, must be canonized. Several European nations have long sought to immortalize their culture—and particularly their primary modeling system, verbal language—through the institutions of academies (*Académie française* in France, *Accademia della Crusca* in Italy, *Real Académia de la Lengua* in Spain). Yet attempts at entrenching language into unchanging heritage have systematically failed.

On the other hand, indeed, feeble vibrations or telluric movements constantly destabilize the semiospheres, pulling old signs out of a culture's heritage, pushing new signs into it. The invention of "world heritage" and the establishment of an international cultural bureaucracy seek to centralize and stabilize the global definition of value. Yet students of UNESCO procedures know that its acts result from the convergence of national pressures and socioeconomic lobbies. Again, power stems from the ability of certifying value, from placing new *Mona Lisas* into novel sancta sanctorum (Leone, Dinamiche dell'innovazione culturale: patrimonio e matrimonio [forthcoming]). UNESCO increasingly places food in its lists of intangible cultural heritage. Local agencies enact the same practice in relation to specific products. Italian labels and institutions were established in order to attest the veracity of Italian wine, cheese, and Slow Food. Their the purpose is simultaneously symbolical and economic: Exclusivity generates value both politically—as the fundament of a community's identity—and economically—as an entity that can be exported and sold. International trade is the result of mutual recognition among semiospheres. Money is the measure of the extent to which a culture's rhetoric is successful. The reason for which French consumers are not ready to pay for Moroccan wine what they pay for Italian wine is not ontological. It does not rest on the chemistry of wine. It is rather semiotic: Italy's rhetoric successfully places "its" wine at the center of the global semiosphere, in competition with France and few other nations. Much of the economic success of Italy in the aftermath of WWII pivoted on the ability to persuade the world about the value of drinking, eating, driving, and especially wearing cultural elements stemming from the imaginary core of the Italian semiosphere.

Yet the creation of value systematically backfires under the form of kitsch. Parasitic reproductions daily abrade *Mona Lisa*'s aura as the symbolical center of French aesthetics. Similarly, cultural falsification forgery constantly attempts at the value of intangible heritage no matter how intensely protected. But different signs show various degrees of resistance to falsification. Everything that means can be falsified but not with the same easiness. Falsifying *Mona Lisa* would require exceptional skills. This is why *Mona Lisa* is at the core of the European semiosphere. Placing this painting at the heart of its most prestigious museum, Europe celebrates the glow of authenticity that emanates from it. Looking at *Mona Lisa*, despite the copies, the parodies, and the kitsch, reassures the viewer about the stability of culture. As long as *Mona Lisa* is in the Louvre—thus goes the illusion—the gods will not migrate from Paris to Dubai (or from the first arrondissement to the suburbs).

But does a wheel of Parmesan cheese show the same degree of resistance to falsification as *Mona Lisa*? Despite all the efforts of specialists, bureaucracies, and institutions; despite the invention of labels, seals, and certificates; and despite even the establishment of special "private detectives" who roam the world looking for fakes to chastise, a wheel of Parmesan cheese results from technique, not from genius. It is craft, not art. Whereas technical reproduction imperils *Mona Lisa*'s aura, a form of Parmesan cheese has never had any aura because not only its reproduction but also its production is mechanic. Take some milk, salt, and rennet; apply the right technique, and *voilà!* A falsifier might well have access to Leonardo's pigments but not to Leonardo's technique, because no technique is sufficient to falsify *Mona Lisa*. This is the ultimate paradox of semiospheres: They attribute utmost value and topological centrality to signs whose signifier cannot be reproduced but only represented. We venerate and represent *Mona Lisa* because we cannot reproduce Leonardo.

On the other hand, current attempts at bestowing an aura of uniqueness to local food are preposterous and, to a certain extent, pathetic. Moved by economic interests and identity anxiety, they often resort to rhetorical invention of the territory and its tradition: Only cows from Reggio Emilia that eat local grass and breathe local air can produce the milk indispensable to "create" authentic Parmesan cheese (Greene 2008). Bureaucratic efforts to protect the authenticity of food, however, are doomed to fail more ruinously than royal attempts at canonizing languages. The authenticity of food cannot be certified because, put bluntly, there is no such thing as authentic food. There is an authentic Leonardo—not immune from episodes of falsification—but not authentic Parmesan cheese. Not only is the latter much easier to imitate than the former—despite the mystique of Italian cows—but it also answers to a completely different logic of recognition. A Canadian lady who has bought a copy of *Mona Lisa* on her honeymoon to Paris might well believe that what hangs over her fireplace in Toronto is the original painted by Leonardo, whereas that in Louvre is a fake. The rest of the world will be ready to contradict her. But what about the "fake"

Parmesan cheese that she keeps in her fridge, thinking that it is authentic Italian Parmesan cheese? Reggio Emilia detectives might well try to persuade her of the contrary, but they will have to persuade as well the millions of Canadians who believe exactly the same. Since food can be produced mechanically, beliefs about its authenticity are a matter of rhetoric, not of ontology.

This is another paradox of semiospheres: What defines the sancta sanctorum of cultures cannot be reproduced; moreover, it cannot be sold either; its value is definitional but not economic. Pictures, reproductions, and glimpses of *Mona Lisa* can be sold, not *Mona Lisa* itself. Its cultural centrality is such that cannot be turned into exportable meaning. When a society thinks of selling the core of its cultural heritage, as the Greeks envisaged selling the Parthenon during the recent economic crisis, that is the beginning of its end as a cultural semiosphere. On the other hand, what of a cultural heritage can be sold *must be* inauthentic.

The current attempt at selling food as ultimate aesthetic experience is giving rise to a preposterous discourse of uniqueness, with a chauvinistic undertone. Technically reproducible goods are bestowed an aura of sacredness to be sold and bought as quintessential expressions of cultures. Yet since the quintessence of cultures has no price, stereotypes and their entrenched discourse of marketing populate more and more the core of semiospheres. Champagne and its Heideggerian relation to *terroir* is purported to embody the French Weltanschauung as intimately as Poussin's *Seven Sacraments*. No matter if an exact copy of an eighteenth-century castle towers over the Taittinger estate in California and no matter if the sparkling wine that is produced there is chemically identical to that produced in France, the former is just "sparkling wine", the second true Champagne, for Californian bubbles lack inmost relation to the French *genius loci*.

Semiotically, food producers' titanic efforts to lay claim of authenticity strive to impose an *intentio auctoris*. The intrinsic quality of food and its aesthetic reception do not count. What matters is only the ritual baptism of the product. Brands are given semantic status of proper names. They are attributed a signature. But faking the logo of the Italian label for the protection of authentic wine (DOC or DOCG) is not the same as faking Leonardo's signature on *Mona Lisa*. It is rather like faking the logo of Adidas on a pair of shoes (Crăciun 2013). Leonardo's signature is an index that means the presence, in time and space, of a unique, irreproducible hand, able to create *Mona Lisa ex nihilo*. Brands' signatures are not indexes but symbols, conventional statements about the authenticity of the relation to their producer/product. The former, *Mona Lisa*, signifies because there cannot be any more instances of it; it is a token whose type does not survive the body that has produced it. The latter, the Adidas logo, signifies because there can be infinite instances of it; it is a sign with no connection to life, despite the rhetoric efforts to turn it into archetypical expression. A logo is no archetype. It is a stereotype. A perfect reproduction of a signature that is not an index of its body is a fake. A perfect reproduction of a logo that is not a symbol of its brand is not a fake of the same kind. It becomes a fake signature only by virtue of an enchanting discourse of naturalization, as if a company were a body able to sign its products one by one.

Food rhetoric of proximity invents shibboleths whose content is not only environmental sustainability but also signifies political identity under aesthetic travesty. Economic agencies behind it are evident: They seek to create and sell value. Yet food is not art; it is technique. Technically produced shibboleths are paradoxical. On the one hand, they must preserve the indexical sacredness of authenticity, the signature. On the other hand, they must indefinitely reproduce that signature in order to sell it. As a consequence, they fill the core of semiospheres with stereotypes of authenticity, whose populist mindset is only a by-product of marketing. "Not in my plate" becomes just another expression of "not in my backyard".

The subversion of sensorial hierarchy

Semiospheres hierarchically arrange not only signs, discourses, and texts but also the senses. Religious cultures have fought for centuries over which senses should better receive the sacred: through the ears only (*ex auditu fides*) or through images as well (Leone 2010c *The Sacred*). They have crossed swords also over the place of taste in human existence. Complex systems of fasting characterize almost all religious cultures, whose bio-political control of communities stems from determining not only what but also whether they eat and when (Leone 2013a *Digiunare*). "Secular" semiospheres vary too, both historically and contextually, as regards their ways of ranking taste in relation to the other senses.

The Greco-Roman culture would often include contempt for food among its criteria of philosophical excellence. Unrestrained talking about food was particularly stigmatized as a sign of a poor spirit. Thus, Theophrastus,[4] the successor of Aristotle in the Peripatetic school, in *The Characters of Men* (3) ironizes over the garrulous men who "tell[s] dish by dish what he had for supper" (Loeb translation). Plutarch[5] in the *Moralia* (686 c–d) pillories the irrelevance of food as topic of philosophical discourse:

> To reminisce about eating and drinking, the sorts of pleasures that are as fleeting as yesterday's perfume or the lingering smell of cooking, is not the mark of a free-born man: only the delights of philosophical discussion will remain perennially fresh, feasts that be enjoyed again and again. If pleasure were only a physical thing, Xenophon and Plato would have left a record in their Symposia not of the conversation, but of the relishes, cakes, and sweets served at Callias and Agathon's houses.

No Latin author better than Petronius,[6] however, poured scorn on the intellectual vacuity of the man who prattles on about food. The venomous passage from *Satyricon* (66) deserves a long quotation:

> "But," demanded Trimalchio, "what did you have for dinner?" "I'll tell you if I can," answered he, "for my memory's so good that I often forget

my own name. Let's see, for the first course, we had a hog, crowned with a wine cup and garnished with cheese cakes and chicken livers cooked well done, beets, of course, and whole-wheat bread, which I'd rather have than white, because it puts strength into you, and when I take a crap afterwards, I don't have to yell. Following this, came a course of tarts, served cold, with excellent Spanish wine poured over warm honey; I ate several of the tarts and got the honey all over myself. Then there were chick-peas and lupines, all the smooth-shelled nuts you wanted, and an apple apiece, but I got away with two, and here they are, tied up in my napkin; for I'll have a row on my hands if I don't bring some kind of a present home to my favorite slave. Oh yes, my wife has just reminded me, there was a haunch of bear-meat as a side dish, Scintilla ate some of it without knowing what it was, and she nearly puked up her guts when she found out. But as for me, I ate more than a pound of it, for it tasted exactly like wild boar and, says I, if a bear eats a man, shouldn't that be all the more reason for a man to eat a bear? The last course was soft cheese, new wine boiled thick, a snail apiece, a helping of tripe, liver pate, capped eggs, turnips and mustard. But that's enough. Pickled olives were handed around in a wooden bowl, and some of the party greedily snatched three handfuls, we had ham, too, but we sent it back.

Even more peremptorily, Stoicism epitomized the classical disdain not only for food talk but also for food itself in Epictetus's[7] words:

> It is a sign of a stupid man to spend a great deal of time on the concerns of his body — exercise, eating, drinking, evacuating his bowels, and copulating. These things should be done in passing; you should devote your whole attention to the mind.
>
> *(Enchiridion 41)*

The imperative to neglect the body and exclusively concentrate on the mind reflected the Stoic mindset. Present-day commentators might be relieved that modernity has rejected the separation between the mind and the body. Feuerbach's materialism even dignified food as substance of the spirit. Yet one thing is acknowledging the continuity between what we eat and what we think, and the other thing is wallowing in a semiosphere where all we think about is food. All we talk about is food. Exploring the public as well as the private Italian arena, one garners evidence that obsession for food, typical of this culture, has reached unprecedented levels. Institutions, media, and people are not alone in focusing on food. Food is becoming the primary modeling system of the Italian semiosphere as a whole. Italy is turning, in its self-awareness and image abroad, into the land of "good food". In the hierarchical topology of senses, taste attains prominence and comes to be the measure of all other senses and experiences. Again, semioticians face their professional question: "What does it mean?" What does it mean when a culture identifies so convincingly not with its literature, arts, music, and philosophy but with its food? Why has the profession of chef become the most coveted by young Italians?

There is no simple answer to these questions. The "aesthetic immediacy" of taste plays a significant role. In a semiosphere that more and more rejects, in the name of pragmatism, any mediation as well as any complex system of judgment, food is the sensorial frame that perfectly embodies the anti-intellectualism of the current Italian society. Of course, great skills and a long training are necessary to become a "master chef"; yet in the popular imagination, turning into a kitchen virtuoso follows a different path as becoming a reputed surgeon. The chef's training, it is believed, rests on innate talent, socially diffused competences, and apprenticeship through imitation. It is a training that, like that of singers or soccer players, is not burdened with verbally encoded knowledge and a formal, bureaucratic control of learning. It is not the institution that will judge who is a great chef but its audience.

This is the second element of food that appeals the present-day popular culture. Food is not only popular but also populist. In the contemporary imagination, the culinary experience entails an aesthetic judgment that is both Manichean and unconstrained by complex forms of evaluation. I like, I dislike: Food turns into the material version of Facebook aesthetics, where the sensorial immediacy of ingestion sweeps away any need to verbalize complex nuances. Words are important in the culinary world but are ancillary. They struggle to present food but must stay in the background. The unfathomable smell of the kitchen takes the foreground and lingers well after words have lost their meaning. In a semiosphere so inclined to dismiss the value of words and articulation, food therefore evolves into the perfect metaphor of aesthetic naturalness: One becomes a great chef through developing natural talent; one receives the pleasure of great food through simply ingesting it.

But what is problematic about that, in the end? After all, the apprenticeship of painters is similar to that of chefs, and the nonverbal rhetoric of judgment in the arts is germane to that of food: Artworks captivate us beyond words. Although many ultramodern voices have flagged as snob conservatism the intellectual resistance to include food among the arts, it is, however, evident that food is not painting. Painting has no recipes, and its artworks are not consumed by aesthetic reception. Is therefore the art of food more similar to that of music? It is, but with the fundamental difference that in music we certainly value execution, but we value composition much more. There would be no Celibidache without Beethoven. But who first composed the "carbonara"? Despite all the ennobling efforts of the present-day media, the art of food is not art but craft. As a consequence, a semiosphere that is engrossed in food will not display the same semiotic features as a semiosphere for which music or painting or literature is the central activity. By relishing food and food talk, contemporary societies celebrate the ultimate pop degradation of aesthetics, one in which creativity has no individual creators and aesthetic value coincides and disappears with its consumption.

Conclusions

Paul Ricoeur famously contended, through a monumental array of works (1983–85), that narratives are cultural devices for coming to terms with the paradoxical experience of time. Semiospheres are macro-narratives too, and time is one of their main concerns (Leone 2014a). Ultimately, a semiosphere's complex topology of meaning is about time. It is not about temporality, which is the structural rendering of time in discourse. It is rather about existential time. A semiosphere's topology is both the consequence and the embodiment of the way in which a culture and its members collectively cope with the idea of death, with the ghost of existential finitude.

Most of the phenomena that originate from the contemporary frenzy for food, including marketing endeavors, revolve around the concept of experience. More than ever, people are ready to credit the aesthetics of food because they are hungry not only for delicious dishes but also for what they embody: an immediate, engrossing, and simultaneous confirmation of existential presence. I eat, ergo I exist. I feel the pleasure of ingestion, ergo I am alive. New technologies facilitate cultural acceleration and the consequent loss of collective memory. Everything looks more impermanent than ever: ideas, words, and institutions. Voices coming from a distant past through literature and the arts are no longer able to soothe existential starvation. People want to be and want to be now. They want to see and be seen, touch and be touched, feeling that they exist not through reconnection with a remote past or projection into a threatening future but through present experience. And what more than the ingestion of a succulent bite, or an exquisite sip, will confirm existence?

A nervously suckling humanity it is, scared more than ever to detach its lips from the breast of the world, lest the insignificance of it all swallow existence at the first abstinence.

Notes

1 "To reminisce about eating and drinking, the sorts of pleasures that are as fleeting as yesterday's perfume or the lingering smell of cooking, is not the mark of a free-born man" (Engl. trans. by Paul A. Clement and Herbert B. Hoffleit 1969).
2 Milan, May 11, 1928–Paris, May 9, 1997.
3 Our translation.
4 Eresos, Greece, c. 371 BC–Athens, c. 287 BC.
5 Chaeronea, Boeotia, c. AD 46–Delphi, Phocis, c. AD 120.
6 Titus Petronius Niger; Massilia, AD 27–Cuma, AD 66.
7 Hierapolis, Phrygia (presumed), c. AD 55–Nicopolis, Greece, AD 135.

8

RECOVERING SIGNIFICANCE

The value of singularity

Quid? Formae ipsae et habitus nonne arguunt
ludibria et dedecora deorum uestrorum?[1]
(Marcus Minucius Felix, *Octavius*, 38, 5)

Introduction

An ideology of progress is implicit in the practice of technology. The domains
of law and religion are not excluded. In both, the conviction persists that a different arrangement of technical signs is able to grant better access to an invisible
realm: On the one hand, religions fine-tune liturgies with the certitude that a
change in words, gestures, architectures, and other sensorial devices shall lead to
a shortening of the metaphysical distance between immanence and transcendence, between the community and the divinity; on the other hand, legal systems
adopt increasingly sophisticated strategies and tools so as to look into the truth
of human life and its legal predicament. Ideologies of technological improvement, however, are seldom neutral, and often introduce a dimension of bias,
a polarization between two or more abstract polarities of signification. In the
present chapter I explore one of these polarities, which affects the domain of
law, that of religion, and, more generally, the gnoseological approach of human
cultures to the invisible. Modernity seems to consist in the more and more pervasive spreading of a quantitative prejudice, according to which "seeing more"
is equivalent to "seeing better". From the genesis of modern anatomy in the late
Renaissance until the development of extremely sophisticated machines for the
analysis of "visual big data", such prejudice suggests that religious, legal, and
other representations linking the visible and the invisible gain a firmer grasp on
their object and—as a consequence—a more effective agency by simply increasing the quantity of items that are included into the sensorial scope, and by merely

subjecting these items to a sort of computation. In the chapter I seek to relativize this ideological turn through focusing on early objections to it, essentially deriving from two sources: on the one hand, philosophers like Thomas Browne, yielding to a sort of mystical reading of nature in contrast with the empirical and diagrammatic perusal of it promoted by coeval rationalist philosophers and on the other hand, artists like Rembrandt, casting an ironic meta-gaze on the gaze of anatomy so as to downplay its epistemological buoyancy and underline, on the contrary, the virtue of the painter's gaze.

Ideologies of transparency and opacity

Throughout the chapter, I shall explore a dialectics between two kinds of optical ideologies: on the one hand, a visual rhetoric of transparency, whose social and political counterpart is a hierarchy of control; on the other hand, an opposite visual rhetoric of opacity, which tends to spot fallacies in the former so as to subvert its strategy of optical dominion. In simpler, more evocative words, and from a historical point of view, I shall deal with that which could be defined, with a slightly tongue-in-cheek expression, the "jealousy of visual media": Every time that, in history, societies develop and adopt more perfected means of visual representation and, therefore, control of the environment, previous and less efficient visual media can be referred to so as to build a metaphor of social liberation. This dialectics between transparent and opaque media, in which transparency and opacity are always relative to the specific media at stake, inevitably affects the domain of law.

Legal systems customarily intertwine the epistemological dimension and the optical one (Resnik 2004). All senses can be important in the construction of a legal judgment, yet none of them is as prominent as sight. A sometimes naïve visual rhetoric permeates the entire history of law, a rhetoric according to which seeing better is tantamount to becoming closer to truth. This connection between visually grasping the environment and cognitively controlling the relations between causes and effects in it is deeply and cross-culturally rooted in legal anthropology (Marrani 2011). Legal societies, however, show an enormous range of variations as regards the particular definition of "seeing better" that they adopt. The effort of elaborating a categorization of these ideologies of optical and, therefore, epistemological excellence has not been fully undertaken yet.

An important divide across such categorization is that between quantitative and qualitative optical utopias. On the one side, societies and, hence, their legal systems adhere to the idea that encompassing a larger quantity of objects in the visual scope will result in more apt assessing of the visual and legal scene. During the campaign preceding recent Italian administrative elections, a right-wing local candidate had as a key point of his program installing "a security camera for every condominium", as his political manifestos would loudly promise. Quantitative ideologies of visual excellence always tend to end up advocating a panopticon. Against such utopia of "seeing it all, ergo, seeing it better", contrasting ideologies propend for a more selective visual exploration of reality. From a certain point of view, the dialectics between these two approaches can be juxtaposed with the one opposing smooth and striated spaces in Deleuze and Guattari's famous philosophical topology (1980).

Quantitative optical utopias are inclined to implicitly believe in a mono-dimensional model of space, which can, therefore, be perused without envisaging any insurmountable obstacles. In technological terms, the combination of a panoptical ambition with a smooth environment topology often gives rise to delusions of total automatizing. Societies that embrace this kind of utopia invest important cognitive and also economic resources in engineering all sort of automatic eyes, able to scan the environment in a way that would be precluded to organic sight.

On the other side, though, qualitative ideologies of optical excellence suggest, often in a contrastive, dialectical relation to quantitative views, that the visual environment is not smooth but striated. In particular, they are keen on positing a multidimensional model of the social space, as a consequence of which what matters is not to scan reality but to acquire the ability to navigate across the various layers of it. If quantitative explorations of a smooth topology bring about automatic utopias, qualitative meandering through a striate topology results in extolling that which could be called "metaphorical utopias": What matters is not to see it all, but to see behind it all.

Needless to say, humanities and especially semiotics are almost naturally inclined to endorse the second kind of visual and also legal understanding of the environment. The primary object itself of the discipline, that is, the sign, actually is a theoretical hymn to the conviction that there is always a "something else" behind the "something", and that this "something else" can never be accessed directly but only through the somehow mysterious and unfathomable mediation of a third element, for instance, the interpretant in Peirce's semiotics.

Transparent and opaque anatomy

Positing this dialectics is perhaps not as relevant as pinpointing the passages marking the transitions between them, passages in which tensions and torsions arise in a collectivity's ways of looking, representing, and judging. A fundamental step in the construction of the modern visual ideology has been constituted by the birth of anatomical science. Anatomical investigation had been performed since antiquity, and had reached an extraordinary level of sophistication in the Renaissance. Yet even one of the greatest masters of it, that is, Leonardo da Vinci, although offering to posterity paramount insights in this field, still associated the exploration of the body with the pictorial representation of it. The best way to know what was inside a corpse was not only dissecting it, and looking through it, but also turning this pragmatic, haptic, and optic experience into an inevitably subjective representation. Constructing the syntagmatic of knowledge as based on both dissecting and drawing meant seeking to reconcile two apparently opposite semiotic movements: on the one hand, the analytical decomposition of the corpse, so as to turn its striated topology into a smooth field of visual and surgical perusal; on the other hand, the synthetic re-composition of the body, so as to pass from the three-dimensional smoothness of its dissection to the bidimensional striatedness of its representation.

The birth of anatomy as modern science coincided with the breaking of this equilibrium between analysis and synthesis, dissection and representation. Seventeenth-century anatomical treatises are still lavishly illustrated, as present-day handbooks of anatomy are. Yet an epistemological abyss seems to divide Leonardo from Andreas van Wesel: In modern and contemporary anatomy, images do not artistically recompose the dissected corpse but offer a mere rendering of its verbal articulation. If in Renaissance anatomy one still witnesses the transition from the indexes of disarticulation to the icons of representation, in modern anatomy icons do not directly transpose the body but illustrate its symbolical and, therefore, standardized verbal articulation.

As was suggested at the onset of this chapter, skepticism toward this new visual rhetoric of truth first materialized under the form of "media jealousy". Whereas displays of anatomical achievements attained great popular success and gained widespread acclaim, those who refrained from partaking in the general enthusiasm were exactly the heralds of a previous modality of visual exploration of the body: painters. Facing the visual and epistemological arrogance of the new science of the body, the old art of the body skeptically wondered: Is this really the best way to look at things? Is it the best way to know things? Is it the best way to judge over things? Isn't there perhaps a mystery, within the body, in its folds, in its consubstantially striated topology, that only the indirect, oblique, and metaphorical gaze of the painter can attain? These questions became particularly thorny when anatomy, as it was soon the case since its modern inception as science, turned into an instrument of legal knowledge, assessment, and judgment: Is it possible to infer a visual truth from the dissection of a corpse, if this corpse is not visually and also artistically recomposed into a body, into the relic of a living individuality?

The dialectics between old, artistic anatomy and new, scientific anatomy transposes at the level of representation a more abstract epistemological opposition between universality and singularity. If painters like Leonardo dissected generic corpses in order to subsequently recompose them through drawing and, above all, through painting, into the singularity of a represented body, anatomists like Andreas van Wesel would, inversely, draw individual bodies in order to visually render the objective universality of human anatomy. The disappearing of color from most seventeenth-century anatomical drawings is certainly due to the technicalities of the history of printing but it also befits a visual ideology according to which anatomical engravings must not, like painters, "resurrect" a body through the color of an incarnate but simply propose an iconic transliteration of the scientific anatomy's verbal knowledge.

The jealousy of Rembrandt

In no early modern visual work is the skeptical "media jealousy" of painters toward anatomists more provocatively visible than in Rembrandt's[2] famous *Anatomy Lesson of Dr. Nicolaes Tulp* (Figure 8.1).

On January 16, 1632, in the Waagebouw of Amsterdam, the famous Dutch surgeon Nicolaes Tulp[3] executed the public dissection of the corpse of Adriaan Adriaanszoon, alias Aris Kindt, a forty-one-year-old robber who had just been hanged. The dissection was part of the public lesson of anatomy yearly offered by the Amsterdam guild of surgeons. Doctors, anatomy students, scholars from several countries, as well as curious citizens attended the show, sitting on the benches of the circular tribune.

The dead body of Aris Kindt, its dissection, and the surgeon who executed it would have been soon forgotten, hadn't Rembrandt, then aged twenty-six, immortalized them through depicting them in one of his most famous and enigmatic paintings, presently at the Mauritshuis Museum at the Hague. Reams of paper have been used so as to unveil the mystery of this canvas, in which a detail, in particular, has attracted the still unsatisfied curiosity of art historians, philosophers, and simple spectators: The left hand of the corpse, whose tendons one sees exposed up to the forearm by Dr. Tulp's forceps, has been wrongly represented; judging from the disposition of the hand bones, indeed, one would say it was a right hand (Koolbergen 1992; Ijpma, van de Graaf, Nicolai, and Meek, 2006; Jackowe, Moore, Bruner, and Fredieu, 2007; Masquelet 2011).

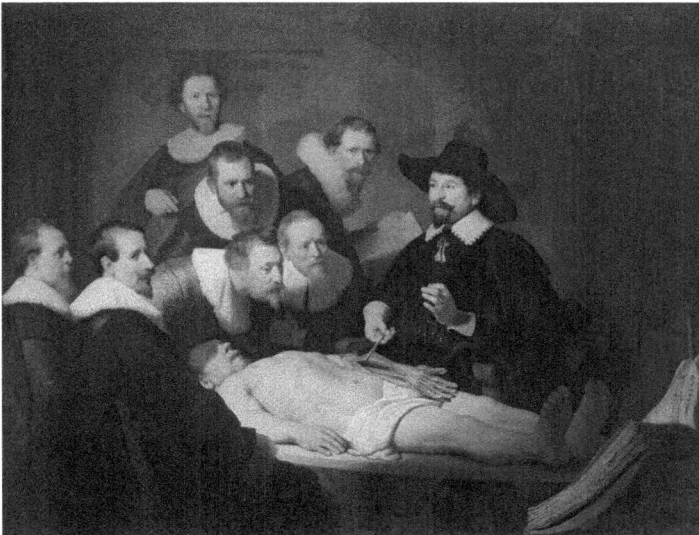

FIGURE 8.1 Rembrandt Harmenszoon van Rijn. 1632. *The Anatomy Lesson of Dr. Nicolaes Tulp*. 216.5 cm × 169.5 cm (85.2 in × 66.7 in). Oil on canvas. The Hague: Mauritshuis

The sight of this corpse with two right hands is likely to spur the hermeneutic fantasy of interpreters, as it is often the case when an unexpected double shows in an image (Heidegger *docet*; Leone 2012e). The hypothesis of a mistake due to the painter's ignorance has been immediately discarded: Rembrandt was an infallible specialist in matters of human anatomy (O'Bryan 2005: 64–7); furthermore, it would be hard to believe that such a coarse ignorance of the discipline could find place in a painting supposed to celebrate it. The meaning of this monstrosity must, therefore, be intentional. The following paragraphs propose a semiotic reading of it.

It is striking that such radical a gap manifests itself between the gaze of the implicit observer of the image—that is, the gaze that the painting predisposes thanks to Rembrandt's pictorial mastery—and the gazes of the observers represented as "simulacra" in the painted scene. Whereas our own gaze is supposed to be immediately captured by the detail of the flayed forearm—which attracts us because of its central position in the visual structure of the scene, because of the brutality of the exposition of flesh, and because of its anatomical deformity—the eyes of the observers within the scene, instead, do not even glance at the dissected corpse. It is among them, at the center of the scene; they surround it with their own bodies, their gestures, and their faces; yet it remains as though invisible and absent to their eyes.

What are they looking at, then? Dr. Tulp, on the right, does not look at the corpse. By his forceps he pulls its skin, cut wide open so as to better uncover its internal mystery, but he does not direct his gaze toward it. Instead, his eyes are addressing the audience, not as much the one that is closer to him but rather the crowd of curious spectators filling the amphitheater all around. The four characters on his right—the one with a sheet of notes in his hand as well as the other three bending toward the corpse—do not look at it either, neither they reciprocate the gaze of Dr. Tulp. On the contrary, as they stretch their bodies toward the center of the scene, that is not in order to better observe the dissected flesh of the robber but in order to better read from a volume that Dr. Tulp, during the dissection, keeps well open at the feet of the corpse, a copy of the *De humani corporis fabrica* by Andreas van Wesel, 1543. No image appears in this big in-folio, but only writing. It is precisely on this writing, indeed, that the four characters in the middle of the scene cast their gazes, thus neglecting the corpse under their eyes; it is with the lines of this writing, moreover, that one of the characters, the farthest one, compares his own notes.

As regards the two observers sitting at the left of the corpse, they constitute a sort of diptych, meant to suggest—through the static disparity of their gazes and the resemblance of their visages—the movement of a single man: On the right, he looks at Dr. Tulp's face; on the left, he turns to the open volume. Neither of them, however, looks at the corpse. What is the reason for this macroscopic distraction? Why, in an amphitheater filled to capacity with spectators and gazes, during the ritual spectacle of anatomic dissection that decorticates the corpse of a hanged robber—thus discovering two right hands therein—this killed, open, exposed, and monstrous body is left alone, looked at by none, and at the center of the scene?

Perhaps, the key to the mystery hides in the posture, the visage, and, above all, the gaze of the character who, standing above the others, looks neither at the corpse, at Dr. Tulp, or at the open volume at his side. This character, on the contrary, looks at us; he beckons us by a gaze that is simultaneously calm and inquisitive. What does it mean, this gaze directed at us, and what does it wonder about our own gaze, about the way in which we, prisoners of Rembrandt's pictorial trap, cast our eyes on the center of the scene, where none of our simulacra looks at, on the impossible flesh of a forgotten corpse?

Descartes *versus* Browne

In the first chapter of *Die Ringe des Saturns* (*The Rings of Saturn*, 1992), W.G. Sebald[4] subtly suggests some paths for the identification of this character, his history, and his gaze. An unusual work, mixture of travelogue, biography, philosophical meditation, and many genres more, *Die Ringe des Saturns* opens and develops by an irregular path, whose subtle semantic unity deploys in a sibylline manner, as barely visible filigree (Leone 2004a, 2004b). Through a chain of digressions whose logic remains mysterious, Sebald takes an interest in the seventeenth-century English doctor and polymath Thomas Browne.[5] The German writer surmises that Browne, in a period in which he was fascinated by the mysteries of the human body, attended the anatomy lesson of Dr. Tulp. Sebald does not identify the mysterious character in Rembrandt's painting with Thomas Browne but provides some veiled clues for such identification, whose consequences are of paramount importance for the interpretation of the painting itself.

The first clue that Sebald offers consists in reminding the reader that another great scholar probably observed the autopsy of Aris Kindt in Amsterdam: René Descartes.[6] The second clue, ensuing from the first one, consists in suggesting that although the precise perspective by which Browne observed the dissection of the corpse is not for us to know, it might be, nevertheless, inferred from what he wrote about the mysterious white fog that, on November 27, 1674, fell on ample regions of England and Holland. According to Browne, as Sebald reminds us, this fog was emanating from the hollows of a corpse that had just been dissected; Browne was convinced that, during our lives, such fog surrounds our brain when we sleep or dream.

To summarize, a mysterious character who looks at us from a pictorial scene in which nobody looks at what we are looking at, that is, the flayed and monstrous hand of a hanged and dissected robber; the presence of Descartes among the spectators of the autopsy; the presence, among the same spectators, of Thomas Browne; the intuition, suggested by the evocation of the fog, that the gaze of Descartes and that of Browne are somehow opposed, and that both hide among the characters of Rembrandt's painting: Sebald proposes a *literary* enigma whose ultimate finality seems to be that of helping us to solve Rembrandt's *pictorial* enigma; a sort of meta-enigma, then.

The key of the mystery hides in the following pages, in a new chain of digressions. Browne's fog looks to Sebald like the fog that had once blurred his sight because of the analgesics that he was taking in the aftermaths of a surgical operation. Through the window of his hospital room, Sebald could therefore observe the trail of a plane, realizing that the aircraft that had traced them was as invisible as the passengers within it: "*Die Maschine an der Spitze der Flugbahn war so unsichtbar wie die Passagiere in ihrem Inneren*" (Sebald 2001: 29). This biographic digression, apparently random, works in reality as all Sebald's digressions: It discloses a novel perspective on the profound meaning of the tale. As he wonders on Rembrandt's painting, and as he speculates, on the other hand, about the perspectives by which Thomas Browne and Descartes observed the anatomy lesson represented by it, what is at stake is, deep down, the relation between gaze, distance, and knowledge. The characters surrounding Dr. Tulp are close to the object of their perusal, yet they try to know it not through direct observation but rather by concentrating their gazes on writing, probably that of a treatise of anatomy. Moreover, they do not develop their knowledge through comparing the writing of the treatise with the image of the body; Rembrandt underlines it with sharp irony: One of them compares the teacher's writing to his own notes; the other three compare the writing of the teacher to his word; none of them, however, looks at the corpse, none of them compares the teacher's writing to the body.

Therefore, the beckoning gaze that the mysterious character whom Sebald identifies with Thomas Browne casts on us could be interpreted as follows: We are not like the bystanders of the dissection; thanks to the mediation of the painting, we do not simply concentrate on writing but we do not see the corpse either; rather, we look at the pictorial image of it. That which we discover in it, undetected by the gaze of both anatomy and anatomists, is both simple and terrible: *an exception*. A typical early modern polymath, Thomas Browne was obsessed with the central questions of epistemology: What can be known? What cannot be known? And what distance, what gaze should be adopted so as to pass from ignorance to knowledge? Thomas Browne's epistemology, Sebald points out, develops in a paradoxical way. On the one hand, like other scholars of his time, Browne contributes to the development of the new sciences through seeking a unitary system of knowledge (Leone 2010a). The British scholar never fails, hence, to find in the flabbergasting variety of nature some constant configurations, whose detection and description can lead one to decipher the reality of both nature and culture.

In *The Garden of Cyrus* (1658), Browne identifies one of the secret models that constitute reality in the quincunx, a disposition of five elements that he considers a sign of "the wisdom of God" (Leone 2005). He finds it everywhere: in the disposition of trees in the garden of Cyrus—whence the title of Browne's work; in some crystal formations; in sea stars and sea urchins; in the vertebrae of mammals; in the backbone of fishes and birds; in the skin of several species of reptiles; in the footprints of quadrupeds that ambulate obliquely; in the body configurations of caterpillars, butterflies, and silk worms; in the root of water ferns; in the shell of sunflower seeds and parasol pines; in the heart of young chestnut burgeons or in horsetail stems; and also in human works, such as the Egyptian pyramids and Augustus's mausoleum, or the garden of Solomon with its pomegranate trees and its lilies planted in mathematical order. Browne dreams of reducing the entire reality—nature and culture—to a single mathematical formula, to a diagram that, in its extreme simplicity, can, nevertheless, explain the generation and appearance of it all.

After following to its extreme this dream of geometrization of reality, however, he radically changes register. By a typical twist of his thought and prose, he writes that the constellation of Hyades, the quincunx of the sky, already disappears beyond the horizon, "and so it is time to close the five ports of knowledge. We are unwilling to spin out our thoughts into the phantasms of sleep, making cables of cobwebs and wilderness of handsome groves" (Browne 1658: 70).

In Thomas Browne, indeed, the ambition of uncovering the secret regularities of the universe and decrypt its ultimate meaning coexists, as it was typical in the baroque mindset, with an opposite passion, that for the exceptional, the irregular, and the monstrous. In the *Paradoxia Epidermica*—whose first edition dates from 1646, the fifth and last from 1672—Browne focuses precisely on this subject: He wonders about the reality, or about the fiction, of monstrous beings, found or imagined during centuries of human history. Somehow anticipating Borges's[7] *Libro de los seres imaginarios* [*Book of imaginary beings*], the English polymath takes an interest in the chameleon, in the salamander, in the ostrich, in the griffin, in the phoenix, in the basilisk, in the unicorn, in the amphisbaena. Moreover, he keeps in his laboratory a Eurasian bittern, whose song as deep as that of a bassoon fascinates him. He searches for the regularities of the universe, for the geometrical principles of its secret structure, and at the same time never stops collecting pathologies, exceptions, and monstrosities that, in both nature and culture, transform this geometry, disfigure it, and introduce chaos and unintelligibility in its order (Leone 2014b).

The chapter will now conclude by expounding on the relation between this dichotomy "geometrization of nature and culture" *versus* "search for monstrosity"—a dichotomy that is typical of Browne's scientific works and characterizes those of many of his contemporaries—and the dichotomies masterfully evoked by Rembrandt in his pictorial representation of Dr. Tulp's anatomy lesson: "gaze on the corpse" *versus* "gaze on writing"; Descartes *versus* Browne. Even more fundamentally in this context, the following paragraphs will focus on the relation between these oppositions and the dialectics of optical ideologies sketched at the beginning of the chapter.

Beyond the microscope

The earliest recorded working refracting telescope appeared in the Netherlands in 1608. Also in the Netherlands, the first compound microscope appeared by the 1620s, less than a decade before the hanging of Adriaan Adriaanszoon, the public dissection of his corpse by Dr. Nicolaes Tulp, and their depiction in Rembrandt's painting. First in Amsterdam, then in the rest of Europe, the eye and the hand of the painter were challenged not only by optical instruments able to look into the imperceptibly far and into the imperceptibly close but also by an optical technique, autopsy, promising to reveal the secrets of the body with no impediments. "Media jealousy"—stemming from the contraposition between the old visual technique and the new ones—prompts painting to elaborate a rhetoric of opacity, contrasting the rhetoric of transparence incarnated in the new scientific usage of lenses and scalpels. His visual primacy challenged, Rembrandt reclaims the dignity of his art through an ironic visual scene, in which anatomists are so confident in their scientific optics that they literally forget to look at the corpse, while the painter organizes the representation of it so that we, its observers, cannot miss the singularity that the anatomists so ridiculously overlook: This corpse has two right hands. That is a lesson of singularity opposed to the universal claims of anatomy, but it is also a moral lesson (Leone 2013b): Rembrandt's painting is implicitly suggesting that the truthful secret of the body will be discovered only by looking into the complex folds of human individuality through the metaphorical, striated gaze of painting rather than through the smooth, automatic look of autopsy. Opposing, as Sebald points out in *The Rings of Saturn*, the smooth epistemology of the Cartesian diagrammatics and endorsing, on the other hand, Brown's labyrinthine epistemology of order and chaos, Rembrandt reveals that this robber, hanged few hours before, brutally dissected by the anatomists, and obscenely exposed in an arrogant display of new optical power, in reality had no left hand, the hand traditionally associated with evil, sin, and guilt. The moral judgment that the painting passes on the life of this body therefore subverts the adjudication of the panoptical law, discovering the intrinsic innocence of humanity where anatomists, microscopes, and the automatisms of law had only found deviation and culpability.

Conclusions

This chapter proposes a complex and tortuous path across several epochs, disciplines, practices of representations, and epistemological domains. This path can be summarized as a plea for singularity; for attention toward singularity. The technological progress of digital devices of representation and control promises to bestow upon their users an increasingly perfected mastery of the real, conceived as a collection of items on which direct and computable agency can be exerted. In the domain of law, the discourse of technicians swerves more and more toward an imaginary of cold revelation, in which the patient accumulation of data and their quantitative treatment lay the ultimate truth of human nature bare. The contemporary religious discourse too does not escape this ideology. Beyond spiritual differences, indeed, the digital versions of all present-day religions seem to stress the preponderance of accountability: Counting one's sins and one's prayers, calculating festive dates, and arranging the bureaucracy of faith appear as more important than igniting the risky duel between the singularity of an existence and its spiritual counterparts. Even more disquietingly, the digital casing itself of reality seems to turn into a sort of new spiritual credo, uncritically embraced by human communities across the globe and revolving around the belief that computational representation is tantamount to knowledge or, worse, morality. Every domain of representation today is inexorably prey to such demons of digital calculus, to a semiotic ideology that, inaugurated by early modern optical science, advocates for an orderly exploration of the human predicament, until its secret is turned into the tetragon structures of a diagram. The humanities must not deny the triumphal emergence of this attitude but must not blindly endorse it either. Recuperating alternative genealogies of the gaze from mystical philosophers, ironic painters, and visionary writers might, indeed, work as an antidote against an excessive rigidity of the representation, a rigidity that, by compressing the singularity of life into quantifiable grids, paradoxically risks losing track of that which is at the core itself of the modern understanding of reality, that is, the treasure of singularity.

Notes

1 "What are the very forms and appearances (of the gods)? Do they not argue the contemptible and disgraceful characters of your gods?" (Engl. trans. by Robert Ernest Wallis 1923).
2 Rembrandt Harmenszoon van Rijn, Leiden, July 15, 1606–Amsterdam, October 4, 1669 (aged 63).
3 Claes Pieterszoon; Amsterdam, October 9, 1593–The Hague, September 12, 1674.
4 Wertach, Germany, May 18, 1944–Norfolk, England, December 14, 2001.
5 London, October 19, 1605–Norwich, October 19, 1682.
6 La Haye en Touraine, Kingdom of France, March 31, 1596–Stockholm, February 11, 1650.
7 Jorge Francisco Isidoro Luis Borges, Buenos Aires, August 24, 1899–Geneva, June 14, 1986.

9

NEGOTIATING SIGNIFICANCE
The value of compromise

Introduction

Once, a colleague of mine, a famous semiotician, told me that semiotics will have the place it deserves in the world when, upon the occurrence of a certain "semiotic accident", someone will shout out, "Is there a semiotician around? Please, we urgently need a semiotician!" in the same way as doctors are anxiously called for in a plane when someone suddenly suffers a heart attack.

A similar situation of semiotic emergency can, indeed, be imagined or even modeled after anecdotes from everyday life. On August 24, 2014, United Airlines Flight 1462 from Newark to Denver was forced to divert to Chicago. The reason was a fight between two passengers, a man and a woman. The former was sitting in row twelve of the plane, working at his laptop, when the latter, sitting in row eleven, decided to recline her seat but realized that it was impossible. Indeed, the man had deployed a knee-defender, a gadget for air travellers that at that time was available for few euros at most US airport shops. The knee-defender locks in place the fold-out tray on the back of airline seats, preventing passengers in front to recline their seat. The company that produced it would advertise for it as follows:

> It helps you defend the space you need when confronted by a faceless, determined seat recliner who doesn't care how long your legs are or about anything else that might be 'back there'.

Readers of this conflictive narrative have several options for identification. On the one hand, they can identify with the man: He is a tall person, his legs barely fit in the empty space between two seats, and, moreover, he must work in such conditions. He is therefore perfectly entitled to defend his vital and working space through the ingenious little device. On the other hand, readers can identify with the woman: She is tired, she wants to sit back, and the airline allows her to do so at her will. Why should she give up such comfort? She is perfectly entitled to request that the passenger behind her remove the knee-defender so that her seat could be reclined. Identification depends on a variety of factors, such as genre, body size, and travel habits but also on a more abstract variable that could be called "ideology of space". Both passengers share a common way of positing the relation between their intentionality, their bodies, and the space these bodies occupy. They both imagine the empty space between seats as a product that airlines have sold to them and that they have bought together with their flight tickets. The man has bought the space in front of him and can use it as he pleases. The woman has bought the space behind her and she can also use it as she pleases. A problem arises for they have actually bought the same space and do not agree as regards their intentions about using it in relation to their bodies.

The question whether there is an alternative solution to conflict is not only ethical but also economic. The solution that United Airlines staff came up with, that is, diverting the plane to Chicago, was extremely costly for the two contenders, for the other passengers, and also for the airline itself, which proved unable to handle such apparently banal conflict. The following paragraphs will suggest how a semiotician could, instead, ease the situation, if called to intervene in the emergency, exactly through turning the invisible insignificance underpinning the tension into visible meaning.

On needing a doctor

As a term of comparison, it is useful to consider how a doctor would intervene when summoned upon a suspected heart attack. She (let us imagine a female doctor) would first listen to the patient, talk to him (let us posit a male patient) if he is still conscious, and abduce that the chest pain that the patient complains of, radiating from the chest up to his ears and gums, is a clear symptom of myocardial infarction. The doctor could abduce that because she has studied semiotics in medical school and learned that a patient complaining of such kind of pain is most likely suffering a heart attack. Clinical experience then confirms the doctor about the trustworthiness of what she has learned in school. Hence, on the basis of this inference, guided by a semiotic rule corroborated by experience, the doctor has the passenger moved in the emergency exit area of the plane. She then starts practicing cardiopulmonary resuscitation (CPR). Up to 2010, the doctor, if well trained, would have performed first airway, then breathing, and then chest compressions (ABC). In 2010, though, the American Heart Association and International Liaison Committee on Resuscitation updated their CPR guidelines to first chest compressions, then airway, and then breathing (CAB).

The well-trained and well-informed doctor in this fictional example, intervening on a plane in 2014, would therefore perform CAB, not ABC. She would do so because the medical association she refers to, on the basis of accumulated scientific evidence, judges CAB as more efficacious than CAB. This judgment is sound and trustworthy for it is based on a falsifiable hypothesis: If CAB is better than ABC, then more patients will be resuscitated through the former than through the latter. A maverick doctor could seek to deconstruct the corroboration of this hypothesis, quoting Latour about the constructivist nature of experiment results; yet few readers of Latour would like to be assisted by such a doctor upon suffering a heart attack on plane. They would prefer to fall into the hands of a doctor who believes CAB is better than ABC, and acts accordingly.

The fictional story of the example goes on. While the doctor is performing CAB, a flight attendant dashes with an automated external defibrillator (AED). An AED is a portable electronic device that automatically diagnoses the life-threatening heart arrhythmias of ventricular fibrillation and ventricular tachycardia. AED is able to treat them through defibrillation, the application of electrical therapy that stops the arrhythmia and allows the heart to reestablish an effective rhythm. The U.S. Federal Aviation Administration requires all flights to carry AED. That, however, is not an international mandate. As a consequence, most passengers with heart conditions would rather travel on a US plane than on a plane where no AED is available, exactly because they would trust the efficacy of such device, like the doctor in the fictional example above. That which passengers and the doctor trust in an AED is, again, empirical evidence; or, more abstractly, mathematics, that is, numbers. There is empirical evidence, translatable in quantifiable figures, that AEDs are able to detect and defibrillate arrhythmias. A particularly Nietzschean passenger could claim that the efficacy of AEDs is a matter of interpretation, not a fact, and evoke a scenario in which the flight attendant would dash with a rosary instead. With all respect to rosaries, though, most well-informed people with heart conditions would still go for AEDs, or succumb if they do not.

In this fictional example, the AED, indeed, restores blood flow to the patient's brain and vital organs. Later, unfortunately, the man goes again into an irregular rhythm because of cardiogenic shock, and then goes back into cardiac arrest. But this patient is lucky. There is also a pharmacist on the plane. As the doctor strives to resurrect the patient again, the pharmacist intravenously injects him epinephrine from the plane's medical kit. Such medical kit contains epinephrine and not, for instance, balsamic vinegar because of more empirical evidence, also translatable in quantifiable figures, and because of falsifiable hypotheses, tested through decades of controlled experiments. Again, one might choose to deconstruct them, but still few would like a pharmacist to inject them with balsamic vinegar when suffering a cardiac arrest.

That is all to say that behind the desperate shout, "Is there a doctor on the plane?" there lies not only a habit, reinforced by scenes seen in movies more than in real life but, also and above all, the human trust in how empirical observation of reality, production of falsifiable hypotheses, elaboration of laboratory experiments, and translation of reality into quantifiable data can improve human life. What lies behind such shout is, in a nutshell, the idea that reality shows some regularities that human beings can analyze and translate into numbers and that such translation can lead to the production of behaviors (CAB), devices (AED), and substances (epinephrine) that improve human existence. The fictional patient will be able to land alive, and celebrate the first birthday of her grandson. A patient on another plane, where ABC is performed instead of CAB, rosaries are considered as efficacious as AEDs, and balsamic vinegar as trustworthy as epinephrine, will not, unless a miracle occurs.

On needing a semiotician

One should now wonder whether a semiotician could intervene in the same way as a doctor, an engineer, or a pharmacist in a situation of emergency, and dramatically improve the quality of life of those involved in the emergency on the basis of a training, an epistemological framework, and a methodology.

A comforting point of departure might be to realize that there are situations of emergency that sciences cannot yet effectively deal with. In general, all situations that involve human language, meaning, and alternative potential decisions cannot be dealt with by natural sciences with the same efficacy by which they deal with a muscle in the human body, a circuit in an electronic device, or a chemical reaction. Indeed, whereas the correct functioning of an AED is a matter for medical engineers, the rapidity by which a flight attendant is able to resort to it is already something that lies outside the scope of natural sciences only (unless until a full development of neurosciences will be able to give full account of humans' reactions to stress situations).

That is a point in favor of semiotics and other humanities but is also simultaneously a weak point. Pharmaceutics, based on chemistry, is not a discipline of freedom but one of necessity: When given an injection of epinephrine, a human body must react in a certain way. There are no alternatives. Empirical observation, formulation of falsifiable hypotheses, and laboratory experiments are carried out exactly with the aim of reaching a situation in which no alternatives can be envisaged anymore: Given a cardiac arrest, you inject epinephrine, nothing else. On the contrary, semiotics, as the other humanities, will never be able to exclude alternatives because alternatives are exactly what they are about. Let's consider showing a diagram to a flight attendant so that she could understand how to use an AED: No matter how much semioticians investigate, they will never come up with a diagram that is the communicational equivalent of what epinephrine is for a cardiac arrest. A heart reacting to epinephrine is a non-semiotic process, a necessary act, and a natural phenomenon, while a flight attendant reacting to a diagram is a semiotic process, an act of freedom, and a cultural phenomenon.

Those who dream for humanities the same efficacy and social status of natural sciences should therefore accept this intrinsic limitation: A semiotician, or a philosopher, or even a jurist, will never be summoned for help with the same conviction and trust with which a doctor, an engineer, or a pharmacist are called for in a situation of emergency. That is a shortcoming of humanities but also simultaneously a position of force. In order to realize it, one should imagine that a problem involving language, meaning, alternatives, and freedom of choice be entrusted to natural sciences or to one of the "disciplines of necessity". That has occurred in history, although mostly in those sociopolitical contexts that can be characterized as totalitarian, in those utopias (or rather, dystopias) that have imagined, programmed, and engineered a supposedly perfect human being with no alternatives. The search for the perfect language has often had the same disquieting totalitarian connotations: Not only the perfect language cannot exist, but even the project of it is symptomatic of an ideology where one of the basic mechanisms of linguistic ability, that is, freedom of enunciation, is denied, often for the sake of the perfect linguistic harmony of a group. Those rigid interpretations of digital sciences that tend to equal human beings and their minds to mechanisms with no alternatives are as reminiscent of dark ideological ages, a reminiscence that accounts for the usual (but sometimes equally ideological) mistrust of humanities toward any reductionism.

Laws of necessity *versus* laws of freedom

One should not conclude that, given that intrinsic freedom characterizes the object of humanities, humanities cannot develop any scientific thought, detecting regularities in reality, formulating falsifiable hypotheses, and conducting experiments. Freedom is not necessarily chaos. Human beings are able to formulate infinitely various thoughts and express them through an equally unlimited array of signs, for instance, through verbal language. The nature of this both semantic and expressive infinity, though, should be specified: As C.S. Peirce first intuited, human thoughts do not normally develop randomly, although they potentially may always do so, but tend to converge toward certain regularities, which eventually crystallize into habits. The proliferation of interpretants in Peirce's model of cognition is absolute freedom. There is no need for an interpretant to take such and such semiosic direction in interpreting another sign. Yet this absolute freedom is only potential, for actual semiosis inevitably entails a series of constraints. Whereas the absolute freedom of semiosic potentiality cannot be the matter of any scientific operation, for it escapes, by definition, all kind of regularity and, therefore, predictability, the coagulation of habits into the social dynamic of semiosis does create repetitions, for habits would be impossible without redundancy. Semiotics can scientifically analyze this redundancy, as well as variations that stem from it, in the same way as chemistry analyzes regularities in the molecular structure of a material.

Positing language at the core of humanities has triggered their potential transformation into scientific endeavor not only in Peirce's tradition of thought but also in that of structural linguistics. In Saussure's lineage too, language is, on the one hand, the dimension along which human beings continuously exert their freedom, as there is no grammar that is so cogent as to oblige its speakers to select a certain combination of signs, and only that, from the socially shared deposit of symbolical forms. Humans must abide to the rules of a linguistic game if they want to play it but at the same time they are constantly free to do so with their own style. Some of them, indeed, develop such a powerfully idiosyncratic style as to change the rules of the game itself (and again, societies in which the free verbal play of poetry is banned or submitted to rules are to be dreaded).

Yet, on the other hand, the revolutionary aspect of structural linguistics exactly consisted in providing evidence that the human exercise of linguistic freedom is built on sophisticate dialectics between regularities and exceptions, repetitions and variations. The structural understanding of phonetics introduced in humanities the idea that language too, and culture with it, could be modeled through a sort of calculus, through combinatorics. Such turning point resulted from a specific semiotic ideology (i.e., a certain way of imagining meaning), yet it was precisely in the domain of language that the study of culture first seemed to give rise to a capacity for prediction analogous to that of natural sciences.

For instance, Bopp's study of Indo-European languages had already established in 1820 that, starting from middle Iranian and applying the same rules, the morphology of Gaelic words at the other end of the Eurasian continent could be predicted. Albeit tentative, Bopp's theory was capturing the regularities of language by observing empirical evidence, formulating falsifiable hypotheses, and testing them in relation to the morphology of Indo-European idioms.

Analogously, Greimas's betting on the possibility of modeling the semantics of languages according to the same lines and principles along which structural phonetics had modeled their sound patterns was tantamount to positing not only the signifier of language but also its signified as structured by regularities, repetitions, and rules. Societies, groups, and individuals do not think meaning randomly but according to cultural patterns that turn to be linguistically structured, if language is defined in a sufficiently abstract and broad way: That is the assumption that Greimas developed on the basis of what had already been found by Claude Lévi-Strauss in the structural study of native American myths, by Vladimir J. Propp in the study of Russian folklore, and, even more ambitiously, by Georges Dumézil in the study of Indo-European mythology and religious cultures.

From a certain point of view, these theories were predictive in the same way as scientific theories are. Albert Einstein's relativity theory was able to prove its theoretical superiority to Isaac Newton's theory of gravity since it was able to predict not only the planets' orbits but also irregular fluctuations in the orbit of Mercury that the former theory was not able to foresee. In the same way, Greimas's model of narrativity can be considered as superior to that of Propp since the former is able to capture variations in narrative structures that the latter could and can account for only through multiplication of individual functions. In other words, Greimas's theory pushes forward Propp's theory because the former is able to see regularity, redundancy, and combinatorial variation (order) where the latter could see only difference and chaos (disorder).

It is not a coincidence, then, that Greimas's term for designating the individuation of semantic regularity in a text, "*isotopie*" ["isotopy"], is modeled after a scientific term. While physical isotopes are variants of a particular chemical element that display different neutron numbers, semantic isotopes are variants of a particular semantic element that display different contextual features. As every metaphor, that of narrative isotopy too is imperfect, since semantic nuclei and contextual particles do not have the same ontology as physical isotopes and neutrons, for the former are epistemological entities posited by the metalanguage of the analyst. Yet the metalinguistic ontology of Greimas's narrative isotopes does not entail that their empirical observation, as well as the formulation of hypotheses on their semiotic functioning, do not generate falsifiable predictions: For instance, the semiotic analyst can predict that a text endowed with a certain isotopic structure will be received by a certain range of cognitive, pragmatic, and emotional reactions.

Moreover, the Greimasian term "*isotopie*" also refers to the scientific term "isobar", which designates the ideal lines that, on geographical maps, run through the points that present equal atmospheric pressure on the level of the sea or at a certain altitude. Analogously, "isotopic lines" are those that ideally run through those points of a narrative that display the same semantic nuclei. It is through spontaneously connecting these points that receivers of a text infer its intended meaning, exactly as a meteorologist can forecast weather by observing the morphology of isobars.

Yet forasmuch as the structural study of language has introduced in humanities the possibility of empirical observation, falsifiable modeling, and prediction of still unknown occurrences, linguistics and semiotics are still part of the humanities. Linguistics and semiotics, indeed, formulate hypotheses and predictions whose nature differs from that of hypotheses and predictions in chemistry or biology as regards an extremely significant element. Seeking to find regularities in the domain of necessity, natural sciences can rely on the relative stability of nonlinguistic matter. Neutrons will not randomly change their behaviors while the physicist is studying them and formulating hypotheses and predictions about them. Heisenberg's principle, in its last formulations, asserts the fundamental limits characterizing any interaction between classical and quantum objects. Yet it is only metaphorically that anthropologists could adopt such principle in order to describe the way in which participant observation transforms both the observer and the observed. In the domain of nonlinguistic matter, indeed, observation can change it, but the way in which that happens is actually further evidence of what matter essentially is: extension without agency, ontology without intentionality, and kingdom of necessity. In the case of Heisenberg's principle, for instance, physicists have found that the loss of precision in observation of complementary variables does not impact on formal mathematical results, which remain valid. In other words, even quantum physics seems to bet on the inertia of matter, although its internal regularity cannot be fully grasped from the point of view of classical objects.

On the other hand, linguists, and all the more semioticians, are constantly and dramatically confronted with the consubstantial mutability of their object. Language and sign systems, indeed, not only change when they are observed but also change, more disquietingly, when nobody observes them. Being the outcome of interaction among many free and intentional agencies, language and meaning evolve according to tendencies whose prediction is not comparable with that which seeks to capture the evolution of nonlinguistic matter. Meaning usually manifests along habits, as Peirce would suggest, yet there is no certainty that it will. New interpretants could break known semiotic patterns at any moment, falsifying all hypotheses and predictions based on previous empirical observation. Chaotic phenomena also exist in nature, yet they are the exception, more than the norm; moreover, the unwritten agenda of every scientist is based on hope that all such chaotic manifestations will one day be proved nothing but extraordinarily complex expressions of necessity, which only scientific ignorance currently interprets as "chaos".

Linguists and semioticians, on the contrary, are constantly aware that the regularity of their object, and therefore its predictability, is not consubstantial to it but rather the ephemeral social outcome of interaction among freedoms, whose unpredictable evolution could, nevertheless, disrupt such equilibrium at any moment. Semioticians study meaning and strive to understand its laws but they are convinced that these laws are paradoxical and oxymoronic "laws of freedom", rather than the laws of necessity that characterize nonlinguistic matter. As soon as linguists and semioticians start believing that what they are after are laws of necessity, whose stringency will determine interaction among human beings as cogently as chemical laws determine interaction in chemical compounds, they cease situating themselves in the humanities and dream a reductionist dream, adhering to an essentially non-semiotic model of the human being.

Methodological competition

A practical consequence of uncertainty of prediction is methodological competition. Laws of necessity can be studied in many different ways, yet it can be eventually demonstrated that these ways can be ranked according to a gradient of efficacy. The same does not apply to the laws of freedom, that is, to all phenomena involving human intentionality, agency, and language. The clear-cut urgency by which, upon a heart attack, the flight attendant shouts out, "Help! Is there a doctor on the plane?" also and foremost depends on the fact that alternatives are hardly conceivable, at least given the present state of the art of cardiology. Alternatives may only be ironically conceived. If someone shouted out, upon the same emergency, "Help! Is there a priest on the plane?" that would not be extremely comforting for the patient. Indeed, at least in most present-day Western cultures, summoning a priest instead of a doctor would be a strong signal that little can be done to resurrect the patient. Similarly, if someone shouted out, "Help! Is there a sorcerer on the plane?" that would be definitive evidence of a sociocultural episteme that is far removed from that of modernity. Such appeal would sound absurd because it is radically at odds with the context: A culture that engineers airplanes is hardly compatible with irrational rejection of modern medicine in favor of religion or magic.

Nevertheless, one can imagine a time in future history in which, upon some-one suffering a heart attack on a plane, the shout, "Help! Is there a doctor on the plane?" will be replaced by the shout "help! Is there a medical engineer on the plane?" That, however, will not be a sign of sharp change as regards the place of sciences in the popular imagination but rather a consequence of scientific and technological evolution. The medical engineer will run toward the patient and inject him a nano-device that will run through the veins up to his heart and re-pair the damage in a matter of seconds. In other words, the medical engineer will be summoned instead of the doctor because the former will have proved more efficacious than the latter.

Increase in efficaciousness will essentially result from decrease in discretion-ary agency. The doctor's agency relies on scientific evidence corroborated by physics, chemistry, and biology. Yet the doctor must also inferentially connect this background scientific knowledge with a course of action. He must interpret symptoms, for instance. The heart reaction to injection of epinephrine is not a matter of debate and escapes semiotic analysis. As Umberto Eco wittily wrote, semiotics studies all that can be used to lie (Eco 1976: 7), but the chemical effect of epinephrine on the heart has no alternative; given such injection, the same re-action will always occur; and likely so: The effectiveness of epinephrine precisely depends on its straightforward and unmediated effect on the body, independently of the patient's state of mind.

On the other hand, semiotics can, and actually does, study the inference through which the doctor, after observing the patient's behavior, decides that he is having a heart attack, whence a whole series of medical procedures ensue. The doctor may wrongly interpret symptoms. Being distracted, or simply being a bad doctor, she could mistake a panic attack for a heart attack, with tragic conse-quences for the patient. But that would also be the ground on the basis of which, in a maybe not-so-distant future, a medical engineer will be summoned instead of a doctor. The engineer will not have to interpret anything. She will not have to rightly infer the presence of a medical state from its potential symptoms. On the other hand, she will simply inject a nano-device that will travel to the heart and ascertain whether there is a heart attack or not. The nano-device will not be human. It will be a very sophisticated machine but it will still be a machine. It will measure certain physical, chemical, and biological data and act accordingly. No alternative will be involved in the process and, therefore, no mistake. It is only metaphorically, indeed, that we attribute a malfunction to a machine. A technical device malfunctioning, indeed, does not result from wrong intention-ality, and therefore wrong choice, but from bad engineering. Behind a malfunc-tioning machine, there must be, somewhere, a malfunctioning human agency.

On the one hand, reductionists dream of explaining human evil too as a con-sequence of necessity; on the other hand, futurologists envision a time in which technical devices will be so complex as to become paradoxically able to make their own mistakes. Yet for the time being, and perhaps also in the near future, technological progress will consist in displacing more and more activities from the domain of necessity to that of choice. In more abstract terms, technological progress will consist in expelling language from life. That is why the medical engineer (or, rather, the medical nano-device) will be called for instead of the doctor: because it will treat the body of the patient according to the laws of necessity instead of treating it according to the laws of freedom. Only mechanical deduction and no human abduction will be involved in the treatment, to the point that the human presence in the process will be progressively diminished. For instance, what if the patient, or a relative of the patient, shouted out, "Help, a medical nano-device is needed!" in a language that nobody in the plane would understand? Well, in that case too, the automatic treatment of language would solve the problem, further eliminating the discretional potential attached to such situation of emergency.

More generally, finding a technological, scientifically based solution to a human problem means moving that problem into the domain of linguistic discretion, and therefore also into the domain of humanity. The more the heart becomes a machine to be fixed, the less room for wrong treatment. Nevertheless, the level of complexity of our example dramatically increases if it considers, instead, a patient suffering a panic attack. In that case too, one could envisage an incredibly sophisticated medical nano-device that enters the brain of the patient and stimulate serotonin receptors, so that panic attack ceases on the spot.

This case, however, is more complicated. First, the brain being infinitely more complex than the heart, the second medical nano-device is much more difficult to imagine than the first. Given the state of the art of neurology, it is hard to engineer, or even imagine to engineer, such a cerebral appliance. Will it work on serotonin receptors? On the production of sodium lactate and carbon dioxide? Or will panic attacks have to be cured before birth, through specific genetic modification? The most serious problem in imagining such a medical nano-device is that it cannot be excluded that panic attacks are actually a semiotic problem, depending on the way the patient remembers her past, experiences her present, and imagines her future. In other words, for the moment being, and perhaps also in a remote future, the best procedure in case of panic attack on a plane will not be to call for a doctor but to summon a nice flight attendant, who will have witnessed hundreds of similar cases, sit next to the patient, take her hand and, most importantly, talk to her.

One could imagine a technological device that talks to the patient, yet most would still rather prefer the company of a flight attendant in case of panic attack on a plane. Most would want to be addressed by something that responds freely to symptoms, that is able to improvise and, most significantly, that is likely to be able to imagine the other's suffering in order to respond to it. In other words, most would desire to be comforted by someone, not by something, by an empathic device, not by a robotic one. But for the time being, the only empathic device on earth is the human being (or other living animals: most sufferers of a panic attack on planes would prefer the company of their dog or cat instead of that of a machine).

But what if knowledge of the brain improves so dramatically that an effective cerebral nano-device can be engineered? What if automatic language devices become so elaborate so as to become undistinguishable from human psychologists? What if brain activity too is removed from the realm of language? There are two main objections to this futurologist reductionism. The first is that eliminating a problem from the domain of language results in removing it from the domain of complexity. That is the case in both medical examples mentioned above. One might want a medical nano-device to rescue someone from a heart attack, and yet it would be simplistic to think that the adoption of such medical technology would eliminate the problem of cardiac pathologies. A heart attack, indeed, is not only a muscular problem but an existential one. What lifestyle has led to the pathology? What social pressures? In order to solve the problem of heart pathologies not only locally but also globally, the operation to be carried out is that of actually resituating the problem into the domain of language and, therefore, complexity. That is even more compellingly evident in the case of a panic attack; treating it simply as a local malfunction in the brain means ignoring what a panic attack globally is: the consequence of a complex semiotic tangle, which must be disentangled if the problem is to be dealt with and solved at its roots.

The second objection is even more radical: Although future linguistic automata will be able to sound exactly like humans, that will not eliminate the human awareness that they are automata, an awareness that will influence, in turn, their own efficacy. There is no way to removing a mental problem from the domain of language, for the act itself of removal becomes part of the mental landscape of the patient, thus changing the nature of the problem. Psychiatric medication, for instance, can certainly be effective but cannot eliminate, in the patient, the awareness of being treated with it (unless medication is surreptitiously administered, which most would find ethically dubious). More generally, scientific evidence that our feelings of intentionality, agency, self-awareness, empathy, and consciousness are the direct consequence of biological, chemical and, ultimately, physical substrata, would not eliminate those feelings. A flight attendant will continue feeling empathy toward someone suffering a panic attack on a plane despite her scientifically based knowing that the panic attack results from a chemical reaction and, above all, despite her scientifically based knowing that her own empathy ultimately is nothing but the outcome of a chemical reaction. In other words, evolution seems to have programmed human beings as endowed with a semiotic interface, which cannot be ignored even if science explains both its evolution and functioning.

That is, on the one hand, reassuring, especially for those who have spent most of their lives studying the laws of freedom: Despite scientific and technological progress, there will always be problems in human life that are best dealt with by the humanities. All sciences and technologies denying the arguments above, therefore, do something quite different than searching scientific solutions to human problems. They rather search human beings for scientific solutions, meaning that they implicitly invoke a different model of humanity, wherein distinctively human features (which humans share with other living beings), such as empathy in spite of realistic knowledge, are considered as undesirable relics of an obscurantist past, to be eliminated through scientific education. Such judgment could be shortsighted, though. In the future, a deeper knowledge of the human evolution might prove that human beings have survived not in spite of their anti-realistic behaviors but because of them. In other words, science might one day find out that what made human beings a fit-to-survive species was not only their capacity of disenchanting reality from language but also that of enchanting and re-enchanting reality through language.

The downside of "the need for humanities" should be thoroughly discussed too. The argument that certain human problems—such as the social context and lifestyle of someone suffering a heart- or a panic attack on a plane—will always remain in the domain of language and will therefore always be best treated by humanities, leaves an important question unanswered: what humanities? Up to a certain level of complexity, there is a straightforward way to rank sciences and scientific theories dealing with problems that, at least locally considered, appear as outside of the domain of language. Modern medicine is better than medieval medicine in dealing with heart attacks, no doubt. And beta-blockers are certainly better than clinical bloodletting through leeches in treating hypertension, no doubt either. The "observation of reality–hypothesis–experiment–falsification or corroboration" circuit proves it. Alternative medicine might seek, as its name says, to introduce alternatives in the domain of necessity, and argue that, for instance, "natural medicaments" are as or even more effective in treating cancer than mainstream medical procedures. Symmetrical to reductionist therapies, though, these unconventional therapies do not propose alternative solutions to medical problems, but rather alternative definitions of them. They displace the human body and its pathology from the domain of necessity and science to that of freedom and language. A cancer patient treated with medicaments that are not scientifically tested is likely to die sooner than patients who undergo mainstream therapy, and no speculation should be allowed by those who claim the contrary.

There are instances, however, in which medical science is impotent too: In this case, that which the patient and her relatives and friends are after is not any longer a solution but an illusion. Again, science tells humans that they shall die, and that there is no way to prove the contrary. Yet believing in a religious miracle or in a palingenesis through alternative medicine makes the pain of physical and mental suffering more bearable. From this point of view, alternative medicine should be considered as a pointer to that aspect of the human being that "technological" medicine is increasingly neglecting. Nevertheless, it remains that the scientific primacy of modern medicine over medieval or alternative treatments can be doubted only by rejecting modern rationality.

Unfortunately, the issue is much more complicated as regards humanities. In the fictional example exposed at the beginning of the present chapter, the problem at stake is clearly one that lies in the domain of language, abstractedly conceived (i.e., in the domain of the laws of freedom). Yet there is no certainty about what specific humanistic methodology would be the most efficacious in dealing with such problem. Should a semiotician or a sociologist or an economist or a psychologist or all of them together be summoned? Moreover, and even more disquietingly, there is no certainty that a present-day semiotician would deal with the problem more efficaciously than her 1960s colleagues. The wonderful assurance by which contemporary physics affirms its superiority over ancient Greek physics is not to be found in any of the humanities. Semioticians, for instance, are not so sure that they know signs so much better than Stoics did. Present-day scholars pursue different questions and give different answers than their ancient predecessors, but in general humanities can rank their methodologies neither synchronically (what methodology is the best?) nor diachronically (which stage in the history of methodology is the best?). Should therefore the dream of an anxious flight attendant urgently summoning a semiotician on a plane be mercilessly abandoned?

Conclusions

For the reasons exposed above, there will never be any way to demonstrate that a certain discipline within the humanities is better equipped than others to deal with the laws of freedom. Whereas the present-day medicine can prove its superiority to medieval and alternative medicine, contemporary semiotics cannot prove its primacy over 1980s semiotics or over sociology in the same way. Designed to find regularities in freedom, humanities will never be able to come up with methodologies of necessity. As a consequence, the urgency by which a flight attendant might call for a semiotician, or a philosopher, or a sociologist on a plane will always depend on fashion and on the rhetorical force by which the various humanities manage to affirm their validity. There is no factual reason, for instance, that explains why present-day semiotics is less invoked to tackle social and cultural issues than 1960s semiotics. That is just a matter of fashion. It ultimately comes down to the triviality that later semioticians have been less effective than their 1960s forerunners in rhetorically supporting the validity of the discipline (a lack of efficacy that might also be a sort of boomerang-effect of the typical semiotic tendency to deconstruct culturally and socially constructed habits, including that of the belief in such and such methodology!).

The question above, though, whether one day a semiotician might be urgently summoned in a plane upon a symbolical emergency could be reformulated as follows: Provided that future semioticians will succeed in claiming for themselves the same useful role that 1960s and 1970s semioticians could vindicate for the discipline, what is the specific contribution that semioticians could give to the solution of problems falling in the domain of language and its laws of freedom? In the example given above, two passengers fight over the same space on a plane, to the point that the pilot is obliged to land and have the two contenders get off at the closest airport. Each of the humanities has a specific way to frame and seek to find a less disrupting solution to the problem. Within the present chapter, full justice cannot be done to the internal complexity of each of the humanities; their approaches will therefore be somewhat caricaturized for the sake of clarity.

For economists, the issue on the plane is clearly a matter of offer and demand. The same space is claimed as having been bought by both contenders. The solution is simple: pricing plane space so that offer and demand might coincide. In certain airlines, for instance, economy class passengers cannot recline their seats anymore. If one wants more space, one must pay extra for it. This approach is refreshing in its straightforwardness but at the same time does not really solve the problem. It just moves it from the domain of space to that of price, that is, to the domain of access to wealth. As on a plane, so in society, allocating resources according to a mechanism of offer and demand regulated by price does not introduce a principle in the distribution of resources but rather differ or even mask the issue of who can access the resource by referring it to the issue of who can access money.

For jurists, the contention results from failure in regulation: If passengers are entitled to both recline their seats and buy and use gadgets that prevent other passengers from reclining their seats, then usage of these devices on a plane should be outlawed. This approach too might seem elegant in truncating the dispute by introducing a prohibition. But this approach has a downside too. It fails to see that the production, sale, and use of knee-defenders points to a problem: For some people, it is impossible to sit and even less work comfortably while sitting on a plane. Prohibition of knee-defenders, moreover, will not prevent passengers from fighting with passengers in front of them when the latter wish to recline their seats.

Sociologists, anthropologists, and semioticians look at the issue from the same angle, although through different methodologies. For all these scholars, space is not only a physical container but a cultural variable that relates to many other aspects of individual and collective life. Hence, the conflict above tells much more than a simple anecdote on lack of room among seats. It reveals, for instance, that miniaturization of working and entertainment devices presently allows passengers to continue studying, working, or playing while traveling, and that this miniaturization cannot be matched by a miniaturization of the body: No matter how small computers might become, humans will still have to look at their screen by bending their necks at a certain angle, or else they'll feel unbearably uncomfortable. The same applies to our arms, legs, eyes, and the rest of our bodies: Despite the efforts of computer engineers, a modicum of space will still be needed for accommodating working or playing limbs on a plane.

Second, the fight between the two passengers reveals that marginal profits in travel industry come at a cost. The era of low cost airlines might be saluted as one of democratization of traveling, but generating huge profits through selling extremely cheap flight tickets is possible only because something else, besides flying, is sold on low cost planes: nerves. More generally, low cost industry—in travel as in tourism, in entertainment as in food—seems to give wider access to goods and activities that would have been previously precluded to many, but it is simultaneously profiting on the wearing of the human body and mind. Travellers are increasingly trading their comfort and health for the low price of airfares.

But the anecdote above also discloses something else: Passengers are increasingly disinclined to courtesy and, more generally, to the practice of compromise. That is, ultimately, the issue with the episode of that about which the knee-defender: I do not want to ask the passenger in front of me, with a kind voice, a big smile, and an appropriate politeness formula, whether she would consent to recline her seat a little less. Instead, I impose my will on her through an impersonal gadget. In a way, I automatize the protection of my life space so that I do not have to do it anymore personally, that is, through language.

All in all, the specific contribution semiotics can and must give to present-day societies is as simple as that: providing evidence—albeit not a scientific but a discursive one—that problems that fall in the domain of language cannot be solved by technology, no matter how smart it might be. Problems that fall in the domain of language can be solved only by talking, compromising, and finding an agreement. The knee-defender is apparently more rapid, more efficacious, and less time-consuming than semiotically interacting with another human being. But is this device really the best option, when a whole plane must be diverted because of its usage? On a larger and more dramatic scale, military solutions to issues emerging from conflicts over ethno-religious frontiers also seem drastically efficacious. But are they really so in the long term?

Should semiotics succeed in affirming its role among the humanities, a flight attendant will one day shout out, "Help! Is there a semiotician on the plane? We have an emergency!" And then the semiotician will rise from her or his seat, walk toward the passengers who are fighting over a knee-defender, and calmly say, "Please, calm down, I'm a trained semiotician. You can solve this problem by just talking, I'll show you how".

10

SHARING SIGNIFICANCE

The value of common sense

Le bon sens est la chose la mieux partagée car
chacun pense en être si bien pourvu, que même
ceux qui sont les plus difficiles à contenter en
toute autre chose, n'ont point coutume d'en
désirer plus qu'ils en ont.[1]
(Descartes, *Discours de la méthode*, I, i (1637))

Introduction

It would be useful to develop a semiotics of faux pas (Puckett 2008). Abundant case studies would be provided by unfortunate events, such as accidents, divorces, or deaths (Idone Cassone, Thibault, and Surace 2018). In these circumstances, interaction among individuals must be highly codified, sometimes even ritualized, for any straying from the usual formulae of speaking and behavior risks generating embarrassment. What could be said, for instance, to someone who has just divorced? Sentences like "I'm happy, your wife was a witch" or "I knew it, she was too beautiful" are definitely to be discarded, but sentences like "it must be such an existential failure for you" would also not be very appropriate for the context. As a consequence, verbal exchanges around tragic events tend to be stereotypical and devoid of any creativity: The sentence "I hope you'll both find your happiness again" is a totally empty and, therefore, appropriate sentence for commenting on the news of a divorce.

No law, however, determines the perimeter within which one must move when interacting in society in tragic circumstances. No written rule specifies that, for instance, when someone lets us know that her or his old mother has passed away, one should not comment, "Anyway, she was very old!" But the inappropriateness of such comment is not inscribed in institutionalized culture either: That which should or should not be said at a funeral is not taught and learned in school but absorbed by people through immersion in real-life environments and experience, through observation of how more mature people behave in such circumstances. Faux pas result from the fact that such immersion and absorption were not sufficient and constitute the unpleasant social accidents through which the unwritten laws of a community are revealed and reinforced.

Someone might transcribe and codify these unwritten rules in handbooks of correct behavior, such as those common in Europe, at least since the Middle Ages on,[2] prescribing right manners in various mundane circumstances. Yet the appropriateness of these manners is not crystallized once and for all but varies in time and, above all, in space. Even when they are compiled in a handbook, their status will remain always uncertain, for uncertain is the speed by which manners themselves have evolved meanwhile. What allows us to avoid faux pas in society does not have the same semiotic nature of what allows us to avoid mistakes in language.[3] It is well known that grammars too are social constructions, whose cogence is destined to vary in time under the pressure of language evolution and statistics; given the centrality of verbal language in human life, however, this system of signs in most cultures undergoes a level of codification and institutionalization that is absent in other semiotic domains.

Both how to speak correctly and how to behave correctly are learned since childhood in contact with a sociocultural environment, but the former pertains to a series of grammatical rules, whereas the latter to a deposit of appropriate, exemplary behaviors. We can correctly use the subjunctive of a verb because the rules of its formation and usage are inscribed in a grammar; we can correctly dress at a wedding because such manners are transmitted from generation to generation as intangible symbolical patrimony of the community.

Invisible rules not only prescribe correct behaviors in recurring circumstances but also encourage one to cultivate stereotypes (Ponzio 1976: 115). These are not always necessarily negative (Lescano 2013). Stereotypes are implicit models that the members of a community follow so as to receive guidance as regards the best way to interpret a given circumstance (Dahl 2016). When a new young professor is appointed in a department, for instance, no written rule specifies the way in which her or his behavior will be interpreted and judged by senior colleagues. An intangible and loosely codified matrix of stereotypes, however, will push them to believe that the young colleague will tend to be overzealous and even a little arrogant or, on the contrary, that she or he will be overmodest and subservient, independently from the actual character of the novice herself or himself. This prejudice or, rather, prejudgment, relies on the experience that it will take a new young professor a certain time, and also a certain amount of professional faux pas, before she or he finds the exact measure of her or his insertion in the preexisting group.

Another good example, which has been thoroughly studied by ethnomethodologists, can be found in conversation, specifically in the way in which participants determine how much they want to expose themselves in verbal exchange (Perinbanayagam 2011). A newcomer, or someone who does not belong to the group, will be inclined to overexpose himself or herself, seeking to gain space and attention in conversation; or, rather, she or he will tend to underexpose herself or himself, struggling to find a moment and a way to appear under the best possible light within the new conversation environment.

Although we rarely realize it consciously, most of our everyday life, and especially the interactions we daily have with other human beings, heavily depend on knowledge that is not transcribed and is not taught anywhere, except, perhaps, in the peremptory indications that we receive during childhood, and that we interiorize without remembering their exact source, or the exact moment and place in which such indications were given to us. It is, indeed, mostly through imitation, intuition, and, sorely, exposition to faux pas, that we learn "how to be in society". Mastering these unwritten rules is an important element of that which usually goes under the name of "belonging" (Leone 2012a). Belonging to the academic community means also interiorizing the unwritten rules that govern, for instance, the way in which questions should be asked after a talk in a symposium.

Young and inexperienced participants might commit the classical faux pas of trying to show off their knowledge by asking long, winding, and erudite questions, that of being too provocative in their critical remarks, that of being exceedingly flattering in their praising comments, and so on. Only after a certain number of symposia, and after being exposed to the negative feedback of frowning colleagues, as well as to the positive models of appropriately asked questions, will young conference goers learn how to participate in that delicate rhetorical ballet that is the Q&A session following a paper or a lecture.

Mastering these unwritten rules is so important in order to develop a feeling of belonging for they determine not only the watershed between appropriate and inappropriate behaviors but also the frontier between insiders and outsiders. Outsiders, those who do not belong, are exactly those who do not partake of the common implicit knowledge that underlies interaction in a community. They might be voluntary or involuntary. The latter case has already been described: It is the case of those who, insufficiently conversant with the rules of the group, fail to abide by them, incurring in faux pas; the former case is more interesting, since it concerns those who, while knowing these implicit rules perfectly well, decide to ignore it. Most of the outrageous behavior that the masses frequently find so attractive in populist leaders precisely consists in disregarding unwritten laws of social life while hinting at the fact that this is not the result of ignorance but, rather, the outcome of Nietzschean superiority (Aalberg 2017).

In both cases, however, either unintentionally ignoring the implicit and unwritten rules of a community or intentionally disregarding them, configures a hierarchical social topology: in the first case, the ignorant individual is placed outside of the circle of belonging; in the second case, he or she tries to place herself or himself above it. The first behavior gives rise to stigmatization and exclusion; the second, to outrage as well as to fascination, to hostility as well as to power. In other words, voluntary or involuntary faux pas subvert the customary topology of the community because they create an area of immunity outside or above it.

The content of common sense

That which is usually called "common sense" is nothing but the complex deposit of implicit cognitive, pragmatic, and emotional rules through which the members of a society interact with each other and, simultaneously, affirm their belonging to the group.[4] This sense is called "common" both because it is current—meaning that it permeates the daily life of the group in all its manifestations—and because it is shared: It is something that belongs to the community as a whole and something through which, at the same time, the members of the community can belong.

What is the relation between "sense" and "common sense"?[5] This question is extremely relevant to semiotics, hermeneutics, and the other disciplines and philosophies of interpretation. When a beholder observes a painting in a museum, it is inevitable that this image, with its configuration of forms, colors, and positions, exudes meaning. The painting makes sense, or rather manifests sense, because it tends to orient the gaze, attention, and cognitive processes of the beholder in a certain direction. The main difference between a painting and the wall from which it hangs in a gallery precisely consists in the fact that the painting tends to orient the cognitive faculties of the beholder in a more cogent and restrictive way than the wall does. In other words, the painting makes sense because it shows a sense, a direction for its observation, contemplation, and interpretation. The beholder is empirically alone in front of the painting, yet something in the sense that emerges from the interaction between the image and the gaze is not idiosyncratic but depends on the sociocultural context in which both happen to be placed. Not all in the sense of a painting is common, but not all in it is uncommon, in both the meanings of "unusual" and "private".

How would a totally private interpretation of a painting be, for instance? Some years ago, during a symposium at the University of Bilbao, Spain, I was invited to a party, with drinks and music, taking place in the magnificent central hall of the Guggenheim Museum. Visitors could drink their cocktails, listen to loud music, and then proceed to explore as they pleased the extraordinary retrospective dedicated to Francis Bacon. It is highly probable that, cocktail after cocktail, some of the spectators were actually quite heavily intoxicated while admiring the paintings of the Irish artist. But were their reactions to them, hence, totally idiosyncratic? They were probably not. Even when we abandon ourselves to extremely personal and intimate reverie in front of a painting, or even when we admire it under the effect of intoxicating substances, it does not cease, for that matter, to guide both our gaze and our interpretation through both its internal semiotic structure and through the complex, multiple ways in which this structure refers to the context of contemplation: the *hic et nunc* of the exhibition, with all its heavy load of sociocultural determinations.

Despite our efforts of creativity, originality, and individuality, common sense systematically reemerges in the experience of sense. It is exactly this reemergence, moreover, that the first semiologists of nonverbal languages were tempted to identify as language. As our experience of verbal meaning is never completely idiosyncratic but is, on the other hand, constantly guided by both our implicit and our explicit adhesion to the grammar and, more generally, to the *langue* of the language we speak, our apperception of nonverbal meaning is guided by something that also represents the impact of a community on individual hermeneutics, something that, for that reason, resembles language. Nevertheless, the most serious mistake of the first semiologists of the fine arts exactly consisted in neglecting the difference between that which constricts our relation to verbal meaning, that is, grammar, and that which limits our relation to nonverbal meaning, that is, common sense (Calabrese 2003). When we interpret a painting, and realize that our interpretation considerably overlaps those of other beholders, what causes such overlapping is not a codified grammar but a non-codified set of implicit hermeneutic rules composing the common sense of a museum visitor.

What does this common sense contain? Here follows a trivial example. When we go to the Louvre, and finally reach the hall where the Gioconda is exhibited, our interaction with the painting, and the sense that emerges from it, is guided by some explicit knowledge, such as what we might have learned in school or from books about Leonardo and his art. The hermeneutic relation with the painting, moreover, will also be guided by the structure of the painting itself, by the way in which Leonardo arranged forms, colors, and positions so as to trap our gaze within the canvas and have it move and interpret in a certain way (Calabrese 2006). The first kind of guidance is codified through verbal language in art history handbooks and other similar meta-texts; the second kind of guidance stems from a micro-code that the painting itself institutes, also with reference to the specific visual grammar of an epoch, a style, and an artist (Segre 2003). Our interaction with the painting, however, also depends on some implicit knowledge that is neither codified in meta-texts nor inscribed in the text. That is the case, for instance, of the so-called para-text (Genette 1987). Nobody has explicitly taught us that we should pay attention to what is inside the frame, and not to what is outside of it; nobody has explicitly taught us either that we should focus on this inside, taking the frame as a frontier that delimits an autonomous micro-universe of meaning; and nobody, moreover, has explicitly discouraged us to challenge the frame, for instance through reading the painting in relation to the wall or to the architecture that surrounds it, or in relation to other paintings in the same gallery (Thürlemann 2013). If we look inside the frame, focus on this inside, and separate it from any outside, it is because we have absorbed, mainly through exposition to appropriate models of observation, what a frame is and how it should be visually used.

As art historian and theoretician Victor I. Stoichita has demonstrated (1993), the para-textual device of the frame resulted from a complex cultural evolution, which distilled it as the main para-textual artifact through which the modern Western civilization separates images from their context. Such evolution might have taken place in a totally different way, for instance, through selecting elliptical frames instead of the squared ones as prototypical devices of visual focusing (after all, the frame that our own sight projects on reality is not squared at all).

Once this device becomes a constituting element of the visual semiosphere of Western modernity, however, it turns into a sort of collective second nature. That is what common sense ultimately is: a deposit of implicit rules that guides our hermeneutic interaction with the cultural environment. Para-textual signs, although shaped through centuries of cultural history, work as common sense meta-signs. Punctuation also works this way. Before its "invention", texts were not segmented (Fasseur and Rochelois 2016). Once this device is interiorized by culture, however, there is no way one can feel familiarity for a text that is not punctuated (Olsen, Hochstadt, and Colombo-Scheffold 2016). In other words, both the frame of a painting and the punctuation of a novel are part of the common sense through which the members of the Western society transmit and receive meaning.

Common sense is enshrined in syntactic arrangements and para-textual devices but it is also deposited in the semantics of texts, or rather in the pragmatic rules through which meaning is "extracted" from a text. Visiting a gallery of abstract art can sometimes be puzzling for those who are not familiar with it. Confronted with long arrays of nonfigurative canvases, the neophyte will certainly wonder, "What do they mean?" (Barrett 2017). This question, as naïve as it might sound, actually derives from the common sense that, for centuries, has guided the human interpretation of visual artifacts. Such common sense implicitly suggests to an image's beholder: "If there is an image, and if this image has been intentionally made by someone, then this image must have a sense, it must make sense, it must try, that is, to convey a certain meaning to its observers" (Gell 1998). Although nonfigurative art has now challenged such common sense for more than two centuries, many museum visitors still abide by the previous implicit rules of visual hermeneutics; they cannot contemplate that a visual artifact intentionally made by another human being actually means nothing. That is why, in this circumstance too, the divide between those who still visually function according to this traditional common sense and those who have accepted to challenge it, adhering to the new common sense of modern and contemporary art critique, is a divide between outsiders and insiders, between those who belong to the world of contemporary art and those who do not.

The elements composing the common sense that orients the emergence of meaning within a community can be ranked in order of complexity. At the lowest level, one shall find non-written syntactic hermeneutic rules, such as those that implicitly prescribe that we look at that which is inside the frame and not at that which is outside of it; at higher levels of complexity, then, one shall come across implicit rules that govern the pragmatics of a meaningful artifact, for instance, the idea that, in order to understand the meaning of a painting, one should not concentrate only on a part of it, but on its totality. At the highest level of abstraction and complexity, finally, one will be confronted to and affected by unwritten rules that determine the specific semiotic ideology in accordance with which a group tends to interpret its meaningful artifacts. At this level, very abstract but fundamental precepts will reside, for instance, the idea—central in many human groups—that there must be a correlation between the way in which the artifact appears, and the intimate world relying on which the artist created the artifact itself. We might reach a stage in our civilization at which this common sense disappears under the blows of technical evolution. We might, one day, be left wondering whether, for instance, the image that we are beholding is the outcome of human intentionality or, rather, that of a sophisticated but emotionless machine, programmed to trick us into believing that what we are watching is the expression of an intimate world we can empathize with.

Sharing the common sense that pervades a semiosphere means abiding by these unwritten rules at all levels; the more abstract the level, the more indirect, implicit, and subterranean the absorption of such rules will be. Some of this common sense, indeed, might be common not only to a specific human group but to humanity as a whole, stemming from the very long period of contextual conditions in which human groups have found themselves interacting with the environment and attaching meaning to it. The way in which we implicitly conceive of the agency of images, for instance, albeit not necessarily hardwired in our biology, nonetheless results from such a long period of human history as to have become a sort of second nature, a consolidated common sense that no human being can now disavow without, by the same move, exiting the community of reasonable image interpreters.

Common sense and community

There is, indeed, a complicated but essential relation between common sense, community, and reasonableness. Italian philosopher Roberto Esposito has convincingly explored the concept of community taking as a metaphoric point of departure its Latin etymology (1998). A "*communitas*", Esposito argues, is a social formation wherein each member donates ("*munus*" in Latin means "gift") to all the others, and to the community itself, a part of her or his identity, in a sort of symbolical sacrifice of it. It is precisely this sacrifice that allows the community to emerge from the voluntary curtailing of individualities. Every time we abide by the laws of language, implicitly we also adhere to an ethical community, meaning that we voluntarily (albeit often implicitly) restrain the idiosyncrasies of our own mind and body so as to conform to a certain syntactic, semantic, and pragmatic grammar. We do not speak how we please, about what we please, and in the context that we please; we maneuver, on the contrary, within an ample and yet limited space, provided by a *langue* and coinciding with the others' adhesion to the same linguistic and cultural community. We might, as it is often the case, pursue individualistic and even narcissistic goals within this frame (for instance through our aspirations as poets or novelists), yet if we do not want to be excluded from the circle of the community, we should be careful enough not to play too hard with its frontiers, or we'll be ostracized as speakers who are actually "incomprehensible" within such circle.

Attempts at creating, along a contrary anthropological dynamic, islands of "immunitas" within the semiosphere take place all the time (Esposito 2002): Just think about the way in which totalitarianisms often forge their own political lingo so as to better separate insiders from outsiders, affiliates from opponents. Nevertheless, in such cases too, the exclusive lingo cannot be so arcane as to prevent the elite to decide whether to co-opt new members exactly through teaching the new language to neophytes. Analogously, every avant-garde requires to be surrounded by a porous semio-linguistic frontier, which functions as a channel between the avant-garde and the mainstream.

The mechanism of the dialectic between semiotic *communitas* and semiotic *immunitas* should now be clear: By adhering to the language of the group, I sacrifice my own identity but enjoy the identity of the community; by creating my own semio-linguistic variations, I reclaim my identity but run the risk to be ostracized by the group (Leone 2009b). The most problematic condition in this dialectic is that of those who either lose themselves completely by drowning their individual identity into the collective one, or find themselves completely isolated because their narcissistic proposal is banned from the semiosphere; the first extreme gives rise to the robot, the second to the madman. The most felicitous condition, on the contrary, is that of those who, while inventing their narcissistic language—sometimes through exploring ways of meaning and expression that are quite at odds with the mainstream—manage to transform their individual creation into the backbone of a new collectivity. The leader, from this point of view, is the one who, by the force of her or his semio-linguistic proposal, convinces an entire community to sacrifice its gifts of identity to the proposal itself, turning it into the new common sense. Picasso, for instance, leads the formation of the twentieth-century visual common sense because he managed to concoct, at the margins of the semiosphere, an entirely new way of seeing and depicting but had, then, his narcissistic proposal adopted as the mainstream visual episteme of the century.

Explaining why certain proposals fail, whereas others triumph, requires a case-by-case analysis of the micro-context in which the proposal is formulated and received. That which rather matters, at this stage, is to underline the relation between this notion of community and the parallel notions of common sense and reasonableness. A community is at the same time more and less than common sense. It is both the élan and the procedure through which individual identities partially empty themselves, so as to create a vacuum within the semiosphere in which the common ground of the community might arise and, in turn, refill, in a transformative way, the narcissistic vacuums left by the gift. In this dynamic, the existential plenitude of the individual is sacrificed but only in order to be restored at a different level through the community. This movement of emptying and filling bestows upon the members of the community itself both a superior sense of belonging and, crucially, a superior sense of existential fulfilling. The reason for that is quite understandable: Whereas the narcissistic semio-linguistic status is constantly precarious (Will anyone ever speak my language? Does anybody understand me?), the status that individuals find in the community is not one of arbitrariness but one of motivation. It is a cultural motivation, of course: There is nothing natural, as Saussure first intuited and demonstrated, in the way communities collectively "decide" to speak.

Yet the fact that this *langue* emerges from abiding by the implicit and explicit rules of a community makes it not naturally but culturally motivated. The grammar according to which speakers create their sentences results from a historical and cultural evolution but gives rise to the second nature of the collectivity, as is demonstrated by the fact that no one, in the community, will single-handedly be able to decide to change such rules (unless she or he is a dictator or a "genius"). Expelled from nature by the evolution of their cognition, human beings find in culture the possibility to recreate, although always imperfectly, and although always precariously, a feeling of necessity. Adhering to a community of speakers, they need to speak as they must, not simply as they want.

Common sense is what is left in the empty space created by the sacrifice of individual identities; it is the *secretum* of the community, meaning that it is at the same time what is secreted by the community in the sense of "producing, discharging, distilling", what is secreted by the community in the sense of "hidden, concealed, protected", and what is made sacred through the sacrifice of individualities. Common sense is an instance of second nature too, meaning that the implicit and unwritten rules that it contains, albeit stemming, them too, from historical and cultural processes of complex negotiation, nonetheless, become the patterns in automatic and spontaneous adhesion to which the members of a community interpret the environment, including the cultural artifacts that circulate through it.

As individual, narcissistic, and idiosyncratic readers we might decide to discard a novel after reading the first page, after looking at the cover, or even after smelling its paper. Were we to intersubjectively share our opinion of the book with other readers, however, we should rather respect the rules of common sense that the human community of readers has set for its members as a consequence of a long but determinant cultural evolution. We should, for instance, read, or at least claim to have read the book from cover to cover before being able to convince our community that we are entitled to pass judgment on it. In other domains of judgment, for instance when a chemist must vouch for the salubrity of water in a city, other rules of common sense apply, often refined into a rigorous scientific methodology. The chemist will be able to sample the water and claim, to both the scientific and the lay community, that the sample was extracted according to such a sound methodology as to make it perfectly representative of the totality of the water in the city. The same procedure could not be included in the common sense that inspires readers of literature. Anyone claiming, in the context of an academic discussion, to be able to estimate the value of a novel upon reading the first chapter of it would be immediately ostracized from the community of specialized readers, since it is common sense, in it, to believe that the totality of a literary artwork is not always necessarily represented, like in a fractal, in its parts.

Common sense, from this perspective, is not only what is left in common from the sacrifice of individual identities but also that which indicates, in accordance with the second meaning of "sense", the direction toward which the community must explore the semiosphere. Common sense is both shared meaning and shared vectoriality.

Common sense and reasonableness

The relation of community and common sense with reasonableness and rationality should now be explored. Reasonableness entails the idea of a dialogue with an abstract interlocutor, that is, with a recipient than places herself or himself within a community (Leone 2018). That is so because a reasonable interpretation is not simply a statement but it is a proposal addressed to the future. In proposing a reasonable semiotic appraisal of a certain aspect of the environment, including that which is constituted by cultural artifacts, the interpreter submits her or his product to the scrutiny of a virtual audience, which will have to decide whether to agree with the new development in the semiosphere or, rather, to reject it. Common sense guides the proposition of a reasonable interpretation but does not fully determine it, for the act of interpreting is, even within the community, an individual one, essentially based on freedom (Zhang [Forthcoming]). "Public interpretation", therefore, cannot mean that the public becomes the subject of the grammar of meaning-making in a society. On the other hand, meaning is always the outcome of individual semiotic work, although this might more or less yield to the explicit constrictions of a grammar or to the implicit rules of common sense. If the public plays a role whatsoever in the scheme of interpretation, it is rather that of the sender, encouraging the individual to produce an interpretation, or that of the receiver, evaluating the individual interpretation once it is produced.

A thorny question to ask at this stage is whether the guidance that common sense provides to the emergence of reasonable interpretations is itself rational, that is, whether the social resistance that individual creations of meaning come across in the semiosphere is able to select the most appropriate ones (Leone 2016a). History seems to deny it. Common sense shared by a community has historically included plenty of interpretations that, in hindsight, proved to be wrong, harmful, or detrimental to the subsistence of the community itself. Should one conclude that the sedimentation of common sense in a society is actually not only irrational but also unreasonable, meaning that there is neither coherence nor logic in the way in which individual interpretations are selected in the semiosphere and constitute the framework in relation to which other individual identities yield to the pressure of the community?

Take, as an example, the value of originality. The genesis of modernity from Renaissance on coincides, at least in the Western civilization, with the raising of the idea that value, glory, and public memory should be attributed to those individual creations that manage to somehow detach themselves from previous patterns of meaning and to propose something new. The extent of such novelty might vary, as well as the specific semio-linguistic procedures through which it is achieved, but the principle underpinning the pursuit of originality remains unchanged: Creating new meaning in the semiosphere is better than simply reproducing artifacts that are already present therein. In many domains of creation, that is not the object of a written rule, but rather the content of common sense. Codes of evaluation in universities prescribe, that is true, that students who copy their dissertations should be banned, so as economic laws seek to defend the copyright of artworks. Both the bureaucratic and economic protection of originality, however, is based on a principle that is enshrined not in law but in common sense. It is common sense, in the Western civilization, and maybe in the human civilization as a whole, that creating something new is more praiseworthy than replicating an existent model.

Nevertheless, it is not difficult to imagine, in the distant future, a development of the semiosphere according to which an increasingly combinatorial aesthetics progressively downplays the value of creativity in the digital world, emphasizing, instead, that of assembling existing pieces in a novel manner (Leone 2012d). It is not difficult to imagine, either, that the progressive disappearance of non-digitalized materiality from the semiosphere will make the defense of originality increasingly harder: Every piece of human creation will be immediately replicable in a matter of seconds, so that the distinction between the original and the copy will be lost (Svašek and Meyer 2016). We, the teachers, already witness the epochal change of episteme that the digitalization of knowledge is triggering in our students: For many of them, taking from the digital semiosphere what is already there and injecting something new therein are not so far apart as they would look like to the previous, non-digitally native generation.

The problem, however, is not whether originality as a central aesthetic principle of the semiosphere will be lost and replaced by other values, for instance, by the principle of skillfulness in recombining existing digital fragments. The question is, rather, whether there might be any reasonable logic in the appearance and advancement of this second value in the common sense that permeates the semiosphere or if, on the other hand, there might be any reasonable logic in contrasting such change. In simpler words, "Is there an intrinsic value in recommending students not to copy their dissertations, or should a present-day teacher rather encourage them to copy well, by selecting the appropriate sources and skillfully hiding the traces of their 'theft'?"

After all, if one considers the history of citations in Western scholarship, one realizes that, to most medieval thinkers, it was not so important to defend the authorship of a thought, provided that such thought, when judged appropriate, was given further opportunities to circulate in culture, be transcribed, memorized, and propagated in the future. Should one come to the conclusion that, given the technical conditions of production and reproduction of knowledge that characterize the current digital semiosphere, common sense should not defend originality any longer, but welcome in its kernel new aesthetic values, values that better adapt to the new context in which meaning is exchanged in present-day human communities?

Conclusions

That might sound like a hard question but it is maybe the easiest of all, not because it can be answered without trouble but because it is not actually up to us to answer. In other terms, deciding how common sense should be shaped is not a problem, for common sense cannot be shaped through the intervention of individuals or cultural lobbies. As there is no way to prevent present-day European languages to lose certain verbal morphologies, such as the subjunctive, for instance (although we might personally attach a nostalgic value to it or even rationally justify its persistence), so there is no way to prevent common sense to take a direction that we might dislike. Verbal languages as well as cultures evolve as a result of complex holistic interactions that escape the control of power. Common sense is uncontrollable exactly because it is common. That might seem frustrating but it is also somehow liberating, not as much because it relieves intellectuals from the responsibility of taking action in the semiosphere and advocating such and such development of its common sense as because it somehow relieves them from the responsibility of failure. If we really deem it reasonable to preserve the usage of subjunctive, for it allows the expression of nuances of thought that are not as appropriately expressed through other verbal morphologies, or the value of originality, for it induces human beings to retain an essential aesthetic difference from machines, we should absolutely continue advocating these developments of common sense, seeking to influence the evolution of the semiosphere according to our agenda. We should not, however, become prone to disappointment, dissatisfaction, or even sterile cynicism in realizing that, despite our efforts, common sense evolved in a completely different or even opposite way. After all, being a member of a semiotic community of meaning makers also entails sacrificing the childish thought that our individual desires will always be endorsed by a majority, given strength and value over time, and preserved at the kernel of the semiosphere. The semiosphere might one day evolve in a direction that we had not expected and wished for, but the span of human life is probably too short to let us witness the moment at which future history will avenge our dissatisfaction, or rather confirm that we were, indeed, on the wrong path.

Notes

1 "Good sense is, of all things among men, the most equally distributed; for everyone thinks himself so abundantly provided with it, that those even who are the most difficult to satisfy in everything else, do not usually desire a larger measure of this quality than they already possess" (Engl. trans. The Harvard Classics, 1909–14).
2 Examples and studies on the topic are numerous; see, for instance, Whelan (2017). Literature on early modern "courtesy books" is particular abundant; see, for example, Berger (2000).
3 See Neumaier (2007) and Reason (2013); on linguistic "errors", see Kindt (2010).
4 Forguson (1989) explores the philosophical and psychological foundations of common sense; Briault (2004) reconstructs the history of the philosophical reflection on common sense and advocates for its critical and deconstructive potential; Rescher (2005) specifically investigates the relation between philosophy of common sense

and communication; Ledwig (2007) surveys the history, method, and applicability of common sense, with reference to philosophers such as Hume, Kant, Reid, Austin, Searle, Moore, and Wittgenstein (and digressions on folk psychology, proverbs, and game theory); on common sense in contemporary philosophy (especially McDowell and neo-Kantian metaphysics), Boulter (2007). On the "disappearing" of common sense, see Lawrence (1994); a "defense" of common sense as philosophical point of departure is in Lemos (2007); for a comparison of common sense and folk psychology, Hutto and Ratcliffe (2007); on the rhetoric of common sense in politics, Rosenfeld (2011); on the relation between common sense and science, Lavazza and Marraffa (2016). Various studies focus on the status of "common sense" in different historical epochs, such as that of ancient Rome (Jehne and Lundgreen 2013), eighteenth-century Great Britain (Henke 2014), and so on.

5 On common sense in Greimas's semiotics, see the entry "monde naturel" [natural world] and "figurativization" [idem] in Greimas and Courtès's *Dictionary of Theory of Language* (1979); for a comment, Marrone (2006). On the role of common sense in Greimas's semiotics, Nöth (1995: 98); Umberto Eco often critically refers to the notion of common sense, particularly in (1973) and (1990: 238). On discourse semiotic analysis and common sense, Geninasca and Greimas (1990); on semiotics as the "common sense" of the twenty-first century, Evans (1999); on common sense in the semiotics of law, Pencak (1988: 277); a partially semiotically inspired contribution on common sense is Starobinski (2005); on common sense in cultural semiotics (and the semiotic implications of Geertz's anthropological insights on the topic), Lorusso (2015); a recent contribution on common sense in semiotics is Sedda (2015).

11

COURTING SIGNIFICANCE

The value of interpretation

> Wise men have interpreted dreams, and the gods
> have laughed.
> H. P. Lovecraft, *Hypnos* (1922)

Introduction

If everyone were spontaneously inclined to interpret reality, be it nature or culture, in the same way, interpretation would not be needed. It would be pleonastic. In the relation between two different natural languages, interpreters are necessary, for they master the language of departure and that of arrival better than any of the speakers of the two languages. That is why they are not only needed but also somehow admired for this capacity, which inevitably leads to power (Fawcett, Guadarrama García, and Hyde Parker 2010, Part III and 147, 150–2). Analogously, the interpreter of a text is someone who, thanks to a superior methodological training, a wider encyclopedia, and a better acquaintance with the text, can provide insights on its meaning that are to be judged as deeper and more truthful than those that the interpreter's audience might bring about. In other words, interpretation begets intermediation, but intermediation is inseparable from an idea of hierarchy. Interpreters, because of the fact itself of being interpreters, will be situated in a higher sociocultural and pragmatic level than the community that they address. That is evident in the whole history of interpretation in the Western civilization (Barnstone 1993). In the Jewish Bible, for instance, all those who are able to read the signs of transcendence better than their fellow human beings acquire a special status, often becoming the leaders of the community. The same happens to prophets and haruspices in the Jewish, Greek, and Roman culture (Struck 2016: 48, 221, 223). In a similar way, when professors of semiotics address the audience of their students and undertake the task of describing, analyzing, and interpreting a text—a painting, for instance— immediately a topology of symbolical power materializes in the classroom, having often as its concrete counterpart also a spatial topology (the professor at the center of the amphitheater, with the students all around) (Oblinger 2006: chapters 1 and 6).

Lectures of this kind, however, constantly reach the bittersweet moment when the professor finally concludes the analysis and shows, with masterful assurance, that the meaning of a novel, a painting, or a song can be encompassed in such and such sentences of the metalanguage. Through the rigorous application of a method and the careful consideration of arguments and counterarguments, the analyst reaches the conclusion that the meaning of a text can be only that expressed through the analysis. Like in the final stage of the solution of a puzzle, all the pieces seem to come together and to find the most suitable place in the organic gestalt of the interpretation (Danesi 2002: chapter 7). When the professor, then, invites the audience to ask questions, a couple of students might propose alternatives to the reading of such and such detail or even point out that some aspects of the text were not taken into sufficient consideration. The masterful professor, though, will not be confounded by such objections but welcome those additions that fit well within the general design of the interpretation and, simultaneously, calmly but vigorously argue against alternatives that would disrupt the whole hermeneutic picture. At the end of the lecture, and even more at the end of the session of questions and answers, the interpretation will stand like a Doric temple in front of the minds of the audience, akin to a conceptual architecture wherein nothing, not even the smallest element of decoration, is now missing.

On the one hand, this moment is sweet: The professor will have demonstrated her or his superior ability to decode culture and its texts, to extract the most coherent patterns of meaning from them, and to translate such meaning into a smooth metalanguage, enhancing the students' comprehension of what the *Divine Comedy* or the Sistine Chapel or the Fifth Symphony of Beethoven actually mean. Yet to the professor who will not fall completely and blindly prey to the inebriation that accompanies teaching and, more generally, any display of a supposedly superior ability to interpret, this apex of the analysis will have a bitter taste too. The professor will mentally look at the tetragonal façade of the interpretation, behold its cold splendor, but then she or he will inevitably be seized, in a moment of sincerity, by a tragic doubt: What if this is all wrong? What if I am just trying to delude myself, and my students together with myself, into believing that meaning is something that can be captured once and for all, transcribed into a formula, transmitted across the ages and the generations, agreed upon?

The "reluctant interpreter" will look at the poem, at the painting, at the song, and wonder whether that which lies in front of her or his eyes is not a living animal anymore but a prey from whose corpse the last sparkles of life are nervously fleeting away. At the same time, she or he will not be able to suppress the intuition that, under that beautiful but cold architecture, the swarming life of meaning is still going on, undetected by anyone except those who have not been entirely convinced by the professor, perhaps including the professor herself or himself. At the end of the analysis, indeed, only the arrogantly distracted, pompously boastful interpreter will be able to tacit the inner voice that stealthily suggests that the beautiful architecture is not made out of marble but of clay. Are the students really convinced or are they just bored and eager to abandon the classroom? More disquietingly, do they accept the professor's interpretation because it is objectively the best, or because they rather yield to the professor's authority and to the social habit of respecting, or even fearing, her or his hierarchically superior level of judgment? Even more puzzlingly, the professor will ask herself or himself whether she or he too is actually not convinced either, and is simply pretending to be persuaded of the soundness of the interpretive solution, in faithful keeping with the interpreter's the role. The ghost of insignificance mars the pantomime of understanding.

The big gap

What causes this excruciating doubt, however, is neither the fragility of the method nor the suspect of the students' insincerity, nor the idea that out there, elsewhere, some other professor might interpret the text in a better way. What causes the doubt, instead, is life. Life itself. The reluctant interpreter, indeed, will not be able to discard the sneaking idea that there is a close and poisonous relation between the practice of interpretation taking place in vitro, that is, in the artificial atmosphere created in the laboratory of a classroom, and the practices of interpretation that, instead, occur spontaneously all around the academic world and that, in most cases, lead to tragedy and disaster. Is the approach through which a poem is analyzed perhaps so different from the approach that, day after day, leads a human being to completely misunderstand a friend, or to blindly fail to notice a partner's infidelity, or to let the lies of a politician go totally undetected, or to be spectacularly mistaken about the future directions of society or economy? Every day, all around the world, people suffer or even die because they wrongly interpret the environment in which they are immersed (Reason 2013: 10). That is why only the foolish human being will not have, at some stage of her or his life, the tremendous thought: I don't understand anything; I have never understood anything; I had the impression that I was able to decode life and reality but I was not; it was just an illusion, whose tragic price will be paid all of a sudden, and all at once. Life is, in reality, insignificant.

The contrast between what happens to interpretations in a classroom and what happens to them in life "out there" is so striking that it must, at a certain stage, prompt a reflection on the status of the former in relation to the latter. The reassuring pedagogical vulgate of academic teaching is that education, and higher education in particular, exactly is that physical and conceptual place in which young minds, guided by more experienced minds, can learn how to produce those interpretations that will improve the quality of their life and that of other people. Young biologists, doctors, psychologists, and semioticians are familiar-ized with heuristic strategies and tactics that have proven effective in the past and that are likely to prove effective in the future as well. Members of a cognitive elite, students will guide the rest of the population in its daily interpretations, influencing the way in which people build their houses, educate their children, cure their diseases, choose their novels, talk about their private life, and interact with other human beings. In other words, that position of hierarchically superior interpretive status that the professor currently holds in front of them will be the same that they themselves will hold in their social and professional environments, exactly thanks to their being exposed to a series of methodological habits, which they absorbed, and whose mastery will be certified by their diplomas.

Why, then, is the passage from the classroom to the street, or to the square, or to the world, experienced as increasingly painful by the majority of students? Why do more and more of them believe that what they have learned from uni-versity lectures does not prepare them at all to deal with what they will face as adult architects, physicians, or lawyers? Is it just a matter of updating the infor-mation that students receive during their training or filling the gap between university and "reality" through multiplying those experiences that students can gain across these two worlds, such as stages or internships? Will a generation of younger professors help in refreshing and sharpening the interpretive skills of students?

Unfortunately, semioticians that look with satisfaction at the complex diagram through which they are explaining to students the meaning of a poem, a pho-tograph, or a theatre performance, will have to admit that the problem is not as simple as that. They might, of course, update the methodology, read the latest books in the field, attend symposia that deal with the most current developments of the discipline, and so on. The feeling of dismay at the thought of the enormous distance between the epistemological atmosphere of the classroom and that of the world is destined to persist or even to be embittered by the experience of how useless any effort of methodological upgrade turns out.

Methods of corroboration

The feeling of this distance, which is at the same time a cognitive, an emotional, and a pragmatic one, has to do with some central issues not only in semiotics but also in any other discipline involving a systematic reflection on interpretation. Such issues affect the jurist as well as the medical scientist, the art curator as well as the journalist (Maitland 2017: "Introduction"). In a nutshell, such distance can be measured in relation to the following question: What are the acceptable pro-cedures of interpretation that are usually adopted during a university lecture, and what are, on the contrary, those that prevail outside of the academic laboratory? In order to answer such question, one should posit an epistemological, meth-odological, and analytical distinction between rationality and reasonableness. As pointed out by most modern philosophy of science, a great divide separates the procedures through which natural scientists reach their conclusions through interpreting the data deriving from the observation and analysis of reality and the procedures through which "human scientists" do the same with both socio-cultural reality and the texts that it produces (Popper 1935: chapter 4—"Grade der Prüfbarkeit"). In the first case, the replicability of the experiment allows scientists to test hypotheses in order to either corroborate them or falsify them, so that they might be replaced by better and more encompassing speculations about the nature of nature.

When semioticians describe, analyze, and interpret a text, their hypotheses cannot be tested in the same way. In a recent article, for instance, I have claimed that one of the most famous and discussed upon sequences in the history of cinema, the "sequence of the vase" in *Late Spring* by Ozu (1949), should be interpreted by taking as a point of departure not only the famous vase that all previous interpreters had exclusively focused on but also the strange object that appears, unnoticed by all, in a shadowy corner of the same sequence (Leone 2016b) (Figure 11.1).

I have proposed this interpretation to my Japanese colleagues, to my Turin colleagues that are experts of Japanese cinema, and, last but not least, I have discussed about my reading at length with the students of my master course of semiotics. I have also published this interpretation online and in journals, both in Italian and in Japanese. All the concerned audiences seemed to

FIGURE 11.1 The sequence of the vase; photogram from 晩春 [*Banshun*], *Late Spring* (1949), by 小津 安二郎, Ozu Yasujirō (1949), picture from Wikimedia Commons

be convinced by my interpretive move, and no major objections were leveled at it. But how can this semiotic hypothesis be corroborated, and how can it be falsified? According to the theory of semantic intentionality formulated by Umberto Eco, there are three different ways to test the hypothesis above (Eco 1990: chapter 13—"Semantics, Pragmatics, and Text Semiotics"). They will be considered in the following paragraphs.

Asking the author

The first is to contrast the interpretive hypothesis with the semantic intentionality of the author, that is, with that which the author meant to signify and communicate through the sequence. This modality of verification, however, is not the most effective one, for two reasons. A contingent reason is that, since Ozu is no longer alive, we cannot ask him what he meant by the sequence of the vase. He might have left some meta-texts, such as notes and interviews, explaining the meaning of the sequence. One could not rely on these meta-texts, however, in the same way as one would rely on Ozu's own words. Determining in what way these meta-texts explain the meaning of the sequence, indeed, would require further interpretations, some of them being as, if not even more, speculative than the one seeking to interpret the sequence in the first instance.

The second reason for the unviability of this procedure is that Ozu himself cannot be regarded as the highest possible authority on the meaning of his movies. He might have had an idea of what the sequence of the vase might signify, or rather of what he wanted to communicate through it, and he might have tried to arrange all the elements of the sequence so as to signify it. Given the nature of the cinematic language, however, which does nothing but magnifying an aspect that is present in verbal language too (Aumont 1990: chapter 6—"Les pouvoirs de l'image"), the sequence itself signifies despite and beyond Ozu's intentions. There is no signification without the potentiality of alternative interpretations. Even those texts that are constructed so as to reduce such alternatives, like the instructions of a drug's leaflet, for instance, can generate diverging interpretations, exactly because of the intrinsically undetermined nature of verbal language (Eco 1976: chapter 1—"Signification and Communication"). Such indeterminacy is even higher when images, instead of words, are used in order to assemble the signification of a message, especially when the former are not meant to refer to reality but to tell a story and, even more ambiguously, to convey a moral message about abstract human values.

To this difficulty one should add that even if Ozu could perfectly explain to us the meaning of the sequence, the explanation would be a fragment of verbal meta-discourse and, therefore, adopt a different expressive substance, syntactic structure, and semantic behavior than the sequence itself (Calabrese 2000). Ultimately, Ozu's interpretive indications on a sequence of one of his movies cannot be considered as its definitive interpretation because that which Ozu really wished to signify with that sequence, he signified it precisely through it, whereas when requested to explain the same signification by translating it into a verbal metalanguage, he would face the same difficulties that most critics do and without even the benefit of detachment.

Asking the reader

A second viable option to test the interpretive hypothesis above might be to compare and contrast it with those of other spectators. That in a way happens every time that an interpretive hypothesis is communicated: In my case, the reading of the sequence was put to the test of its reception by Japanese colleagues (including a historian of Japanese pottery), an Asian cinema specialist at the University of Turin, and students. In all of these circumstances, as pointed out earlier, no objection was made. Is that sufficient as a means to corroborate the reading of the sequence as the best possible interpretation? The problem here arises to designate the community of interpreters that would exert the highest authority in matters of judgment over the extent to which an interpretation of the famous sequence of the vase in Ozu's *Late Spring* might or might not be correct. How and by whom is this community going to be shaped, perhaps by Japanese spectators, since they are supposed to be those whose interpretive encyclopedia is geographically and culturally the closest to that which Ozu referred to in creating the sequence itself? But, then, how should one select and shape such cohort of Japanese spectators? What age should they be, from what sociocultural background, of what gender, and so on?

The major problem in adopting a corroboration strategy based on the notion of "*intentio lectoris*" (the meaning that the reader of a text, or the spectator of a movie, attributes to such cultural artifact) is its representativeness. In other words, against what kind of range of subjective interpretations should mine be tested? The answer is not clear and might even lead to solutions implying intolerable ethnocentrism. Should only Italians interpret Dante, and Molière be interpreted only by the French? Is the native command of a natural language enough to determine the circle of those who are supposed and entitled to correctly interpret a text? And is this applicable also in the case of predominantly nonverbal texts, such as the famous sequence of the vase in Ozu's movie? The most serious difficulty of this second method, however, resides in the fact that one should clearly establish beforehand the criteria according to which a subjective interpretation is going to be judged as more or less apt to falsify or corroborate a hypothesis.

Statistic methodologies would not be a solution either. Should one conclude that, for instance, since in a survey more than seventy-five percent of spectators have declared that they interpret the famous vase as symbol of the solitude of the male protagonist of the movie after the demise of his wife, this should be considered as the correct interpretation? And would this statistic argument imply that, should a subsequent survey show different statistics, the correct interpretation should change accordingly? Such way of testing, falsifying, and corroborating interpretive hypotheses would be unacceptable for most scholars in the humanities, although some of them are exploring these procedures in the field of quantitative aesthetics (Kreuz and MacNealy 1996).

The aspect that is particularly problematic in this statistic methodology is that it would export a method of political determination (the majority wins) in a field where the opinion of the majority is not necessarily the lesser evil. On the contrary, one could claim that one of the objectives of the critical analysis of artworks is not to comply with the average opinions expressed by a community of receivers but rather to alter this average reception through showing that more complex and all-encompassing interpretive hypotheses are possible and potentially lead to farther exploit the moral content of an artwork. In the humanities, art historians and literary critics have not been usually seen as those who certify the interpretations of the average receiver but rather as those who, through engaging with the artwork at length, discover in it paths of meaning that most readers were not able to detect.

Asking the text

The third major strategy for testing an interpretive hypothesis does not consist in asking directly or indirectly the author (which, moreover, is impossible in some cases, for instance in the case of the supposedly transcendent authorship of most "sacred" texts) or in seeking to determine a majority of readers but in comparing and contrasting different interpretations in relation to the artwork itself. In our example, this heuristics consists in comparing my interpretation of the sequence of the vase with other interpretations that different spectators might have produced about the same sequence. Although this strategy seems similar to the second one, it is, on the contrary, a completely alternative one. In the subjective method, different interpretations are compared and contrasted, but there is no rational standard for doing it, save for that of ethnocentric or similar conventions (someone is Italian, so her or his interpretation of Dante must be better; someone is a Japanese man, so his interpretation must be better than that of a Japanese woman) or that of statistic measurements. In the third way, instead, different interpretations are compared and contrasted not subjectively but intersubjectively, not in relation to the supposed primacy of a certain sociocultural category of readers or to that of the majority, but in relation to the text itself. That is why this method leads to a rational comparison of interpretations: The way in which they differ can be articulated and measured in relation to the text, that is, to features of the texts that are visible to everybody. To give an example, one could say, "let us compare the Japanese interpretations of Ozu with the Italian ones", which is a comparison that makes reference to extra-textual and quite slippery elements, such as the nationality of spectators; if not, one could say, "let us compare the interpretations of the sequence that only consider the vase with those that consider both the vase and the mysterious object appearing in a shadowy corner of the scene" or "let us compare the interpretations that explain why the vase is shown twice in the sequence to the interpretations that do not".

In relation to the first two methods, this third one implies a significant advantage, which is the possibility of rationally ranking interpretations. In the first method of testing, there was no particular reason to believe that Ozu's interpretation of his own sequence was superior to those of his spectators, unless one relied on a naïve idea of signification, an idea whose weaknesses have been exposed supra; similarly, there was no particular rational argument to believe that an interpretation is superior to the others because of its ethnocentric or statistic force. The third method, instead, introduces a simple but irrefutable logic of ranking: Since the whole of the text signifies, those interpretations coherently taking into account more elements of this signification will be preferable to those that take into account only a part of them (Hjelmslev and Uldall 1957).

That is an axiom, but it is one that is difficult to refute. It rests, indeed, on the concept itself of semiosis. In verbal language, for instance, given a sentence, or even a complex assemblage of sentences such as a literary text, it is hard to demonstrate that an interpretation that takes into account only its incipit is better than that which, on the contrary, describes, analyzes, and interprets the totality of verbal signs woven within the text. Similarly, it is hard to prove that a reading of a painting of Piero della Francesca explaining only the meaning of the characters appearing therein but not that of the background is preferable to an interpretation where both receive an analytical reading. This axiom also relies on the principle that culture is made by both texts and para-texts, that is, meta-signs that are supposed to tell readers (observers, listeners, and so on) where a text starts and where it ends, from where the analytical effort must be exerted and where it should stop (Genette 1987). Postmodern artists and texts can play with such para-textual meta-signs, producing, for instance, artworks whose frontiers are not neat but blur with that of their contexts. This blurring effect, however, is possible only for, in most circumstances, culture clearly signals the limits of a text. Since culture tells us how and where to look at in order to understand where and when a text begins, and where and when it ends, it is reasonable to believe that culture also requires to exert our interpretive attention throughout the text and not only through part of it.

Interpretive temporality

This criterion of exhaustiveness is in a way superior to any criterion adopted either in the objective or in the subjective methods of testing, because it is an intrinsically cooperative one. Whereas the first method implicitly affirms that only the author knows the meaning of a text and the second intrinsically claims that only a certain group of readers knows it, the third method leaves open the question of who might better interpret a text: It is not the author; it is not a certain category of readers; it is, on the contrary, the one or those who will look more attentively into the text and explain more carefully what they can see and read. The first method is oriented toward the past: The author conceived of a meaning, expressed it through an artwork, and it is now upon the reader to retrieve that meaning from the text, if possible by faithfully adhering to the author's first communicative intention. The second method, on the other hand, is oriented toward the present: It is here and now that the text means, for a reader x or y, and its meaning is not to be searched in the past intentions of an author—intentions that preceded the creation of the artwork—but in the current perception of a selected group of readers, whose features or number make them the artwork's best interpreters. A farther reason for which the third method of testing is preferable to the first two is that it is, instead, open to the future: An interpretation is put forward, but if in the future someone will propose an interpretation that explains all the elements taken into account by the previous interpretation, and explicates, moreover, some farther elements, neglected by the former, then this future interpretation will have to be judged as superior.

In the first and in the second method, a better interpretation can also emerge, but not in relation to the text; in the first case, a better interpretation will be one that, for instance, relies on novel information concerning the intentions of the author, information that was hitherto ignored or neglected; in the second case, a change in the ethnocentric polarization of the semiosphere or in statistics will make a better interpretation emerge: Now that women more than men interpret *Hamlet*, for instance, a feminist interpretation must be preferred to a macho one (on the weaknesses of this approach, see Zhang 2016). The dynamic of improvement implied by the third method is intrinsically different and superior to the first two because it does not relate to extra-textual elements but to intra-textual ones; in other words, in order for someone to come up with a better interpretation, it is not necessary to look for it outside of the text, because such interpretation is already available to everyone inside of the text, and all that is needed is to better look into it.

To return to the example given above, the sequence of the vase in Ozu's *Late Spring* has always contained two objects, not only the vase. It was always possible for someone to notice the second object and to include it into the interpretation. For some reason, however, this second object was neglected, until someone took notice of it and included it in a coherent interpretation of the sequence. This new interpretation, which takes into account more elements of the textual manifestation than the previous ones, is better than them not because it better grasps the intentionality of the author, or because it fits better with the inclinations of a group of readers, but simply because it explains more and better that which all might have seen and interpreted in the text.

Along this line, interpretations of *King Lear* that propose a coherent view of more textual elements of it are to be preferred to those interpretations that are sketchy, or partial, or neglect to fit some major portions of the text within the architecture of the interpretation. Similarly, interpretations of the Sistine Chapel that coherently read more visual details of it, without neglecting those that are placed at the margins of the visual scene, are also to be preferred. In a way, this strategy for ranking interpretations is not dissimilar from that which guides natural sciences too: If someone formulates a hypothesis that might explain more of that which can be seen in the image produced by a microscope, then that hypothesis must be preferred to that which neglects some of the elements of the image.

Textual laboratories

Something central, however, still distinguishes the third method for testing the value of a textual interpretation from Popper's idea of scientific corroboration. All the interpreters of a text deal with the same materials. They can take into consideration a smaller or a greater quantity of them but they cannot exit the perimeter of the para-text. Interpreters of Shakespeare's *King Lear*, for instance, can propose different readings of some of the passages of the text, but they cannot add new materials to it. In natural sciences, instead, the fact that an experiment can usually be replicated allows scientists to control the changing of conditions that surround the interpretation of reality. In a textual reading, an interpretation can improve a previous interpretation by taking into consideration neglected elements of the text, but not by adding new elements to it; in natural reading, since the experiment is supposed to be not the ultimate object of interpretation, but a controlled simulacrum of reality (nature), then its para-textual frontiers are not as clear: Through varying the frontiers of the simulacrum and, therefore, its semiotic relation with reality (nature), better interpretations can be formulated, interpretations that are preferable not simply because they explain neglected elements of the experiment but also because they introduce neglected elements into it.

Mutatis mutandis, one might affirm that a textual reading cannot be compared with a scientific reading, but rather with the designing of an experiment leading to a scientific reading, the only but crucial difference being that the humanist's experiment cannot vary, because the laboratory coincides with the object that is to be interpreted. The frustration of the humanist interpretation in relation to the scientific one derives from the fact that the textual materials that eighteenth-century scholars had at their disposal so as to interpret Shakespeare's *King Lear* are actually the same as those that contemporary interpreters have. Shakespeare's text is both the object of the reading and its laboratory, and the same syllables, words, sentences, and rhymes constitute the perimeter of that which the interpreter can read and to which she or he can attribute meaning.

If the para-textual perimeter of a text does not vary, though, in the sense that it offers always the same elements to any interpreter who might come across the significant surface of the text itself, the lenses of the microscope through which these elements are observed, instead, might change. The psychoanalyst of literature and the semiotician look into the same text, but they see different elements in it.

Interpretive lenses

The way in which readers, spectators, listeners, and so on look at the significant surface of a text is never completely casual, or merely guided by personal taste. It is, on the contrary, shaped by a series of patterns, some of which derive from the historical and sociocultural coordinates of the reader, whereas other stem from her or his subjective training as reader and interpreter. It is known, for instance, that being an assiduous reader of the literary works of a certain author turns one into a different kind of interpreter of that author, one who is able to detect, within that author's texts, elements and nuances that less accustomed readers tend to ignore. In this case, it is not the text that varies, but the cognitive and emotional filter through which its significant surface is sifted. A novel invests the readers with a myriad of words, sentences, and stories; a movie solicits the beholder with a frantic sequence of images; and so on. The novel and the movie are the same for everyone, meaning that they present all readers with the same significant surface, and yet not the entirety of it can be retained and deciphered on the spot. Exiting a movie theater, or closing a book, some more attentive and perceptive interpreters will have retained a greater amount of information, and some of them will have almost naturally conflated this information into a coherent interpretation. The value of an interpretive method, therefore, can be measured in relation to the extent to which it leads interpreters to discover, within the perimeter of a text, elements that they would not have otherwise detected. If Greimasian semiotics has a merit, for instance, exactly consists in working as a lens that, pointed at a certain text, allows one to see elements within it that would have been otherwise gone unseen and neglected (Greimas 1976).

That is possible because every interpretive method essentially consists in a translation. In the Greimasian method of textual interpretation, that which matters the most is not the exactitude of the theoretical proposal, many aspects and nuances of which are both debatable and, indeed, debated. Just to give an example, this method imagines the meaning of a text as though it was generated through a series of logical operations, whose dynamics and results can be ranked at different levels of abstractedness. Despite what Greimasian fundamentalists tend to affirm, there is no intrinsic motivation for singling out a certain number of such logical levels (that of deep values, that of narrative grammar, that of discourse, and that of figuration). This largely depends on the accidents of the history of the elaboration of the semiotic method, such as the fact that some aspects of the theory were developed more than others.

The major usefulness of the Greimasian method, instead, emerges from the fact itself of translating the features of a (literary, filmic, visual, etc.) text into a new analytical simulacrum, whose features coherently derive from the inter-defined metalanguage that the analysis adopts. In other words, when the Greimasian method translates the meaning of a text through rendering it into a metalanguage, that which matters is not as much the metalanguage itself, which could be replaced by other metalanguages, but the coherence of the analytical translation. Translating the meaning of a text into the code of a metalanguage, indeed, allows the analyst to see, within the perimeter determined by the text's para-textual marks, new elements and new dynamics. A lay reader will see, when reading Shakespeare's *King Lear*, a complex array of syllables, words, and sentences; she or he will also see a protagonist, perhaps a co-protagonist, some secondary characters, and the line of a narrative plot. When a semiotician trained in the Greimasian method looks at the same text, she or he will see the same elements, but she or he will simultaneously detect also elements that the lay reader does not perceive, exactly for they emerge from the application of the metalanguage to the text itself. The Greimasian semiotician, for instance, will single out not only characters but also macro-narrative functions that complexly intertwine with them.

That is why the application of a method enhances interpretation: not in the trivial and somehow misleading sense that such method leads to the discovery of a textual truth that non-trained approaches are unable to spot but in the sense that, through the operation of metalinguistic translation, the method multiplies the possibilities of elaborating interpretive hypotheses concerning the text itself. As stated earlier, unlike in natural sciences, in human sciences, the text is both the object under investigation and the investigation laboratory; its perimeter must remain the same. The application of a new method, that is, of a new way of metalinguistically translate the text, introduces new possibilities for the analysis. The text is always the same, but now the meta-text allows one to peruse it under a different angle.

This metalinguistic translation is not without problems: It must be faithful to the significant surface of the text and, at the same time, render its structures in a creative way. If one looks at this matter with unbiased eyes, however, one must admit that the so-called "lay" approach to a text is not naturally unproblematic either. The fact that we recognize "sentences" in a literary text might appear as a spontaneous operation, but such spontaneity actually is the result of interiorizing a grammatical analysis whose evolution required a long and sometimes conflictive elaboration. The fact that we recognize a subject, a verb, and an object in *King Lear*'s sentences is not less conventional than the fact that we recognize an actant subject, an actant object, or an actant observer in the narrative plot of the text. The difference between the two approaches is not as much a question of abstractedness as one of centrality, within the semiosphere, of such and such method of interpretive reading. In most contemporary societies, readers are trained to analyze the syntax of a text, whereas they are not trained to decode its semantics, which is usually still dealt with through impressionistic methods. Nothing, however, intrinsically prevents a structural method of semantic analysis to become equally central in the semiosphere, to be taught and learned in schools, and to become a "second nature" of most readers and readings.

Toward an interpretive liturgy

That leads one to consider the major advantages of this third method for testing the interpretive hypotheses concerning a text, which is the possibility of sharing and inhabiting a common space for intersubjective discussion. In the first method, there is no need to debate about interpretations: Those who have the closest access to the supposed mind and intentionality of the author occupy the highest hierarchical rank in the sphere of interpretation. Such method is dangerously inclined to authoritarianism, especially in those cases in which the identity of the author is not clear or is mystified. In the "religions of the book", for instance, power can be held also as a consequence of the claim that someone, be it a scribe or a priest, is closer to the intentionality of the author, the problem in this case being that there is no way to prove or disprove such pretense of proximity (Leone 2013c). In the second method too, discussion is not a viable option, because diverging interpretations are not meant to reconcile their differences and converge toward a negotiated version of them, adopting those tenets that better fit the reading of the text at stake, but to coagulate into statistical clusters: As long as an interpretation is shared by a majority of readers, it is to be considered the correct one, no matter what.

In the third method, instead, which is the one that targets the *intentio operis*, discussion is not only an option but is the natural outcome of how this approach works. When the meaning of a text is translated into a diagram that renders it through a specific metalanguage, then competition must arise among all the beholders of such diagram, in order to determine who is able to see more elements into it and, more importantly, who is able to connect the greatest quantity of such elements into a coherent interpretation. There is no more exciting moment, in academic seminars, of that magic atmosphere that takes shape when the analyst has delivered her or his interpretation—for instance the interpretation of a painting by Rembrandt—and all the attendees are left with the image, the method, and the proposed reading, implicitly challenged by the speaker herself or himself to further improve that which has been proposed. Typically, at this stage two different kinds of questions are raised: On the one hand, someone points at an element of the painting that has not been taken into account by the metalinguistic translation. Objections of this kind are interesting, but somehow fail to work as devices of corroboration.

That happens, on the contrary (second kind), when some of the attendees not only point out at a neglected element in the painting and its metalinguistic description: In addition, they are also able to reformulate the proposed interpretation in a way that encompasses all the elements that such interpretation takes into account, plus the neglected one. Confronted with remarks of this kind, the analyst will have to rejoice, since cooperative interpretive work has actually achieved more than a single analyst, albeit a genial one, could. In the third method, indeed, the community of scholars sharing the same method is more important than the single scholars, and it is actually more important than the method itself. What matters, in fact, is sharing: Familiarity with the same metalanguage, albeit at different levels of precision and sophistication, allows the analytical work to become a *liturgy of interpretation*, which etymologically means "work of the people". This liturgy will be guided by an expert but will necessarily be followed by a series of practitioners of the analysis that share the same methodology and can advance each other's perception of the text. That is the way in which the Greimasian seminar in Paris, or Eco's seminars in Bologna and Urbino, or Lotman's seminar in Tartu worked in their halcyon days.

But why, then—given that focusing on the *intentio operis* allows one to create an intersubjective arena where to debate, through the lenses of a metalanguage, about the meaning of a text and, more generally, about interpretations—should analysts be seized by that bittersweet melancholy that, as has been described at the beginning of this chapter, subjugates them when the suspect arises that this laboratory of interpretation is actually an empty one, both because it does not resonate with the practices of interpretation that take place in the "real world", outside of the academe, and because students and colleagues themselves seem to just pay lip service to the ritual of interpretation, turned into a sort of cold liturgy to which no one any longer attach any faith?

One could not answer this question without accepting the saddening hypothesis that, in interpretation, it is not the method that creates the community, but the community that creates the method. That does not mean that some methodological proposals might not be more articulated and sophisticated than others. Greimas's proposal of a methodology for textual analysis was certainly more complex and rich than any method proposed by Roland Barthes, for instance. That, however, is not the point. The force of a method, like the force of a language, does not stem uniquely from its internal structure, or from the internal structure of the metalanguage, but from the fact that a community speaks such languages. Italian can work as a language not because it is phonetically, syntactically, or semantically coherent, but because a community of speakers believes and interiorizes the belief of such coherence. Similarly, Greimas's method is effective not only per se but for a community takes shape around this methodological proposal and is willing to sacrifice interpretive idiosyncrasies in order to create a common arena for discussing interpretations.

That is the real cause for the interpretive melancholia that, nowadays, strikes many academics, especially those who lived in cultural epochs and contexts where, on the contrary, a feeling of the existence and the activity of an interpretive community would be stronger. Looking outside of the classroom, what is it that the professional analyst sees? A chaotic cacophony of narcissistic voices, each boasting itself not only as a voice but also as the ultimate method that everyone should adopt; the transformation of relativism into the absence of dialogue; the conflation of the subjective method of interpretation with the intersubjective one, a conflation wherein each interpreter claims to own and dominate the entire arena of interpretation; the total inability to embrace a principle of humbleness, according to which one's interpretive identity is at least partially sacrificed in the name of sharing a common space for discussion. In this interpretive semiosphere, it is natural that conspiracy theories, trolling, cynicism, and sectarianism thrive. Nobody wants to yield to a common method of interpretation for a fundamental mistake is made, consisting in the inability to distinguish between accepting a common space in which to debate over interpretations, and accepting a common interpretation. The two options are completely different. A society in which all are forced to accept a single view is a dictatorial one. A society in which nobody accepts a space where a single view might arise, however, is an anarchist one.

The two models are dangerous because they both entail the possibility of violence, meant as agency that resolves interpretive conflicts in nonsymbolic ways, not through persuasion but through force.

The melancholy of the interpreter arises even more when she or he sees that also in the purified atmosphere of the laboratory of interpretation, in the classroom, for instance, or in the conference hall, the pernicious cynicism that pervades society contaminates the instruments, disrupting any feeling of an interpretive community also among colleagues, or between professors and students.

Conclusions

Is there any antidote to such melancholy? Again, a viable solution seems to lies in what Umberto Eco has underlined all through his career, that is, the essential difference between rationality and reasonableness (Eco 1992). What is reasonableness, also etymologically? It is the potentiality of rationality. Something that is reasonable is not rational per se but can be recognized as such within the continuous exchange and negotiation of a community devotedly sharing a public discourse. Claiming that an interpretation is the only rational one, especially in the field of humanities, dangerously resembles an act of authoritarianism. There is no single way to interpret the meaning of a novel, a painting, or a film, and fortunately there will never be. Language is slippery and mutable, not a solid but a liquid substance, or even an airy one in the case of poetry or similar discursive formations. One should strongly object, however, that claiming that there is no single rational interpretation of a cultural fact is tantamount to claiming that there is no single reasonable interpretation of it. When I affirm the rationality of my interpretation, I impose my view, mostly by authority if not even by force. But when I affirm the reasonableness of my interpretation, I do not impose it; on the contrary, I offer it to a community to which I myself subscribe, by curtailing my cynicism, narcissism, envy, and by sharing a methodology that, although it might not be perfect and although it might be perfected, is nevertheless able to create a space of intersubjective recognition, where the correctness of an interpretation might always be recognized.

Admitting and preserving this difference is fundamental not only to protect an arena for the discussion and corroboration of interpretive hypotheses but also because such arena is essential for their falsification too. Claiming that reasonable interpretations do not exist, indeed, is tantamount to both thwarting any possibility of ranking them positively and undermining any opportunity to ranking them negatively. In a society that is unable to humbly turn itself into a structured community of interpreters, one can neither hope that a new interpretation of Shakespeare will be proven as more encompassing and satisfying than any previous one nor that a new conspiratorial revisionism will be disproven as less reasonable and, therefore, less tenable than any preceding interpretation of history or society.

After all, what is needed for a society to work as an interpretive community is not a perfect method of interpretation. It is reasonable manners.

CONCLUSIONS

The clash of semiotic civilizations

> La civilisation n'est autre chose que le mode de
> végétation propre à l'humanité.[1]
> (Victor Hugo, *Œuvres complètes*, 4: 495–6)

Introduction

There is no better way of honoring a scholar than critically assessing and prolonging his or her work. There is nothing more fastidious to great scholars than worshipping epigones. Unfortunately, Greimas's theory was thus compelling that attracted both the best minds of his generation and the most intellectually subservient ones. Several decades after Greimas's demise, the frenzy first generated by the novelty of his method long gone, it is time not only to reevaluate structural and generative semiotics but also to defend it: in recent years, semiotics-bashing has become a popular sport, mostly performed through cliché arguments and very little knowledge of semiotics itself. Even the most authoritative critics of semiotics have often "thrown the baby with the dirty water" (Leone 2015a: 2–3).

There is only one serious way of talking about Greimas's contributions to semiotics, and it is to read, reread, and comment on his texts, better if perused in the original French. The prose of the Franco-Lithuanian scholar might seem abstruse to many or old-fashioned in its rhetorical choices, yet it is increasingly evident that what came after Greimas and is now more and more pervading both highbrow and lowbrow culture, is such a shallow combination of superficial cultural studies and, worse, conspiracy thought that one can only be nostalgic about the glorious time of humanities in which scholars like Greimas still believed that a rational grasp of cultural and social facts could be attained through designing and applying a rigorous method (Leone 2016c: 1–5). Detractors of methods especially in the humanities now abound and write bestsellers, yet where are these Pied Pipers leading their readers? To a world where no reasonable understanding of reality and language is promised but a dreamland where all are left free to run after their wildest interpretations of texts and people, including those interpretations that are bound to be harmful to society.

The present conclusive chapter, nevertheless, does not encourage its readers to adopt a nostalgic gaze on Greimas and his semiotics, as though they were a golden age of the human thought, lost forever. On the contrary, it will claim that the best attitude to look at Greimas's marvelous theoretical castle is *vintage*: Contemporary semioticians should understand the principles of the internal harmony of Greimas's semiotics, pinpoint those elements of it that, like wooden clogs in the Seventies or shoulder pads in the Eighties, should never become fashionable again—not only because they are objectively ugly beyond any possible redemption but also because they are unpractical—and select those elements that, instead, are sorely needed in the contemporary design of humanities. One of them is particularly precious, as the present chapter will seek to demonstrate: rational enthusiasm.

No "vintage" assessment and refashioning, however, will be ever possible without a merciless critical assessment of Greimas's foundational texts. It is a pity that they are not read anymore as they would deserve, partially because the mindset that they express is now dangerously out of fashion, partially because they are badly or poorly translated or not translated at all, and partially and mostly because they are too often diluted in companions and handbooks that transmit the superficial charm of Greimas's theory but not its fundaments. What follows is, to begin with, a critical analysis of the foundations of Greimas's semiotic theory, which were first laid with the publication of *Sémantique structurale: recherche et méthode*—the (more catious) title of the English translation is: *Structural Semantics: An Attempt at a Method* (1983)—published in 1966 by the prestigious French publisher Larousse.

Reality and signification in Greimas

In a paragraph entitled "Signification and the human sciences" Greimas writes that "[…] if the natural sciences ask questions in order to understand how man and the world are, the human sciences pose the question, more or less explicitly, of what both of them signify" (Greimas 1966; Engl. trans. by Daniele McDowell, Ronald Schleifer, and Alan Velie, 1983: 1). This sentence posits a neat separation between knowledge of the being of reality and knowledge of the signification of reality. That could be regarded as a postulate of Greimas's semiotics. Indeed, both his works and those of his followers tend to drastically "de-ontologize" semiotics, reframing and deconstructing in structural terms any possible indentation of "reality" into "language". For Greimas and his school, reality might well exist but it is not semiotically relevant, unless it is translated into semiotic forms, that is, into patterns of signification.

The way in which Greimas approached the issue of images and their capacity to "represent reality" is the most efficacious example of such attitude. As the Franco-Lithuanian semiotician pointed out in the essay "Sémiotique figurative et sémiotique plastique" ["figurative semiotics and plastic semiotics"] (1984), images do not represent reality; admitting that would mean tainting the immanence of the semiotic metalanguage with a reference to the ontological dimension. Instead, Greimas contends that images are "visual texts" that refer to the articulation of the semantic plane of the "macro-semiotics of the world" in order to shape the articulation of their own expressive plane. In simpler words, and with an example, we do not recognize grapes in Caravaggio's *Basket of Fruit* because the painting faithfully represents reality but because it skillfully refers to the semantic articulation of fruit in most Western European visual culture in order to construct its own expressive plane though usage of appropriate plastic formants (lines, colors, and positions). For Greimas, then, images do not depict reality but the semiotic appraisal of it that circulates in a given cultural context.

An even more macroscopic example of Greimas's attitude of de-ontologization is his treatment of time. As it is well known, most of the disagreement between Greimas and Paul Ricoeur stemmed from the fact that, whereas for the French philosopher, narratives are one of the most powerful means though which human beings account for time, for the Franco-Lithuanian semiotician, time does not matter as much as temporality, that is, the illusion of a temporal dimension that, again, texts and narratives construct through their internal dynamics, whose analysis should therefore be independent from any preoccupation about the ontology of time (Greimas and Ricoeur 2000).

Greimas's rationality and Eco's reasonableness

Some exponents of the Greimasian school have radicalized the immanentism of structuralist and especially generative semiotics to an unbearable extent, translating into the inner labyrinth of the theory any potential reference to "extra-textual reality". The philosophical purposes of this attitude were clear to Greimas and, to a certain extent, also perfectly understandable and laudable in the context of twentieth-century humanities. Greimas used to summarize such attitude through the saying "hors du texte, point de salut" ["outside of the text, there is no salvation"], paraphrasing the famous theological sentence "extra ecclesiam nulla salus" ["outside of the church there is no salvation"], contained in the catechism of the Catholic Church and attributed to the third-century bishop Cyprian of Carthage.

Greimas was thus attached to the idea that semiotics should deal with what is inside texts, and not with what is outside of them, for he believed that keeping faith to methodological immanentism was the only way to guarantee the rationality of interpretation. Talking about the meaning of texts as something that emanates from their inner structures and not as something that is attributed to them from the outside (by the psychology of the interpreter, by the interpretive tendencies that predominate in societies according to ethnicity, class, gender, and so on, or according to reference to a reality supposed as existing outside of the text) was meant to preserve the rationality and, therefore, the intersubjectivity of interpretation: How can an agreement about the meaning of something be reached, if this something is not seen as a structure, as a text, and as a system that inherently forbids or discourages certain interpretations and encourages certain others, guiding the reader toward them?

On the one hand, Greimas's ambition—prolonging, to a certain extent, that of previous structural students of narratives, such as Vladimir J. Propp—was that of providing a rational method to grasp meaning, not only in plain discourse but also, and above all, in the elaborate, duplicitous, and subtly ambiguous linguistic creations of literature. The acme of this ambition manifested itself in Greimas's *Maupassant* (1976), a didactic exploit meant to display the utmost potentialities of the Greimasian method for the analysis of literary narratives.

On the other hand, such project of rational description of meaning joined, also to a certain extent, that of Umberto Eco's interpretive semiotics: In Eco too, the so-called *intentio operis* is central; readers who attentively decode a text should aim neither at their subjective reading of it (*intentio lectoris*) nor at the meaning that the author supposedly intended to instill in the text (*intentio auctoris*)—which is frequently, and especially in literature, radically different from the actual meaning of the text; they should seek to seize, instead, the *intentio operis* of a text, that is, the way in which the text itself designs a "model reader" by encouraging or discouraging certain interpretive moves (Eco 1979). Drawing his philosophical semiotic framework from Peirce's vision of the sign and semiosis rather than—like Greimas—from Saussure's linguistics and, even more keenly, Hjelmslev's glossematics, Eco's proposal of a method for the intersubjectively sustainable interpretation of texts and narratives does not strictly claim to be a rational but a reasonable one.

That is the main difference between Eco and Greimas, and that is also their strength or weakness, depending on the point of view from which their divergences are observed. Eco does not doubt that a reasonable agreement can be found, within a community of interpreters, when seeking to determine the meaning of a text (Eco 1990). Faithful to Peirce's dynamic semiotic philosophy, however, Eco does not affirm that this agreement is a permanent one, eternally inscribed in the structure of a text like a Platonic idea. He suggests, on the contrary, that such reasonable agreement will essentially depend on the interpretive encyclopedia shared by the community of interpreters. This encyclopedia is mutable by definition; Eco does not primarily focus on the causes and laws of such mutation but aims at providing some abstract guidelines that, independently from the community and the text at stake, might guide the interpretive work of readers. From this point of view, he provides a sort of semiotic version of Jürgen Habermas's theory of communicative rationality, in which what matters is not prescribing the rationality of the content of communication but that of the empty framework in which such content is communicatively dealt with (Habermas 1981).

Moreover, Juri Lotman's semiotics can be considered, according to this perspective, as the natural complement of Eco's theory, since it precisely bears on the semiotic analysis of those sociocultural dynamics that modify the communitarian setting in which a given interpretation takes place (Lotman and Uspenkij 1984). Lotman does not focus either on causes or on agencies of changes in the semiosphere but, at least, envisages a systematic study of how the "environment of meaning" mutates over time (Lotman 1990).

Greimas disregards time. He does not contemplate that changes in the semiosphere will affect the ways in which readers interpret texts. His ambition is to propose not a reasonable but a rational method for the analysis of meaning, which could be valid both cross-culturally and trans-historically. He does not want only to define the framework in which interpreters will reasonably discuss about the meaning of a text, like Eco, or the dynamics that affect the characteristics of this framework through time and space, like Lotman. Greimas wants to define the range of meaning of a text; its immutably and intersubjectively valid content; its inherent voice. That is Greimas's strength and charm but that is also his weakness, and perhaps the ingredient that has made many of his texts age much faster than those of other less ambitious semioticians.

Relativizing Greimasian semiotics: trends and dangers

Perhaps exactly as a reaction or even as a provocation against the universalism of structural anthropology and generative semiotics, anthropological research has increasingly focused, in the last decades, on the extreme variability of meaning. Moreover, such research has found out that, in the passage from culture to culture both in time and space (a robust school of historical anthropology has developed in parallel with sociocultural and mainly synchronic anthropology), it is not only meaning that changes but also its framework. On the one hand, semiotic anthropology has investigated the variety of linguistic and semiotic ideologies, that is, ways of conceiving the production, circulation, and also the destruction of meaning in society (including those semiotic ideologies that deny the existence of a separate dimension called "meaning") (Silverstein 1979; Silverstein and Urban 1996); on the other hand, certain trends of post-structural anthropology itself (e.g., Descola) have proposed that human groups vary even in the way in which they conceive the ontology of the world in which they live (Descola 2005). Hence, how is it possible to still maintain the universality of certain Greimasian theoretical ingredients and the corresponding analytical tools, given the extreme variability of semiotic and even ontological ideologies? How can one apply the semiotic square to the analysis of a non-Western and/or noncontemporary text, if the framework of meaning in which this text is usually read, for instance native American cosmologies, systematically disregards that principle of dialectic opposition on which the semiotic square is essentially based?

At the same time, as suggested earlier, one should not throw the baby away together with the dirty water. First, while acknowledging the profound and sometimes extreme variety of "cultures of meaning", the semiotic anthropologist should not give up the ambition of comparing cultures, lest anthropology be turned into a poorly descriptive and quite sterile exercise, as it has been the case with much recent post-colonial anthropology; furthermore, such theoretical stance would justify a fragmentary view of human culture, ignoring its lines of continuity and, what is worse, disintegrating any ground for a common ethics. In a world with no common framework for meaning, misunderstanding is the only option. Abstract semiotic models like the very articulate and powerful one developed by Greimas and his school should, therefore, be conceived not as point of arrival but as point of departure of the comparative analysis, offering a solid framework in relation to which contrasts could be observed and differences pinpointed.

To give an example: Greimas's treatment of actors, time, and space in discourse is quite Cartesian. Meaning effects of discursive choices in the construction of these narrative coordinates are explained with reference to an abstract instance of enunciation, as though all narrative was the result of a projection of simulacra departing from this abstract point. While perfectly suitable to analyze actorial, temporal, and spatial structures in most Indo-European languages and narratives, this framework is incompatible with languages and cultures in which the articulation of space and time is radically different from the Western one, for instance in cultures where the past is spatially seen as something that lies before speakers, since it is already known, and not behind them (Leone 2014a: 12–13). Nevertheless, one cannot deny that, in this case too, relying on the Greimasian theory of discourse and enunciation and realizing that it does not properly capture the construction of space and time in some linguistic and semiotic cultures is an indispensable point of departure, for it provides a negative framework in contrast to which the specificities of even the most "exotic" semiotic ideology can be described at least in relation to what it is not.

Second, admitting that the claimed universality of the Greimasian method is shaky when confronted with texts distant in time and space does not necessarily mean that it should be rejected or that more universal frameworks of meaning, yet to be elaborated, should replace it. On the one hand, from such interpretive difficulties one should deduce that semiotics, even the most abstract one, never grows outside of a specific culture of meaning. Greimas opened one of his most important books, *Du Sens* ["on meaning"] (1970), by saying that "it is extremely difficult to speak about meaning and to say something meaningful about it" (Engl. trans. by Paul Perron, 1987: 7); he did not say, "It is difficult to say something definitive about meaning". No matter how the metalanguage of the semiotician seeks to detach itself from the language-object that it analyzes, it will always remain that such metalanguage stems from a precise "culture of meaning", from a semiotic ideology that "contaminates" the designing of frameworks within which the rationality of a textual interpretation is gauged.

Methods should, therefore, be considered in the same ways as Louis T. Hjelmslev would consider interpretations: Even if they cannot be exhaustive, they can, nevertheless, be ranked (1957). Greimas's method, like any other method, cannot be completely immune from being biased: It was conceived within a specific meta-semiotic ideology.

It is, however, much less biased and more encompassing than less ambitious frameworks of meaning. To give an example, it is certainly true that Greimas's way of conceiving of narratives as essentially centered on an object of value longed for by a subject does not precisely adapt to narrative cultures that either lack such a strong idea of "subject" or do not define it as a "chasing agent"; at the same time, it is also true that Greimas's model is more abstract, flexible, and, as a consequence, encompassing than Propp's narrative framework, on which it elaborates.

On the other hand, while refining one's awareness of the cultural specificities of the adopted meta-language, one should not give in to the intellectual cliché that all biases are to be immediately condemned and discarded from the researcher's compass. There are no humanities without biases. Furthermore, in humanities and perhaps also in social sciences, biases one is aware of are nothing but a manifestation of the point of view, as well as the specific interest, from which other cultures are observed, analyzed, and interpreted. The idea that every interpretation should be in function of the "Other", from the point of view of the "Other", and in total obliviousness of one's "local knowledge" is not only utopian but also, from a certain point of view, counterproductive. It generates a paradoxical semiotic ideology according to which the only way to know the "Other" is to forget oneself or, worse, to hide oneself behind a curtain of pseudo-neutrality.

The desire of interpreting texts should, indeed, never be detached from the awareness that such desire enfolds in a conversation that links one's cognitions, but also one's emotions, with the idea of an audience. Semioticians as well as anthropologists do not interpret other cultures for an abstract, universal readership; they do so because they somehow anticipate the interpretive needs of a community to which they more or less belong, although in the guise of "outposts outside of the semiosphere". Cultivating one's biases means also refining the awareness that one's interpretation stems from a community and for a community, although it seeks to reach out to distant worlds, times, and spaces.

Toward a politics of interpretation

Admitting the inevitability of biases entails a politics of interpretation. To return to Greimas's structural semantics and the complex method that, on such premises, the Franco-Lithuanian semiotician developed all along his career, one might look at their specific biases not as something to be stigmatized and purged but as something that hints at the specific interpretive community to which Greimas's theory spoke and still speaks. Such community essentially coincides with the

"Western culture", meant as that complex ontological and semiotic ideology that stemmed at the genesis of the Greek thought and culminated in the philosophy of the Enlightenment. Entire libraries have been dedicated to describe the development, ramifications, and main characteristics of this huge and hugely influential tradition. Its features cannot be properly summarized or even hinted at in a single book. But one should at least underline that Greimas's semiotic theory adopts as its center a fundamental feature of the Western episteme: the idea of truth. In Greimas, truth does not consist, like in most logic, in a correspondence between reality and representation, ontology and semiosis. As it was indicated at the onset of this chapter, for Greimas, reality is an extra-semiotic element that should not intrude in the analysis of language. But truth is an essential idea in the Greimasian semiotics too, in two even more fundamental regards.

First, Greimas's generative path is articulated in such a way that distinction between truth, secret, lie, and falsity is inherent to it. "Truth" is an effect of meaning largely independent from reality, yet that does not mean that it is independent from discourse too. In other words, Greimas seems to postulate that, within a text, it is always possible to rationally determine whether its structures convey a message of truth, disguise it under a secret, mask it in a lie, or subvert it as falsity. Truth is an effect of meaning that it would be impossible to grasp if the idea of a hierarchy of values of veridiction were not part of the epistemic background of structural semiotics. Not all cultures cherish the value of truth in the same way. The distinction between that which is and appears and that which is not and does not appear (truth/falsity), as well as the distinction between that which is not but appears and that which is but does not appear (lie/secret) is not as sharp and does not configure such a stark hierarchy in all cultures of meaning. In certain oriental philosophies, for instance, such as some trends of Zen meditation, separating these four modalities of discursive veridiction is not as important as accepting their indistinctiveness, to the point that deconstructing the hierarchy of epistemic values even turns into the main goal of signification.

The preeminence of truth in the ideological semiotics that gave rise to Greimas's method is, instead, evident in the internal structure of its generative path as well as in the kind of conversation implicitly entertained by those interpretations that, thanks to this path, Greimas and his followers have been producing. As underlined earlier, humanities inexorably utter their meta-discourse "for someone", although they are not always necessarily aware of it (but they should). The "someone" for whom the Greimasian semiotic theory has worked over the last five decades can be variously defined but it is certainly an abstract member of the community for which the distinction among a truthful interpretation, a false interpretation, a conspiracy theory, and a lie is essential. Greimas implicitly worked all his life for a community of interpreters to which determining whether an interpretation is truthful or not—in the sense that it is more or less in keeping with the nature of the semio-linguistic features that are intersubjectively attestable in discourse—crucially matters.

That is not always necessarily the case. One could easily think of con-temporary non-Western cultures in which the efficacy of interpretation is, for instance, more important than its truthfulness (think about the way in which religious fundamentalists, for example, conceive of the hermeneutic work). Moreover, one could as easily conceive of a historical and anthropo-logical development as a consequence of which the epistemic impulse given by the Greeks to the Western culture more than two millennia ago slowly but inexorably dwindles. One could imagine a scenario in which Western Europeans will not care anymore about truth as their ancestors did and will adhere, on the contrary, to an ontological and semiotic ideology of meaning in which, for instance, a Nietzschean idea of interpretation prevails, one in which the value of an interpretation is not a measure of its structural accuracy but a result of the rhetorical and sometimes even brutal force by which it is promoted.

It should not be forgotten that also the second pillar of the Western civiliza-tion, Jerusalem, underlined the importance of truth in one of its commandments, "Do not lie". Why is such a commandment there? Because in the Judeo-Christian civilization too, the prevailing ontological and semiotic ideology was meant to push forward a social scenario in which the members of a community can live with each other only if they at least constantly strive to be truthful, to treasure the correspondence between what they think, feel, and see, and what they say, write, and represent. The Judeo-Christian idea of the morality of presenting the truth to the world has complemented, in the history of the Western civilization, the Greek idea that the world has a truth to be presented.

A sophisticate perspective on the history of the Western civilization, how-ever, should suggest that such ethical and gnoseological preeminence of truth is not a biological feature of humanity but a long-term cultural choice, which could admit alternatives and be subverted. Semiotics inherently conceives of human beings as free agents, able to use their signs in order to lie as well as in order to tell the truth, or to combine both in various manners. As pointed out earlier, Eco famously defined semiotics as the "discipline studying everything which can be used in order to lie" (1976: 7); he didn't mean, though, that signs "*must* be used to lie"; they can be used for either saying the truth or lying. At a meta-level, however, the epistemic freedom of human beings in relation to language—that is, the fact that they are not bound to use signs as truthful sig-nals as other animal species are, but they can actually weave them to present an untruthful depiction of reality or an untruthful interpretation of discourse—entails the possibility of different epistemic ideologies. It entails, for instance, the possibility that such a kind of society exists or develops in which lies are not only tolerated but also encouraged; a society in which what matters is not the correspondence between discourse and reality or the harmony between discourse and interpretation but the efficacy of simulacra and their ability to grant their utterers a modality to "get by" among more or less conflictive re-lations in a society.

The mutability of the communities of interpreters

Eco's emphasis on the importance of the "community of interpreters" complements in a dynamic sense Greimas's theoretical proposal in two ways: It points at the changing nature of interpretive frameworks and ideologies and, as a consequence, makes the urgency of a "politics of interpretation" more cogent. As pointed out earlier, unlike Greimas, Eco does not seek to provide a methodology for the rational determination of the content of a textual interpretation; he rather tries to outline the empty framework and the general rules for the reasonable interpretation of a text. That ultimately means that, whereas in Greimas there is only one way in which the abstract narrative direction of a text can be seen as shaping its meaning—that is, a direction that flows from the contract between the sender and the subject to the sanction between the subject and the receiver— nothing in Eco intrinsically forbids that the cultural evolution of a community slowly transforms this narrative standard to the point that, at some stage, the community actually considers as meaningful those narratives in which, on the contrary, the hero is positively sanctioned by the receiver exactly because he or she *did not attain* the object of value or even voluntarily gave up the purchase of it (like in those "cultures of meaning" that extol martyrdom, sacrifice, and even defeat, like the Shia one).

To give an example, the evolution of new religious communities stemming and often violently departing from older ones often entails dramatic changes in the way they construct not only meaning (e.g., the meaning of "sacred" texts) but also the "meaning of meaning" (i.e., the way in which they maintain that a sacred text should be read in order for it to transmit some cultural value to the community). In the contemporary religious world, as an increasing number of individuals is attracted by the so-called "fundamentalism", new communities are being shaped around the idea that sacred texts—which these new communities apparently share with the nonfundamentalist ones—should be read in a completely different way in order for them to exude that meaning which will subsequently inform the entire life of the community itself at every level, from the regulation of finance to sexual behaviors.

From the point of view of Greimasian semiotics, one could argue that these fundamentalist interpretations of sacred texts are wrong or, at least, that they are poorer than mainstream interpretations, for they do not adopt a rational method in order to pair the expressive plane of such religious texts with what they are supposed to mean. For instance, for Greimas and his school, as well as for most mainstream interpreters of sacred and nonsacred texts, the syntagmatic continuity of discourse must be taken into account when determining its meaning; the fact that a lexeme comes before or after another one is an essential component of the *intentio operis* of the text, suggesting readers how to progressively pinpoint its proposal of signification. In the fundamentalist reading, instead, the rationality of this very basic interpretive rule is subverted; excerpts are detached from the syntagmatic chain of the text and rearranged in its interpretation without particular attention to the original disposition of elements; such work of textual bricolage—which allows the interpreter, for instance, to put together "quotations" whose ingredients do not actually belong to the same textual place—is evidently irrational in Greimasian terms. But is it also unreasonable in Eco's terms?

It is, of course, unreasonable, but only to the extent to which a community of interpreters holds it as such. In other words, it is unreasonable to cherry-pick words or sentences from the continuity of a text in order to set them together into pseudo-citations that supposedly reveal its meaning and declare its stance and guidance as regards a certain aspect of social life, but if and only if the semiotic ideology of the community perceives that the integrity of the text as it has been composed by the author or recomposed by a rigorous philological tradition is a hierarchically superior value in the community. What if, however, under the pressure of alternative semiotic ideologies and, therefore, models of meaning and methods of interpretation, a community slowly but inexorably starts to find it more reasonable to obtain a pragmatic effect through the manipulation of a text than to remain faithful to its original syntactic construction? What if a rhapsodic, transient, and "bricoleuse" textual ideology ends up belittling the value of textual integrity?

To a certain extent, such devaluation of philological accurateness is already perniciously gaining momentum and space in the Western semiosphere, also as a consequence of revolutionary changes in the technology of communication. Today more than ever, interpreters can decompose not only a verbal text but also an image or a video and reassemble them at their will, producing new physical signifiers for the global interpretation. On the one hand, the easiness by which the texts that circulate in the digital semiosphere can be decomposed and recomposed allows interpreters to access a degree of freedom and creativity that would have been impossible under the previous technical conditions. On the other hand, though, technical possibilities are transforming the prevailing textual ideology, replacing it with one in which what a text is becomes less important of what a text is used for.

The predominance of strategic pragmatics over philological syntax is undermining and subverting one of the pillars of the interpretive framework emphasizing the reasonable character of which Eco spent most of his intellectual prestige: The difference between interpretation and use (Eco 1990). In other words, while not prescribing rigid rules for the rational definition of the meaning of a text like Greimas, Eco considered it fundamental for the reasonableness of the social exercise of interpretation in the Western world that such difference between how texts materially are and what readers want to achieve through their interpretation be maintained and preserved. Eco probably did not believe that this standard of interpretive reasonableness was universal. Being not only a semiotician but also a historian, he perfectly knew that semiospheres, with their textual, semiotic, and even ontological ideologies, are subject to change due to external forces that want to subvert and replace them; he knew the Middle

Ages too well (and perhaps he studied it exactly for this reason) to ignore that, in certain historical epochs, "barbarians" arrive, and it is not only material destruction that they bring; they bring, instead, a new interpretive community that disrupts the older criteria of reasonable interpretation (Leone 2012f). During the Middle Ages, unflagging monasteries preserved not only manuscripts but also the very abstract idea of textual integrity, allowing the continuity of the Western civilization between the classical epoch and the Renaissance.

Such historical continuity was also an ideological one: Despite the fact that our interpretation of texts is in many cases radically different from that which the ancient Greeks were keen to give, our way of distinguishing between what is reasonable and what is unreasonable to do with a text is essentially the same, and it was handed down from the Greeks and the Jews and subsequently the Christians to us because it was preserved as an irreplaceable value. If, today, we consider—as Aristotle would in his time—that the meaning of a text can be obtained only by considering the integrality and the integrity of the text, and not through its capricious excision, we also owe it to the fact that this textual mindset was placed at the core of the Western semiosphere and defended against external attacks.

Waiting for the semiotic "barbarians"

Does this mean that the "clash of civilizations" exist? Does it mean that the "Western civilization" exist? Does it mean that it must be defended from "attacks" coming from different civilizations? In the semiotic perspective, these questions make sense only if the notion itself of "civilization" is deconstructed and reconstructed in semiotic terms. If by "Western civilization" one means a certain way of conceiving of the relation between reality and signification; a certain way of construing the "meaning of meaning"; and above all, a certain way of positing the exercise of textual interpretation as a means to retrieve the meaning of a signifying reality, then the "Western civilization" certainly exists. Moreover, that entails that other civilizations also exist as adoptions of different ontological, semiotic, and textual ideologies.

Being defined as a conceptual semiosphere, the "Western civilization" marks its borders through sundry means (Leone 2010b). The geographical frontiers of this semiosphere are not perhaps the most fundamental ones but they are, nevertheless, among the series of signs that concretize the threshold between what is inside and what is outside. In other words, it is not sufficient for an interpreter to be geographically in France to guarantee that his or her interpretation will actually adhere to the standards of reasonable handling of texts that characterizes the Western civilization. At the same time, France is what it is exactly because its geographical frontiers more or less coincide with those of an interpretive community for which a given set of interpretive standards and criteria are considered as valuable and even binding.

On the one hand, it would be meaningless to ignore the geographical nature of interpretive communities: For a long time in human history, communication has been based on physical proximity; and even now, in an era in which it is tremendously easy to communicate and establish communities with individuals that do not share at all our own geographical space, the fact of occupying the same portion of physical territory still is a fundamental ingredient of most communities. That is the reason for which the Western civilization is *not only* that which is marked by precise geographical borders—although constantly renegotiated through communication or fight—but it is *also* that geographical space. Being born in Europe means coming to the world in a geography with a precise history in terms of what ontological, semiotic, and textual ideologies have prevailed over a very long period in such space.

On the other hand, it would be equally meaningless to think that defending the "Western civilization" exclusively means protecting its geographical borders. The geographical borders of a civilization must be protected not only because they physically outline a space but also, and more fundamentally, because, in many cases, they are the concretization of ideological borders. But geographical and ideological frontiers do not always coincide. Unfortunately, the "enemies of the Western civilization" are not only beyond its geographical frontiers but also within them, thriving inside their internal geographical space while ideologically exerting a centrifugal and disruptive agency.

Pinpointing the ultimate nature of the "clash of civilizations" comes down to the irreverent question "who are our barbarians?" During the Middle Ages, it was clear that the barbarians were those whose political aims entailed also the destruction of the European Judeo-Christian cultural heritage, which was, therefore, protected through strategies of isolation and reproduction of the core texts of the civilization under attack. The "barbarians" that, today, seek to undermine the fundaments of the Western civilization cannot be primarily conceived in geographic terms, although, as pointed out above, a civilization is also embodied by the physical space that it occupies. On the other hand, it is in abstract semiotic terms that the current "barbarians" must be defined.

If the "Western civilization" is defined as the one in which a community of interpreters active over several millennia painfully selected as its core interpretive habits the standards that allow its members to determine what is true and what is fake, what interpretation is coherent with the text and what is not, how the limits of a textual unit should be considered and preserved and how, on the contrary, the textual integrity of discourse is dismantled and disrupted, then the "barbarians", that is, the enemies of such civilization are not necessarily the "eastern", or the "non-Christian", or the "non-Jewish", but all those who, geographically reunited into different physical communities outside of the Western semiosphere or seeking to ideologically undermining it from the inside, intentionally or unintentionally operate so that, under their continuous collective pressure, the geographical space of the Western civilization comes to adopt an alternative ontological, semiotic, and textual ideology, producing effects of meaning and, above all, relations among members in a completely different way.

To give an example, Islamic fundamentalists that seek to create a state at the doors of Europe certainly are its "barbarians", for they aim at injecting more and more into the European civilization ideas of truth, meaning, and text that are completely at odds with that which such civilization has singled out over the centuries of its history as its core semiotic standards of reasonable interpretation. ISIS represents the barbaric counterpart of Europe not only because it tramps the rule of law but also and perhaps more disquietingly because it seeks to destroy the semiotic ideology that underlies such rule of law, a semiotic ideology that, for instance, considers that a certain degree of certainty in adjudication can be reached only when unbiased witnesses are taken into account (the idea that the rape of a woman must be attested by four male witnesses, for example, is against the Western legal civilization but is also, and even more, fundamentally against the Western *semiotic* civilization).

Nevertheless, the Western civilization is threatened not only by these "barbarians outside" but also by those individuals and groups that could be defined as "barbarians inside" (inside the semiosphere of the Western civilization). A long, painful, and often bloody history has brought about in the west the idea that being civilized means determining and respecting the "human rights" of others but also, even more fundamentally, determining and respecting the "semiotic rights" of others. Paul Grice's conversational maxims are an example of attempt at distilling these rights in a tremendously concise form (1975). Even more generally, a fundamental "semiotic right" that the Western civilization has learned to place at the center of its semiosphere is the idea that there should be a certain amount of correspondence between what the member of a conversation thinks and what this member says in the conversation. It is not difficult, however, to imagine an evolution of the Western semiotic civilization in which the final result will see the prevailing not only of fundamentalist hermeneutics but also of *trolling hermeneutics*, that is, of a semiotic ideology in which the correspondence between signified thought and signifying word is less important than the fun that one proves at witnessing the disruption of the conversation and at actually contributing to it. Or one may equally witness the raising of a semiotic civilization of conspiracy, in which, again, the aesthetic pleasure of detecting secret plots beyond any sociopolitical phenomenon will be more important than gathering coherent evidence supporting one's interpretation of facts.

Greimas's gigantic efforts to elaborate a theory and a method able to rationally determine the meaning of texts might well be regarded as démodé nowadays, given the proliferation of alternative textual ideologies and, above all, given the increasing affirmation of a semiotic ideology according to which discrepant hermeneutics can coexist in a community of interpreters. Nevertheless, accepting this relativization of Greimas would be tantamount to ignore that, behind his method, a long and complex history lies, through whose painful vicissitudes a certain idea of text and interpretation became fundamental in the Western world. The historical forces that led Greimas to envisage his complex and powerful theory are the same that allow a Western judge to choose among different interpretations of facts and make this choice intersubjectively viable for all the members of the same legal conversation. If one rejects Greimas—not in the details of his theoretical creation but in the overall spirit that animates it—then one rejects an important and perhaps definitional ingredient of the Western semiotic civilization, that according to which meaning is not created through force but through communication, though rules and not through violence.

On the other hand, Eco's theory of semiotics is there to warn us all about the fact that what Greimas considered as the only possible rational method of interpretation is actually the result of what a community of interpreters came to recognize and actually defend for a long time as a reasonable framework for signification. In other words, Greimas tells us what the meaning of texts is, whereas Eco tells us what the meaning of texts should be, suggesting that the semiotic ideology of the Western civilization is binding also, and above all, by virtue of the historical process that resulted in its triumph.

We might abandon ourselves to the currents of history and think that, whatever we do or say, eventually the semiosphere will shape itself according to mysterious, unfathomable laws. We might fatalistically accept that, for instance, one day we'll lose the meaning of "truth" as this idea was conceived from the Greeks until Greimas. But that is not the message of most twentieth-century semiotics. Greimas, Eco, and also Lotman implicitly suggested that what we do and say actually shape the semiosphere and that we should therefore take responsibility for the maintenance of the semiotic core that lies at the center of the Western civilization. If a clash of civilizations exists, it exists, above all, in the form of continuous tension among different ways of conceiving of meaning, including the way that eliminates the very idea of meaning from the human horizon. If we think that this idea is important, because it is nothing but the counterpart of the ethical idea of freedom, then a clash of semiotic civilizations not only exist but should also give rise to a continuous battle for the defense of a reasonable conception of meaning.

Note

1 "Civilization is nothing but the modality of vegetation characteristic of humanity" (Engl. trans. by Massimo Leone).

REFERENCES

Aalberg, Toril, Frank Esser, Carsten Reinemann, Jesper Stromback, and Claes H. de Vreese. 2017. *Populist Political Communication in Europe*. New York, NY: Routledge.

Adami, Elisabetta and Gunther Kress. 2010. "The Social Semiotics of Convergent Mobile Devices: New Forms of Composition and the Transformation of *Habitus*", 184–97. In Gunther Kress, ed. 2010. *Multimodality: A Social Semiotic Approach to Contemporary Communication*. London, UK and New York, NY: Routledge.

Albritton, Robert. 2009. *Let Them Eat Junk: How Capitalism Creates Hunger and Obesity*. London, UK and New York, NY: Pluto Press.

Andrews, Geoff. 2008. *The Slow Food Story: Politics and Pleasure*. Montreal, Canada and Ithaca, NY: McGill-Queen's University Press.

Archetti, Cristina. 2013. *Understanding Terrorism in the Age of Global Media: A Communication Approach*. Houndmills, Basingstoke, Hampshire and New York, NY: Palgrave Macmillan.

Ariès, Philippe. 1974. *Western Attitudes toward Death: From the Middle Ages to the Present*. Engl. trans. Patricia M. Ranum. Baltimore, MD: Johns Hopkins University Press.

Ariès, Philippe. 1977. *L'homme devant la mort*, 2 vols. Paris, France: Editions du Seuil. Engl. trans. Helen Weaver. 1981. *The Hour of Our Death*. New York, NY: Knopf; distributed by Random House.

Aron, Matthieu. 2014. *Folles rumeurs: les nouvelles frontières de l'intox*. Paris, France: Stock.

Ata, Mehmet. 2011. *Der Mohammed-Karikaturenstreit in den deutschen und türkischen Medien: eine vergleichende Diskursanalyse*. Wiesbaden, Germany: VS Verlag.

Aumont, Jacques. 1990. *L'image*. Paris, France: Armand Colin. Engl. trans. Claire Pajackowska. 1997. *The Image*. London, UK: British Film Institute.

Avon, Dominique. 2010. *La caricature au risque des autorités politiques et religieuses*. Rennes, France: Presses universitaires de Rennes.

Bahamón, Alejandro and Patricia Pérez. 2008. *Inspired by Nature: Minerals: The Building/ Geology Connection*. New York, NY: W.W. Norton.

Balick, Aaron. 2014. *The Psychodynamics of Social Networking: Connected-Up Instantaneous Culture and the Self*. London, UK: Karnac Books.

Barbieri, Gian Luca. 2014. *Il laboratorio delle identità: dire io nell'epoca di internet*. Milan, Italy: Mimesis.

Barnstone, Willis. 1993. *The Poetics of Translation: History, Theory, Practice*. New Haven, CT: Yale University Press.

Barrett, Terry. 2017. *Why Is That Art?: Aesthetics and Criticism of Contemporary Art*. New York, NY: Oxford University Press.

Baudrillard, Jean. 1981. *Simulacres et simulation*. Paris, France: Galilée. Engl. trans. Sheila Faria Glaser. 1994. *Simulacra and Simulation*. Ann Arbor: University of Michigan Press.

Benjamin, Walter. 1936. "Das Kunstwerk im Zeitalter seiner technischen Reproduzierbarkeit". *Zeitschrift für Sozialforschung*, 5, 1; now in Id. 1972–89. *Gesammelte Schriften*, ed. Rolf Tiedemann and Hermann Schweppenhäuser, 7 vols in 14. Frankfurt am Main: Suhrkamp, 1: 471–508. Engl. trans. Harry Zohn. 1969. "The Work of Art in the Age of Mechanical Reproduction", 217–52. In Id. 1969. *Illuminations*, ed. Hanna Arendt. New York, NY: Schocken.

Benveniste, Émile. 1966. *Problèmes de linguistique générale, I*. Paris, France: Gallimard. Engl. trans. Mary Elizabeth Meek. 1971. *Problems in General Linguistics*. Coral Gables, FL: University of Miami Press.

Benveniste, Émile. 1971. *Problèmes de linguistique générale II*. Paris, France: Gallimard.

Benz, Nadine. 2013. *Zeit des Wartens: Semantiken und Narrative eines temporalen Phänomens*. Göttingen, Germany: V&R Unipress.

Berger Jr., Harry. 2000. *The Absence of Grace: Sprezzatura and Suspicion in Two Renaissance Courtesy Books*. Stanford, CA: Stanford University Press.

Berger, John. 1972. *Ways of Seeing*. London, UK: British Broadcasting Corporation and Penguin Books.

Berry, David M. and Michael Dieter, eds. 2015. *Postdigital Aesthetics: Art, Computation and Design*. Houndmills, Basingstoke, Hampshire; and New York, NY: Palgrave Macmillan.

Bersani, Leo. 2006. "Psychoanalysis and the Aesthetic Subject", 161–74. *Critical Inquiry*, 32, 2.

Berzano, Luigi. 2012. "Dal *cult* al culto. L'irritazione della *vicarious religion*", 233–46. In Massimo Leone, ed. *Culto / Worship*, special issue of *Lexia*. Rome, Italy: Aracne.

Bhatti, Anil and Dorothee Kimmich, eds. 2015. *Ähnlichkeit: esin kulturtheoretisches Paradigma*. Konstanz, Germany: Konstanz University Press.

Bleich, Erik. 2011. *The Freedom to Be Racist?: How the United States and Europe Struggle to Preserve Freedom and Combat Racism*. Oxford, UK and New York, NY: Oxford University Press.

Böhme, Antje. 2012. *Ästhetischer Schein und gesellschaftliches Sein am Beispiel des Shoppingcenters*. Bielefeld, Germany: Aisthesis Verlag.

Boler, Megan. 1997. "The Risks of Empathy: Interrogating Multiculturalism's Gaze", 253–73. *Cultural Studies*, 11, 2.

Bompiani, Ginevra. 1988. *L'attesa*. Milano, Italy: Feltrinelli.

Bond, Robert. 1999. "Links, Frames, Meta-tags and Trolls", 317–23. *International Review of Law, Computers & Technology*, 13, 3.

Boomgaarden, Hajo G. and Claes H. de Vreese. 2007. "Dramatic Real-world Events and Public Opinion Dynamics: Media Coverage and its Impact on Public Reactions to an Assassination", 354–66. *International Journal of Public Opinion Research*, 19, 3.

Botan, Carl H. and Francisco Soto. 1998. "A Semiotic Approach to the Internal Functioning of Publics: Implications for Strategic Communication and Public Relations", 21–44. *Public Relations Review*, 24, 1.

Boulter, Stephen. 2007. *The Rediscovery of Common Sense Philosophy*. Houndmills, Basingstoke, Hampshire and New York, NY: Palgrave Macmillan.

Bower, Anne L. 2004. "Romanced by Cookbooks", 35–42. *Gastronomica: The Journal of Food and Culture*, 4, 2.

Briault, Thierry. 2004. *Les philosophies du sens commun: pragmatique et deconstruction*. Paris, France: L'Harmattan.

Browne, Thomas, Sir. 1658. *Hydriotaphia, Urn-Burial, or, A Discours of the Sepulchral Urns Lately Found in Norfolk Together with the Garden of Cyrus, or, The Quincuncial Lozenge, or Network of Plantations of the Ancients, Artificially, Naturally, Mystically Considered: with Sundry Observations*. London, UK: Printed for Henry Brome.

Buckels, Erin E., Paul D. Trapnell, and Delroy L. Paulhus. 2014. "Trolls Just Want to Have Fun", 97–102. *Personality and Individual Differences*, 67, September.

Calabrese, Omar. 2000. "Lo strano caso dell'equivalenza imperfetta. (Modeste osservazioni sulla produzione intersemiotica)", 101–20. *Versus*, 85–87.

Calabrese, Omar. 2003. "Semiotic Aspects of Art History: Semiotics of the Fine Arts", 3212–33. In Roland Posner, Klaus Robering, and Thomas A. Sebeok, eds. 1997–2003. *Semiotik: Ein Handbuch zu den zeichentheoretischen Grundlagen von Natur und Kultur*, 3 vols. Berlin, Germany and New York, NY: Walter de Gruyter, vol. 3, section 14.

Calabrese, Omar. 2006. *Come si legge un'opera d'arte*. Milan, Italy: Mondadori.

Campbell, Heidi A. 2012. *Digital Religion: Understanding Religious Practice in New Media Worlds*. Abingdon, Oxon, UK and New York, NY: Routledge.

Campion, Nicholas. 2016. *The New Age in the Modern West: Counter-Culture, Utopia, and Prophecy from the Late Eighteenth Century to the Present Day*. London, UK and New York, NY: Bloomsbury Academic.

Canetti, Elias. 1960. *Masse und Macht*. Hamburg, Germany: Claassen. Engl. trans. Carol Stewart. 1984. *Crowds and Power*. London, UK: Continuum.

Cariello, Vincenzo. 2014. *Achille, o, dell'attesa: per una genealogia sovverziente dell'attesa, per un'attesa che sovverta*. Genoa, Italy: Il melangolo.

Cary, Phillip. 2008. *Outward Signs: The Powerlessness of External Things in Augustine's Thought*. Oxford, UK and New York, NY: Oxford University Press.

Castelli, Richard, Berliner Festspiele, and Martin-Gropius-Bau, eds. 2007. *Vom Funken zum Pixel: Kunst + Neue Medien*. Berlin, Germany: Berliner Festspiele and Nicolai.

Centre de recherches sémiologiques. 1991. *La Négation: le rôle de la négation dans l'argumentation et le raisonnement*; actes du colloque, Neuchâtel 11–12 October 1990. Neuchâtel, Switzerland: CdRS, Université de Neuchâtel.

Ceriani, Giulia. 2000. *Du dispositif rythmique: Arguments pour une sémio-physique*. Paris, France: Éditions L'Harmattan.

Chaw, Andrew. 2003. "'La grande bouffée': Cooking Shows as Pornography", 46–53. *Gastronomica: The Journal of Food and Culture*, 3, 4.

Comte-Sponville, André. 2015. *Du tragique au matérialisme, et retour: vingt-six études sur Montaigne, Pascal, Spinoza, Nietzsche et quelques autres*. Paris, France: Presses universitaires de France.

Contemori, Lido and Paolo Pettinari. 1993. *Il segno tagliente: meccanismi comunicativi e pragmatici della satira politica grafica*. Alessandria, Italy: Edizioni dell'orso.

Crăciun, Magdalena. 2013. *Material Culture and Authenticity: Fake Branded Fashion in Europe*. New York, NY: Bloomsbury.

Dahl, Øyvind. 2016. *Human Encounters: Introduction to Intercultural Communication*. Oxford, UK: Peter Lang Ltd, International Academic Publishers.

Danesi, Marcel. 2002. *The Puzzle Instinct: The Meaning of Puzzles in Human Life.* Bloomington, IN: Indiana University Press.

Dawkins, Richard. 2008. *The God Delusion.* Boston, MA: Houghton Mifflin Co.

Deleuze, Gilles and Félix Guattari. 1980. *Capitalisme et schizophrénie: mille plateaux.* Paris, France: Éditions de Minuit. Engl. trans. and foreword Brian Massumi. 1987. *A Thousand Plateaus: Capitalism and Schizophrenia.* Minneapolis, MN: University of Minnesota Press.

Descola, Philippe. 2005. *Par-delà nature et culture.* Paris, France: NRF-Gallimard. Engl. trans. Janet Lloyd; foreword by Marshall Sahlins. 2013. *Beyond Nature and Culture.* Chicago, IL and London, UK: The University of Chicago Press.

Di Nola, Alfonso M. 1995a. *La morte trionfata: antropologia del lutto.* Rome, Italy: Newton Compton.

Di Nola, Alfonso M. 1995b. *La nera signora: antropologia della morte.* Rome, Italy: Newton Compton.

Doll, Martin. 2012. *Fälschung und Fake: zur diskurskritischen Dimension des Täuschens.* Berlin, Germany: Kulturverlag Kadmos.

Donà, Massimo. 2004. *Sulla negazione.* Milan, Italy: Bompiani.

Ebbighausen, Rodion. 2010. *Das Warten. Phänomenologisches Essay.* Würzburg, Germany: Königshausen & Neumann.

Eco, Umberto. 1973. *Il costume di casa. Evidenze e misteri dell'ideologia italiana.* Milan, Italy: Bompiani.

Eco, Umberto. 1976. *A Theory of Semiotics.* Bloomington, IN: Indiana University Press.

Eco, Umberto. 1979. *The Role of the Reader: Explorations in the Semiotics of Texts.* Bloomington, IN: Indiana University Press.

Eco, Umberto. 1985. "Pirandello ridens", 261–70. In Id. 1985. *Sugli specchi e altri saggi.* Milan, Italy: Bompiani.

Eco, Umberto, ed. 1987. *Fakes, Identity, and the Real Thing,* special issue of *Versus,* 46. Milan, Italy: Bompiani.

Eco, Umberto. 1990. *The Limits of Interpretation.* Bloomington, IN: Indiana University Press.

Eco, Umberto. 1992. *Interpretation and Overinterpretation;* with Richard Rorty, Jonathan Culler, and Christine Brooke-Rose; edited by Stefan Collini. Cambridge, UK and New York, NY: Cambridge University Press.

Eco, Umberto and Thomas A. Sebeok. 1983. *The Sign of Three: Dupin, Holmes, Peirce.* (Advances in Semiotics). Bloomington, IN: Indiana University Press.

Ehrat, Johannes. 2010. *Power of Scandal: Semiotic and Pragmatic in Mass Media* (Toronto Studies in Semiotics and Communication). Toronto, Canada: University of Toronto Press.

El Refaie, Elisabeth 2009. "What Makes Us Laugh? Verbo-Visual Humour in Newspaper Cartoons", 75–89. In Eija Ventola and Arsenio Jesús Moya Guijarro, eds. 2009. *The World Told and the World Shown: Multisemiotic Issues.* London, UK and New York, NY: Palgrave.

Esposito, Roberto. 1988. *Communitas: origine e destino della comunità.* Turin, Italy: Einaudi. Engl. trans. Timothy Campbell. 2010. *Communitas: The Origin and Destiny of Community.* Stanford, CA: Stanford University Press.

Esposito, Roberto. 2002. *Immunitas: protezione e negazione della vita.* Turin, Italy: Einaudi. Engl. trans. Zakiya Hanafi. 2001. *Immunitas: The Protection and Negation of Life.* Cambridge, UK and Malden, MA: Polity Press.

Esposito, Roberto. 2014. *Le persone e le cose.* Turin, Italy: Einaudi. Engl. trans. Zakiya Hanafi. 2015. *Persons and Things: From the Body's Point of View.* Cambridge, MA: Polity Press.

Evans, Malcolm. 1999. "Semiotics, Culture, and Communications: The Common Sense of the 21st Century". Proceedings of the Australian Market Research Society Conference; available at www.teleensm.ummto.dz/pluginfile.../Semiotics-Introduction.pdf (last access March 7, 2018).

Fasseur, Valérie and Cécile Rochelois, eds. 2016. *Ponctuer l'oeuvre médiévale: Des signes au sens.* Geneva, Switzerland: Droz.

Fawcett, Antoinette, Karla L. Guadarrama García, and Rebecca Hyde Parker, eds. 2010. *Translation: Theory and Practice in Dialogue.* London, UK and New York, NY: Continuum.

Ferguson, Kennan. 2012. "Intensifying Taste, Intensifying Identity: Collectivity through Community Cookbooks", 695–717. *Signs,* 37, 3.

Field, Mike and Martin Golubitsky. 1992. *Symmetry in Chaos: A Search for Pattern in Mathematics, Art, and Nature.* Oxford, UK and New York, NY: Oxford University Press.

Floch, Jean-Marie. 1984. "Pour une approche sémiotique du matériau", 165–85. In Alain Renier. 1984. *Espace: Construction et signification.* Paris, France: Éditions de la Villette.

Floyd, Juliet and James E. Katz, eds. 2016. *Philosophy of Emerging Media: Understanding, Appreciation, Application.* New York, NY: Oxford University Press.

Fontanille, Jacques. 2006. *Pratiques sémiotiques: Immanence et pertinence, efficience et optimisation.* Monographic issue of *Nouveaux Actes Sémiotiques,* 104–6. Limoges: PULIM.

Forguson, Lynd. 1989. *Common Sense.* London, UK and New York, NY: Routledge.

Freidenreich, David M. 2011. *Foreigners and their Food: Constructing Otherness in Jewish, Christian, and Islamic Law.* Berkeley, CA: University of California Press.

Frindte, Wolfgang and Nicole Haussecker, eds. 2010. *Inszenierter Terrorismus: mediale Konstruktionen und individuelle Interpretationen.* Wiesbaden, Germany: VS, Verlag für Sozialwissenschaften.

Gaines, Elliot. 2010. *Media Literacy and Semiotics.* New York, NY: Palgrave Macmillan.

Gantrel, Martine. 2002. "La Gastronomie française au cinéma entre 1970 et 1990", 697–706. *The French Review,* 75, 4.

Gell, Alfred. 1998. *Art and Agency: An Anthropological Theory.* Oxford, UK and New York, NY: Clarendon Press.

Genette, Gérard. 1987. *Seuils.* Paris, France: Seuil. Engl. trans. Jane E. Lewin; foreword by Richard Macksey. 1997. *Paratexts: Thresholds of Interpretation.* Cambridge, UK and New York, NY: Cambridge University Press.

Geninasca, Jacques and Algirdas J. Greimas. 1990. *Le discours en perspective.* Limoges, France: PULIM.

Gerhards, Jürgen, ed. 2011. *Terrorismus im Fernsehen: Formate, Inhalte und Emotionen in westlichen und arabischen Sendern.* Wiesbaden, Germany: VS, Verlag für Sozialwissenschaften.

Giarelli, Ellen and Lorraine Tulman. 2003. "Methodological Issues in the Use of Published Cartoons as Data", 945–56. *Qualitative Health Research,* 13, 7 (September).

Giorda, Maria Chiara and Sara Hejazi, eds. 2013. *Spazi e luoghi sacri.* Special issue of *Humanitas.* Brescia, Italy: Morcelliana.

Girard, René. 1977. *Violence and the Sacred.* Baltimore, MD: Johns Hopkins University Press.

Goody, Jack. 1986. *The Logic of Writing and the Organization of Society.* Cambridge, UK and New York, NY: Cambridge University Press.

Graham, Mark and William H. Dutton, eds. 2014. *Society and the Internet: How Networks of Information and Communication are Changing our Lives*; with a foreword by Manuel Castells. Oxford, UK: Oxford University Press.

Grande, Maurizio. 1980. *Marco Ferreri*. Florence, Italy: Nuova Italia.

Graw, Isabelle and Ewa Lajer-Burcharth, eds. 2016. *Painting Beyond Itself: The Medium in the Post-Medium Condition*. Berlin, Germany: Sternberg Press.

Greenaway, Peter. 2008. *Ultima cena di Leonardo / Leonardo's Last Supper*. Milan, Italy: Charta.

Greenberg, Bradley S., ed. 2002. *Communication and Terrorism: Public and Media Responses to 9/11*. Cresskill, NJ: Hampton Press.

Greene, Carlnita. 2008. "Shopping for What Never Was: The Rhetoric of Food, Social Style, and Nostalgia", 31–47. In Lawrence C. Rubin, ed. 2008. *Food for Thought: Essays on Eating and Culture*. Jefferson, NC: McFarland.

Greif, Mark, ed. 2012. *Hipster: eine transatlantische Diskussion*. Berlin, Germany: Suhrkamp.

Greimas, Algirdas Julien. 1966. *Sémantique structurale: recherche de méthode*. Paris, France: Larousse. Engl. trans. Daniele McDowell, Ronald Schleifer, and Alan Velie; with an introduction by Ronald Schleifer. 1983. *Structural Semantics: An Attempt at a Method*. Lincoln, NE: University of Nebraska Press.

Greimas, Algirdas Julien. 1970. *Du Sens*. Paris, France: Seuil. Partial Engl. trans. Paul J. Perron and Frank H. Collins. 1987. *On Meaning: Selected Writings in Semiotic Theory*; foreword by Fredric Jameson; introduction by Paul J. Perron. Minneapolis, MN: University of Minnesota Press.

Greimas, Algirdas Julien. 1976. *Maupassant: La sémiotique du texte: Exercices pratiques*. Paris, France: Éditions du Seuil. Engl. trans. Paul Perron. 1988. *Maupassant: The Semiotics of Text: Practical Exercises*. Amsterdam, The Netherlands and Philadelphia, PA: J. Benjamins Pub. Co.

Greimas, Algirdas Julien. 1983. *Du Sens II. Essais sémiotiques*. Paris, France: Seuil.

Greimas, Algirdas Julien, ed. 1984. "Sémiotique figurative et sémiotique plastique". *Actes sémiotiques*, 60, 24.

Greimas, Algirdas Julien and Joseph Courtès. 1979. *Sémiotique: dictionnaire raisonné de la théorie du langage*. Paris, France: Hachette. Engl. trans. Larry Crist. 1988. *Semiotics and Language: An Analytical Dictionary*. Bloomington, IN: Indiana University Press.

Greimas, Algirdas Julien and Jacques Fontanille. 1991. *Sémiotique des passions: des états de choses aux états d'âme*. Paris, France: Editions du Seuil. Engl. trans. Paul Perron and Frank Collins; foreword Paul Perron and Paolo Fabbri. 1993. *The Semiotics of Passions: From States of Affairs to States of Feeling*. Minneapolis, MN: University of Minnesota Press.

Greimas, Algirdas J. and Paul Ricoeur. 2000. *Tra semiotica ed ermeneutica*, ed. Franscesco Marsciani. Rome, Italy: Meltemi.

Grenda, Christopher S., Chris Beneke, and David Nash, eds. 2014. *Profane: Sacrilegious Expression in a Multicultural Age*. Oakland, CA: University of California Press.

Grice, Paul 1975. "Logic and Conversation", 41–58. In Peter Cole, ed. 1975. *Syntax and Semantics 3: Speech Acts*. New York, NY: Academic Press.

Griffin, Robert J., ed. 2003. *The Faces of Anonymity: Anonymous and Pseudonymous Publication from the Sixteenth to the Twentieth Century*. New York, NY: Palgrave Macmillan.

Habermas, Jürgen. 1981. *Theorie des kommunikativen Handelns*, 2 vols. Frankfurt am Main, Germany: Suhrkamp. Engl. trans. Thomas McCarthy. 1986–9. *The Theory of Communicative Action*. Cambridge, UK: Polity Press.

Hage, Ghassan. 2009. *Waiting*. Carlton, VC: Melbourne University Publishing.

Hagener, Malte and Vinzenz Hediger, eds. 2015. *Medienkultur und Bildung: Ästhetische Erziehung im Zeitalter digitaler Netzwerke*. Frankfurt, Germany and New York, NY: Campus Verlag.

Haiman, John. 1998. *Talk Is Cheap: Sarcasm, Alienation, and the Evolution of Language*. New York, NY: Oxford University Press.

Handelman, Don. 1977. "Play and Ritual: Contemporary Frames of Meta-Communication", 185–92. In Anthony J. Chapman and Hugh C. Foot, eds. 1977. *It's a Funny Thing, Humour* (Reports of papers presented at the International Conference on Humour and Laughter held in Cardiff, July 13th–17th, 1976 and organized by the Welsh Branch of the British Psychological Society). Oxford, UK and New York, NY: Pergamon Press.

Handelman, Don. 2006. "Framing", 571–82. In Jens Kreinath, Jan Snoek, and Michael Stausberg, eds. 2006. *Theorizing Rituals*. Leiden, The Netherlands: Brill.

Hardaker, Claire. 2010. "Trolling in Asynchronous Computer-Mediated Communication: From User Discussions to Academic Definitions", 215–42. *Journal of Politeness Research. Language, Behaviour, Culture*, 6, 2.

Hardt, Michael and Antonio Negri. 2004. *Multitude: War and Democracy in the Age of Empire*. New York, NY: Penguin Press.

Hart, William B. II and Fran Hassencahl. 2002. "Dehumanizing the Enemy in Editorial Cartoons", 137–55. In Bradley S. Greenberg, ed. 2002. *Communication and Terrorism: Public and Media Responses to 9/11*. Cresskill, NJ: Hampton Press.

Hayes-Conroy, Allison and Deborah G. Martin. 2010. "Mobilising Bodies: Visceral Identification in the Slow Food Movement", 269–81. *Transactions of the Institute of British Geographers* (new series), 35, 2.

Hébert, Louis. 2006. "Le carré sémiotique", online; accessible at www.signosemio.com/greimas/carre-semiotique.asp (last access April 29, 2015).

Henke, Christoph. 2014. *Common Sense in Early 18th-century British Literature and Culture: Ethics, Aesthetics, and Politics, 1680–1750*. Berlin, Germany: De Gruyter.

Herring, Susan, Kirk Job-Sluder, Rebecca Scheckler, and Sasha Barab. 2002. "Searching for Safety Online: Managing 'Trolling' in a Feminist Forum". *Center for Social Informatics – Indiana University*; available at www-bcf.usc.edu/~fulk/620overview_files/Herring.pdf (last access January 16, 2017).

Hine, Christine. 2015. *Ethnography for the Internet: Embedded, Embodied and Everyday*. London, UK and New York, NY: Bloomsbury Academic.

Hjelmslev, Louis. 1943. *Omkring sprogteoriens grundlæggelse*. Copenaghen, Denmark: Ejnar Munksgaard. Engl. trans. Francis J. Whitfield. 1961. *Prolegomena to a Theory of Language*. Madison, WI: University of Wisconsin Press.

Hjelmslev, Louis T. and Hans Jørgen Uldall. 1957. *Outline of Glossematics: A Study in the Methodology of the Humanities with Special Reference to Linguistics*. Copenhagen, Denmark: Nordisk Sprog- og Kulturforlag.

Holtzman, Jon D. 2006. "Food and Memory", 361–78. *Annual Review of Anthropology*, 35.

Hutto, Daniel D. and Matthew Ratcliffe, eds. 2007. *Folk Psychology Re-Assessed*. Dordrecht, The Netherlands and London, UK: Springer.

Ibo, Lydie. 2012. "Négation et conflit: la double face passionnelle et culturelle", online. In *Nouveaux Actes Sémiotiques*, 115; available at https://www.unilim.fr/actes-semiotiques/1497.

Idone Cassone, Vincenzo, Mattia Thibault, and Bruno Surace, eds. 2018. *Semiotica della catastrofe* (I saggi di Lexia, 28). Rome, Italy: Aracne.

Ijpma, Frank F.A., Robert C. van de Graaf, Jean-Philippe A. Nicolai, and Marcel F. Meek. 2006. "The Anatomy Lesson of Dr. Nicolaes Tulp by Rembrandt (1632): A Comparison of the Painting with a Dissected Left Forearm of a Dutch Male Cadaver", 882–91. *Journal of Hand Surgery*, Amsterdam, 31, 6.

Jackowe, David J., Michael K. Moore, Andrew E. Bruner, and John R. Fredieu. 2007. "New Insight into the Enigmatic White Cord in Rembrandt's the Anatomy Lesson of Dr. Nicolaes Tulp", 1471–6. *Journal of Hand Surgery*, Amsterdam, 32, 9.

Javarone, Marco Alberto and Serge Galam. 2015. "Emergence of Extreme Opinions in Social Networks", 112–7. In Luca Maria Aiello and Daniel McFarland, eds. 2015. *Social Informatics: Lecture Notes in Computer Science*. Cham, Switzerland: Springer International Publishing.

Jehne, Martin and Christoph Lundgreen, eds. 2013. *Gemeinsinn und Gemeinwohl in der römischen Antike*. Stuttgart, Germany: Franz Steiner Verlag.

Johnson-Laird, Philip Nicholas. 1988. *The Computer and the Mind: An Introduction to Cognitive Science*. Cambridge, MA: Harvard University Press.

Johnston, Lucy, ed. 2015. *Digital Handmade: Craftsmanship and the New Industrial Revolution*. London, UK: Thames & Hudson.

Kandinsky, Wassily. 1926. *Punkt und Linie zu Fläche: Beitrag zur Analyse der malerischen Elemente*. Munich, Germany: Albert Langen. Engl. trans. Howard Dearstyne and Hilla Rebay; edited Hilla Rebay. 1979. *Point and Line to Plane*. New York, NY: Dover Publications.

Keane, Webb. 1997. "Religious Language", 47–71. *Annual Review of Anthropology*, 26, 1. Palo Alto, CA: Annual Reviews.

Keane, Webb. 2003. "Semiotics and the Social Analysis of Material Things", 409–25. *Language & Communication*, 23.

Keane, Webb. 2007. *Christian Moderns: Freedom and Fetish in the Mission Encounter*. Berkeley, Los Angeles, CA and London, UK: University of California Press.

Keen, Suzanne. 2006. "A Theory of Narrative Empathy", 207–36. *Narrative*, 14, 3.

Kindt, Walther. 2010. *Irrtümer und andere Defizite in der Linguistik: Wissenschaftslogische Probleme als Hindernis für Erkenntnisfortschritte*. Frankfurt am Main, Germany and New York, NY: Peter Lang.

Klausen, Jytte. 2009. *The Cartoons that Shook the World*. New Haven, CT: Yale University Press.

Koch, Walter A. 1989. "Toward a Theory of Empathy", 111–20. In Walter A. Koch, ed. 1989. *For a Semiotics of Emotion* (Bochumer Beiträge zur Semiotik, 4). Bochum, Germany: N. Brockmeyer.

Koolbergen, Michiel. 1992. "De R van Rembrandt. Waarheen wijst de tang van dokter Tulp?" 13. *Trouw*, 31, January.

Kostioukovitch, Elena. 2009. *Why Italians Love to Talk about Food*. Engl. trans. Anne Milano Appel. New York, NY: Farrar, Straus and Giroux.

Krappitz, Stefan. 2012. *Troll Culture*. Diplomarbeit, Merz Akademie – Hochschule für Gestaltung, Kunst und Medien, Stuttgart 2011/ 2012; available at wwwwwwwww. at/downloads/troll-culture.pdf#77 (last access January 16, 2017).

Kreuz, Roger J. and Mary Sue MacNealy, eds. 1996. *Empirical Approaches to Literature and Aesthetics*. Norwood, NJ: Ablex Pub.

Krishnendu, Ray. 2007. "Domesticating Cuisine: Food and Aesthetics on American Television", 50–63. *Gastronomica: The Journal of Food and Culture*, 7, 1.

Landowski, Éric. 2004. *Passions sans nom*. Paris, France: Presses Universitaires de France.

Landowski, Eric. 2012. "Régimes de sens et styles de vie", online. In *Nouveaux Actes Sémiotiques*, 115; available at https://www.unilim.fr/actes-semiotiques/2647.

Lange, Patricia G. 2007. "Publicly Private and Privately Public: Social Networking on YouTube", 361–80. *Journal of Computer-Mediated Communication*, 13, 1.

Lavazza, Andrea and Massimo Marraffa, eds. 2016. *La guerra dei mondi: scienza e senso comune*. Turin, Italy: Codice edizioni.

Lawrence E. Joseph. 1994. *Common Sense: Why It's no Longer Common*. Reading, MA: Addison-Wesley Pub. Co.

Ledwig, Marion. 2007. *Common Sense: Its History, Method, and Applicability*. New York, NY: P. Lang.

Leitch, Alison. 2009. "Slow Food and the Politics of 'Virtuous Globalization'", 45–64. In David Inglis and Debra Gimlin, eds. 2009. *The Globalization of Food*. Oxford, UK and New York, NY: Berg.

Lemos, Noah Marcelino. 2007. *Common Sense*. Cambridge, UK: Cambridge University Press.

Leone, Massimo. 2002. "Shoah and Humor: A Semiotic Approach", 173–92. *Jewish Studies Quarterly*, 2, 9.

Leone, Massimo. 2004a. "Literature, Travel, and Vertigo", 513–22. In Jane Conroy, ed. 2004. *Cross-Cultural Travel: Papers from the Royal Irish Academy Symposium on Literature and Travel*, National University of Ireland, Galway, November 2002 (Travel writing across the disciplines, v. 7). New York, NY: Peter Lang.

Leone, Massimo. 2004b. "Textual Wanderings: A Vertiginous Reading of W.G. Sebald", 89–101. In Jonathan J. Long and Anne Whitehead, eds. 2004. *W.G. Sebald: A Critical Companion*. Edinburgh, UK: Edinburgh University Press.

Leone, Massimo. 2005. "On the Quincunx", 289–304. In Claus Clüver, Véronique Plesch, and Leo Hoek, eds. 2005. *Orientations: Space/Time/Image/Word*, Proceedings of the 6th Congress of the International Association for Word and Image Studies held in Hamburg, July 2002; with an introduction by Charlotte Schoell-Glass (Word & image interactions 5). Amsterdam, The Netherlands: Rodopi.

Leone, Massimo. 2007. "Appunti per una semiotica della frontiera"; available at the website www.academia.edu/174662/2007_Appunti_per_una_semiotica_della_frontiera (last access February 2, 2018).

Leone, Massimo. 2009a. "Virtual Cities and Civic Virtues: The Semiotics of Space in Gated Communities", 67–87. In Asunción López-Varela Azcárate and Mariana Net, eds. 2009. *Actual and Virtual Cities (Intertextuality and Intermediality)*. Bucharest, Romania: Univers Enciclopedic Press.

Leone, Massimo. 2009b. "The Paradox of Shibboleth: *immunitas* and *communitas* in Language and Religion", 131–57. In Giusy Gallo, ed. 2009. *Natura umana e linguaggio*. Monographic issue of RIFL – Rivista italiana di filosofia del linguaggio, 1; available at http://www.rifl.unical.it/index.php/rifl/article/view/137.

Leone, Massimo, ed. 2009c. *Attanti, attori, agenti: senso dell'azione e azione del senso; dalle teorie ai territori / Actants, Actors, Agents: The Meaning of Action and the Action of Meaning; from Theories to Territories*. Monographic issue of *Lexia: International Journal of Semiotics*, 3–4. Rome, Italy: Aracne.

Leone, Massimo. 2010a. "Ancient Tradition and Modern Audacity: On the (Proto-) Semiotic Ideas of Juan Caramuel y Lobkowitz", 247–68. *Semiotica*, 182, 1–4.

Leone, Massimo. 2010b. "Invisible Frontiers in Contemporary Cities: An Ethno-Semiotic Approach", 59–74. *The International Journal of Interdisciplinary Social Sciences*, 4, 11.

Leone, Massimo. 2010c. "The Sacred, (In)Visibility, and Communication: An Inter-Religious Dialogue Between Goethe and Hāfez", 373–84. *Islam and Christian–Muslim Relations*, 21, 4.

Leone, Massimo. 2011. "The Reasonable Audience of Religious Hatred: The Semiotic Ideology of Anti-Vilification Laws in Australia", 112–34. In Nadir Hosen and Richard Mohr, eds. 2011. *Law and Religion in Public Life: The Contemporary Debate*. New York, NY and Oxford, UK: Routledge.

Leone, Massimo. 2012a. "From Theory to Analysis: Forethoughts on Cultural Semiotics", 23–38. In Valentina Pisanty and Stefano Traini, eds. 2012. *From Analysis to Theory: Afterthoughts on the Semiotics of Culture.* Monographic issue of *Versus*, 114. Milan, Italy: Bompiani.

Leone, Massimo. 2012b. "Introduction to the Semiotics of Belonging", 449–70. *Semiotica*, 192.

Leone, Massimo. 2012c. "Petition and Repetition: On the Semiotic Philosophy of Prayer", 631–64. In Massimo Leone, ed. 2012. *Culto / Worship.* Special issue of *Lexia: International Journal of Semiotics*, 11–12. Rome, Italy: Aracne.

Leone, Massimo. 2012d. "Quanta and Qualia in the Semiotic Theory of Culture", 281–302. In Ernest W.B. Hess-Lüttich, ed. 2012. *Sign Culture / Zeichen Kultur.* Würzburg, Germany: Königshausen & Neumann.

Leone, Massimo. 2012e. "Scarpe abbandonate: sul senso dei resti", 51–64. In Gianluca Cuozzo, ed. 2012. *Resti del senso: ripensare il mondo a partire dai rifiuti,* (I saggi di Lexia 6). Rome, Italy: Aracne.

Leone, Massimo. 2012f. "Semiótica de lo bárbaro: para una tipología de las inculturas", 551–65. *Signa: revista de la Asociación Española de Semiótica*, 21.

Leone, Massimo. 2013a. "Digiunare, istruzioni per l'uso: la mistica dell'inedia nel Giainismo", 47–58. In Alice Giannitrapani and Gianfranco Marrone, eds. 2013. *Mangiare: istruzioni per l'uso.* Special issue of *E/C*, the E-Journal of the Italian Association of Semiotic Studies, 14; available at http://www.ec-aiss.it/monografici/14_mangiare_ istruzioni/14_mangiare_leone.pdf.

Leone, Massimo. 2013b. "L'aritmetica di Gesù: un esperimento semiotico", online. In *E/C*, the e-journal of the Italian Association for Semiotic Studies, 28 October; available at www.academia.edu/4902345/2013_-_L_aritmetica_di_Ges%C3%B9_ un_esperimento_semiotico (last access February 2, 2018).

Leone, Massimo. 2013c. "The Semiotics of Fundamentalist Authoriality", 227–39. *International Journal for the Semiotics of Law – Revue Internationale de Sémiotique Juridique*, 26, 1.

Leone, Massimo. 2013d. *Annunciazioni. Percorsi di semiotica della religione,* 2 vols. Rome, Italy: Aracne.

Leone, Massimo. 2014a. "Longing for the Past: The Nostalgic Semiosphere", 1–15. *Social Semiotics*, 25, 1.

Leone, Massimo. 2014b. "Semiotica dello slancio mistico", 219–84. In Massimo Leone, ed. 2014. *Estasi / Ecstasy,* numero monografico di *Lexia*, 15–16. Rome, Italy: Aracne.

Leone, Massimo. 2014c. *Sémiotique du fondamentalisme religieux: messages, rhétorique, force persuasive.* Paris, France: l'Harmattan.

Leone, Massimo. 2014d. *Spiritualità digitale: Il senso religioso nell'era della smaterializzazione.* Milan, Italy: Mimesis.

Leone, Massimo. 2015a. "Double Debunking: Modern Divination and the End of Semiotics", 433–77. *Chinese Semiotic Studies*, 11, 4.

Leone, Massimo. 2015b. "La pallavolo sacra", 63–84, online. In *E/C*, E-Journal of the Italian Association for Semiotic Studies, 5 May; republished in Mattia Thibault, ed. 2016. *Gamification urbana: letture e riscritture ludiche degli spazi cittadini* (I saggi di Lexia, 20). Rome, Italy: Aracne.

Leone, Massimo. 2016a. "El murmullo de la cultura: semiótica y sentido de la vida", 110–27. *Religación: Revista de Ciencias Sociales y Humanidades*, 2, June.

Leone, Massimo. 2016b. "Metafisica del design: il senso degli oggetti in De Chirico, Kiarostami, Ozu", online: 1–37. *E/C*, E-Journal of the *Italian Association for Semiotic Studies*, 31 December; available at www.ec-aiss.it/index_d.php?recordID=753 (last access February 2, 2018).

Leone, Massimo. 2016c. "On Depth: Ontological Ideologies and Semiotic Models", online. In Kristian Bankov, ed. 2016. *New Semiotics. Between Tradition and Innovation.* Proceedings of the 12th World Congress of Semiotics. IASS Publications & NBU Publishing House (ISSN 2414–6862); available at www.iass-ais.org/proceedings2014/view_lesson.php?id=48 (last access February 2, 2018).

Leone, Massimo. 2016d. "Saints Smashing Idols: A Paradoxical Semiotics", 30–56. *Signs & Society*, 4, 1 (Spring).

Leone, Massimo. 2016e. "Silence Propaganda: A Semiotic Inquiry into the Ideologies of Taciturnity", 154–82. *Signs and Society*, 5, 1.

Leone, Massimo, ed. 2016f. *Censura / Censorship.* Monographic issue of *Lexia: International Journal of Semiotics*, 21–22. Rome, Italy: Aracne.

Leone, Massimo, ed. 2016g. *Complotto / Conspiracy.* Monographic issue of *Lexia: International Journal of Semiotics*, 23–24. Rome, Italy: Aracne.

Leone, Massimo, ed. 2017. *Aspettualità / Aspectuality.* Monographic issue of *Lexia: International Journal of Semiotics*, 27–28. Rome, Italy: Aracne.

Leone, Massimo. Forthcoming. "Dinamiche dell'innovazione culturale: patrimonio e matrimonio"; available at www.academia.edu/1726797/2012_Dinamiche_dell_innovazione_culturale_patrimonio_e_matrimonio (last access February 2, 2018).

Leone, Massimo. 2018. "Rationality and Reasonableness in Textual Interpretation", 53–70. In Alin Olteanu, Andrew Stables, and Dumitru Borțun, eds. 2018. *Semiotics and Communication.* Dordrecht, The Netherlands: Springer.

Leone, Massimo and Richard Parmentier, eds. 2014. *Representing Transcendence.* Special issue of *Signs and Society*, 2, s1. Chicago, IL: University of Chicago Press.

Lescano, Alfredo. 2013. "Stéréotypes, représentations sociales et blocs conceptuels", online. *Semen*, 35; available at the website http://semen.revues.org/9835 (last access July 8, 2017).

Liebes, Tamar and James Curran, eds. 1998. *Media, Ritual, and Identity.* New York, NY and London, UK: Routledge.

Lipovetsky, Gilles and Jean Serroy. 2013. *L'esthétisation du monde: vivre à l'âge du capitalisme artiste.* Paris, France: Gallimard.

Liu, Hugo. 2007. "Social Network Profiles as Taste Performances", 252–75. *Journal of Computer-Mediated Communication*, 13, 1.

Lorusso, Anna Maria. 2015. *Cultural Semiotics: For a Cultural Perspective in Semiotics.* Houndmills, Basingstoke, Hampshire and New York, NY: Palgrave Macmillan.

Lotman, Jurij M. 1985. *La semiosfera: l'asimmetria e il dialogo nelle strutture pensanti*; It. trans. Simonetta Salvestroni. Venice, Italy: Marsilio.

Lotman, Jurij M. 1990. *Universe of the Mind: A Semiotic Theory of Culture.* Engl. trans. Ann Shukman. Bloomington, IN: Indiana University Press.

Lotman, Yuri M. and Boris A. Uspenskij. 1984. *The Semiotics of Russian Culture*, ed. Ann Shukman. Ann Arbor, MI: Department of Slavic Languages and Literatures, University of Michigan.

Maitland, Sarah. 2017. *What Is Cultural Translation?* London, UK and New York, NY: Bloomsbury Academic.

Manetti, Giovanni. 2008. *L'enunciazione: dalla svolta comunicativa ai nuovi media.* Milan, Italy: Mondadori Università.

Marks, Laura U. 2010. *Enfoldment and Infinity: An Islamic Genealogy of New Media Art.* Cambridge, MA: MIT Press.

Marrani, David. 2011. *Rituel(s) de justice?: essai anthropologique sur la relation du temps et de l'espace dans le process.* Fernelmont, Belgium: E.M.E.

Marrone, Gianfranco. 2006. "Le monde naturel, entre corps et cultures", 47–55. *Protée*, 341.

Marrone, Gianfranco. 2011. "*Brand on the Run*: mirada semiótica sobre Slow Food", 59–92. *Tópicos del Seminario*, 26.

Marrone, Gianfranco. 2013. "Cucinare senza senso. Spazialità e passioni in Masterchef", 235–51. *Studi culturali*, 10, 2.

Masquelet, Alain Charles. 2011. "Rembrandt's Anatomy Lesson of Professor Nicolaes Tulp (1632)", 773–83. *Bulletin de l'Académie Nationale de Médecine*, 195, 3.

Matrix, Sidney Eve. 2006. *Cyberpop: Digital Lifestyles and Commodity Culture*. New York, NY: Routledge.

Mcbride, Anne E. 2010. "Food Porn", 38–46. *Gastronomica: The Journal of Food and Culture*, 10, 1.

Meise, Bianca. 2015. *Im Spiegel des Sozialen: zur Konstruktion von Sozialität in Social Network Sites*. Wiesbaden, Germany: Springer VS.

Meneley, Anne. 2004. "Extra Virgin Olive Oil and Slow Food", 165–76. *Anthropologica*, 46, 2.

Mereghetti, Paolo. 2002. *Il Mereghetti. Dizionario dei film 2002*. Milan, Italy: Baldini & Castoldi.

Mitchell, William J. 2005. *Placing Words: Symbols, Space, and the City*. Cambridge, MA: MIT Press.

Modigliani, Franco. 2007. *Crisi del sistema economico, prezzi politici e autarchia: cinque articoli giovanili, Roma 1937–1938*, ed. Daniela Parisi. Milan, Italy: Vita e pensiero.

Moutat, Audrey. 2013. "Stratégies énonciatives et imaginaires gustatifs dans les émissions télévisées", 151–74. *E/C*, 7, 14.

Mueller, Tom. 2012. *Extra Virginity: The Sublime and Scandalous World of Olive Oil*. New York, NY: W.W. Norton.

Mullan, John. 2007. *Anonymity: A Secret History of English Literature*. Princeton, NJ: Princeton University Press.

Neumaier, Otto, ed. 2007. *Fehler und Irrtümer in den Wissenschaften*. Wien, Austria and Berlin, Germany: Lit.

Nöth, Winfried. 1994. "The Semantic Space of Opposites: Cognitive and Localist Foundations", 63–82. In Kei I. Yamanaka and Toshio Ohori, eds. 1994. *The Locus of Meaning: Papers in Honor of Yoshihiko Ikegami*. Tokyo, Japan: Kurosio.

Nöth, Winfried. 1995. *Handbook of Semiotics* (1990). Bloomington, IN: Indiana University Press.

O'Bryan, C. Jill. 2005. *Carnal Art: Orlan's Refacing*. Minneapolis, MI: University of Minnesota Press.

Oblinger, Diana G., ed. 2006. *Learning Spaces*. Washington, DC and Boulder, CO: Educause.

Olsen, Ralph, Christiane Hochstadt, and Simona Colombo-Scheffold, eds. 2016. *Ohne Punkt und Komma: Beiträge zu Theorie, Empirie und Didaktik der Interpunktion*. Berlin, Germany: RabenStück Verlag.

Ono, Aya. 2007. *La Notion d'énonciation chez Émile Benveniste*. Limoges, France: Lambert-Lucas.

Osbaldiston, Nick, ed. 2013. *Culture of the Slow: Social Deceleration in an Accelerated World*. Houndmills, Basingstoke, Hampshire, UK: Palgrave Macmillan.

Ott, Corinna. 2012. *Zu Hause schmeckt's am besten: Essen als Ausdruck nationaler Identität in der deutsch-türkischen Migrationsliteratur*. Frankfurt am Main, Germany: Peter Lang.

Pabst, Stephan, ed. 2011. *Anonymität und Autorschaft: zur Literatur- und Rechtsgeschichte der Namenlosigkeit*. Berlin, Germany and Boston, MA: De Gruyter.

Paul, Gerhard. 2016. *Das visuelle Zeitalter: Punkt und Pixel.* Göttingen, Germany: Wallstein Verlag.

Paxson, Heather. 2005. "Slow Food in a Fat Society: Satisfying Ethical Appetites", 14–18. *Gastronomica: The Journal of Food and Culture,* 5, 1.

Peace, Adrian. 2006. "Barossa Slow: The Representation and Rhetoric of Slow Food's Regional Cooking", 51–59. *Gastronomica: The Journal of Food and Culture,* 6, 1.

Peace, Adrian. 2008. "Terra Madre 2006: Political Theater and Ritual Rhetoric in the Slow Food Movement", 31–39 *Gastronomica: The Journal of Food and Culture,* 8, 2.

Peirce, Charles Sanders Sebastian. 1982–2000. *Writings of Charles S. Peirce: A Chronological Edition,* 6 vols. Bloomington, IN: Indiana University Press.

Pencak, William. 1988. "Eric Voegelin's Semiotics of History", 2: 277–92. In Roberta Kevelson, ed. 1988. *Law and Semiotics*: Proceedings based on the Second Round Table on Law and Semiotics, held May 12–15, 1988, at Pennsylvania State University, Berks Campus, Reading, PA, 2 vols. New York, NY: Plenum Press.

Perinbanayagam, Robert S. 2011. *Discursive Acts: Language, Signs, and Selves.* New Brunswick, NJ: Transaction Publishers.

Petrini, Carlo. 2003. *Slow Food: The Case for Taste.* Engl. trans. William McCuaig. New York, NY: Columbia University Press.

Phillips, Whitney. 2015. *This Is Why We Can't Have Nice Things: Mapping the Relationship between Online Trolling and Mainstream Culture.* Cambridge, MA: The MIT Press.

Pike, Kenneth Lee. 1967. *Language in Relation to a Unified Theory of the Structure of Human Behavior* (Janua linguarum. Series maior, 24). The Hague, The Netherlands: Mouton.

Poletti, Anna and Julie Rak, eds. 2014. *Identity Technologies: Constructing the Self Online.* Madison: The University of Wisconsin Press.

Pongratz-Leisten, Beate and Karen Sonik, eds. 2015. *The Materiality of Divine Agency.* Boston, MA and Berlin, Germany: De Gruyter.

Ponzio, Augusto. 1976. *La semiotica in Italia: Fondamenti teorici.* Bari, Italy: Edizioni Dedalo.

Poole, Matthew and Manuel Shvartzberg. 2015. *The Politics of Parametricism: Digital Technologies in Architecture.* London, UK and New York, NY: Bloomsbury Academic.

Popper, Karl. 1935. *Logik der Forschung: zur Erkenntnistheorie der Modernen Naturwissenschaft.* Vienna, Austria: J. Springer.

Power, Andrew and Grâinne Kirwan, eds. 2014. *Cyberpsychology and New Media: A Thematic Reader.* London, UK and New York, NY: Psychology Press.

Puckett, Kent. 2008. *Bad Form: Social Mistakes and the Nineteenth-Century Novel.* Oxford, UK and New York, NY: Oxford University Press.

Reason, James. 2013. *A Life in Error: From Little Slips to Big Disasters.* Farnham, Surrey, England: Ashgate.

Rescher, Nicholas. 2005. *Common-Sense: A New Look at an Old Philosophical Tradition.* Milwaukee, WI: Marquette University Press.

Resnik, Judith. 2004. *Processes of the Law: Understanding Courts and their Alternatives.* New York, NY: Foundation Press.

Revillard, Anne. 2000. "Les interactions sur l'Internet", 108–29. *Terrains & Travaux,* 1, 1.

Ricœur, Paul. 1965. *De l'interprétation.* Paris, France: Éditions du Seuil.

Ricœur, Paul. 1983–5. *Temps et récit,* 3 vols. Paris, France: Seuil. Engl. trans. Kathleen McLaughlin and David Pellauer. 1984–8. *Time and Narrative.* Chicago, IL: University of Chicago Press.

Ritzer, George. 2001. *Explorations in the Sociology of Consumption: Fast Food, Credit Cards and Casinos.* London, UK and Thousand Oaks, CA: SAGE.

Ritzer, George. 2013. *The McDonaldization of Society,* 7th ed. Thousand Oaks, CA: SAGE.

Röbkes, Marion. 2013. *Religion, Ernährung und Gesellschaft: Ernährungsregeln und -verbote in Christentum, Judentum und Islam*. Hamburg, Germany: Diplomica Verlag.

Rockwell, Patricia Ann. 2006. *Sarcasm and Other Mixed Messages: The Ambiguous Ways People Use Language*. Lewiston, NY: Edwin Mellen Press.

Roesler, Silke. 2007. *Identity Switch im Cyberspace: Eine Form von Selbstinszenierung*. Frankfurt am Main, Germany and New York, NY: Peter Lang.

Romero, Juan and Penousal Machado, eds. 2008. *The Art of Artificial Evolution: A Handbook on Evolutionary Art and Music*. Berlin, Germany and New York, NY: Springer.

Rose, Susan. 2011. *The Wine Trade in Medieval Europe 1000–1500*. London, UK and New York, NY: Continuum.

Rosenfeld, Sophia. 2011. *Common Sense: A Political History*. Cambridge, MA: Harvard University Press.

Sacks, Jonathan. 2003. *The Dignity of Difference: How to Avoid the Clash of Civilizations*. London, UK and New York, NY: Continuum.

Saponari, Angela Bianca. 2008. *Il rifiuto dell'uomo nel cinema di Marco Ferreri*. Bari, Italy: Progedit.

Scalabroni, Luisa, ed. 2011. *Falso e falsi: prospettive teoriche e proposte di analisi*. Pisa, Italy: ETS.

Scandola, Alberto. 2004. *Marco Ferreri*. Milan, Italy: Il Castoro Cinema.

Schneider, Stephen. 2008. "Good, Clean, Fair: The Rhetoric of the Slow Food Movement", 384–402. *College English*, 70, 4 (Special Focus: Food).

Schwarz-Friesel, Monika and Jan-Henning Kromminga, eds. 2014. *Metaphern der Gewalt: Konzeptualisierungen von Terrorismus in den Medien vor und nach 9/11*. Tübingen, Germany: Francke Verlag.

Sebald, Winfried Georg. 2001. *Die Ringe des Saturn: eine englische Wallfahrt* (1992). Frankfurt am Main, Germany: Eichborn. Engl. trans. Michael Hulse. 1998. *The Rings of Saturn*. New York, NY: New Directions.

Sedda, Franciscu. 2015. "Semiotics of Culture(s): Basic Questions and Concepts", 675–96. In Peter P. Trifonas, ed. 2015. *International Handbook of Semiotics*. Dordrecht, The Netherlands: Springer.

Segre, Cesare. 2003. *La pelle di San Bartolomeo: discorso e tempo dell'arte*. Turin: Einaudi.

Shachaf, Pnina and Noriko Hara. 2010. "Beyond Vandalism: Wikipedia Trolls", 357–70. *Journal of Information Science*, 36, 3.

Silverstein, Michael. 1979. "Language Structure and Linguistic Ideology", 193–247. In Paul R. Clyne, William F. Hanks, and Carol L. Hofbauer, eds. 1979. *The Elements: A Parasession on Linguistic Units and Levels*. Chicago, IL: Chicago Linguistic Society.

Silverstein, Michael and Greg Urban. 1996. *The Natural History of Discourse*, 1–20. In Michael Silverstein and Greg Urban, eds. 1996. *Natural Histories of Discourse*. Chicago, IL and London, UK: University of Chicago Press.

Simonetti, Luca. 2010. *Mangi, chi può. Meglio, meno e piano. L'ideologia di Slow Food*. Florence, Italy: Mauro Pagliai Editore.

Sinram, Jana. 2015. *Pressefreiheit oder Fremdenfeindlichkeit? Der Streit um die Mohammed-Karikaturen und die dänische Einwanderungspolitik*. Frankfurt, Germany and New York, NY: Campus Verlag.

Sniderman, Paul M., Michael Bang Petersen, Rune Slothuus, and Rune Stubager, eds. 2014. *Paradoxes of Liberal Democracy: Islam, Western Europe, and the Danish Cartoon Crisis*. Princeton, NJ: Princeton University Press.

Spieler, Reinhard and Barbara J. Scheuermann, eds. 2012. *Punkt.Systeme: Vom Pointillismus zum Pixel*. Heidelberg, Germany: Kehrer.

Spineto, Natale. 2014. "Aurum: da voce di catalogo a tema culturale", 413–21. In Marisa Tortorelli Ghidini, ed. 2014. *Aurum. Funzioni e simbologie dell'oro nelle culture del Mediterraneo Antico*. Rome, Italy: "L'Erma" di Bretschneider.

Spruds, Andris, Anda Rožukalne, Klavs Sedlenieks, Martins Daugulis, Diana Potjomkina, Beatrix Tölgyesi, and Ilvija Bruge. 2016. *Internet Trolling as a Hybrid Warfare Tool: The Case of Latvia.* Riga, LV: NATO Strategic Communications Centre of Excellence (published 28 January 2016)

Staglianò, Riccardo. 2006. *L'impero dei falsi.* Rome, Italy: GLF editori Laterza.

Starobinski, Jean. 2005. *Donner à penser.* Paris, France: Seuil.

Stehlé, André. 1982. "Théophile Bader", 84. In Fédération des sociétés d'histoire et d'archéologie d'Alsace, ed. 1982. *Nouveau dictionnaire de biographie alsacienne*, 13 vols. Strasbourg, France: Fédération des sociétés d'histoire et d'archéologie d'Alsace, 1.

Stoichita, Victor I. 1993. *L'instauration du tableau: Métapeinture à l'aube des temps modernes.* Paris, France: Méridiens Klincksieck. Engl. trans. Anne-Marie Glasheen. 1997. *The Self-Aware Image: An Insight into Early Modern Meta-Painting.* New York, NY: Cambridge University Press.

Stoller, Paul. 1997. *Sensuous Scholarship.* Philadelphia, PA: University of Pennsylvania Press.

Struck, Peter T. 2016. *Divination and Human Nature: A Cognitive History of Intuition in Classical Antiquity.* Princeton, NJ: Princeton University Press.

Stryker, Cole. 2012. *Hacking the Future: Privacy, Identity, and Anonymity on the Web.* New York, NY: Overlook Duckworth.

Sullivan, Winnifred Fallers, Robert A. Yelle, and Mateo Taussig-Rubbo, eds. 2011. *After Secular Law.* Stanford, CA: Stanford Law Books.

Svašek, Maruška and Birgit Meyer, eds. 2016. *Creativity in Transition: Politics and Aesthetics of Cultural Production across the Globe.* New York, NY: Berghahn Books.

Tao, Terence. 2008. *Structure and Randomness: Pages from Year One of a Mathematical Blog.* Providence, RI: American Mathematical Society.

Thibault, Mattia. 2016. "Trolls, Hackers, Anons. Conspiracy Theories in the Peripheries of the Web", 387–408. In Massimo Leone, ed. 2016. *Complotto / Conspiracy*, special issue of *Lexia – International Journal of Semiotics*, 23–24. Rome, Italy: Aracne.

Thürlemann, Felix. 2013. *Mehr als ein Bild: Für eine Kunstgeschichte des hyperimage.* Munich, Germany: Wilhelm Fink.

Turton-Turner, Pamela. 2013. "Villainous Avatars: The Visual Semiotics of Misogyny and Free Speech in Cyberspace", 1–18. *The Forum on Public Policy*; available at www. google.de/url?sa=t&rct=j&q=&esrc=s&source=web&cd=10&ved=0ahUKEwiM3t 6yp8fRAhUIK8AKHd_eBPQQFghWMAk&url=http%3A%2F%2Fforumonpub licpolicy.com%2Fvol2013.no1%2Fvol2013archive%2Fturton.pdf&usg=AFQjCNGle KjyJqmeocCltjzgeDERF8MqoA (last access January 16, 2017).

Uffelen, Chris van. 2009. *Fine Fabric: Delicate Materials for Architecture and Interior Design.* Berlin, Germany and London, UK: Braun and Thames & Hudson.

Urroz, Javier. 2008. "La gastronomía en los medios de comunicación. Una visión crítica", 18–33. *Ábaco*, (2 Epoca) 57 (El impacto mediático de la gastronomía).

Valeri, Mark R. 2010. *Heavenly Merchandize: How Religion Shaped Commerce in Puritan America.* Princeton, NJ: Princeton University Press.

Van der Ploeg, Irma and Jason Pridmore, eds. 2016. *Digitizing Identities: Doing Identity in a Networked World.* New York, NY: Routledge.

Virno, Paolo. 2002. *Grammatica della moltitudine.* Roma, Italy: Derive Approdi. Engl. trans. Isabella Bertoletti, James Cascaito, and Andrea Casson. *Multitude: Between Innovation and Negation.* Los Angeles, CA and Cambridge, MA: Distributed by MIT Press and Semiotext(e).

Walter, Tony, Rachid Hourizi, Wendy Moncur, and Stacey Pitsillides. 2011. "Does the Internet Change How We Die and Mourn? Overview and Analysis", 275–302. *Omega: Journal of Death & Dying*, 64, 4.

Wason, Peter Cathcart. 1962. *Psychological Aspects of Negation: An Experimental Enquiry and Some Practical Applications.* London, UK: Communication Research Centre, University College.

Werner, Axel Roderich. 2010. *System und Mythos: Peter Greenaways Filme und die Selbstbeobachtung der Medienkultur.* Bielefeld, Germany: Transcript.

Whelan, Fiona. 2017. *The Making of Manners and Morals in Twelfth-Century England: The Book of the Civilised Man.* Abingdon, Oxon, UK and New York, NY: Routledge.

Wilk, Richard, ed. 2006. *Fast Food/Slow Food: The Cultural Economy of the Global Food System.* Lanham, MD: Altamira Press.

Wise, Amanda and Selvaraj Velayutham, eds. 2009. *Everyday Multiculturalism.* Houndmills, Basingstoke, Hampshire, UK and New York, NY: Palgrave Macmillan.

Yang, Young-Im. 2005. *Das Phänomen der Verneinung: philosophisch, psychologisch und im Kulturvergleich untersucht.* Würzburg, Germany: Königshausen & Neumann.

Zhang, Jiang. 2016. "The Dogmatic Character of Imposed Interpretation", 132–47. *Social Sciences in China*, 37, 3.

Zhang, Jiang. Forthcoming. *Thesis on Public Hermeneutics.* In *Versus*, forthcoming.

Zhou, Yuqiong and Patricia Moy. 2006. "Parsing Framing Processes: The Interplay Between Online Public Opinion and Media Coverage", 79–98. *Journal of Communication*, 57, 1.

Zilberberg, Claude. 2011. *Des formes de vie aux valeurs.* Paris, France: PUF.

INDEX

abduction 12, 153
absentification 110
abstraction 164
acceleration 84, 132
accountability 142
actant 2, 27–28, 99–101, 184
action 23, 25, 32, 43, 46–47, 57, 84, 100, 124, 152, 170
actors 34, 48, 82, 99, 116, 193
addiction 7, 17
Adidas 128
adjudication 142, 201
Administration 146
Adoration 81
Adriaanszoon, Adriaan 137, 142
Adulterous woman 44
AED 146–147
aesthetics 3, 28–30, 57, 59, 67, 70–71, 76, 79, 82, 87, 93, 118, 127, 131–132, 169, 179
affects 44, 71, 106, 123, 133–134
affordance 66, 71
agency 60–64, 68–69, 71–72, 74, 77–78, 118, 120–124, 133, 142, 150–152, 154, 165, 187, 200
agents 53, 103, 119, 124, 126, 196
agnosticism 107
airlines 144–5, 157
airplanes 109, 151
airports 4, 76, 79, 109, 144, 156
Alexandria 95
algorithms 4, 21, 81
alienation 1, 3, 19, 82, 114

allegory 118
alligator 67
alpaca 70
alphabet 65
Alsace 91, 94
altar 93, 108
alternatives 5, 15–16, 32, 40, 48, 50–53, 57, 60, 77, 120, 143, 145, 147, 152, 155–156, 177, 179, 198, 200–201
amphisbaena 141
amphitheater 138, 173
Amsterdam 137, 139, 142–143
anagrams 8
analgesics 140
analogy 85–87
analysis 1, 5, 22, 28–29, 32, 44, 46, 48–49, 54–55, 91, 97–98, 100, 106–108, 113–115, 133, 136, 152, 166, 171, 173–174, 176, 179, 183–186, 189–193, 195
anaphora 43
anatomy 4, 133–142
ancestor 22
anchorman 52
anecdote 112, 157–158
anger 23
animals 16, 71, 76, 153
annihilation 86
anonymity 2, 25–27, 34, 42–43
antagonism 41
anthropology 1, 8, 15, 90, 104, 115, 134, 192–193
anthropomorphism 68
antidote 143, 187

antiracist behavior 39
antisocial behavior 41
anxiety 84, 99, 107, 120, 127
apology 44, 46
apperception 163
applause 108–111
Apple 86, 104
Apulia 124
Arabophobia 53
Aramaic language 89
arbitrariness 85, 89, 91, 167
archetype 128
architecture 57, 92–93, 103, 106, 163,
    173–174, 181
Arduino 80
argumentation 24, 29
arguments 26, 28–29, 36, 154, 173, 188
Aristotle 129, 199
arithmetic 85
Aron 54
arrhythmia 146
arrogance 4, 136
art 3, 21–23, 28, 56–57, 60–62, 70, 78, 92,
    114, 127, 129, 131, 136–137, 142, 151,
    153, 163–164, 175, 179
articulation 98, 131, 136, 190, 193
artifacts 70, 76, 82, 104, 164, 167–169
artificiality 85
artists 47, 69, 111, 113–114, 162–163, 165
artworks 61, 68, 131, 169, 179–180
ashrams 98
aspectuality 28, 32
asphalt 65–68
assassins 41, 43, 49
asymmetries 52
atheism 107
atmosphere 38–42, 63, 91, 93, 130, 142,
    161–163, 174–175, 180, 185, 187, 198
audience 2, 27–28, 41, 45–48, 111, 113, 131,
    138, 168, 172–173, 194
Augustine 22, 91
Augustus 141
Austin, John 171
autarchy 125
authenticity 71, 122–123, 125, 127–129
author 5, 18–19, 38, 42–43, 49, 62, 66,
    68, 70, 72–73, 75–77, 79, 81, 92, 96,
    102–103, 105, 112, 129, 177, 179–181,
    183–185, 191, 198
authoritarianism 185, 187
authority 174, 177–178, 187
authors 8, 22, 43, 115
authorship 169, 179
automata 19, 154

automatisms 142
autopsy 139, 142
avanguardia 119
avatar 26, 43–44, 86
Avellino 55
awareness 9, 20, 52, 111, 122, 130, 154, 194
axiology 28, 50, 52, 90
axiom 180
azulejos 81–82

Babel 88–89
ballet 161
Banksy 39
baptism 107, 128
bar 52
barbarians 117, 199–201
bards 16
baroque 96, 141
Barthes, Ronald 186
basilisk 141
Baudrillard, Jean 84
beach 65
beauty 64, 69, 82–83
bees 69
Beethoven, Ludwig van 131, 173
beginnings 8, 82
behavior 9, 14, 29–30, 106, 108, 152,
    159–161, 177
Belgium 65–66, 68
Belgrade 79
belief 24, 33, 110, 112–113, 125, 143, 156, 186
belonging 4, 31, 71, 82, 122, 161–162, 166
Benjamin, Walter 87, 125
Benveniste, Émile 35
Berlin 97, 121
Bershka 97
biases 53, 194
Bible 172
Bilbao 162
Bildpunkt 60
binding 43, 124, 199, 202
biological 152, 154, 196
biology 150, 152, 165
birth 85, 88, 107, 135–136, 153
bishop 19, 91
blasphemy 53
blindness 13, 15–16, 34
blood 103, 146
bloodletting 155
blurring 2, 34, 45–46, 50–51, 180
boar 130
body 8–9, 16–17, 27, 42–43, 53, 61, 84–86,
    91, 97, 123, 128, 130, 135–137, 139–140,
    142, 145, 147, 152–153, 155, 157–158, 165

Boeotia 132
Bologna 185
borders 122, 199–200
Borges, Jorge Luis 141, 143
Botticelli 69
boundaries 25–26, 29, 43, 89
brain 139, 146, 153–154
Brandenburg 121
branding 104
brands 86, 97, 125
bricolage 108, 110–111, 198
brightness 56, 61–62, 77–78
brilliance 112
Britain 171
Browne, Thomas 134, 139–141
Bulgaria 111
bureaucracy 3–4, 19–21, 82, 126, 143
burial 105, 109–110, 113–114
Burri, Alberto 68
bus 1, 6–7, 9–11, 13–14, 17–18
butterflies 141

Caen 115
Caesarea 33
Calabrese, Omar 163, 177
California 128
Calvin, John 89
camera 62, 134
Canada 117
Canetti, Elias 36, 43, 115
Cannes 116
canon 74
capitalism 3, 111, 114, 116, 118, 122
Caravaggio 190
carbonara 131
cardiology 151
career 18, 187, 194
carpets 3, 70–71, 75, 77
Carthage 190
cartoonists 35–36, 39, 42, 45
cartoons 35–36, 54
catechism 190
categorization 2, 31, 33, 93, 134
Catholicism 96, 107–108, 110, 190
causality 14, 26, 28–29, 37–38, 43–44, 52,
    84–85, 117, 120, 186
Celibidache, Sergiu 131
censorship 42, 44
center 28, 74, 101, 111, 124–127, 138–139,
    173, 195, 201–202
centrality 3, 50, 53, 118, 126–128, 160, 184
centrifugal 57, 62, 200
centripetal 62
ceremonies 10, 12, 107

Chaeronea 132
chain 12, 16, 42, 119, 121, 139–140, 197
chameleon 141
Champagne 128
change 17, 24, 53, 69, 71, 74, 118, 121–122,
    124–125, 133, 149–150, 152, 167, 169,
    178, 181–182, 198
chaos 70, 141–142, 148–149, 151
chapel 106–108
characterization 29, 101
Charlie Hebdo 2, 35–54
chauvinism 124
chemistry 17, 126, 147–148, 150, 152
chemtrail 48
cherry 198
chessboard 31
chestnut 141
Chicago 144–145
childhood 7, 160–161
children 14, 31, 97, 107
chimera 46
Chinese 124
Christianity 89–90, 97
circularity 62
circulation 36, 88, 192
cities 15, 65, 113
citizens 34, 45, 47, 103, 112, 137
civilization 5, 15, 119, 121, 163, 165,
    168–169, 172, 196, 199–202
classics 1, 57, 104
cleavage 2, 34–37, 40–41, 45, 50
clothes 91, 95, 114
clowns 29, 107–108
cobblestones 65–67, 69, 77
code 8–9, 11, 13–15, 85, 106, 109, 163, 183
codification 160
cognition 148, 167
cohesion 4, 30
collectivity 37, 39–40, 43, 103, 110, 114,
    118, 121, 135, 166–167
Colombo 164
colonization 85
color 7, 14, 56–57, 59, 61–62, 64, 66, 71, 74,
    81, 136
combination 26, 45, 135, 148, 188
combinatorics 149
comedian 40, 45–47
Commandments 123, 196
commercialization 84, 91, 93, 97–98,
    100–101, 104–105, 111, 125
communication 2, 4, 7–8, 22–24, 26, 29–30,
    34, 37, 42, 44, 49, 53–54, 57, 85–86, 88,
    90, 97, 109, 171, 191, 198, 200, 202
communitas 165–166

communities 5, 8, 16, 20, 31, 33, 88–90, 101, 107–108, 110–111, 113, 125, 129, 143, 167, 169, 197, 200
Como 62
comparison 5, 27, 37, 45, 47, 50, 71, 84, 87, 122, 145, 171, 179
competence 99, 101
competition 59–60, 99, 116, 126, 151, 185
complexity 4, 51–52, 69, 72, 153–155, 157, 164
compromise 4, 144, 158
computer 56, 84, 157
conception 12, 50, 202
confession 106
configuration 15, 39, 59, 63, 71, 92, 105, 110, 115, 162
conflicts 2, 4, 30, 33, 158, 187
connection 43–44, 98, 105, 124, 128, 134
connoisseurs 74
connotation 65, 81, 98, 100–101, 114
conscience 87, 90–91
consciousness 122, 154
consensus 27, 31, 46–47, 52–53
conservatism 131
conspiracy 2, 30, 32, 34, 47–49, 55, 186, 188, 195, 201
consumption 3, 20, 65, 83, 93, 104, 116, 118, 120, 122, 124, 131
contemplation 60, 162
content 2, 7–13, 17, 19, 30, 34–36, 39, 41, 44–46, 49–52, 60, 78, 84, 90, 98, 107, 114, 118, 129, 162, 169, 179, 191–192, 197
context 28–29, 31, 47, 53–54, 60, 62–63, 84, 109, 114, 121, 141, 151, 155, 159, 162–163, 165–167, 169, 190
contiguity 85
continuity 130, 193, 197–199
contradiction 12, 50, 52
contrarian 36, 40, 42, 44, 46, 82, 123
contrariety 50, 52
controversies 32, 34, 43, 47
convergence 87–88, 126
conversation 2, 21, 23–32, 38, 44, 53, 129, 160–161, 194–195, 201–202
conviction 18, 104, 109, 133, 135, 147
cookbooks 116
coordinates 183, 193
cosmologies 192
counterargument 17
counternarratives 41
counterpart 25, 28–29, 44, 104, 108, 134, 173, 201–202
counterreaction 37
counterstrategy 120

Courtès, Joseph 171
courtesy 17, 158
craft 20, 56, 70, 127, 131
creation 4–5, 30, 47, 53, 55, 74, 100, 109–110, 114, 127, 166, 169, 181, 202
creativity 20, 39, 73, 82, 106, 131, 159, 162, 169, 198
crisis 18, 29, 122, 128
criticism 30, 37
cross 16, 134, 192
crowd 3, 27, 36–37, 39–41, 43–44, 97, 105, 110–112, 115, 138
crucifix 108
crying 48–49
crystallization 15, 88, 118, 123, 148
culatello 122
culture 3, 5, 10, 13–14, 17, 32, 59–60, 78, 83, 86–87, 114, 117–118, 120, 122–127, 129–132, 140–141, 149, 151, 159, 164, 167, 169, 172–173, 180, 188, 190, 192–193, 195–196
cultures 2–3, 6–7, 10, 29, 33, 85, 88, 101, 109, 113, 118, 122–125, 128–129, 133, 149, 151, 160, 170, 193–197
cyberwarfare 32
cynicism 170, 186–187
Cyprian 190

Dadaism 79
Dahl, Robert 160
danger 3, 15
Dante 178–179
data 19–20, 88, 133, 142, 146, 152, 176
Dawkins, Richard 93
dead 47, 106, 109, 111, 137
death 8, 13, 20, 29, 32, 37, 44–45, 48–49, 87, 99, 106, 109–111, 114, 116, 132
debayering 81
debunking 48
Decartes 139
deceased 29, 105–106, 109
deciphering 7
decoding 6, 173–174, 184, 191
deconstruction 75–6, 189, 195
deduction 153
defibrillation 146
deictic 35
deity 7, 90–91
Deleuze, Gilles 135
deliverance 104, 109, 121
Delphi 132
dematerialization 5, 84, 86–87
democracy 53
democratization 157
demons 143

demosaicing 81
Denver 144
deontic 118–120, 124
Descartes, René 139–141, 159
Descola, Philippe 192
description 31, 80, 97, 140, 185, 191
desecration 46, 108
desertion 121
design 38, 86, 91, 173, 189
desire 7, 24, 48, 59, 84, 90–91, 98–101, 116, 118, 124, 153, 170, 194
devaluation 3, 83, 86–87, 89–90, 198
devices 86, 98, 132–133, 142, 147, 152, 154, 157, 163, 185
devotion 96
diagnosis 146
diagram 49, 141, 143, 147, 175, 185
dialectics 2, 4, 67–68, 70–74, 76, 78, 82, 93, 101, 104, 134–136, 141, 149
dialogue 16, 36, 121, 168, 186
dichotomies 88, 141
dictators 167
dictatorships 40
Dieudonné M'bala M'bala 40–42, 44–47, 49–52
differentiation 2, 10, 34–35, 37, 39–41, 43, 47–48, 50, 52, 55, 90
digital communication 1–5, 18–22, 26–30, 32–33, 36–37, 39–40, 42, 50, 53, 55–57, 59–62, 73, 76, 78–82, 84–87, 93, 104, 107, 110, 113, 142–143, 148, 169, 198
digitalization 1–2, 20–21, 59, 84–87, 169
dioxide 153
diptych 138
disarticulation 136
discipline 8, 12, 22, 87, 113, 125, 135, 138, 147, 156, 175, 196
discourse 2–3, 5, 22–23, 27–28, 30–32, 34–37, 39, 49–51, 59, 86, 88–89, 98, 101, 104, 108, 113–114, 118–121, 123–124, 128–129, 132, 142, 171, 177, 183, 187, 191, 193, 195–197, 200
discursive 2, 4–5, 22–23, 26–32, 37–39, 51–52, 106, 123, 158, 187, 193, 195
disembodied 90–91
disenchantment 108
dispute 118, 157
dissidents 42–3
divine 88–90, 97, 106
divinity 89–91, 120–121, 133
dogma 110
dogmatic 89
Doric 173
drug 177
drum 85

Dubai 126–127
Duchamp, Marcel 126
Dumézil, Georges 149
durativity 99–100
dynamic 5, 37, 48, 82, 84, 114, 118, 148, 166, 181, 191, 197
dynamism 100
dysphoria 99
dystopia 20–21, 148

earthquakes 69
Eataly 117, 122
eBay 59
economy 59, 101, 118, 124, 157, 174
Eco, Umberto 5, 8, 12, 55, 57, 105–106, 110–111, 113, 125, 152, 171, 177, 185, 187, 190–192, 196–198, 202
ecstasy 103
Ecuador 72, 75–77
education 88, 155, 174
effect 26–29, 43, 62–63, 68–70, 75, 78, 82, 91, 101, 152, 156, 162, 180, 195, 198
efficacy 36, 41, 106–108, 111, 114, 146–147, 151, 154, 156, 196
efficiency 12, 67
Egyptian 141
eidetic 62–64
Einstein, Albert 149
embodiment 116, 120, 126, 132
emergence 3, 21, 39, 71–72, 83, 143, 164, 168
Emilia 127–128
emoticons 43
emotions 4, 23–25, 27, 30, 32, 194
empathy 26, 29, 35–40, 43, 45, 49–51, 54, 154–155
Empire 126
Empirical knowledge 11, 134, 146, 149–151
emptiness 60, 89, 92
enchantment 108, 110, 114, 123
encyclopedia 172, 178, 191
energy 19–20, 25, 29, 64, 91, 95, 121–122, 125
England 139, 143
enjoying 17, 43, 104
Enlightenment 5, 195
enunciation 35, 77, 148, 193
environment 3, 7–9, 18–20, 82, 93, 120, 123–125, 134–135, 160–161, 164–165, 167–168, 174, 192
Epictetus 130
epigones 188
epinephrine 146–147, 152
epistemological dimension 83, 134, 136, 142, 147, 150, 175

epistemology 84, 140, 142
Eresos 132
errors 170
ethics 2, 29–30, 118, 193
ethnocentric 179–181
ethnocentrism 178
ethnography 54, 107
etiology 52, 84
etymology 23, 60, 77, 165
Eucharist 81, 89
Eudes, Jean 96
eulogy 84
euphoria 17, 47, 99
Europe 126–127, 142, 160, 200–201
evangelism 117, 122
evolution 2, 18, 33–34, 69, 74, 84, 86–87,
    90, 151–152, 154–155, 160, 163, 165,
    167, 170, 184, 197, 201
existence 1, 4, 7–8, 11, 15, 17, 21, 51, 54,
    82, 86–87, 106, 123, 129, 132, 143, 147,
    186, 192
experiment 25, 59–60, 112, 146, 155,
    176, 182
expression 2, 9, 11, 15, 24, 30, 35, 44–45,
    47, 57, 71, 90, 96–97, 118, 120, 128–129,
    134, 165–166, 170
eyes 44, 64, 135, 138–139, 157, 173, 184

face 21, 26, 42, 44, 78, 85, 124, 130, 138,
    175, 178
Facebook 40, 45, 131
faith 17, 143, 186, 190
falsification 125–127, 155, 187
familiarity 6, 10, 164
Fascism 30
Fawcett, Percy 172
feminism 117, 181
Ferreri, Marco 116, 118
Feuerbach, Ludwig 130
figuration 70, 73, 183
figurative 59, 61, 75, 77, 82, 190
figurativization 171
filmmaking 82
films 187
flickering 78–79, 81
flight 145–147, 151, 153–154, 156–158
Floch, Jean-Marie 93
flood 91
flowerbeds 68–69, 71–72, 74, 82
folklore 149
Fontanille, Jacques 54, 99
food 3, 116–117, 119–124, 126, 129–131
formula 39, 68, 141, 158, 173
fractals 167
France 55, 115, 125–126, 128, 143, 199

freedom 18, 42, 69, 71, 82, 147–149, 151,
    153–156, 168, 196, 198, 202
Freud, Sigmund 119
fundamentalism 34, 183, 196, 201
funerals 3, 47–48, 106, 111, 160
futurologists 152

gadfly 29
gadget 84, 144, 157–8
Gaelic 149
gastronomic 117, 124
Geertz, Clifford 171
Gell, Alfred 164
gender 178, 191
genealogies 143
generations 86–87, 173
generative 188, 190, 192, 195
Genette, Gérard 18, 163
Geneva 115, 143
Geninasca, Jacques 171
genius 13, 15, 47, 60, 84, 127–128, 167
Genoa 55
genocide 37
genre 23, 29, 47, 51, 53, 145
geography 200
geology 65, 69
geometrization 141
geometry 141
German 54, 60, 89, 139
Germany 143
gestalt 54, 61, 63–64, 66–67, 69, 71–72, 173
gestures 9, 24, 114, 133, 138
ghiordes kmot 71
Gioconda 163
globalization 4, 29, 39, 53, 84, 86, 97, 111,
    117–118, 121, 123–126, 198
glossematics 191
Goethe 12
Goody, Jack 88
Gospels 112
graffiti 42
grammar 148, 160, 163, 165, 167–168, 183
Gramsci, Antonio 120
gratification 116
gravel 62–64, 66
gravity 149
Greece 49, 54, 156, 172, 195–196
Greeks 5, 128, 196, 199, 202
Greenaway, Peter 93
Greimas, Algirdas J. 49–50, 55, 93, 99, 115,
    118, 149–150, 171, 183, 186, 188–195,
    197–198, 201–202
Greimasian, semiotics 27–28, 50, 99, 150,
    183–185, 190–193, 195, 197–198
Grice, Paul 201

griffin 42
Grillo, Beppe 48
grimaces 103
grocery 117, 122–123, 125
Gropius, Walter 78
grotesque 32, 108
Guattari, Félix 135
Guayaquil 76–77
Guggenheim Museum 162
guilt 142
guru 96, 98, 117

Habermas, Jürgen 191–192
habits 15–16, 20, 112, 119, 145, 148, 151,
    156, 175, 200
Hage, Ghassan 115
Hague 137, 143
halcyon 185
Hamlet 181
handmade 70–72
happiness 159
Hardt, Michael 115
harmony 70, 97, 148, 189, 196
haruspices 172
Harvard 170
heart 24, 90, 96–97, 127, 141, 144–147,
    151–155
heaven 120
hegemony 118, 120
Heidegger, Martin 128, 138
Heisenberg, Werner Karl 150
heritage 125–128, 200
hermeneutics 5, 8, 138, 162–164, 173,
    196, 201
heterogeneity 63, 69, 72, 76
heuristic 83, 175
Hierapolis 132
hierarchy 2, 27, 42, 99–100, 103, 110, 129,
    134, 172, 195
hilarity 27
hipster 21, 80, 87
hiragana 6
history 8, 12, 14–16, 18, 22, 38, 47, 60, 66,
    70, 87–88, 94, 101, 104, 121, 126, 134,
    136, 139, 141, 148, 152, 156, 163–165,
    169–172, 176, 183, 187, 196, 200–202
Hjelmslev, Louis T. 49, 180, 191, 194
hoax 48
holistic 63, 65, 68–70, 170
Holland 139
Holmes, Sherlock 8, 12
homogeneity 63, 66, 69, 72, 76
homologation 40
honeymoon 127
horizon 15, 57, 87, 141, 202

horror 78
horsetail 141
hostility 99, 123–124, 161
Hugo, Victor 188
humanities 4–5, 84, 93, 135, 143, 147–151,
    154–158, 178–179, 187–190, 194–195
Hume, David 171
humor 24, 47, 55
hydrogen 78
hymn 135
hypertension 155
hypertrophy 53
hypnotic 69
hypocrisy 29
hypothesis 2, 33, 48–49, 86, 107, 118, 138,
    146, 155, 177–179, 181–182, 186

iconic 62, 85, 136
iconoclasm 89
icons 12, 76, 87, 89, 108, 136
identification 36, 39, 41, 45–46, 50–52,
    139, 144
identity 7, 21, 32, 36–37, 44–46, 48, 50,
    54, 56, 59–60, 97, 122, 126–127, 129,
    165–166, 185–186
ideology 36, 50, 52–53, 84–90, 120–121,
    125, 133, 135–136, 142–143, 145,
    148–149, 164, 193–196, 198, 201–202
idiolects 91
idiosyncrasies 165, 186
imagery 3
imaginaire 67
immanence 91, 133, 190
immanentism 190
immediacy 131
immunitas 166
impermanence 113
impoliteness 32
indecipherability 12
indexes 11, 85–6, 128–9, 136
India 98, 115
Indifference 49
indignation 23, 46
individualism 37, 40, 165
individualization 36
inertia 15, 70
infarction 145
inference 145, 152
information 27, 31, 46, 86, 175, 181, 183
ingestion 120, 131–132
insects 26, 66
insignificance 1–5, 7–21, 23–32, 34–55,
    57, 59–82, 84–94, 96–101, 103–115,
    117–132, 145, 174
institutionalization 160

intellectualism 131
intellectuals 4, 46, 129, 131, 194, 198
intention 2, 30, 45, 93, 107, 181
intentionality 5, 30, 61, 71, 145, 150–152,
    154, 165, 177, 181, 184–185
interaction 32, 69–71, 98, 104, 109,
    150–151, 159, 161–164
interlocution 23–24, 28, 31, 50, 85,
    89, 168
intermediation 90, 172
internalization 17
Internet 22, 32, 39, 41–44, 54, 57, 59–60
interpretant 12–13, 16, 135, 148
interpretation 5, 12–13, 15, 36, 47, 53, 88,
    112, 139, 146, 162–164, 168, 172–187,
    190–202
interpreter 12, 168, 172–174, 182–183,
    186–187, 191, 198–199
intersubjective 5, 184, 186–187
intimacy 84, 89
invention 42, 85, 88–89, 126–127, 164
I-Phone 68
Iran 149
irony 24, 27, 30, 46–47, 55, 111, 126, 140
Isaac 149
ISIS 201
Islam 34
Islamic 35, 201
Islamophobia 53
islands 111, 166
isobars 150
isolation 200
isotopy 149–150
Israel 48
Italy 19, 48, 62, 108–112, 115–118,
    124–126, 130

Japan 9–10, 13–14, 117
Japanese 1, 6–7, 9–14, 17–18, 176,
    178–179
jargon 1
jealousy 134, 136–137, 142
Jerusalem 196
Jesus 112–113
Jews 199
Jihadism 41
Jihadist 34–35, 44, 48
Job 32
journals 42–43, 117, 176
Judaism 89–91, 172, 200
judges 145
judgment 46, 131, 134, 136, 142, 145, 155,
    167, 174, 178
justice 90, 157
justification 36

Kandinsky, Vasilij Vasil'evi? 56–57, 60–61, 77
kanji 6–7, 9–10, 12
Kant, Immanuel 89–90, 171
katakana 6
kebab 124
killings 34–35, 37–38, 48
kinesics 101
kinetics 114
kitsch 127
knots 3, 33, 70–72, 75, 77
Kyoto 6–7, 18

labyrinth 19, 48
Lafayette, Galeries 91–93
Landowski, Eric 54, 115
landscape 21, 69, 154
language 4, 6–7, 9, 13, 17, 31, 53, 61, 86,
    88–91, 97–98, 107, 113–114, 123, 126,
    147–151, 153–156, 158, 160, 162–163,
    165–166, 172, 177–178, 180, 186, 189,
    193–196
languages 7, 34–35, 39–40, 43, 60, 90, 114,
    127, 149, 162, 170, 172, 186, 193
langue 163, 165, 167
lanterns 124
laptop 144
Latin 6, 23, 129, 165
Latour, Bruno 146
laughter 46–47
Lavazza 171
Law 30, 42, 85, 106, 133–134, 142, 159,
    169, 171, 201
laws 124, 148, 151, 153–156, 160–161, 165,
    169, 191, 202
lawyers 175
LCD 56, 61, 76–78, 80–82
leaders 42, 44, 48–50, 52, 161, 172
legitimation 55
Leonardo da Vinci 87, 126–128,
    135–136, 163
Leuven 65–66, 68
Lévinas, Emmanuel 3, 78
Lévi-Strauss, Claude 149
lexeme 197
liberation 104, 119, 134
libido 120–121
lilies 141
limbs 97, 157
linguistics 32, 97, 100, 106, 114,
    148–150, 191
Lisbon 81
literature 32, 54, 107, 131–132, 167,
    182, 191
Lithuania 115
liturgy 91, 93, 98, 100, 107, 110, 184–186

liver 130
logic 7, 9, 28, 33, 45, 86, 113, 127, 139, 168–169, 180, 195
London 14, 143
Lotman, Jurij M. 5, 50, 98, 113, 118, 122, 124, 185, 192, 202
Louvre 125–127, 163
love 86
Lovecraft, Howard Phillips 172
lying 28, 196
Lyon 34

machine 17, 19, 31, 71–72, 74, 78, 82, 87, 93, 119, 152–153, 165
madman 166
madness 120
Madrid 3, 14, 95–98, 101–105, 113
magazine 35–37, 40–41, 54
magic 151, 185
majorities 122
Malaysia 115
male 145, 178, 201
malfunction 81, 152, 154
mammals 140
Manchester 54
Manichean thought 131
manifestation 23, 33, 37, 53, 60, 78, 110, 181, 194
Slow Food Manifesto 119
manipulation 52, 83, 198
map 2, 33–34
marble 71, 97, 174
margins 166, 181
market 70, 78, 84, 87, 97, 104, 113, 118, 125
marketing 3–4, 21, 82, 100–101, 104, 111, 113–115, 122, 124, 128–129, 132
marks 6, 101, 103, 107, 183, 199
marriage 106–107
Mars 65
martyr 42
martyrdom 197
marvel 63
Marx, Karl 119, 121
mask 157, 195
masochistic 116
material 3–4, 7, 11, 21, 63, 65–68, 71–72, 82–84, 86–87, 90, 93, 95, 108, 110, 114, 116, 120, 131, 148
materialism 83–84, 130
materiality 21, 83–84, 86–87, 169
materials 10, 66, 69, 80, 91, 182
mathematics 57, 77–78, 85, 141, 150
matrix 17, 59, 80–81, 160
Maupassant, Guy de 191
mausoleum 141

maverick 46, 123, 146
meaning 1, 3–5, 7–12, 15–18, 20, 23, 25, 28, 43, 50, 52–53, 59–60, 66, 74, 82–91, 93, 98, 103, 107, 110, 114, 123, 128, 131–132, 138, 140–141, 145, 147–151, 154, 162–170, 172–175, 177–183, 185–187, 190–199, 201–202
meaningfulness 3–4, 8–9, 13–14
meaninglessness 1, 6, 8–11, 13–14, 31, 82
meat 130
mechanism 15, 60, 78, 122, 157, 166
media 3, 32, 34, 37–38, 40–42, 46, 48, 50, 54, 93, 130–131, 134, 136–137
mediation 131, 135, 140
medicine 8, 151, 155–156
meditation 61, 98, 139, 195
melancholy 67, 186–187
memory 29, 86, 88, 118, 125, 129, 132, 168
merchandizing 93
message 7, 14, 21, 27, 35, 37–39, 43, 45, 88, 124, 177, 195, 202
messianism 121–2
metalanguage 87, 150, 173, 178, 183–186, 190, 193
metaphor 31, 104, 116, 118, 131, 134, 150
metaphysical 34, 77, 106–107, 119–120, 133
method 5, 171, 173–174, 178–188, 191–195, 197, 201–202
microscope 63, 141, 182
migration 20
Milan 117, 124, 132
military 26, 34, 84, 158
milliondollarhomepage 58
mind 12, 23–24, 27–28, 71, 84, 97, 106, 130, 152, 158, 165, 184
minerals 69, 76
miniaturization 86, 157
minority 36, 40, 42, 46, 48, 87
miracle 88, 112–113, 147, 155
mirror 28, 57, 59–60, 78
mistakes 15, 87, 152, 160
misunderstanding 8, 193
mockery 108
modalities 1, 75, 110, 125, 195
modernity 89–91, 118–119, 130, 151, 164, 168
Modigliani, Amedeo 125
modules 111
molecules 71
Molière 178
monad 61
Mona Lisa 125–128
monarchy 103
monasteries 199
monde 6, 171

monitor 78
monochrome 103
monologue 36
monotheism 85
monsters 8, 16, 78, 139, 141
monumentality 132
morality 31, 143, 196
Morocco 123, 126
morphogenesis 22
morphology 61, 64, 71, 74, 76, 91, 149–150
mortality 8
mosaics 76–77, 80–81, 93
mothers 97, 159
motility 72
motivation 167, 183
mourning 106, 109–111
mouth 117
movies 56, 78, 87, 146, 177
mullah 106
multitude 26, 43, 63–64, 67, 69, 71, 78, 97–98, 100–101, 103–105
murderers 46–47, 49, 51
museums 126–127, 162–164
music 131, 162
mutability 69, 150, 197
mutation 74, 191
Muybridge, Eadweard 80
myocardial 145
mystical 18, 87, 89, 92, 98, 134, 143
myth 9, 88
mythology 149

narcissism 4, 40, 53, 59, 187
narrative 54, 79, 87, 100–101, 113, 115, 121, 144, 149–150, 183–184, 193–194, 197
narrativity 149
nationalisms 122
naturalization 128
nature 3, 11–12, 14–18, 24–25, 28, 30, 50, 53, 57, 59–60, 62, 71, 76, 78–79, 82–83, 97, 101, 104, 106, 123, 134, 140–142, 146, 148, 150–151, 154, 160, 164–165, 167, 172, 176–177, 182, 184, 195, 197, 200
necessity 17, 36, 85–86, 91, 107, 147–148, 150–153, 155–156, 167
negation 34, 36, 39–41, 47, 54–55
Netherlands 141, 143
networks 2, 20, 26, 33–39, 41, 45, 47–48, 50, 52–56, 86, 117
neurology 153
neurosciences 147
neutrality 51–52, 194
neutralization 4, 118
neutrons 150

Newark 144
Newton, Isaac 149
Niger 132
nihilism 2
Nipkow, Paul Gottlieb 60
Nola, Alfonso Maria di 115
Norfolk 143
Normandy 115
norms 3, 16
nostalgia 108, 114
Novedrate 62
novel 34, 61, 126, 140, 164, 167, 169, 173, 181, 183, 187
nutrition 117, 121

obliviousness 194
obnubilation 17
obscurantism 20, 35, 39, 46
observation 11, 14, 39, 65, 67, 71, 74, 107, 140, 146–147, 150–151, 155, 160, 162–163, 176
observer 2, 27–28, 52, 63–64, 67, 138, 150, 184
obsession 13, 117
obstacle 43, 81
ocean 42, 84
Octavius 133
offers 32, 83, 139, 182
olives 130
olivine 65
Olympus 126
OMG 80
ontology 128, 150, 190, 192, 195
opacity 134, 142
Opéra 93, 119, 121
opposition 31, 36, 88, 136, 192
oppression 14
optical effect 63, 69, 134–135, 141–143
orchard 123
orderliness 66
organs 146
orient 162
Oscar 117
Osho 98
ostracism 123, 167
ostrich 141
Otavalo market 70
outsiders 30, 161, 164, 166
oxygen 78
OYSHO 97–98, 100, 103–104
Ozu 176–181

Pabst, Georg Wilhelm 42
Paedagogus 95
painters 131, 136–137, 143

paintings 78, 137, 162–163
palingenesis 155
Panama 72–76, 78
panopticon 135
Pantheon 92–93
pantomime 32, 174
papaya 123
paradigm 93
paradox 21, 84, 89, 127–128
paralysis 4, 23
parametricism 57
Paris 14, 34–35, 40, 43, 47, 53, 55, 91–94,
    115, 119, 125, 127, 132, 185
Parliament 48
Parmesan 125, 127–128
parodies 127
parody 108, 126
paroxysm 38
Parthenon 128
pasquinades 42
passengers 4, 6, 9–11, 14, 109, 140, 144–146,
    156–158
pathologies 141, 154
patients 146, 155
patterns 1–2, 9, 29, 34, 36, 41–42, 44, 47, 49,
    51–53, 55–56, 62, 64–65, 67–68, 70, 72,
    74, 76–77, 107, 110–111, 113–114, 149,
    151, 167–168, 173, 182, 189
pebbles 16, 63–64
Peirce, Charles S.S. 8, 10–11, 31, 93, 113,
    135, 148, 151, 191
Pentecost 89
perception 3, 9, 63–66, 69, 74–76, 83, 100,
    113, 123, 181, 185
perfection 56, 71, 78, 82
perfectionism 89
performance 101, 104, 111, 175
perfume 129, 132
perimeter 60, 62, 89, 159, 182–184
persecution 44
persuasion 24, 187
Petersen 54
Petrini, Carlo 117
Petrograd 115
Petronius 129, 132
phantasms 141
phenomenology 91, 115
philology 5
philosophy 20, 22, 32, 47, 88, 93, 115,
    117–118, 131, 170–171, 175, 191, 195
phonetics 149
photograph 62–63, 65, 70, 72, 75–76, 81, 175
photographs 64, 73, 101
physicians 8, 175
physicists 150

physics 150, 152, 156
pictures 29, 48, 65, 67, 79, 91, 96
Piedmont 124
Pike, Kenneth L. 15
pilgrimage 93
pilgrims 113
pineapples 123–124
pines 141
pixels 56–60, 62, 76–78, 80, 82
pixies 82
pixilation 82
placebos 20, 113
planet 3, 64, 117
plants 69, 71, 76
Plato 88, 129
play 2, 24, 76, 109, 112, 125, 149, 165, 180
pleasures 75, 120, 123, 129, 132
plenitude 166
Plutarch 116, 129
poetics 80
poetry 67, 149, 187
poets 54, 165
poisons 30
polarities 4, 63–64, 133
polarization 28, 133, 181
police 34, 42–43
policy 88
politics 5, 171, 194, 197
Pollenzo 117
pollution 123–124
polyethylene 111
polyglots 7
polymath 139–141
polyphony 36
pomegranate 141
Pope 110, 117
Popper, Karl 176, 182
populism 31, 124
populisms 124
portrait 126
Portuguese 81
postmodern 31, 91, 93, 104, 110, 126
postures 70
potentiality 12, 28, 148, 177, 187
pottery 178
power 25, 27, 35, 42, 44, 47, 50, 54, 69,
    86–88, 104, 110, 114, 122, 124, 126, 142,
    161, 170, 172–173, 185
practice 11, 22–23, 25, 28–32, 78, 126, 133,
    158, 174
practices 2, 19, 22, 27, 89, 142, 174, 186
Prado 102
pragmatics 25, 28–29, 47, 100, 107, 164, 198
pragmatism 131
prediction 149–151

preeminence 195–196
prejudgment 160
prejudice 16, 133
premodernity 126
presentification 110
priest 101, 106–108, 151, 185
procedures 126, 152, 155, 169, 175–176, 179
processions 101
producers 117, 125, 128
propaganda 42, 169
prophet 35, 89, 172
Propp, Vladimir Jakovlevi? 149, 191, 194
proprioceptive 104
prosody 107
protagonist 109, 178, 183
protest 21, 38
Protestantism 85, 89
proverbs 171
provocation 2, 22–23, 25, 27–28, 42, 46, 59, 192
psychoanalysis 7, 118, 182
psychology 55, 171, 191
punctuation 164
puppet 25
pyramids 141

quadrupeds 140
qualitative dimension 74, 88, 134–135
quantifiable dimension 20, 74, 143, 146
quantitative dimension 59, 74, 78, 82, 88, 118, 133–135, 142, 179
quantum 150
quincunx 140–141
Quito 72, 75

readers 8, 144, 146, 167, 179–185, 189, 191–192, 197–198
reality 3, 5, 8, 16, 19–21, 37, 39, 46, 48, 64, 75–76, 85–87, 111, 116, 135, 140–143, 146, 148, 155, 163, 172, 174–177, 182, 189–191, 195–196, 199
realization 17, 25, 30
reasonableness 5, 16, 165–166, 168, 175, 187, 190, 198
reception 22, 34, 85, 128, 131, 178–179
recognition 109, 126–127, 187
reconstruction 48, 86, 93
reductionism 148, 154
redundancy 148–149
reification 1
reinvention 85
relativism 186
relativity 149
relics 11, 114, 155

religion 3, 36, 83, 88–90, 98, 100, 104, 106, 114–115, 117–119, 133, 151
religions 85–90, 106, 133, 142, 185
Rembrandt 134, 137–143, 185
Renaissance 88–89, 126, 133, 135–6, 168, 199
representation 16, 31, 37, 54, 69, 82, 86, 89, 134–136, 141–143, 195
representativeness 87, 178
reptiles 140
resemblance 85, 89, 138
responsibility 2, 26–27, 34, 43–45, 52–53, 170, 202
restaurants 113, 117, 119, 123–125
resuscitation 145
revelation 13, 25–26, 89–91, 142
revisionism 187
revolution 85, 88, 121
rhetoric 22–23, 29, 51–52, 59, 78, 104, 123–126, 128–129, 131, 134, 136, 142, 171
rhythm 100, 107, 115, 120, 146
Ricoeur, Paul 6, 120, 132, 190
rituals 3, 91, 100, 104, 106–112, 114
robots 17, 19, 166
Roman 92–93, 129, 172
Romanic 106
Rome 14, 92, 171
rosaries 146–147
rules 4, 7, 16, 44, 47, 77, 123, 148–149, 160–165, 167–168, 197–198, 202
Russian 115, 149

sacralization 4
Sacraments 128
sacredness 60, 125–126, 128–129
sacrifice 103–104, 165–168, 186, 197
sadism 28–29
Saint Petersburg 115
saints 96, 101, 115
salamander 141
salience 1
salvation 19, 54
sancta sanctorum 60, 126, 128
Santorini 65
sapiens 119
sarcasm 2, 34, 40, 45–47, 51, 55
satire 30, 116
Satyricon 129
Saussure, Ferdinand de 8, 98, 113, 148, 167, 191
scale 21, 63, 67, 84, 88, 158
scandal 41
scheme 49, 61, 73, 168
scholarship 100, 169

Schopenhauer, Arthur 22
science 87, 118, 135–136, 143, 154–155, 171, 175
scientists 176, 182
screen 26, 56, 60, 73, 76–78, 81–82, 85, 157
Scriptures 88
Searle, John 171
Sebald, Winfried Georg 139–140, 142
Sebeok, Thomas A. 8
secret 17, 42–43, 48, 64, 84, 140–143, 195, 201
secularization 106–107, 110, 114, 118
seductiveness 60
Segre, Cesare 163
self 7, 18–19, 32, 39, 61, 84, 91, 111, 116, 130, 154
semantics 177, 189
sememes 49
semiology 98
semiosphere 5, 8, 13, 26, 28, 32, 36, 40–47, 50–53, 55, 89, 108, 114, 117–118, 122–128, 130–132, 164–166, 168–170, 181, 184, 186, 192, 194, 198–202
semioticians 8, 12–13, 15, 50, 53, 117, 123, 130, 147, 150–151, 156–157, 175–176, 189, 192
semiotics 1–5, 8, 12, 15, 19, 22, 27, 31–33, 47, 49, 52–54, 56–57, 73, 78, 82, 85, 87, 90, 93, 98–101, 106, 108, 114–115, 118, 125, 135, 144–145, 147, 150, 152, 156, 158–159, 162, 171, 173, 175–176, 183, 188–193, 195–197, 202
Semitic world 40, 45
sensibility 39
Serbia 79
serendipity 21, 82
serotonin 153
sexuality 120
Shakespeare, William 182–183, 187
Shanghai 126
Shia Islam 197
shibboleths 122–123, 129
shoes 16, 128
Sibilia, Carlo 48
sibylline 139
signal 7, 84–87, 151
signatures 128
signification 6, 8–12, 15, 57, 61, 107, 109, 113–114, 118, 133, 177–178, 180, 189, 195, 197, 199, 202
signs 6–11, 17, 43, 48, 50–52, 73, 85, 93, 98–99, 108, 114, 118, 122–123, 125–127, 129, 133, 148, 156, 160, 164, 172, 180, 196, 199

silence 14, 17, 40, 48, 82–83, 95
silk 141
Silverstein, Michael 192
simulacra 3, 21, 138–139, 193, 196
simulacrum 85–86, 182–183
simulation 85, 87, 111
singularities 21, 43, 69, 71–72, 82
skeleton 52
skepticism 136
skillfulness 169
slaughter 16
slave 130
sleepiness 17
smartphone 80
soccer 43, 131
societies 1–4, 27, 29, 31, 33–34, 42, 44, 82, 88, 106–107, 109–110, 112–115, 131, 134, 149, 158, 184, 191
sociobiology 84
sociology 1, 32, 104, 156
Socrates 29
solidarity 40–41, 43, 51
solipsism 43
solitude 104, 178
Solomon 141
somaticity 100, 115
sophistication 48, 135, 185
sounds 17, 21, 98
space 4–5, 10, 13–15, 17–18, 35, 38, 43–44, 59–60, 62, 69, 71, 73–74, 85–86, 88–89, 91, 93, 100–101, 103–105, 110, 113–114, 117, 122, 128, 135, 144–145, 156–158, 160–161, 165, 167, 184, 186–187, 192–193, 198, 200
Spain 101, 104, 110, 126, 162
Spaniards 101
spatiality 123
spatiotemporality 100
species 18–19, 69, 71, 82, 86, 119, 140, 155, 196
spectacle 25, 27, 69, 93, 111, 138
spectators 137–139, 162, 178–180, 182
spiral 26, 28
spirit 87, 89–90, 121, 129–130, 202
spirituality 83–84, 98, 114, 118
spontaneous 16, 45, 108, 110, 167, 184
Starobinski, Jean 171
statistics 2, 33, 94, 160, 178, 181
statues 101, 103
stereotypes 1, 4, 122, 124, 128–129, 160
stigmatization 123, 161
Stockholm 143
Stoichita, Victor I. 163
Stoicism 130
Stoics 156

storytelling 37
Stradivarius 97
strangers 25–26
strategies 1, 51, 87, 114, 133, 175, 200
streets 34, 53, 95, 124
striatedness 136
structure 6, 28, 34, 37, 39, 52, 61–62, 66, 69, 71, 92, 100, 108, 110–111, 120–122, 138, 141, 148, 150, 162–163, 177, 186, 191, 195
stupidity 19
style 23, 53–54, 72, 149, 163
subjective 52, 63, 74, 135, 178–180, 183, 186, 191
substance 19, 49, 130, 177, 187
subtext 81, 108, 113
suicide 111
superiority 74, 149, 156, 161
superstructural 121
suspicion 39
sustainability 129
symbol 11, 117, 120, 128, 178
symbology 3, 83
symptom 2, 31, 121, 145, 152–153
synagogue 91
synchronic 101, 104, 192
synchronicity 11, 97
syndrome 31
synergy 96, 100, 104
syntagmatic 135, 197
syntax 2, 29, 34, 44, 101, 184, 198
synthesis 136
system 3, 7, 14, 18, 31, 85, 98, 113–114, 126, 130–131, 140, 160, 191

taboo 29
tachycardia 146
tactics 175
tactility 71
Taittinger 128
talking 4, 19, 21, 85, 129, 158, 188
tangibility 83
tapestry 63, 70, 75, 78, 103
Tartu 115, 185
Taussig, Michael 115
Taylor, Charles 93
teacher 140, 169
technique 82, 88, 127, 129, 142
technology 4, 34, 56, 60, 80–82, 86, 88, 90, 133, 154, 158, 198
telecommunication 84
teleology 118
telephone 85
telescope 141
television 60, 116

temple 3, 6, 57, 60, 83, 91, 93, 101, 110, 173
temporality 99–100, 123, 132, 180, 190
tenability 37
tendency 4, 84, 86–87, 109, 117, 126, 156
tendons 137
tension 26, 61, 63–66, 69, 71–72, 145, 202
territory 2, 127
terroir 128
terror 2, 37, 40, 45, 52
terrorism 40–42, 44, 46–47, 53–54
terrorists 34–35, 40–41, 46, 48
tetragon 143
text 5, 29, 49, 51, 80, 88, 95, 98, 119, 149–150, 163–164, 172–174, 176, 178–186, 190–192, 195, 197–201
textiles 70
texture 63–67, 71, 74
theater 45, 47, 93, 119, 175, 183
theft 169
Theophrastus 129
theory 48, 57, 59, 120, 149, 171, 177, 183, 188–195, 201–202
therapy 146, 155
thresholds 10, 17, 106, 123
Thürlemann, Felix 163
time 1–2, 4–5, 8–9, 12–13, 17–21, 23–27, 29, 32, 35–40, 42–45, 50, 53, 57, 59–60, 63–64, 69, 71, 73–74, 81, 85, 88, 90, 96–97, 99–101, 105, 118, 120, 122, 128, 130, 132, 134, 140–141, 144, 149, 152–153, 157–158, 160, 162, 165–167, 170, 173, 175, 178, 184, 188, 190, 192–194, 199–200, 202
Titanic 36
topology 61, 91, 101, 103–104, 114, 118, 122, 125, 130, 132, 135–136, 161, 173
Toronto 127
torture 27
totalitarianisms 166
Toulouse 55
Touraine 143
tourism 113, 157
tourists 6, 9–10, 13, 66
tradition 65, 89, 97, 127, 148, 195, 198
traditional 2, 29, 31–32, 35, 80, 86, 89, 106–110, 112, 118, 164
tragedy 34–37, 47, 51, 174
transcendence 3, 87–91, 93, 106–107, 133, 172
transduction 122
transformation 67, 101, 121, 148, 186
translation 85–86, 129, 132, 146–147, 183–185, 189
transparency 13, 134, 142

transportability 86
traveling 13–14, 56, 157
travelogue 139
Trimalchio 129
trivialization 120, 126
trolling 2, 21–32, 53–54, 82, 186, 201
truth 5, 14, 133–134, 136, 142, 184, 195–196, 201–202
truthfulness 49, 196
Tulp, Nicolaes 137–142
Turin 38, 117, 176, 178
Tuscany 124
typology 6, 11, 55, 67

undecipherable 9–11, 15–17
undergarments 97
understanding 8, 29, 135, 143, 149, 174, 189
undertexts 107
underwear 97–98, 104
UNESCO 126
unicorn 141
uniform 63–64
uniformity 63, 67–68, 74
unintelligibility 141
unintentionally 29, 161, 200
uniqueness 64, 71, 87, 98, 125–128
universalism 89, 192
universality 63, 70–72, 136, 192–193
universalization 90
universities 18, 117, 169
unpredictability 71
utopia 3, 16, 18, 20–21, 56, 87, 90, 110, 135, 148
utterances 107, 109

vacuum 111, 166
valorization 59, 83
values 5, 13, 17, 36, 38–40, 43, 45, 48–51, 57, 59–60, 63, 71, 74, 77, 100, 104, 118, 123, 125–129, 131, 133, 144, 159, 167–170, 172, 182–183, 194–199
variability 192
variants 149–150
variations 63, 134, 148–149, 166
variety 63, 69, 71, 140, 145, 192–193
vectoriality 168
Verbal language 10, 24–25, 27, 35–36, 43, 97–98, 107, 109, 113–114, 123, 136, 148–149, 159–160, 162–163, 170, 177–178, 180, 198

veridiction 195
vibration 64, 66, 70–71, 75, 78, 81
victimization 46
victims 22, 27, 29, 35–38, 40–41, 43, 45–52, 83
viewer 63, 65, 68, 127
vintage 80, 87, 189
vinyl 86–87
violence 14, 16–17, 20–21, 24, 32, 36, 41–42, 82, 99, 101, 103–104, 187, 202
viral 35–36, 38, 57
virtual 2, 5, 21, 26, 43–44, 52–53, 82, 124, 168
virtue 128, 134, 202
virus 119, 121
visage 3, 87, 138–9
vision 82, 191
visual language 32, 35–36, 48, 54, 57, 59–72, 76–78, 80–82, 133–138, 142, 163–164, 166, 181, 183, 190
vocation 18, 117
voices 14, 27, 29, 33–34, 36, 40, 42–43, 53, 110, 131, 186

Waagebouw 137
waiting 13, 95, 97–101, 104, 115
war 2, 14, 33, 125
weapons 35, 122
weaving 70, 74, 82
web 27, 32, 35, 37–39, 41–44, 46, 54, 57, 59–60, 97–98
website 60, 87, 97–98, 113
wedding 106–108, 160
weighing 14, 111
Western culture 5–7, 10, 42, 44, 52, 54, 61, 85, 107, 125, 151, 163–164, 168–169, 172, 190, 192–193, 195–196, 198–202
wheat 130
wheel 127
WWII 127

xenophobia 124
Xenophon 129

yoga 3, 96–98, 100, 102–105, 110, 113–114
YouTube 44–45

Zara 97
Zen 195
Zilberberg, Claude 54

For Product Safety Concerns and Information please contact our EU
representative GPSR@taylorandfrancis.com
Taylor & Francis Verlag GmbH, Kaufingerstraße 24, 80331 München, Germany

www.ingramcontent.com/pod-product-compliance
Lightning Source LLC
Chambersburg PA
CBHW050350270326
41926CB00016B/3682